Luminos is the Open Access monograph publishing program from UC Press. Luminos provides a framework for preserving and reinvigorating monograph publishing for the future and increases the reach and visibility of important scholarly work. Titles published in the UC Press Luminos model are published with the same high standards for selection, peer review, production, and marketing as those in our traditional program. www.luminosoa.org

D1617030

# The Monastery Rules

# The Monastery Rules

*Buddhist Monastic Organization in Pre-Modern Tibet*

———

Berthe Jansen

UNIVERSITY OF CALIFORNIA PRESS

University of California Press, one of the most distinguished university presses in the United States, enriches lives around the world by advancing scholarship in the humanities, social sciences, and natural sciences. Its activities are supported by the UC Press Foundation and by philanthropic contributions from individuals and institutions. For more information, visit www.ucpress.edu.

University of California Press
Oakland, California

Suggested citation: Jansen, B. *The Monastery Rules: Buddhist Monastic Organization in Pre-Modern Tibet.* Oakland: University of California Press, 2018. DOI: https://doi.org/10.1525/luminos.56

Library of Congress Cataloging-in-Publication Data

Names: Jansen, Berthe, 1980- author.
Title: The monastery rules: Buddhist monastic organization in pre-modern Tibet / By Berthe Jansen.
Description: Oakland, California : University of California Press, [2018] | Series: South Asia across the disciplines | Includes bibliographical references and index. |
Identifiers: LCCN 2018028779 (print) | LCCN 2018031022 (ebook) | ISBN 9780520969537 (Epub) | ISBN 9780520297005 (pbk. : alk. paper)
Subjects: LCSH: Buddhist monasticism and religious orders--China--Tibet Autonomous Region--Rules. | Buddhism--Social aspects--China--Tibet Autonomous Region.
Classification: LCC BQ7744 (ebook) | LCC BQ7744 .J36 2018 (print) | DDC 294.3/657--dc23
LC record available at https://lccn.loc.gov/2018028779

27   26   25   24   23   22   21   20   19   18
10   9   8   7   6   5   4   3   2   1

*The reasonable man adapts himself to the world. The unreasonable man persists in trying to adapt the world to himself. Therefore, all progress depends on the unreasonable man.*

—GEORGE BERNARD SHAW, *MAN AND SUPERMAN*

*How can enough leather be found to cover the surface of this earth? With just the leather under my feet, it is as though the earth's entire surface is covered.*

*Likewise, it is the external things that I cannot control; therefore, I will control my own mind. What need is there to control anything else?*

—ŚĀNTIDEVA, *BODHICARYĀVATĀRA*, CH. 5, V. 6, 7

CONTENTS

# ACKNOWLEDGMENTS

When I tell them of my research topic, Tibetans often joke that I will probably be a monk disciplinarian in my next life and that I must like rules a lot. In fact, working on this book has taught me discipline, but unfortunately not exactly the type of discipline required to live in a monastery. Along the way, inside and outside of the monastery, I have met so many people who have been invaluable to both my research and my private life—the two have become more and more intertwined. Being part of the research project "Buddhism and Social Justice" led by Jonathan Silk at Leiden University has made me realize that to be in the same office with scholars working on different Buddhist traditions is a wonderful and pain-free way of getting different perspectives on this elusive thing we call Buddhism. For this I am grateful to the NWO (Netherlands Organisation for Scientific Research) for financing the project and much thanks and appreciation go out to my fellow project members, Vincent Breugem, Thomas Kim, and Vincent Tournier. I was also fortunate to have been the beneficiary of a visiting research fellowship at Heidelberg University, allowing me to do further work on this book. Another grant, the NWO Veni grant, has helped me further fine-tune ideas in this book and continue my research on the broader topic of "Buddhism and Law" in pre-modern Tibet.

Another project in which I was involved, albeit in a less prominent manner, is "Social Histories of Tibetan Societies," jointly funded by the ANR (French National Agency for Research) and the DFG (German Research Foundation). I was invited to give papers at this project's conferences and workshops. The resulting feedback, input, and friendships have been invaluable. For that I thank the core members and the "passersby" (such as myself): Jeannine Bischoff, Patrick Booz,

John Bray, Christoph Cüppers, Astrid Hovden, Fabienne Jagou, Kalsang Norbu Gurung, Saul Mullard, Fernanda Pirie, Charles Ramble, Nicola Schneider, Peter Schwieger, Elliot Sperling, Alice Travers, Maria Turek, Richard Whitecross, and Liu Yuxuan.

Conferences, it appears, are ideal places to meet those who not only do fascinating research, but also are willing to discuss and share their findings, references, and copies of obscure articles. For this, I am thankful to numerous people, among whom are Chris Bell, Jane Caple, Erden Chuluu, Marc-Henri Deroche, Mathias Fermer, Ann Heirman, Christian Lammerts, Dan Martin, Jann Ronis, Brenton Sullivan, Péter-Dániel Szántó, Tashi Tsering, Markus Viehbeck, and Dorji Wangchuk. I also thank Geshé Ngawang Zöpa for obtaining a rare publication from Sera Je monastery.

During my fieldwork in India the following people were always there to lend a hand, share food and tea, and simply be wonderful company, come rain or shine (mostly rain, as the monsoon was in full swing): Gazellah Abdullah, Mona Bruchmann, Ani Dawa Dolma, and Karma Sichoe. The staff of the Library of Tibetan Works and Archives (LTWA) in Dharamsala has also been very helpful. I am grateful to Jonathan Samuels (Sherab Gyatso), who has made valuable suggestions and corrections. I am further thankful to Leonard van der Kuijp and Shayne Clarke for pointing out mistakes while remaining supportive. Special thanks should also go out to my *Doktervater* Jonathan Silk for his criticism, inspiration, and support, and also for his willingness to remain my friend after he stopped being my teacher. Being a householder, I thank my family, Joost, Pema, and Lorelei, for their love, distraction, and support.

Last of all, I am deeply indebted to my monk informants, who have shared their knowledge, stories, books, and buttertea so generously. Without the monastic community, the Buddhist Teachings would not only die, but this study would never have been born. This book is therefore dedicated to the Sangha—of the present, the past, and the future. May it live forevermore.

# A NOTE ON TRANSLITERATION

I here largely follow the so-called "Wylie system," as set forth in "A Standard System of Tibetan Transcription" (Wylie 1959), except that generally no hyphens or capital letters are used in the transliteration in this book. However, where applicable, the first root-letter of Tibetan works, personal names, and place names is capitalized. Recurring names of authors and place names, which include the names of monasteries, are romanized and the Tibetan transliteration is given in brackets upon first appearance. When Tibetan terms, words, or titles are the topic of discussions that are of a more technical or philological nature, the Wylie system is, in most cases, maintained. Sanskrit terms are, where applicable, given in brackets and indicated by "S." When canonical material—i.e., Kanjur (*bKa' 'gyur*) and Tenjur (*bsTan 'gyur*)—is cited, the Tōhoku catalogue number of the Dergé version is given.

# Introduction

*How on earth do all these thousands of monks spend their time? How are they supported? And what good, if any, do they do?*
—SPENCER CHAPMAN [1938] 1984: 171

## THE SOCIETAL ROLE OF MONKS AND MONASTERIES

Monasteries traditionally played a large role in the lives of ordinary people in Tibet. To date, however, relatively little is known about the role of these monasteries and their inhabitants in Tibetan society. Still, the impact of monastic Buddhism on other expressions of Buddhism as well as on a wide range of aspects of Tibetan culture has been tremendous. By contrast, whereas Christian monasticism is only of secondary importance to its faith,[1] Buddhist monasticism is generally seen as primary to Buddhism. Its importance is brought to the fore both in Buddhist doctrine and Buddhist practice. It should, therefore, not come as a surprise that Buddhist monastic institutions not only were a religious "driving force" but also organizations that dealt with so much more than religion alone. In Tibet, as in other countries where Buddhism was adopted as the dominant religion, monasteries came to be major players in politics, economics, culture, art, and society as a whole. This book investigates the role and position of these Buddhist monasteries in Tibetan societies.

While the Christian monastic institution, as it existed in medieval Europe, is seen as the earliest form of organization and a model for later institutions such as schools, orphanages and hospitals, the Buddhist monastic community, according to Spiro, has provided no model for the organization of lay society.[2] Although it is doubtful that this remark is applicable to all Buddhist cultures, Spiro's comment shows how this notion of religious specialists as guardians of social institutions is ingrained in the psyche of many modern (Western) thinkers and commentators— be they academically or otherwise affiliated. People who are aware of the role that Christian monasticism has played throughout history regularly associate the clerical role with particular worldly concerns, social service, community welfare, economic justice, and charity work. Evidence for this influence is found throughout the history of the Christian church.[3] This is what raises the question of why certain other religions and non-Christian societies have *not* led to the same types of ubiquitous institutions; it is difficult not to view the other through the lens of one's own cultural and religious background. Even though this book does engage the above question—simply put: "why not Buddhism?"—it is not of primary importance. Here, the starting point is the emic position—that is to say, how (monastic) Buddhists view society and the duties and rights of individuals and institutions, and further, how monks actually put these views into practice.

The level of influence of any given religion on a society or a culture and the nature of the relationship between doctrine and reality, theory and practice, are much debated issues. It is difficult, if not impossible, to determine these relationships. As Spiro contends: "It is one thing to assert that religion has a specified influence on one or another of a society's social or cultural institutions, and another to demonstrate it."[4] Until recently, it was seen as acceptable to explain social practices in societies on the basis of their religious doctrine, often with written texts as the sole source. This seems particularly to have been the case with regard to Buddhism, both within Buddhist Studies and outside of it. Such method of inquiry tends to yield the result—perhaps unsurprisingly—that reality and doctrine are often at odds with each other. Or so they seem. The dichotomies, problems, and contradictions that are blatantly obvious to the Buddhist Studies specialist are often invisible to Buddhists themselves, including the Buddhist literati. Rather than continuously looking for paradoxes, it is more useful to take the perspective of Buddhists as the point of departure. At the same time, one also should not uncritically reiterate certain "standard" Buddhist narratives that have evolved over time. Nonetheless, these narratives—and perhaps more importantly—the issues about which they remain silent, need to be tested and investigated.

Collins's *Selfless Persons* investigates "how the fact of social differences in thought and practice are taken account of *by Buddhist doctrine itself*, and how they affect it."[5] Here, I propose the inverse of this approach. In other words, I want to explore the ways in which social differences and relationships existed within a Buddhist society in practice and, subsequently, to examine whether—if at all— these differences were seen to be justified by aspects of Buddhist thinking by figures who had an active, authoritative role within monastic communities. Here the point of departure is not "Buddhist doctrine" but realities on the ground.

In this study the focus is on pre-modern Tibet, by which I mean the period before 1959.[6] When we examine pre-modern Tibetan Buddhism as interpreted and propounded by monastic authors, can we pinpoint a homogenous perception of a certain societal responsibility? Did the rules as stated in the monastic "law" codes imported from India (the Vinaya) and in textual materials on the individual monks' vows (*prātimokṣa*)—shared by all Tibetan monastics—create a uniform set of morals that guided monks when dealing with both internal and external affairs? Or could it be that other factors were at play in the development of monastic rules and regulations and that, more generally, there existed an alternative set of standards that dictated how to treat others?

Naturally, it is to be expected that Buddhist ethics, as communicated by Buddhist texts such as biographies (*rnam thar*), *Jātaka* tales, sūtras, and "introductory" works (*lam rim*), to name but a few, had some influence on the monks' sense of morality. However, it is likely that other factors were at play that, to a certain extent, were decided by cultural, economical, political, and geographical matters. Furthermore, monks were also influenced by the religious and political affiliations of the monastery and the charisma of particular spiritual leaders.

## BUDDHISM AND SOCIETY

*The laity are tolerant both in religious and social matters, but not the priesthood.*
—BELL [1946] 1998: 21

Buddhism is often seen as a religion that contains strong expressions of morality: a religion emphasizing orthopraxy over orthodoxy.[7] This focus on "right practice," however, has not materialized in the pre-modern Buddhist societies' development of well-organized "faith-based" social institutions. This notable absence has opened up varieties of Buddhism throughout Asia—and perhaps Tibetan Buddhism in particular—to the criticism of not being (sufficiently) socially engaged. This accusation did not stem solely from the camp of those who were heavily influenced by certain Judeo-Christian notions or those who had a political or ideological axe to grind. The Japanese Buddhist monk Ekai Kawaguchi, who traveled widely in Tibet between 1900 and 1903, comments on this lack of "social engagement" by "Tibetan priests."[8] He accuses them of being entirely disengaged from societal problems. Kawaguchi sees this social aloofness as a result of the Tibetan ideal of a hermitic lifestyle, in which practitioners willingly cordon themselves off from the outside world. He explicitly did not see this as a shortcoming of Buddhism itself.[9] This is in sharp contrast with attempts by certain non-Buddhist commentators to explain the lack of pre-modern institutions that promote social equality and welfare in Buddhist countries: if the connection with religion is made at all, the finger is usually pointed at the Buddhist faith in general, and the doctrine of karma in particular. In more extreme instances, scholars portray the Buddhist religion as nothing more than a power-grabbing ploy.[10]

That Buddhist societies of old did not give rise to social institutions in the way that they existed in the Christian world does not mean that Buddhism has had no influence on society as a whole. Rather than asking the question of why Buddhist societies have developed differently from Christian ones, it is more rewarding, at least from the outset, to examine the way in which Buddhism as practiced has affected certain societies and conceptualizations of society. In this book then, the focus is on pre-modern Tibetan societies and how monastic Buddhism has affected them.

In historical Tibetan societies, those writing about how Buddhists should behave in society were almost invariably monks. The works they produced were not directly taken from the corpus of Vinaya texts themselves. They were seen as codes of behavior that existed in parallel with the Vinaya, containing rules adapted to a specific time and place. These texts—the primary sources of this research—are monastic guidelines, *chayik* (*bca' yig*). These works were mostly written for the monk populations of specific monasteries, but they also affected the lay population, occasionally explicitly, and—as I shall argue—always implicitly. This is not to say that social norms were not also formed by other members of the "elite" in Tibet, but nevertheless the lion's share of written material to which we have access was written by monastics.

Throughout this book these monastic guidelines are used to understand where *Buddhism*—problematic though that term may be—touches on social policy and practice. From there we can explore whether and to what extent (monastic) social policy was informed by notions implicit within certain Buddhist beliefs or doctrines, at certain points in time. In the context of the study of pre-modern Tibet, even the mere *description* of societal processes is an enterprise that is rarely undertaken, let alone their analysis. One reason is that Tibetan politics on the one hand and religious doctrine on the other have historically taken center stage for most scholars involved in Tibetan Studies, Buddhist Studies, and (World) History.[11]

In addition to making sense of the role and position of monks and monasteries in Tibetan society, I endeavor to understand and analyze the underlying motivations or notions that in some way have a connection to Buddhism. In order to understand the position held and taken by monks, it then also becomes imperative to understand the structure they inhabited: the way the monastery was organized and how it functioned.

## ON SOURCES AND LACK THEREOF

There can be no doubt that monastics played an important role in almost all aspects of Tibetan society. But the exact, or even approximate, nature of that role has been little studied. Carrasco, writing in 1959, comments that since "the church plays such an important role in Tibet, it should be examined as a whole and in its relation to the lay society."[12] To date this research has not been undertaken. Tibetan monasteries have been both lionized and demonized for their impact on pre-modern society in Tibet. Critics chastised the Tibetan monastic institutions in particular for their economic dominance over large sections of the population and apparent lack of social engagement.[13] However, despite the existence of conflicting views on the underlying motivations of monasteries and monastics in their management of affairs, it is undeniable that Tibetan monastic Buddhism is of primary importance for understanding not merely the culture but also the history of pre-modern Tibet.

It is estimated that between 997 and 1959 over six thousand bigger and smaller monasteries were built in political Tibet alone.[14] They exerted great religious, cultural, political, and economic influence over the general populace. Although the literature these monks produced is most often utilized by academics for the study of complicated doctrinal conundrums, some of these texts contain valuable information on various aspects of pre-modern Tibetan society and how it was viewed by monastic authors. It needs to be noted, however, that the majority of the documents that bear direct witness to the role of monasteries in Tibet before the 1950s appear to be lost forever. Land deeds, contracts, monasteries' accounts, official correspondence, and the like were mostly destroyed, first when the People's Liberation Army arrived in Tibet in the 1950s and later during the Cultural Revolution (1966–76).[15] Thus, in the process of examining the monastery's position in Tibetan society, it is important to be aware of the lacunae regarding documents that contain information on social policy.

To better understand the role that monasteries played in Tibet throughout history, it is essential, first, to look at how the monasteries themselves operated and the general mind-set of the monks with regard to Tibetan (lay) society. In other words, any account of pre-modern Tibetan civilization would be incomplete without a more comprehensive appreciation of the impact of Tibetan monasticism on society as a whole. Ellingson similarly remarks upon "the need for understanding the monastic system, the most distinctive and characteristic of Tibetan sociopolitical institutions, on its own terms in order to develop a balanced and integral comprehension of Tibetan polity as a whole."[16]

The way in which scholars of contemporary Tibetan monasticism study the current state of the monastery shows that relatively little is known about the basic organizational structure of the monastery and the extent to which local and global politics, as well as "modernity," have affected this structure.[17] A complicating factor, as this study will demonstrate, is that organizational structures varied over time and place. However, when viewed comparatively, for example by looking at Christian monasticism, Tibetan monastic policies changed surprisingly little. While the political climate has now changed entirely for monks, both in exile and in Tibet, the monkhood is—for the most part—"a continuation of what came before in Tibet."[18]

This book largely deals with Tibetan religion and social history before the 1950s, and therefore, when general statements are made, they are often in the past tense.

This is not to say, however, that these policies, practices, or rationales ceased to exist after 1959. In many cases—of which I highlight only a few—they continue to the present. More research on contemporary Tibetan monasticism, both in exile and in Tibet, is needed to understand what has changed and what has remained the same.

By examining and comparing monastic guidelines, in which basic behavioral and organizational rules are set out and are seen as pivotal to the monastery for which they were written, it becomes possible to understand specific conditions prevailing at a certain monastery, which then influenced monastic behavior. Throughout the book, I supplement this information with materials that provide context: recent scholarship, monastic histories,[19] ethnographic and travelers' accounts, and oral history. The combination of these sources makes it possible to obtain a more comprehensive appreciation of the historical, economic, and political contexts. One type of source material that features in this study is oral history: interviews I conducted with elderly monks and monks in administrative positions. On the basis of the information they provide, it is possible to understand how texts were used and to determine the extent to which their contents affected monastics in daily life. The primary textual sources, the monastic guidelines written for the individual monasteries, are largely prescriptive and may paint an idealized picture of monastic life. However, close reading enables us to gain an understanding of the mainly religious, but also political, economic, and cultural ideas, that influenced the lives of the monks in the monastic institutions as well as those of laypeople.

So far, I have been able to locate more than two hundred sets of monastic guidelines. In order to obtain relatively representative results, texts were selected on the following basis: first, of course, their availability; their locality (center and periphery; historical Tibet and beyond);[20] their religious affiliation (all schools are represented); their respective economic circumstances ("state" sponsored, privately sponsored, partially self-sufficient, maintained by another monastery); and the age of the texts. It is noteworthy that the majority of the currently available *chayik* hail from the seventeenth and eighteenth centuries. This is likely due to the organizational overhaul that took place among monasteries as well as the building of new monasteries after the establishment of the Ganden Phodrang (*dGa' ldan pho brang*) government in 1642. In this year, Tibet became politically unified under one leader, the Fifth Dalai Lama, who took on both temporal and religious authority. However, texts from the twelfth to the sixteenth and from the nineteenth and twentieth centuries also feature widely in this research.

With regard to the religious affiliation of the texts, it is striking that the majority of the *chayik* that are generally available were written for Geluk (*dGe lugs*) monasteries.[21] It is tempting then to assume that the composition of monastic guidelines was largely a Geluk enterprise and to logically conclude that rules and discipline in the monasteries must have been deemed more important in the Geluk school than in others. Taking into account, however, the Geluk school's greater access historically to printing presses and the fact that more collected works (*gsung 'bum*) by Geluk masters have been (re-)printed and digitized, it comes as no surprise that there is a greater wealth of monastic guidelines for Geluk monasteries available at the moment. In fact, *chayik* written for monasteries of *all* other traditions exist. Paying due attention to the unevenness in the number of available materials, this study is based on a broad selection intended to be representative of the variety of monasteries that existed in greater political Tibet and its cultural spheres, thereby including Mongolia, Sikkim, Bhutan, Ladakh, Spiti, and Nepal.

Using the aforementioned sources, this book sets out to address the following questions: What was the role of the monastery and its monks in pre-modern Tibetan society? To what extent is that role a product of, or grounded in, Buddhist thought? What impact has the position of the Buddhist monks had on society as a whole? Before engaging with these issues, the problematic nature of two pivotal terms employed here—monk and monastery—needs to be addressed.

## WHAT MAKES A (TIBETAN) MONK?

There does not appear to be a consensus on the definition of the term "monk" in the context of Buddhist Studies. Silk, while acknowledging that the monastery would have been populated with various kinds of Buddhists, appears to translate the word "monk" only for the term *bhikṣu* (*dge slong*).[22] Similarly, Clarke also excludes "novices" (S. *śrāmaṇera, dge tshul*) from the classification of monks.[23] Were we to follow such an "exclusive" definition of the term "monk" we probably would not be able to classify the majority of Tibetans living in monasteries, today and in pre-modern Tibet, as monks. While the English word itself is of course not without its own semantic problems,[24] nevertheless, in this book, the word "monk" covers a broad range of Sanskrit and Tibetan terms.

In the genre of Tibetan literature under consideration here, we come across several terms referring to (male) inhabitants of a monastery,[25] such as *ban de,*[26] *grwa pa, btsun pa* (S. *bhadanta*), *bla ma,*[27] and *dge 'dun pa.* This overarching group of people who have "renounced" lay life or "have gone forth" (*rab tu byung ba,* S. *pravrajyā*) is most regularly subdivided into *dge slong* and *dge tshul.*[28] Sometimes, when an author wants to include everyone in the monastery, the *dge bsnyen* (S. *upāsaka*) are also mentioned, but in this context the *dge bsnyen* refer not simply to lay practitioners but to "aspiring monks." These are usually young boys who have not yet been allowed to take *dge tshul* vows or are not (yet) able to.[29]

Although Seyfort Ruegg is right in claiming that the division between laymen and monks was not always straightforward throughout the history of Buddhism,[30] the Tibetan normative distinction between a member of the Sangha and a layperson is fairly clear-cut. Of course, there were (and are) what scholars often perceive as gray areas, such as the "yellow householders" (*ser khyim pa*), a community of religious specialists who wore robes but married,[31] and the lay tantric practitioners,[32] who sometimes lived in "monasteries" of their own.[33] In this book, I use the term monk to refer to someone who has taken some sort of vow of celibacy and wears the monastic robes.[34]

A scholar monk at Kirti monastery, whom I interviewed in Dharamsala, remarked that for him—being from Amdo—the word *grwa pa,* which is the Central Tibetan word for "monk," appeared foreign,[35] but that *grwa* in his dialect—as it does in classical Tibetan—means "edge" or "side" (*zur*). In his analysis, this would thus make a *grwa pa,* a monk, someone who lives on the edge of society.[36] As is demonstrated in this study, while the above explanation is unlikely to be etymologically correct, it does describe the position of the Tibetan monk: not outside of society, but on the edge of it. As Collins so aptly puts it, "religious figures do not leave society, but merely exchange one social position for another."[37]

## WHAT MAKES A (TIBETAN) MONASTERY?

In this study, I delimit the monastery as an institution that demands celibacy of its members. By so defining the monastery, I exclude certain types of hermitages (*ri khrod*) and religious encampments (*chos sgar*), to name but a few, within which a commitment to celibacy—although common—was not, and is not, a prerequisite for admittance. The reason for excluding those religious institutions in which celibacy tended to be optional is not because the various religious groups consisting of non-celibate practitioners or a mixture of lay and monk members do not merit scholarly attention, but because one of the objectives of this book is to explore the connections between Tibetan monastic policy and organization and the Vinaya. This approach, furthermore, facilitates comparison with various kinds of Vinaya materials and procedures in place at monastic establishments in other Buddhist cultures that are similarly defined. Thus, despite the fact that there are a number of scholars working in different fields who call places inhabited by noncelibate religious practitioners "monasteries," I define the monastic institution in a narrower fashion. Considering that celibacy is "the *raison d'être* of Buddhist monasticism,"[38] the monastery is the very center of that celibacy.

So far, the English word "monastery" has been used to describe a (Tibetan) Buddhist phenomenon. There is a danger of confusing a number of terms here, however. According to Vinayic texts,[39] a physical establishment of the Sangha was only created by putting down a *sīmā,* a monastic "border,"[40] after which certain essential ritual practices could be performed. To be counted as a place where a Sangha lives, a set of three monastic rituals described in the Vinaya need to be performed (*gzhi gsum cho ga*): the fortnightly confession for *bhikṣus* (*gso sbyong,* S. *poṣadha*), the ritual start of the summer retreat (*dbyar gnas,* S. *varṣā*), and the ritual closing of that retreat (*dgag dbye,* S. *pravāraṇa*).[41] In practice, this does not mean, however, that each individual monastic community is required to have its own *sīmā*. In Dharamsala in India, the established ritual border is so large as to include at least fifteen monasteries and nunneries, all belonging to different schools. The fortnightly confession ritual is performed in the main temple there.[42] Thus, practically, a *sīmā* does *not* define a monastery or a monastic community, at least not in terms of a distinct institutional identity of any kind.

Scholars of Indian Buddhism often translate the Sanskrit *vihāra* as "monastery," introducing another set of problems. *Vihāras* often refer to the (potential) living spaces for monks, but according to Schopen, in the *Mūlasarvāstivāda vinaya*—the sole Vinaya in use in Tibet—they are not "presented here primarily as residences for monks to live in, but rather as potential and permanent sources of merit for their donors."[43] *Vihāra*, translated in Tibetan as *gtsug lag khang*, thus does not represent the "intentional" celibate communities we see in Tibetan Buddhism. There are a number of Tibetan terms, however, that *can* denote these monastic communities that live in well-defined physical spaces, which I choose to translate with the word "monastery": *gdan sa, grwa sa, dgon sde, chos sde, grwa tshang,* and *dgon pa.* In these places, the three rituals mentioned above may or may not be performed.[44]

The word *dgon pa* does not necessarily cover what Tibetans understand to be a living community of monks, for it refers more to a physical space than to a community. The contemporary Tibetan author and monk Rendo Senggé considers the primary meaning of this term to be a secluded place, although more generally Tibetans do not identify remote places of practice as such: "It is more common to understand *dgon pa* to be an institution where there is an organized community of ordained people who maintain the three rituals."[45] This author further emphasizes the educational aspects of the *dgon pa,* but it needs to be noted that this learning does not necessarily imply scholastic knowledge but may also include, or even solely refer to, ritual education.

The word *grwa tshang,* often glossed as "college" although this translation does not apply to all instances, has a stronger communal aspect, even though in contemporary Tibet many monks will primarily refer to their *dgon pa,* and only to their *grwa tshang*[46] when they, for example, belong to one of the Three Great Seats[47] and want to specify the subdivision within the large institution to which they belong, i.e., their college. The sources discussed in this study are selected on the basis of their representation of Tibetan Buddhist monastic communities before the 1950s, but also on the basis of the information they contain. Occasionally, the names of the geographical places mentioned in these works may suggest that they were hermitages (*ri khrod / nags khrod*) or temples (*gtsug lag khang*). However, the texts written for these institutions clearly suggest that they were seen, or saw themselves, as monastic celibate communities, using the word *grwa tshang.*[48]

Although there may be crossovers, monastic communities often have different primary functions, such as education, ritual practice, and meditational retreats.[49]

Tibetan monasteries can be characterized as monastic residencies, as communities organized around the performance of rituals, and as corporate entities.[50] While the specific ritual functions of monasteries are not explicitly examined in this study, the sense of community and identity, strengthened by shared vows, shared spiritual teachers, and shared geographical location—eventually amounting to the whole of the monastery—plays an important role in this study.

## AUTHORITY, THE STATE, AND THE MONASTERY

*Had it not been for the Buddhist dictum of humility . . . the monks could have considered themselves as the ruling elite of Tibet.*
—MICHAEL 1982: 57

While it is unlikely that the "Buddhist dictum of humility"—a highly problematic notion to begin with—had any impact whatsoever, it is important to appreciate the nature of the Tibetan government in order to understand the role of the monasteries in Tibetan society and the extent of their authority. It is a common misconception—particularly from the start of the Ganden Phodrang government in 1642 onward—that the Tibetan state was a single unity, with a high level of control and influence.[51] In fact, the Tibetan government always had a predisposition toward loose government. In other words, it controlled certain aspects of Tibetan society, but it certainly never attempted to govern at a local level. Power vacuums were thus filled by local landlords, chieftains, nobility, *and* monasteries.

At least conceptually, from the mid-seventeenth century onward, all land belonged to the Dalai Lama and his government, which meant that local leaders ultimately answered to the state. The position of monasteries was different from that of other ruling parties, because their authority was regularly both political and religious. This both facilitated and complicated relations with the government. The networks of Geluk monasteries were seen as safeguarding the ultimate authority of the state, whereas the larger monasteries of certain other schools were less likely to eagerly accept the influence of the state. At the same time, it was the influence of the large Geluk monasteries in Central Tibet that occasionally destabilized and undermined the authority of the government. The sheer number of monks living in these institutions was a force to be reckoned with: at one point, the Three Great Seats alone housed up to twenty-five thousand monks.

The broader question has yet to be satisfactorily answered: Why, compared to other countries where Buddhist monasticism thrived, was the number of monks so much higher in Tibet? Various sources give estimates of the monastic population that range from ten to as high as twenty-five percent of the Tibetan male population.[52] I suspect that while these numbers may have been accurate at certain times, from a demographical point of view they are open to misinterpretation. In particular, it is often not taken into account that at the largest monasteries in

Central Tibet (for usually the percentages of monks only pertain to that area), the number of "immigrant monks," e.g., people from Mongolia, Kham, Amdo, and beyond, must have been very high. Most of these monks were not permanent residents at these monasteries. Thus, even though one in four males residing in Central Tibet may indeed have been a monk, this does not mean that a quarter of all boys born in Central Tibet would eventually be sent to the monastery. The percentages—however high or low the estimates—are therefore nearly *always* misrepresentations, for these numbers would not necessarily have a direct effect on Central Tibetan society and its taxable workforce. Immigration and semipermanent residence thus are issues that need to be taken into account when making umbrella statements about the state of Tibet's societal composition.[53]

On a local level, the monastery was a crucial agent in Tibetan society. Taken as a whole, it had more influence on the day-to-day life of ordinary people than the state ever had. Usually, in examining issues of social welfare in a given society, the starting point is the main authority in place, which, in most cases in the modern Western context, is the state. This is taken as the point of departure when scrutinizing how authority deals with the general populace. In the Tibetan context, however, the direct authority was often, though by no means always, the monastic institution. It is for this reason that, while state involvement must be taken into account, the role of the government is not the starting point of this study. In the *longue durée* of Tibet's history, monasteries have been more influential in shaping the government than the government has been in shaping monasteries. Thus, the focus must be placed on these monasteries as *de facto* loci of influence and power.

## A PREVIEW

In order to contextualize the primary sources that form the backbone of this study, Chapter 1 focuses on the genre of the *chayik* as a whole and the way in which these texts relate to the larger corpora of both Indic and Tibetan Vinaya texts. In this chapter, I demonstrate that the *chayik* were often written in reaction to realities on the ground—that is, they deal with issues that were seen to be in need of attention. They thus contain mention of corruption, bribery, nepotism, maltreatment of lay servants, and political scheming. The texts furthermore give us insight into the internal hierarchy and organization of the monastery, its judicial role, monastic economics, and the social stratification within the monastery. For this reason, I argue in this chapter that these works are rich sources for monastic social history. This chapter also explores the parallels of the genre with other Buddhist traditions.

Chapter 2 provides a background of the monastic system that was prevalent in pre-modern Tibet. It looks at the development of monastic Buddhism in Tibet by tracing its history and compares the way the monastery was organized to that of a modern-day corporation. In this chapter the status of both monastery and monk in Tibetan society and how each has influenced monastic attitudes toward social issues is examined. The chapter also explores the extent to which these monastic attitudes are grounded in Buddhist thought.

Chapter 3 looks at the ways in which entrance to the monastery was restricted. Contrary to what is often thought, the monastery was not open to all. The monastic guidelines provide information on who was and was not allowed to become a monk. The works give reasons that are economic, geographical, or that have to do with (ritual) purity. This chapter explores both Vinayic and local justifications for barring certain people from entering the monastery and thereby—potentially— preventing them from social advancement.

Chapter 4 focuses on the organization of the Tibetan monastery, how the community was formed, and how monastic official and administrative roles were divided. Informed by the monastic guidelines, this chapter considers the internal hierarchy and social stratification within the monastery and argues that the monastic institution was two-tiered, in which religious authority and managerial power were often carefully kept separated.

Chapter 5 explores monastic economy: how the monastery balanced the Vinaya- based need for limited possessions and the upkeep of the monastic institution. In this chapter I discuss the issue of an individual monk's commercial enterprises, trade conducted by the monasteries, monastic property in general, the monasteries' function as banks, and the theoretical economic separation of the individual and the institutional as featured in the monastic guidelines and the Vinaya.

Chapter 6 deals with the relations between the monastery and the laity. Here particular attention is given to issues of charity and to the relationship between sponsors and their monastic beneficiaries. The rules regarding monks not just receiving but also *giving* alms are examined, assessing the types of reciprocity that took place. It further considers family ties, the role of the monastery as an educational facility, and issues regarding healthcare in and around the monastic institutions, as featured in the monastic guidelines.

Chapter 7 examines the judicial position of the monasteries in Tibet. It looks at the extent to which these institutions were legally allowed and even *obligated* to punish both laypeople and monks, paying some attention to what kind of punishments were given. The chapter further explores cases in which monks were to be tried according to state law and looks at what happened to monks who broke their vows.

In addition to summing up the main points and arguments made throughout the study, the final chapter discusses the central position of the Tibetan monastery in society and the role of Buddhist monasticism on societal change. The monastic reluctance to change is connected to the Buddhist idea of "the age of decline" (*kaliyuga*), as well as to the position of the Sangha as the guardian of Buddhism. It is argued that monastic perceptions of what is just or morally right are intimately connected to the monk's duty to bring about the happiness of all, but not in the way that most people would presume: monks promote the welfare of others by maintaining order and discipline.

Throughout this study some references to other Buddhist cultures and even to other types of monasticism are offered. This is done in order to emphasize that Tibetan monastic Buddhism cannot and should not be viewed in (geographical) isolation, as has been a general tendency of previous scholarly works. In contemporary academia, the mystification and idealization of the Tibetan monkhood—and more broadly, Buddhist monasticism in its entirety—continues. Ellingson, writing in 1990, notes: "Tibetan monasteries are still widely characterized as mysterious enclaves of 'priests,' Rasputin-like powers behind thrones, and hordes of ignorant fanatics who periodically and inexplicably march forth to topple governments."[54] This depiction is still current, although it alternates with the equally persistent cliché of monasteries filled with enlightened beings, all striving to bring happiness to this world.

Aware that to represent past Tibetan societies is an undertaking "permeated with uncertainty and subjectivity,"[55] this study aims to present a picture of Tibetan monks and monasteries that remains close to the Tibetan sources, without taking them at face value and without the need to pay lip service to any political agenda or theory. Monastic policy and ideology are the focal points of this book, although all assertions are made with the understanding that "to categorize human actions as ideal or material is philosophically absurd, they are always both."[56] The monastic guidelines are works that contain both the ideal and the material, to which I now turn.

# 1

# Documents That Establish the Rules

## *The Genre of* Chayik

### INTRODUCTION

*... a broad survey of bca'-yig ... provides what might be considered a general outline of normative monastic polity.*
—ELLINGSON 1990: 207

The extent to which Indic monastic guidelines, that may have existed in either oral or written form, influenced their Tibetan counterparts is unknown. In any case, Tibetan authors never point to Indian precedents for their monastic guidelines.[1] Rather, the claim most commonly made is that the monastic guidelines address both local and contemporary issues, to which Indian precedents would not be relevant.

A *chayik* or a *chayik*-like text in its most basic form is a formal, written address directed to a group of religious practitioners and concerns the future of that group.[2] It may not necessarily be restricted to religious practitioners.[3] The term is an abbreviation of *khrims su bca' ba'i yi ge*—a document that establishes rules.[4] The most likely origins for the word *chayik* are the works mentioned in the *Mūlasarvāstivāda vinaya*. Schopen notes the existence of the so-called *kriyākāraṃ*, which is found in Tibetan translations as both *khrims su bca' ba* and *khrims su bya ba*. These are texts of which both secular and clerical versions exist. Both types can be found within the vast corpus of the *Mūlasarvāstivāda vinaya*.[5]

An early document that contains "regulations for the monastic community" stems from the third century and is written in Kharoṣṭhī script. It is from Central Asia and unfortunately fragmentary. The regulations for the community of monks contained in this text list the kinds of punishment that were meted out for certain types of offenses.[6] Schopen mentions that not much research has been done

on these "monastic ordinances" and that in all likelihood they were more important to monastic communities than the canonical Vinaya.[7] Mention of *sāṃghikaṃ
kriyākāraṃ* occurs in the *Bodhisattvabhūmi*. In it the bodhisattva's actions through
which he would commit a fault are described, such as not rising to greet his senior.[8]

The earliest Tibetan texts that were later labeled *chayik* are still relatively late,
some four hundred years after monastic Buddhism was supposed to have been
introduced into Tibet. Mention of eleventh-century Kadam (*bKa' gdams*) monastic guidelines is made in a fifteenth-century religious history.[9] In this work, the
author claims not merely to have heard of, but also to have seen, *chayik* authored
by the important Kadam masters Gonpawa (dGon pa ba), Sharawa (Shar ba pa),
and Potowa (Po to ba), as well as four sets of monastic guidelines for the general Sangha (*dge 'dun spyi'i bca' yig*).[10] To my knowledge, these works, which then
would stem from the eleventh century, are not extant.

The oldest existing works containing instructions for religious organizations
hail from the twelfth century. According to Ellingson, the first *chayik*-like text contains prescriptions for aspects of monastic governance and consists of instructions
given by Lama Zhang (Zhang brtson 'grus grags pa, 1123–1193), written down and
preserved in his collected works.[11] The tradition maintains that it was recorded as
an oral testament directed to his successors at the monastery of Tsel Gungtang
('Tshal gung thang). It is said to have been spoken when Lama Zhang was on
his deathbed, thus either in or before 1193.[12] Even though this text contains some
valuable information on the monastic organization of the late twelfth century, the
monastic guidelines did not develop into a more established genre of literature
until the fourteenth century.

Interestingly, a number of *chayik* survive that were written in the Mongolian
language. These texts, however, have imported various technical Tibetan terms,
which are phonetically transcribed, making them difficult to understand for most
Mongolian readers.[13] Several bilingual sets of *chayik* also exist, in which the Mongolian is most likely translated from the Tibetan.[14] These Tibeto-Mongolian texts
merit further study.

## CONSTITUTIONS, REGULATIONS, OR GUIDELINES?

The only scholar to have written on the genre of *chayik* in more general terms is
Ellingson. In his article, he proposes that this genre derived from sources such
as common law and traditional rights. In light of the presumed origination in
Tibetan traditional "secular" law, he translates *chayik* both as "monastic constitution" and as "a monastic constitutional document." He states: "the Tibetan bca' yig
are 'constitutions' in the sense that they are constitutional-documentary outlines
of part of a more extensive body of documentary and traditional fundamentals of
monastic government."[15] He does not give further information on this extensive

body of works but mentions that many of these may be oral.[16] The translation of "monastic constitution" or "monastic ordinances" for the Tibetan word *chayik* is problematic, as a fair number of texts that are called *chayik* are not written for *monastic* communities. We know of *chayik* written for hermitages (*ri khrod*)[17] and for communities of tantric practitioners who are not monks.[18]

Certain legal codes in Bhutan are also called *chayik*, although this is a more recent development.[19] Another interesting occurrence of the word is in the context of modern Amdo, where in certain village communities, the term *chayik* can denote a series of rules jotted down in a notebook. These consist of rules on lay religious gatherings (such as reciting *maṇi* mantras) and state the monetary fines to be paid by those who fail to attend, do not wear Tibetan dress, or arrive late at the gathering.[20] The name *chayik* also crops up in the context of regulations for certain Himalayan communities. There is a text for the inhabitants of Pachakshiri, written by Lama Lodre Gyamtso in the early 1930s and some years later completed by Sonam Gelek Rabtan Lhawang. It gives information on the migration of people to an area and the creation of a so-called Hidden Land (*sbas yul*). The text lays down rules on correct moral behavior, the relationship between the ruler and his subjects, the establishment of law, and social and religious order. It also provides instruction on how to deal with newcomers or tribal neighbors. It can be read as a justification of Pachakshiri's inhabitants' rights as the chosen community.[21] The word *chayik* appears in yet another context: a text that contains guidelines on issues such as aesthetics and punctuation for copyists of the Kanjur.[22]

It is clear that *chayik* is a name for a genre of texts that address multiple audiences. However, here the word *chayik* is translated as "monastic guidelines" because the texts dealt with in this book are by and large limited to the monastic context. I use the word "guidelines," although one might render the word *chayik* as: regulations, constitutions, rules, codes, protocols, manuals, laws, rulebooks, regulatory texts, codified rules, regimens, monastic injunctions, standards, charters, or edicts. Because *chayik* may cover a variety of topics, ranging from the details of punishments to mere spiritual advice, a translation that has a broad coverage is preferred.

## MONASTIC GUIDELINES AND THE LAW

Aside from an etymological connection between the word *chayik* and the term that denotes legal documents (*rtsa tshig*),[23] another possible connection of the *chayik* with legal and secular texts is their appearance. Several pre-modern *chayik* found *in situ* in monasteries do not have the palm-leaf shape most religious texts do, but are scrolls made out of sheets of paper stuck together with glue.[24] They could also be scrolls made out of cloth or silk. The Mongolian author Lopzang Tamdrin (Blo bzang rta mgrin, 1867–1937), the author of the guidelines for a monastery likely to have been established in Mongolia, explains the process of creating the guide-lines: "In the midst of an assembly of old and new studying monks, I, together with friends and enemies, 'made' a big piece of paper and established regulations regarding congregating."[25]

Law codes that were kept in the Tibetan courts had the same scroll-like shape, similar to that of many other official secular documents.[26] Nowadays, Tibetan monasteries in exile still keep the version of the monastic guidelines that is read out by the disciplinarian in the same format, while copies that are handed out to monks usually take the shape of a small book.

While there are indications that suggest that the format of the texts as well as the term (and subsequently the genre of) *chayik* is derived from Tibetan legal sources, the contents and vocabulary of available works that carry the word *chayik* in their title do not suggest a *direct* relationship to Tibetan "secular" law. Most of the monks I interviewed, when asked how they viewed the relationship between secular law ("lay law") and the *chayik,* find there to be considerable overlap, as the monastic rules contain "laws" that could be found in secular society, such as the rule on not killing human beings. One respondent mentioned that for this reason the monastic law[27] is broader in spectrum than the layperson's law, as the latter does not contain rules on religious behavior.[28] This indicates that (at least some) Tibetan monks think of the rules of the monastery as a parallel law.

Another respondent noted that, generally speaking, the monastic guidelines fall under state law: the contents of the guidelines can never contradict the gen-eral law.[29] The compilers of a book published in Tibet in the 1980s, which con-tains a variety of pre-modern law texts, also saw the connection, because aside from numerous important works on secular law it contains five sets of monastic guidelines and a text by the Fifth Dalai Lama that explains the *prātimokṣa* vows.[30] A more elaborate discussion on the role of the monastic guidelines within the monastic organization and its legal authority, as well as a more general treatment of the judicial position of the monastery, can be found in chapter 7.

## MONASTIC GUIDELINES AS AN INSTRUMENT OF GOVERNMENT?

In some cases, monastic guidelines functioned as an instrument of government. At certain times, the monastic guidelines were tools of the state, or of those allied with the state. At other times, they were the instruments of local governing bod-ies or people whose authority was largely religious in nature. This distinction can be easily made by looking at the authors of the monastic guidelines. Some writers were the founders of the monastery for which they wrote the guidelines, others were in one way or another affiliated to the monastery but were requested to write monastic guidelines because of the charismatic authority they enjoyed among the monastic population. Again others wrote monastic guidelines for monasteries that were far removed, both physically and "religiously," beyond the reach of the authors' effective power. Examples of this can be seen in the works of the Fifth Dalai Lama, who authored monastic guidelines for Bon and Nyingma (*rNying ma*) monasteries, and in those of the Thirteenth Dalai Lama, the author of many *chayik,* mostly for monasteries in Kham and Amdo. These monasteries presumably already had monastic guidelines of their own, but it appears that issuing these texts was, to a large extent, a political act—a way to draw Eastern Tibetan monasteries, not well known for their allegiance to the Central Tibetan government, into the political and religious sphere of the Dalai Lama.

It is important to note that the existence of government-issued monastic guidelines at monasteries far removed from the political center is *not* proof of state control or even mere influence; rather, it should be understood to be proof of *an attempt* at state control and nothing more. While the political qualities of the monastic guidelines should never be overlooked and do merit further research, this book deals mostly with the practical usages of the monastic guidelines.

## MONASTIC GUIDELINES AND THE VINAYA

Some see the monastic guidelines as additions to the existing Vinaya code[31] or clarifications and abridged versions of it. Ellingson suggests, for example, that the *chayik* were (and still are) seen as necessary because certain rules in the Vinaya were believed to require clarification.[32] Others view these types of work as presenting the practical message of the Vinaya in a more accessible way,[33] as the Vinaya texts themselves were often—not only conceptually, but even physically—inaccessible. In China, the canonical Vinaya was initially not translated, and the Vinaya texts were often not kept in the monasteries.[34] In Tibet, those who wished to conduct a formal study of monastic discipline were required to be *bhikṣus*.[35] Furthermore, in the monastic educational curriculum of the Geluk school, the Vinaya is a topic only studied for the last four years of the scholastic training that takes a total of at least sixteen years.[36] Moreover, the canonical Vinaya texts themselves are and were not studied in any of the Tibetan monastic educational systems. The main focus lay instead on Guṇaprabha's *Vinayasūtra* (*'Dul ba'i mdo rtsa ba*), a summary of the rules found in the Vinaya.[37]

Thus, while the Vinaya was an integral part of the monastic curriculum, extensive knowledge of the contents was not a requirement for scholastic progress.[38] The number of studying monks in traditional Tibet was relatively small, so the vast majority of monks therefore *never* studied Vinayic texts in any detail; all their awareness of monastic regulations and guidance came through oral instruction and the monastic guidelines. Monastic life was thus directly regulated more by local monastic guidelines than by the Vinaya.[39]

This makes it likely that, at least in Tibet, exactly because they usually addressed *all* monks who inhabited a monastery, the monastic guidelines were *not* mere appendices to Vinayic texts. As noted above, the *chayik* are seen as more comprehensive than secular law codes, and—perhaps in a similar way—they are believed to function as a means to uphold not just the *prātimokṣa*, but all the vows, which include more than just the Vinaya. A contemporary work on Pelyul (dPal yul) monastery formulates this thought in the following way: "Furthermore, the internal rules of the monastery are laid down as a foundation, so as to not go against the duties and prohibitions of the three: *prātimokṣa*, bodhisattva and tantra [vows], as well as the local and religious customs."[40]

Another way in which the monastic guidelines can be said to be more "inclusive" than the Vinaya is that although the monastic guidelines usually overtly address only the Sangha, they demonstrate that laypeople—both monastery employees and lay devotees—were often part of the "jurisdiction" of the monastic institution. In Tibet, for example, hunting on monastic property was forbidden, and a set of monastic guidelines by the Thirteenth Dalai Lama states that hunters caught in the act were forced to leave their weapons in the protectors' chapel and to promise not to reoffend.[41] This regulation thus addresses the behavior of those outside of the monastic community, something that does not occur in the Vinaya itself.

In the case of Tibetan monasteries, there was a need to supplement the general discipline with more specific documents that focused on "the practical aspects of daily life."[42] Such documents have on the whole little to do with clarifying the Vinaya or the *prātimokṣa* vows, but contain practical instructions that seek to regulate monastic life. One set of monastic guidelines, written by the Fifth Dalai Lama in 1664, notes in its opening verses that the text contains the means to "bring about liberation [that is] being disciplined (*dul ba'i rnam thar*) through establishing rules and morality."[43] Here the author connects adhering to the rules with spiritual progress, and inserts a play on words: *dul ba* (S. *vinīta*), meaning control, ease, or being tame(d), is the end result of *'dul ba,* the effort of taming, disciplining oneself, and the translation of the Sanskrit word *vinaya.* Even though the importance of adhering to certain rules is linked to one's religious practice, the *chayik* are neither necessarily clarifications nor new standards, nor merely supplements to the Vinaya, but handbooks or guidelines.

According to the Pāli Vinaya, the first Buddhist Council decreed that the Sangha was not to alter Buddha's laws.[44] The notion that the Vinaya, and in particular the monastic vows, cannot and should not be modified appears very much alive today. Many of the senior Tibetan monks I interviewed insisted that the rules for the monastery have no bearing on the rules contained in the Vinaya, because the monastic rules are flexible, whereas the Vinayic ones—which is to say, the *prātimokṣa* vows—are not.[45] It is perhaps for this reason that one can see the Vinaya rules and the monastic guidelines as existing—at least in theory—alongside each other. As Smith notes: "Although bca' yig have a close connection with the vinaya rules, the two are quite distinct. Monastic morality and individual conduct are the fundamental concerns of the vinaya literature, while institutional organization and the liturgical calendar are emphasized in bca' yig."[46]

The literature that contains local or specific monastic rules is never presented as a commentary to Vinaya material. Nonetheless, the authors of these works regularly emphasize that they write in accordance with the contents of the Vinaya, and they sometimes add that certain Vinaya-like works have been consulted. One such example is the *chayik* for Pabongka hermitage, written in the early 1800s. Toward the end of this work, the author Yeshé Lopzang Tenpé Gonpo (Ye shes blo bzang bstan pa'i mgon po, 1760–1810) states:

> In short, all manners of behavior that have been clarified in these monastic guidelines [have come about] by taking the *Vinayapiṭaka* as a witness. However, there were some slight differentiations that needed to be made due to the time and place here in this Land of Snow. This is not to meddle recklessly and take control of the Dharma, but it is [to follow] the early great and honorable scholar practitioners, in particular Tsongkhapa and his two main disciples.[47]

Here then the Vinaya, or rather the notion of the Vinaya, is used to reaffirm the authority of the rules given in this text.

Several *chayik* cite extensively from Vinayic works, while others make no mention of them whatsoever. This may have to do with the intended audience of the *chayik,* which could have varied, as well as with the expertise of the author. One senior monk, the disciplinarian Ngawang Peljin, comments:

> The monastic guidelines, generally speaking, contain rules pertaining to the relations within the monastic community. If it is relevant, then the Vinaya is quoted in these works, as a support. For example, if I were to say: "Hey, you are a monk, you should not drink alcohol," then some monks will listen but others will simply say: "Well, why is that exactly?" I can then give a valid reason and say that this is the word of the Buddha, and give the appropriate citation. That often makes quoting useful.[48]

It is not the case, however, that these monastic rulebooks were never in contradiction with rules found in the Vinaya corpus. In comparison, the contents of the Sri Lankan counterparts, the *katikāvata,* sometimes did deviate from the canonical law and even directly contradicted it.[49] It is, however, rare for this type of literature to display an awareness of the possibility of a contradiction between Vinaya and monastic rules.

To what extent then did monastic regulations silently "overrule" Vinaya rules rather than merely exist alongside them? Schopen notes that in Buddhist India this process was not even necessarily always silent: "Explicit instances of adaptation of monastic rule to local custom can be found in all vinayas." He sees this preference for local values as a characteristic that also features in Indian *Dharmaśāstra* materials, where the accepted principle appears to have been that "custom prevails over dharma."[50]  *power of local customs/rules*

If this overruling of monastic rule by local custom were a regular occurrence, which set of rules held final authority? This brings us to the place of the Vinaya in Tibetan monasticism. As mentioned earlier, the Vinaya was a subject often only studied in the later years of one's monastic curriculum. This did not mean, however, that Tibetan authors did not encourage monks to study the Vinaya. The Thirteenth Dalai Lama emphasizes the importance of studying the Vinaya along with its commentaries, for without it one would "become blind to correct behavior."[51] It is important to note that the relative lack of emphasis on the study of the Vinaya is not exclusively found in Tibetan Buddhist monasticism; it is equally a feature of the Theravāda tradition. Blackburn writes that in medieval Sri Lanka a monk who had not yet become an "elder" (*thera*) was unlikely to ever encounter the Vinaya. She argues that instead certain sūtras were used to teach monks about monastic discipline.[52]

Not just in Tibet, but throughout the Buddhist world we find that the monasteries are institutions that were (and still are) ultimately pragmatic. The monastic guidelines are witness to this pragmatism. They show the efforts made by the authors to regulate the monastic community and to negotiate its position within society.

## AUTHORSHIP AND AUTHORITY

Monastic guidelines can have various purposes. I distinguish three subgenres among the *chayik*: (1) guidelines for multiple monasteries written by someone whose religious authority is acknowledged by those monasteries; (2) codes written for multiple or all monasteries of a particular region, encouraged or enforced by a political ruler; and (3) rulebooks for individual monasteries that contain references to specific situations and local practices. Often it will prove difficult or impossible to distinguish the first two. An example of this are the Sikkim monastic guidelines in which the author has religious as well as political authority.[53] However, the majority of the extant Tibetan Buddhist monastic guidelines are written for specific monasteries.

Most of the now available *chayik* have been written by famous Buddhist masters. It is likely that many monastic guidelines were, in fact, written by a group of people or by less illustrious monks, which therefore remained without signature. I suspect that the majority of these—as having no authorship equals having no prestige—have not survived the Cultural Revolution. Some of these "anonymous" *chayik* have, however, been preserved. The *Collection of Monastic Guidelines* (*bCa' yig phyogs sgrig*) contains a *chayik* from 1903 written by the "office" (*yig tshang*) for Pelkor Chödè.[54] Another set of guidelines from 1900 suggests that the contents had been written by the higher monastic officials and the community of monks.[55]

Monastic guidelines are in many ways comparable to any set of guidelines for a larger institution such as those of a university, which means that they do not necessarily need an author. The works were often compilations of new and previously existing rules and were even sometimes taken from the guidelines of other institutions. The role of the author becomes pivotal not with regard to the contents of the guidelines but to the way the guidelines were received, perceived, and implemented. Authorship often equaled authority, but at times authorship also *required* authority. A monk who acted as the disciplinarian at Sera Je (Se ra byes) in India some decades ago wrote a set of guidelines for his monastic college, but "when the rules were completed, many [monks] did not like them and for two nights, stones were pelted at my house, which is why . . . shutters had to be made. They did that twice in the night within a gap of about seven days."[56] It appears that—not only in the past, but even today—monastic guidelines were more likely to be accepted by the monk body when they involved either consensus or religious authority, or both.

## THE ACCESSIBILITY AND PRACTICAL USE OF THE MONASTIC GUIDELINES

The monastic guidelines were often inaccessible—to laypeople and to ordinary monks. Although all monks in the Kirti monastery in India have access to the *chayik,* in the Kirti monastery in Amdo, the text used to be restricted solely to the disciplinarian.[57] In Ganden, the *chayik* was kept by the disciplinarian or the monastery's head and it was not disclosed to others.[58] In some monasteries, this is still the case. The texts are oftentimes equally inaccessible to researchers. During my fieldwork, my access to them was occasionally limited. Of the fifteen monasteries I visited, three did not make use of a specific set of guidelines. However, at seven of the monasteries the *chayik* were not public: only the disciplinarian had access to the text. In three cases, I was able to look at or photograph the texts. In the other four instances I was not allowed to see them. Although this is just a small sample, it does not appear to be a coincidence that all seven of these monasteries where the monastic guidelines were in some way restricted are Geluk.[59]

Different informants gave me different reasons as to why these works are kept hidden. Rendo Senggé hypothesizes that the *chayik* at Kirti in Tibet is not public "because it concerns the monastery's rules, the monks' rules. It does not concern the general populace. It is also kept away because it is considered precious."[60] In a similar vein, another informant, who would not let me copy the monastic guidelines, said that the *chayik* is not for everyone to see and that one is not meant to show it to laypeople. He justified this by saying that it is precious, or "holy," and needs to be taken care of. Nevertheless, because the *chayik* in question had already been published in the author's collected works, he did allow me to have a brief look at it. Other Geluk monks I asked simply claimed they did not know why they were not public. The disciplinarian of Nechung monastery, who used to be a monk at Drepung ('Bras spungs) in Tibet, had also heard that monastic guidelines did not use to be public works. They were considered special—even holy—and were well guarded:

> There was a very special work there called *The Great Monastic Guidelines* (*bCa' yig chen mo*), written by the Fifth Dalai Lama. This work could only be kept by the over-arching disciplinarian. During the Great Prayer Festival these Drepung monastic guidelines would be "invited" to Lhasa. The disciplinarian would carry the text, accompanied by the disciplinarian's assistants and deputies, about twenty people in total. According to oral lore this text could fly. When transported to Lhasa, this text would not go underneath a particular stūpa close to the Potala. Instead, it would fly up, circumambulate the Potala, and land back into the disciplinarian's hands. For twenty-one days, during the festival, everyone would abide by the rules of the Great Prayer Festival.[61] On the way back, the text would again fly. This is an anecdote; I have of course not seen this myself. I was told that before 1959, the original text was kept safe at the monastery and that a copy of it would be used for general purposes. All the versions of it must have been destroyed: when I became a monk at Drepung there was no *chayik* there at all.[62]

Although none of the monk informants stated it explicitly, there seems to be a sacred—perhaps even a magical—element to the monastic guidelines.

There may be a parallel with the way the Vinaya was restricted to laypeople as well: "Vinaya texts were not meant for public consumption, but were strictly—*very* strictly—in-house documents."[63] A similar notion also seems to have been upheld in Sri Lanka, where the local monastic rules stipulate that the disputes settled within the monastery should not be made known to outsiders, and that members of one monastery should not meddle in the disputes of other monasteries.[64]

It should be noted that the Geluk school seems to be the exception here, not the rule. As far as I am aware, none of the other schools impose explicit restrictions on access to the monastic guidelines. The Nyingma monastery Pelyul in Kham has its rules posted above the entrance to the assembly hall. All monks were meant to memorize this *chayik* for the assembly hall, which is written in verse. It is recited at all assemblies.[65] Hemis monastery, affiliated with the Drukpa Kagyü school (*'Brug pa bka' brgyud*) in Ladakh, also has a (more recent) *chayik* above the entrance of the assembly hall. One of my informants reported hearing that many monastic guidelines in Tibet used to be written on the walls of the assembly hall. Because all monks had to go there regularly, they would be reminded of the rules.[66]

Most monasteries had, whether publicly accessible or not, one or more *chayik*. The mere presence of guidelines, however, does not mean that they were followed to the letter. For example, Lobzang Döndrup of Spituk monastery told me that only when things go wrong does the disciplinarian consult the text and use it to clarify the rules of the monastery. This relatively small Ladakhi monastery does not, however, hold a ceremonial reading from the monastic guidelines.[67] Sometimes the

*Sacred, but due to tradition/history, not current practice*

opposite is true and then the *chayik* has a purely ceremonial purpose, even though its contents are viewed as unusable. This is the case in Tsechok Ling (Tshe mchog gling), India, where an eighteenth-century *chayik* is read aloud, but only during ceremonies. Practical rules have been added for the day-to-day management of the monastery.[68] Generally speaking, it is likely that the rules were only consulted in unusual situations, or when there was a need to support a decision with a (religious) textual authority. However, again, this appears to be more common in the Geluk monasteries than in the others.

Some parallels to this use of rules as mere tokens of authority can be found in the treatment of secular law in Tibet. According to Schuh, despite the fact that there were formal secular laws in place, so far there is little evidence that they were ever applied in practice.[69] Pirie writes that the legal code in its written form had a symbolic function and that it was only used to support the authority of the person charged with mediating two parties, not for its contents.[70] The notion of a written work that has as its main function the empowerment of the authority that has access to the work seems a pervasive one in Tibetan (and more generally, Buddhist) culture. Various sources show that the *chayik* was used as a tool to lend authority to figures in some kind of official position, in most cases that of the disciplinarian.

Gutschow writes that every year at the Geluk Karsha monastery in Zangskar a new disciplinarian is appointed. The accompanying ceremony is held on the twenty-fifth of the tenth month: the day on which the death of Tsongkhapa is commemorated (*dGa' ldan lnga mchod*). The new disciplinarian arrives at the monastery riding a horse, and is welcomed "like a new bride"—he is presented with ceremonial scarves (*kha btags*) and receives a variety of gifts. He then reads out the monastic guidelines to the congregation.[71] It is likely that this has been a public event, open to monks and laypeople alike. Excerpts of a *chayik* for Amdo's Labrang (Bla brang) monastery written by the second Jamyang Zhépa ('Jam dbyangs bzhad pa, 1728–1791) were indeed read out publicly to laypeople and monks alike. Nietupski presumes that its function was "a formal recognition of authority."[72]

This analysis is possibly incomplete. Assuming that reading parts of the monastic guidelines aloud to an audience of laypeople, as well as monks, was indeed intentional, I believe that it served, naturally, to set a standard for the monks to live by, but also that it gave laypeople an idea of how monks were meant to live. This, in turn, would presumably inspire admiration for the monks' adherence to the rules. This admiration, paired with the general concept that donations given to worthy receivers generate more merit, would strengthen the existing religious and economic relations between monks and laypeople. In other words, making the monastery's rules known to the lay community would increase social cohesion and control. This is because laypeople perceive themselves to have a stake in the correct behavior of the monks they support—rituals and the like are believed to be less effective when performed by monks with poor ethical discipline, and the amount of merit gained by making a donation is dependent on the religious standing of the receiver.[73] The reputation of the monks among the lay community is immensely important and this is corroborated by many of the monastic guidelines. In fact, it is perhaps *the* most common line of reasoning for encouraging or discouraging certain types of behavior among monks.[74]

As previously mentioned, in some monasteries the *chayik* were (and are) public; in others the monastic guidelines were only ever consulted by the disciplinarians and abbots. The latter appears to be a Geluk approach, while several Geluk institutions had their *chayik* read out in public. This does not mean that all people in effect understood what was read out or that they had hands-on access to the actual texts. Although there is no direct evidence to support this hypothesis, as the traditional ways in which the individual monastic guidelines were employed are in many cases unknown or altogether lost, I suspect that the contents of the *chayik* differ according to whether they were intended to be for public or private use. Some works explicitly state that the intended audience are the monk officials,[75] whereas others are less explicit in this regard.

Close reading of the texts is a way to infer their intended audience: the voice of a *chayik* can show the extent of its "insiders' language." This also complicates the understanding of the contents of the monastic guidelines at certain points—they frequently make reference to things and situations only known by monks of that monastery at that particular time. It does allow us to get an idea of the intended audience of specific monastic guidelines. For example, when a *chayik* contains many more technical terms derived from the Vinaya, it seems likely that it was meant for a *specialist* audience, such as the disciplinarian, abbot, or other monastic official. When such terms are largely absent, then the text probably was directed to the general populace of monks. Certain turns of phrases in the works point to the performatory use of some *chayik*: some of these monastic guidelines most certainly were written to be read aloud. One of these, the early twentieth-century *chayik* for Pelyul Darthang (dPal yul dar thang) monastery in Golog (mGo log), Amdo, actually states that it needed to be recited monthly.[76]

## THE ORALITY OF THE MONASTIC GUIDELINES

Some of the longer *chayik* contain a long introduction consisting of the history of Tibet, Buddhism in Tibet, and the monastery in particular. This way of relating history is a common feature of Tibetan oral literature, prevalent in monastic as well as in nonmonastic contexts.[77] Again, this may be another indication of the performative function of the text.

Cabezón, in describing the monastic guidelines of Sera Je monastery, mentions that the text called *The Great Exhortation* (*Tshogs gtam chen mo*) is the transcription of an oral text written down only in 1991.[78] It clearly directly addresses the audience.[79] The text is traditionally read aloud once a year to the assembly of monks at the start of the "summer doctrinal session" by the disciplinarian.[80] It is not generally available to the monks.[81] Even though the monastic guidelines are now written down, when *The Great Exhortation* is performed, the disciplinarian is still at liberty to add certain things, such as proverbs. Certain monks who have misbehaved particularly badly may even be named and shamed at such an occasion.[82] Cech notes that the Bon *chayik* for Menri (sMan ri) monastery was to be read out once a year by the steward (*gnyer pa*), but does not provide any details on its general availability.[83]

Reading aloud the monastic guidelines was a regular occurrence, but not in all monasteries. In Kirti monastery in Tibet the *chayik* is still read out every year by the disciplinarian. Rendo Senggé describes it as a pleasant occasion: someone holds out the scroll and it is slowly unrolled as the disciplinarian reads. Its recitation does not sound like ordinary prayers or reciting other texts, since there is a specific "melody" (*dbyangs*) to it. In general, Kirti monastery has eight doctrinal sessions (*chos thog*), two for each season of the year. The *chayik* is read during one of those sessions but my informant could not remember which one. At that time, all the monks come together, but no laypeople are present. The disciplinarian reads out the *chayik* and explains the commentary (*'grel pa*) to it. If he is well educated then he also adds his own citations, which are usually from the Vinaya.[84] Thus, even in the case where the monastic guidelines are read out in public in a ritual context, they can be adapted as well as explained.

Again, it appears that the performatory aspect of the *chayik* is much stronger in the Geluk school than elsewhere. However, there is no uniformity among the Geluk monasteries when, by whom, and how often the text is "performed." In Gyütö (rGyud stod) monastery in India it is recited on average once every three years, on an auspicious date by the head chant master (*bla ma dbu mdzad*).[85] In other monasteries it is recited only when the conduct of the monks is found wanting.

The Tibetan monastic guidelines do not tend to be concerned with the minute details of the life of a monastic inmate. Instead they largely deal with the upkeep of an institution, the organization of the monks, and the monastery's reputation among patrons and direct neighbors. This is quite unlike the monastic regulations found in China and Japan, in which all mundane daily tasks are painstakingly prescribed. How then did Tibetan monks learn the proper way to conduct themselves, and to understand what was expected of them? From the interviews I have conducted, it has become clear that much of the information a new monk needed to know was passed on orally. A young monk would be assigned a "'teacher,"[86] who would be responsible for the monk's well-being but also ultimately for his financial situation.[87] It appears then that the day-to-day activities of ordinary monks were fairly strictly regulated, despite the fact that detailed descriptions of these activities did not tend to get written down. Geshe Lhundup Sopa notes that everyday matters would be solved by the relevant administrators according to an oral tradition of rules.[88] The monastic guidelines then seem, in one way or the other, to be connected both to rules that had previously just been communicated orally and to "edicts" promulgated by kings or high lamas. A set of monastic guidelines written some time around 1800 by Yeshé Lopzang Tenpé Gonpo in fact states that previously rules for the community of monks at the Pabongka hermitage had solely been communicated orally and that this text was the first to commit these rules to writing. The author also promises to promulgate the rules clearly, possibly suggesting that the oral transmission may have caused certain misunderstandings.[89]

## WHAT MONASTIC GUIDELINES CAN CONVEY

The Tibetan monastery is often described as a micro-cosmos, in which the inhabitants follow their own rules, according to their own standards, without being overly concerned with externalities such as politics, economics, or even the local population. Because of the great variety of monastery types, this description is not entirely accurate. We are aware that there were many monasteries that did have a great deal of independence and were largely self-governing bodies that had economic, political, and judicial power within their respective domains. The monastic guidelines are unique in that they can inform us about the makeup of the monastery, its internal hierarchy, and the (perceived) roles, rights, duties, and obligations of the monks within the institution.

The modern Tibetan work *Monasteries of Tibet* (*Bod kyi dgon sde*) states that monastic guidelines were consulted to decide on legal matters (*gyod don*) by the disciplinarian.[90] To a certain extent, these types of documents were works that could be consulted and possibly cited as justification for their rulings, by those tasked with maintaining the discipline in the monastery. Both jural issues of an internal nature, such as monks' behavior, and of an external nature, such the behavior of laypeople on monastery grounds, feature in these texts.

It is clear that in some cases laypeople were directly affected (and restricted) by the rules laid out in the monastic guidelines, and it is probable that they would have been made aware of their contents. This communication would likely have been oral. It is not probable that written guidelines for laypeople who moved within monastic grounds were expressly composed, although this possibility cannot be dismissed entirely. It is possible that a headman whose village was part of a monastic estate would make sure that his villagers knew the rules of the land. Furthermore, one can assume that, because monasteries in many areas had considerable power, the way that monks behaved had an influence on the inhabitants of those areas.

The mere fact that in particular situations it was deemed necessary to formulate rules tells us something about the interaction between monks and laypeople. These rules and regulations thus shed light on the value that certain people attached to specific societal phenomena. The monastic guidelines contain references, albeit unsystematic and casual ones, to the monks' perceptions of society and their role within it.

Previously I have alluded to how the contents of monastic guidelines may vary greatly from one text to another. Some explicitly contain references to things that have actually happened, while other monastic guidelines are concerned with specific organizational matters. A *chayik* for a Mongolian Geluk monastery, for instance, deals merely with the setup of formalized debating sessions at certain periods in the summer. It speaks of the times at which the debates are to take place, between which classes, and so on. It even comments on what the correct answers to give during a debate are. Such a *chayik* is thus limited to one very specific aspect of monastic organization and is of little use to us here.[91]

Other *chayik* give instructions that are more "spiritually" than practically oriented. *The Eighty Prohibitions* (*bCa' yig mi chog brgyad cu*) is a case in point. Written in 1918 by the head of Pelyul monastery in Kham, it contains, as the title suggests, eighty "prohibitions" written for the monks of Pelyul. Some of these are common in other sets of monastic guidelines and may be interpreted as having some direct practical purpose. Prohibition number fourteen, for example, states that one is not allowed to wear sleeves and laypeople's attire, as "one's robes are the base for the Vinaya."[92] Other prohibitions are clearly less easy to obey, for this *chayik* regularly forbids certain mental activity, such as the last two prohibitions of the text: "It is not allowed to ever forget the instructions of one's guru, [be it during] birth, death, or the intermediate state. It is not allowed to forget the instructions for dying at the time of death."[93]

Clearly then, not all *chayik* were contemporary reactions to the situation of the monastery on the ground. *The Eighty Prohibitions* for Pelyul monks should thus be seen as guidelines of a more spiritual nature. They are instructive when one is concerned with the conduct of the "ideal monk." For the current purpose, however, these rules are hardly relevant. It is important to appreciate that there are several reasons for listing rules in the Buddhist context. With regard to Indian monastic Buddhism, Silk has noted that "it is one of the conceits of the literature of the Buddhist monastic codes, the Vinayas, that they record case law."[94] Likewise, in the Tibetan case we need to be careful not to reify the stipulations that appear in the monastic guidelines. For just as in the case of the Indic Vinaya, in which the "world of monastic law does not appear to be a simple one of fables and fiction or half remembered 'historical' accounts, but a complex one of carefully constructed 'cases' in which concerns of power, access and economics were being or had been negotiated,"[95] the Tibetan monastic guidelines cannot simply be read as reactions to problems.

At the risk of stating the obvious, I here identify some possible motivations for writing these texts, which may help to better distinguish different types of rules: (1) to formally address actual problems and misconduct; (2) to settle organizational matters; (3) to exhaust all possible similar occurrences; (4) to give spiritual guidance. In other words, monastic rules can be firmly based on reality or on hypothetical situations, or on a combination of both. In my treatment of the *chayik* and their suitability as a source of information with respect to the societal place of Tibetan monasteries, I distinguish those texts and sections of texts that are clearly rooted in on-the-ground realities from those that mainly sketch an ideal image of the monk and the monastery. Nonetheless, separating utopian rules from real ones is not always easily achieved. It is also not always necessary, in particular, when it is the goal to examine monastic *attitudes* toward society as a whole, because in that case visions of an ideal society are just as relevant as the tackling of actual problems in the monastery.

When one takes a closer look at the monastic guidelines as a genre, the underlying reasons for which authors may have had to write a text can be summarized as follows:

1. The monastery had just been established;
2. A new building or department had been built at the monastery;
3. The monastery had been taken over by another religious school;
4. The monastery had sided with a losing political party and the winning party saw the need to reform it;
5. A change in the numbers of monks had occurred (significant increase or decrease);
6. The monastery had started a new curriculum;
7. A powerful religious (and political) figure sought to establish (strategic and moral) authority over the monastery in question;
8. Misconduct of the monks had been reported;
9. The monks' ritual practices had become "adulterated";
10. The existing regulations were seen to have become archaic, irrelevant, redundant, or deficient;
11. The economic situation of the monastery had changed.

Ortner notes that when a particular nunnery was newly founded, Lama Gulu of Tengpoche (sTeng po che) monastery was asked to write a *chayik* "to construct the temple for the nunnery."[96] With this document the nuns went from village to village to raise funds to actually build the place. The building was begun in 1925 and completed in 1928. If the composition of a *chayik before* the institution was actually set up was something that occurred more regularly elsewhere, this adds another possible purpose to the monastic guidelines, namely as an official document through which one could raise funds to build or rebuild a religious institution.

In order to understand which rulings are reactions to current situations or problems faced by the institution, it is helpful to read several *chayik* written for the same monastery. Unfortunately, in most cases, we do not have more than one *chayik*. When analyzing a *chayik*, in particular when one is looking for rulings that directly address on-the-ground issues, one needs—in addition to being aware of the possibility that certain rules and phrases were derived from Vinayic texts—to be conscious of the fact that certain rules and expressions are reiterations of (and in a sense tributes to) monastic guidelines that were written by the author's predecessors. The close reading of *chayik* composed for one monastery at different times reveals a certain level of (textual) continuity but also the changes undergone by a monastic community. These changes are highlighted by new rulings and remarks on the contemporary status of the monastery.

Generally speaking, it is safe to say that the vast majority of extant monastic guidelines do address contemporary monastic issues in a pragmatic manner. The texts themselves often explicitly state their local and contemporary purpose. An example is the *chayik* written in 1909 for all Sikkimese monasteries, which states that it is a work "in accordance with all the monasteries' own rules, the local customs, [people's] dispositions, capacities, and intentions."[97] What we then can see is that when structural changes took place in a particular monastery (e.g., it changed affiliation or it had been rebuilt after it had been destroyed), the *chayik* of that monastery was seen to be in need of revision or replacement. This is not unlike the notion prevalent among the authors of the *katikāvatas*: some of these Sri Lankan monastic codes state that they were renewed in accordance with the changing times.[98]

The contemporary nature of most of these works means that they can provide a great deal of information with regard to monastic life and the internal hierarchy of the monastery in general. It is imperative, however, also to stress the provisional character of these works. The monastic guidelines do not claim to be the final mandate on how the monastery should be run and how monks are to conduct themselves. Many of the monastic guidelines express their temporary nature, and this is exactly why a certain monastery can have a number of *chayik* written for it: the later harking back to, but also "overwriting," the earlier ones. Needless to say, the contents of the *chayik* are prescriptive and normative, and it would be naïve to assume that rules in the monastery were followed to the letter. Nonetheless, when one wants to study how the monastic institution and its role in society was conceived, the *chayik* are certainly valuable sources. In the context of the pre-modern Tibetan society, it appears that the point where "philosophy touches social policy"[99] can be found in the monastic guidelines.

2
___

# Historical and Doctrinal Frameworks of Monastic Organization in Tibet

INTRODUCTION

*The Church, yes, She must worry for She is destined not to die. Solace is*
*implicit in Her desperation. Don't you think that if now or in the future She*
*would save herself by sacrificing us She wouldn't do so? Of course She would,*
*and rightly.*
—TOMASI DI LAMPEDUSA [1958] 2007: 29

Even though the position of the monastic institution within Tibetan society has
changed significantly throughout the ages, there is also a distinct level of continuity. This continuity is historical as well as ideological. The way in which Vinayic
literature was interpreted by monastics among the various schools has remained
more or less unaltered for hundreds of years. As we are here concerned not just
with monastic organization but also with attitudes of monks toward the rest of
society, the manner in which certain notions seen as pivotal within Tibetan Buddhism are interpreted is also relevant. This chapter explores the historical and
ideological continuations and concepts thereof discernible at Tibetan monastic
institutions, for these are the building blocks of both the physical and conceptual
space that the monastery occupies within society.

The earliest extant monastic guidelines stem from the late twelfth century, but
according to traditional sources, monastic Buddhism was introduced in the eighth
century with the completion of the monastic complex at Samyé in 779 at the behest
of Trisong Detsen (Khri srong lde btsan, r. 755–797 or 755–804). Samyé was seen
as the first "real" monastery in Tibet because it was a place where monks could
receive ordination. During the eighth century, Tibetans who were ordained elsewhere were apparently already occupying the temples (*gtsug lag khang*) and other

residences that had been built by Trisong Detsen's predecessors.[1] The founding of Samyé has been viewed by Tibetans as a crucial turning point concerning the introduction of Buddhism to Tibet.[2] While the introduction of Buddhism, along with writing and a legal system, during the time of Songtsen Gampo (Srong btsan sgam po, 569–649?/605–649?) was traditionally seen as a civilizing force, the construction of Samyé is thought of as an achievement that ensured the endurance of Buddhism in Tibet. This view demonstrates the widespread conflation in Tibet of religion *tout court* with monastic Buddhism, not unlike what occurred in other countries where monastic Buddhism flourished. Kern argues that early Indian Buddhism was primarily a monastic institution and "the laity but accessory."[3] For Tibet, this conflation signifies the prominence of the monastic institution.

Another important decision, reportedly declared by the last of the Dharmarājas, Tritsuk Detsen (Khri gtsug lde btsan, a.k.a Ral pa can, r. 815–841), who promoted uniformity in Buddhist practice, was to only allow translations of the *Mūlasarvāstivāda vinaya* and its commentaries and no other Vinaya materials.[4] This sealed the fate of Tibetan monasticism, for while religious traditions quarreled over the interpretations of complex philosophical points, the shared ordination tradition brought about a more or less homogenous monastic identity among Tibetan Buddhists. This is particularly striking in comparison to other Mahāyāna countries.[5]

In order to understand how the monastic institutions in Tibet were managed and organized, it is useful to look at the socioeconomic status of the monasteries prior to the period under investigation, i.e., the late twelfth to mid-twentieth centuries. *The Chronicles of Ba* (*sBa' bzhed / dBa' bzhed*), which should be read "as a work of historical fiction,"[6] provides us with clues as to how the first monastery in Tibet was perceived. The dates as well as the authorship of this text are unknown, but passages quoted elsewhere suggest that versions of this text were already in circulation by the twelfth century.[7] This work tells us that, initially, Samyé was to be a temple (S. *vihāra, gtsug lag khang*). The narrative of Samyé's construction does not mention building accommodations for monks, and nowhere does it speak of Samyé as a monastery (*dgon pa*). However, when Samyé was completed, several people took vows there, all of whom reportedly belonged to the aristocracy.[8]

It is important to note that Tibetan monastic Buddhism was from the outset both patronized and controlled by the state.[9] According to *Monasteries of Tibet,* the first monastery of Tibet was populated by over a thousand monks, not long after Trisong Detsen had founded it, and was fully supported by the state: which is to say that the ruler appointed seven families to sponsor the upkeep of one monk.[10] In the beginning Samyé had no estates, no land, and no cattle. During that time all monks received the same allowances, regardless of their status: 25 measures (*khal*) of grain annually, 11 measures of butter, and 30 coins (*srang*).[11]

The widespread Tibetan narrative of the rise, apex, and subsequent decline of (monastic) Buddhism during the early transmission (*snga dar*) is significant for later conceptualizations of monastic ideals. With the completion of Samyé and the first ordinations there the introduction of Buddhism was complete, and the Sangha flourished. Being entirely dependent for its survival on the ruler as its sponsor has been idealized by many later monks as the best way to subsist. Pointing to how the first monks lived solely off the donations they received, they criticized the situation in which many a monastery found itself in later times—monks had to provide their own income by working or doing business, monasteries possessed vast estates, loaned money against interest, and invested in trade.

Although the contemporary state of monastic Buddhism is not the topic of this book, it is worth noting that because monks—both in exile and in the People's Republic of China (PRC)—have had to renegotiate their economic position in relation to both "the state" and the laity, the historical patterns that live on through shared memories play an important role in this process. In much the same vein, Aris once commented that Tibetans, "by comparison with many other peoples of the east or west, . . . maintain a high level of historical consciousness and a deep sense of the vitality of the living past."[12] This makes an awareness of collective memories crucial to any analysis of less ancient history as well as current affairs that concern Tibetans. It appears that in present-day China the recent increased commercialization at the monasteries is seen as problematic by monks and laypeople alike, partly because it is seen as a by-product of tourism (and state intervention) and thereby of "modern times." The collective memory here is thus rather selective, as the monasteries in traditional Tibet in fact played an active role in business. At the same time, begging laypeople for alms is nowadays regarded to be a last resort and often actively discouraged. This is not a recent development: misgivings toward (morally) coercing laypeople into giving to the monkhood are found in some of the older monastic guidelines.[13]

The current drive toward self-sufficiency is seen by many monks as a break from the recent past—during which the monasteries were dependent on state support—as well as a respite from the atmosphere of oppression, often associated with monastic economic policy during pre-modern times. There is the realization that self-sufficiency, by means of setting up businesses, funds, and "providing services to the community," is far from ideal, yet necessary to survive. It is clear that now for many, the purest form of monastic economy is one in which doing business is not needed and sponsors volunteer to make donations, without the monks having to ask for them.[14] This is reminiscent of the earliest situation of the monastery in Tibet—or at least the collective memory of it.

There is another way in which the traditional narrative highlights the position of monastic Buddhism. For later Tibetan historians, the death of Tritsuk Detsen was followed by the disastrous rule of king Lang Darma (Glang dar ma, c. 803–842) and the subsequent period of fragmentation (*sil bu'i dus*). This is projected as the darkest period in the history of Tibet and Tibetan Buddhism. In the

Tibetan histories, especially the genre of "religious histories" (*chos 'byung*), the collapse of the empire after the reign of Lang Darma began with the persecution of the clergy. A large portion of the monks were reportedly forced to disrobe, with some fleeing east and others west. Although it is now evident that certainly not all Buddhist practitioners left Central Tibet during that time, later narratives conflate Buddhism and monastic Buddhism, stating that only the "embers of the Dharma" were left in the region.[15] This demonstrates the importance of the monkhood for the religion—for monks were seen as the keepers of the Buddha's Teachings.

Most Tibetan histories describe a period of political and social unrest following the monastic persecutions. The temples were in disrepair, the Imperial treasury was plundered, and the social order suffered the consequences.[16] During this period of chaos, Tibet not only lacked a central state; social structures also had eroded. Nyangrel Nyima Özer (Nyang ral nyi ma 'od zer, 1124–1192) writes that, at that time: "A son did not listen to his father, a servant did not acknowledge his lord, and the vassal did not hear the noble."[17] We now know that Buddhism had not entirely disappeared under and after Lang Darma, but rather that the monks had lost their royal patronage and that the aristocratic families were divided over the support of the religion. The accuracy of the accounts of events given in the historiographies is thus highly questionable, but for the current purpose this is irrelevant. Here it is important that this narrative was well known throughout Tibet, not just among the learned but also presumably among the ordinary people. The endurance of this semi-historical account is what Halbwachs calls "collective memory,"[18] explained as a group process in which the way the past relates to the present is more important than the historical facts themselves. It is likely that the Sangha's disappearance from (Central) Tibet and the social upheaval that followed were seen to be intimately related.

This pervasive narrative confirms the message that some Indic Buddhist texts are seen to convey: wherever the Sangha remains, there the Dharma will be, and where the Dharma is, the area will prosper and be at peace. The set of monastic guidelines by the Fifth Dalai Lama from 1664, for example, cites the *Vinayottaragrantha*: "As long as there are monks,[19] the holy Dharma will remain."[20] The author of these guidelines further explains: 'Because the *Vinayapiṭaka* is the foundation for all other dharmas of both Hinayāna and Mahāyāna, the Buddhist Teachings depend on the Sangha who maintain that [*Vinayapiṭaka*].'[21] Very similar wording is used in the monastic guidelines for the Sakya (*Sa skya*) nunnery Rinchen Gang (Rin chen sgang), written in 1845. It tells the nuns to study and practice well: "It is said that the Teachings of the Buddha depend on the Sangha."[22] And again, an early twentieth-century *chayik* says: "Whether or not the Buddha's Teachings remain in the world depends on the Sangha that maintains them."[23] This demonstrates an awareness that the Sangha had as its primary role the preservation of the Dharma, making "concern for the happiness of all beings . . . the foundation of the Sangha's very existence,"[24] but only implicitly: the methods to bring about lasting happiness (i.e., *nirvāṇa*) are the Buddhist Teachings that the spiritual community is charged with continuing.[25]

Connected with this responsibility to preserve Buddhism is the notion of what is often translated as the "degenerate times," the *kaliyuga* (*snyigs ma'i dus*).[26] This age of decline implies not only that Buddhism as we know it will one day disappear, but also that before its disappearance it will gradually become more difficult to properly practice. Monks, in particular those who have studied the Vinaya, display an acute awareness of this notion. Some use it to explain the divergence between the original Vinaya rules and the practice found among Tibetan monks: "In this day and age we cannot keep the Vinaya in all its details; this is because of the degenerate times (*snyigs dus*). But we keep the rules as well as we can. The monastic guidelines are written in accordance with the times; these rules are generally more relaxed than the exact stipulations in the Vinaya."[27] The abbot of the nunnery Genden Chöling (dGe ldan chos gling) in India mentions that this allowance for relaxations in the discipline can be found in the Vinaya itself. Here, he may be referring to the exemptions with regard to monastic communities living in the outer regions mentioned in the Vinaya.[28]

One senior monk I interviewed complained that whenever he commented on the lax attitude toward discipline at his monastery, monks commonly retorted: "Oh well, considering the times . . . ," implying that when one takes the current age into account, the monks look good in comparison.[29] This notion of the age of decline was also seen in the past as a valid reason to relax the rules,[30] which affected both the internal organization of the monasteries as well as the way in which monks dealt with the outside world. The monastic guidelines themselves regularly claim that they contain rules that are adapted to the specific place and time, thereby appealing to a mind-set common among monks.

The Sangha, synonymous to most ordinary people with "monks" (and only rarely with "nuns"), did not exist simply in order for the laypeople to gain merit. Similarly, monks were not there solely to perform rituals to appease local spirits on behalf of the ordinary population. Their role was more substantial. Although perhaps not during the initial stages of the introduction of monastic Buddhism, but certainly from the eleventh century onward, monks in Central Tibet started to play a bigger role and were classed among the "important men" (*mi chen po*). According to Davidson, the efforts of these important people to spread the Dharma "were understood as contributing to social cohesiveness and organizations, a trend in Tibetan public life that continues to the present."[31] Their presence alone furthermore provided a shared identity: "Buddhism had always been seen as the core of Tibetan identity, and its clergy the epitome of 'Tibetanness.'"[32] The importance of the Sangha, the monks in Tibetan society, cannot be overemphasized. Their primary position—collectively, though not always individually—should be kept in mind when discussing the societal role of the monastery and the monks.

Yet another aspect of Tibetan monastic Buddhism is its portrayal as the embodi-ment of the continuity of the Indian tradition. The notion of the necessity for unbroken lineages of practice, ritual, and ordination brings with it a notoriously conservative attitude and an aversion toward innovation and invention. Kapstein sees the ideology of monastic Buddhism in Tibet as one "that often appears to systematically devalue innovation and personal inventiveness, considering them sources of deviation and of the transgression of the genius of the past."[33] This is particularly well attested in the Tibetan scholastic tradition, in which accusations that an individual writer was being imaginative, creative, or promoting divergent ideas—all possible translations of *rang bzo*—were particularly damaging to one's scholarly reputation.[34]

Although current scholars acknowledge that the Tibetan variety of Buddhism is most definitely not a carbon copy of the "original" Indian religion and that it was adapted in many ways,[35] the fact remains that the complete preservation of the religion and its accompanying rituals has been idealized among monks. Change—any change—may have been seen as possibly disrupting the process of preserva-tion. This conservative attitude with regard to matters of religion is likely to have affected the behavior of monks within social settings. Furthermore, this type of "inertia, or conservatism, may cause cultural forms to persist, perhaps even for centuries, while material conditions are changing."[36] There are other factors that contributed to this conservatism—or fear of change—and the subsequent status-quo attitude among the monastic agents, which in turn affected the relationship between monks and laity.[37]

Another significant feature of Buddhism in Tibet is that it held a monopoly position. Although there were several schools that sometimes vied for disciples and sponsors, and fought over doctrinal issues and transmission lineages, monks were, generally speaking, united in their vows. Of course the presence of the Bon religion cannot be denied, but in the *longue durée* of Tibetan history its adher-ents played only a minor role in the public sphere. What was then the impact of this monopoly position? According to market theory, a monopoly position of a product or a service is expected to *decrease* social welfare.[38] This monopoly in the religious market is then seen to reduce the level of morality of individual believ-ers, but to "improve the quality of the moral constitution supporting a market society."[39] In other words, a shared religion brings about shared values, which positively influence society. This is why it has been argued that a monopoly in the market for organized religion could in fact increase the "net social welfare."[40] This contemporary argument would not look amiss in the writings of pre-modern Tibetan monastics, although this type of reasoning is rarely explicitly present in the monastic guidelines.

The central role of monastic Buddhism in Tibetan society, the need for the preservation of the religion, the degenerate times, the conservative attitudes, and the religious monopoly position all emphasize both the centrality and continuity of Tibetan monasticism. At the same time, living in the *kaliyuga* meant that potential threats and evils had to be regularly negotiated, indicating change as well as continuity. This continuity makes it possible to look at Tibetan monasticism diachronically and to detect certain patterns. By uncovering these patterns, one may identify changes over the centuries, and the factors that led to those changes.

## THE INFLUENCE OF BUDDHIST LEARNING ON MONASTIC ORGANIZATION

One of the factors that encouraged continuity and homogeneity among monks and, less overtly, even among laypeople is "the Buddhist *Weltbild*." What did people actually know about Buddhism? We first must acknowledge that the level of education—and this includes formal religious education—was relatively low at the monasteries. Among the population of Drepung, for example, it is estimated that ten percent were scholar monks (*dpe cha ba*).[41] These monks at the larger university-like monasteries studied topics that were often highly abstract and philosophical. Works that are now seen as primary texts containing "basic Buddhist values," such as Tsongkhapa's *Stages of the Path to Enlightenment* (*Byang chub lam gyi rim pa*), Atiśa's *Lamp for the Path to Enlightenment* (*Byang chub lam gyi sgron me*), Gampopa's *Precious Ornament of Liberation* (*Rin chen thar rgyan*), and Patrul Rinpoche's *Words of My Perfect Teacher* (*Kun bzang bla ma'i zhal lung*), do not appear to have been part of the general curriculum at most monasteries. These texts were taught—if at all—at public venues, where laypeople and monks gathered to listen to a sermon by a great master. Perhaps the main exception is Śāntideva's *Bodhicaryāvatāra* (*sPyod 'jug*), a text widely studied in centers of Nyingma scholasticism.[42] This leaves us to ask what the monks actually learned and thus knew about Buddhism and about what may now be called "Buddhist ethics." This subject has not been widely studied, perhaps partly because the results of a query into this matter would necessarily be highly speculative. For the current purpose it is important to understand the kind of religious education that monks with positions of power and influence received.

In the *Ratnarāśisūtra*, the Buddha tells Kāśyapa that an administrative monk[43] should be either an arhat, or someone who "is purified, who is fearful of censure in the other world, who has confidence [in the idea that results will come about for him as] the maturation of [his own] deeds, and who feels shame and remorse."[44] In other words, he should be a person who has a deep understanding of karma and who knows how to apply that understanding to his own actions. Most of the Tibetan monastic guidelines take a more pragmatic stance with regard to the religious accomplishments of monks in charge of administrative or managerial tasks. The monastic guidelines for Tashi Lhunpo state that a prospective candidate for the position of disciplinarian needed to have a better standard of education.[45] This was not the only requirement: one also had to be affluent, of an authentic lineage,[46] and have an imposing physical appearance.[47]

In the Nyingma monastery Pelyul in Kham, certain important positions, such as that of the great chant master,[48] required someone who had completed a three-year retreat. If no one of that rank was available, the individual still had to be from the ranks of monks who had completed various other types of retreats.[49] The source for this information is a monk who lived at that monastery before the 1950s. The extant set of monastic guidelines unfortunately does not give this type of information.

It appears that in the past in Geluk monasteries it was unusual for people with a geshé (dge bshes) title, the highest educational degree, to fill administrative positions.[50] In Sakya monastery, however, "a doctor of theology"[51] regularly was appointed to a high managerial position at the Sakya estate (zhabs pad).[52] To become a disciplinarian there during the late 1950s one had to have followed the monastic curriculum up to a certain point, but it was not essential to be a dge slong.[53] Whatever the level of education of monastic decision-makers, the monastic education system itself was clearly not designed to teach "applied Buddhism." Wangchuk mentions that the monastic system expects educated monks to master three activities, namely teaching, debating, and composing. In this way, the monks preserve and spread the Buddhist Teachings and work for the well-being of other living beings. Wangchuk hypothesizes that because helping others is done solely on the basis of the knowledge gained from their education, the educated monks are traditionally not primarily charitable or socially engaged, and that this may be the reason that there are very few charitable undertakings in Tibetan society.[54]

## SOCIAL REALITIES AND BUDDHIST THOUGHT

"Buddhist traditions generally did not develop practical ethical systems which might work to ameliorate the genuine suffering of the world."[55] At least, not in the way current nongovernmental organizations and the like try make the world a better place. In Tibetan Buddhist literature, social realities are not often reflected or commented upon. When this does occur, it seems that these realities, such as the plight of those who transport tea to Tibet,[56] or the hypocrisy of those Tibetans who purport to be pious but crave meat excessively, are highlighted not in order to encourage direct change, but to show the realities of saṃsāra and thereby the need to renounce concerns for the current life alone. The aim of these types of texts is to show the "injustice" of certain common situations, so as to provoke the realization that cyclic existence does not provide a stable base for any type of well-being, which includes justice. Emphasizing human (and other) suffering was thus usually not directly aimed at mustering support to rally against social injustices.

Similar topics that can be recognized as relevant to social welfare are mentioned in religious texts when authors write about compassion. The audience is reminded of the suffering of sentient beings, of the poverty and disease of a stricken populace. The aim is to evoke not only feelings of compassion but also a heartfelt commitment to do something about the suffering of others. This commitment, however, does not translate into social action—or at least, social action is not presented as a necessary expression of this commitment. This is because of the strong awareness that an ordinary human being is unable to structurally alter the plight of others: only a Buddha can.[57] In this way, the attainment of Buddhahood becomes the ultimate goal. Nonetheless, for those committed to the goal of attaining enlightenment for the sake of fellow beings, helping others is presented as a responsibility, as well as a necessary means to accumulate the merit required for the achievement of that goal.

According to the Buddhist doctrine in the Tibetan tradition, understanding the world around us, understanding the unjust and dissatisfactory nature of *saṃsāra*, is necessary to arrive at those most essential of Mahāyāna Buddhist concepts: renunciation (*nges 'byung gi bsam pa*) and the wish to attain enlightenment (S. *bodhicitta, byang chub kyi sems*). For Buddhist practitioners a thorough awareness of the outside realities is therefore warranted, although it is likely that a rather abstract and general understanding of those realities was seen to suffice for most. In fact, meditation was in some cases preferred to directly aiding others. The Kadam master Geshé Tönpa (dGe bshes ston pa, c. 1004/5–1064) was reportedly asked whether it is better to practice in solitude or to help beings by means of Dharma. He replied: "In this current age of decline, it is not the time for an ordinary being to actually help others, while not being involved in developing love, compassion, and bodhicitta in solitude."[58] Thus in degenerate times, practice takes priority over venturing forth to help others.

Traditionally then, the focus on love, compassion, and the resolve to attain enlightenment served first and foremost to change the practitioner's mental attitude and did not appear to have resulted in a push for a structured change of the status quo. To wit, neither secular nor religious institutions in pre-modern Tibet facilitated such undertakings, at least not structurally. Social and economic mobility was limited within the strongly hierarchical Tibetan society. This societal rigidity was in part due to "collective conservatism," which was maintained for a variety of reasons. The influence of the Buddhist *Weltbild* maintained by Tibetan believers—and thereby social agents—should also not be underestimated.

Psychological research on the concept of justice among young monks in a contemporary Tibetan Buddhist monastic community in Nepal suggests:

> The virtues of liberty, equality, and justice are not emphasized in this particular Buddhist environment. Concern for compassion and suffering takes absolute precedence. Perhaps in a worldview where fairness is built into the fabric of the uni-

verse (the concept of karma) one need not be preoccupied with making the world fair or just.[59]

This initially confirms that there are certain issues that take center stage in textual Buddhism and become incorporated in the mind-set of monks. Speculative as the above-cited research may be, it strengthens the hypothesis that doctrinal discussions of (human) suffering were not primarily geared toward, and usually did not lead to, social engagement. In the words of Spiro: "soteriological action provides no support for action in this world. As it is nirvana through knowledge, not through works."[60]

## THE MONASTERY AS A CORPORATE INSTITUTION

Economic historians have described the medieval Catholic Church as a corporation closely connected to economic progress. Weberians have argued that the Church was responsible for slowing down economic development in Europe, whereas others have argued that the Church had a positive influence on economic growth.[61] It is less common to analyze Buddhist institutions in such a way.[62] Considering Buddhist monasticism in China, Walsh defines an institution as "a competitive structure seeking to perpetuate itself." He argues that religious institutions such as monasteries operate as corporate bodies.[63] Miller, who surveyed Tibetan monastic economy, disagrees with this notion of an institution and sees the monastery "as a collection of individuals having individual, transient funds."[64] Indeed, when considering the Tibetan case, it is unlikely that monks ever thought of their monastery as an economic unit (which does not mean that it was not one). However, the stress Miller lays on the individuality of the monks also seems unwarranted. Still, it is often claimed that there is a high degree of individualism in Tibetan Buddhism.[65]

This emphasis on the individual has its precedence in the depiction of Indian Buddhism. Dumont, in his *Homo Hierarchicus,* writes: "Buddhism truly expresses the place of the individual in Indian Society."[66] As argued above, the Tibetan Buddhist monastery *as an institution* is generally not concerned with salvation or liberation, but with continuation and preservation. In that way the monastery's task is to preserve the *facilitation* of salvation on an individual level. This is what gives monks their individuality: they, at least in theory, have the individual choice to make use of the facilities.

Goldstein claims that "the karma-grounded ideology of Tibetan Buddhism saw the enforcement of morality and values as an individual rather than an institutional responsibility."[67] This statement is perhaps only partially correct, for it is true that in the monastery orthopraxy is more important than orthodoxy,[68] but the contents of the monastic guidelines demonstrate that this can never have been entirely the case. These texts show us that the (publicly displayed) lax morality of a few monks would reflect negatively on the whole of the Sangha: firstly, because it would inspire bad behavior in other monks, and secondly, because it would cause the laity to lose faith in the Sangha. This made morality—at least to the extent that it pertained to external behavior—an institutional concern. This concern is highlighted in the monastic guidelines, which compare the danger of harboring a single individual with faulty discipline to the presence of one diseased frog in the pond, potentially infecting all the other frogs.[69]

In most other contexts, it appears that the word "individuality" to describe the lifestyle of monks is misguided, for it bears too many (both Western and modern) connotations that are simply unheard of in a monastic setting, even today. The nature of the monastery as an institution is that of a conglomerate of individuals, each of whom to a large extent retains the socioeconomic status he held in the "lay world." At the same time, they form a socioeconomic unit. The monastic guidelines paint a picture of a monastery as a socioeconomic unit, while acknowledging that individuals are the parts who create the whole. When viewing the monastic guidelines from the point of view of their audience, one finds that they both address the whole (how the monastery ideally should function) as well as the parts (the role individual monks play within the institution).

According to Collins, what monasteries intend to be is not always what they then turn out to be:

> Although it seems that both Buddhist and Christian monasticism aims to incarnate the close sense of community which sociologists often call *Gemeinschaft*, that is a small group with close cohesion, emotional intensity and absence of internal division, it is more likely that the monastic group is a *Gesellschaft*, a society with separate and separable individuals whose relations are governed by contract and whose ultimate goal lies beyond the immediate fact of association.[70]

When it concerns Tibetan monasteries, it seems more likely that the monastic institution is *both* a group with close cohesion and a society with separable individuals governed by contract. This is particularly evident in the larger monasteries, where the internal cohesion is found largely within the separate monastic houses[71] or colleges, whereas solidarity between these houses and colleges was far more tenuous.[72] More generally, the monastic guidelines see a good reputation among laypeople, religious prestige, a steady flow of donations, a stable community of monks, and a conducive political climate as vital to the continuation of a monastic institution. None of these are issues entirely beyond the reach of the monastery.

Justification for Buddhist monasteries holding important positions of power in Tibetan society was found in the doctrinally prevalent notion of the paramount importance of preserving the Sangha: the end justified the means. Viewing the monastic institution as a corporation, in which monastic agents act on (at least) two levels, namely individual and communal, allows one to understand how certain types of behavior that would be unacceptable if they concerned a lone monk would be allowed or even encouraged if the whole community could benefit from them. This bipartite modus of organizing the community is not just an aspect of Tibetan monasticism, but is present in Indic Buddhist texts as well.[73] In Buddhist India, for example, the offerings given to a stūpa could not be redirected to the general nor to the universal community (i.e., the monks present locally and the entire Sangha, respectively).[74] This clearly demarcated division is also apparent in the Vinaya literature, which demonstrates that the monastic community is not in itself liable for the actions of its members. Schopen gives the example of debts left by deceased monks: the debtors had to consider their money lost.[75] This is another instance—and there are many—in which the monastic institution is comparable to a modern-day corporation.

For Ashman and Winstanley, contemporary corporations exist "as legal and economic entities constructed to pursue social and economic objectives."[76] The Buddhist monastery does not fit this definition, for its fundamental aim is the betterment of all beings, and more specifically, the continuation of the Dharma. Contrary to what is claimed by some, I do not believe that the Sangha's primary aim is to "raise the efficiency of religious practice" and that "its beneficiaries are none other than the monks who constitute its membership."[77] Aside from having social and economic objectives, the monastery does have features akin to those of corporations. One such feature is corporate identity. Corporate identity is similar to monastic identity, which is imbued with the notion of belonging to a larger community that has a shared purpose and a sense of belonging.

It is problematic to view the corporation—not an actual entity—"as possessing identity or acting as a conscious moral agent."[78] Velasquez questions the notion that a corporate organization can be held morally responsible (at least in part) for its actions, and dismisses the idea that there is such a thing as corporate moral responsibility.[79] Modern-day lawmakers appear to be in accordance with Velasquez, as they seem to acknowledge that only individuals can be ascribed morality, and thereby culpability.[80] To translate this into Buddhist concepts: just as a corporation cannot be held morally responsible, it also cannot accumulate karma—only individual agents can. What monks did on behalf of the monastic administration, with a benevolent motivation, would not have been seen as reprehensible in any way, regardless of the consequences of those actions. This in turn is a partial explanation for the relatively low level of social responsibility that monasteries appear to have had for their immediate surroundings.

This is by no means to suggest that monastic institutions acted with impunity. Despite the fact that "the moral order of organizations has a powerful effect on individual motivation, morale and performance,"[81] the monasteries were ruled and administered by individuals, usually monks, who had their own sets of values. The religious figures of authority, portrayed in hagiographies, are often depicted as being heavily involved with "serving social ends," of which the bridge-builder

Tangtong Gyelpo (Thang stong rgyal po, 1385–1464) is a famous example. Helping others, however, took place on an individual basis.[82] Presumably, members of the monastery did see themselves as having a certain responsibility regarding the lives of others. However, this generally did not translate into the improvement of the socioeconomic state of others but rather in the facilitation of religious practice and merit-making. Clearly, in Tibet the relationship between the monastery and the laity was not limited to mere religious facilitation. It was much more far-reaching. When this relationship is examined, in particular with regard to the perceived religious responsibilities and justifications of certain socioeconomic practices, a clearer picture of the social embedding and role of monastic Buddhism as practiced emerges.

To move beyond the simplified, yet valuable, model of the bipartite levels of perceived moral responsibility, one needs to look at the monastic organization, the roles the individuals played within it, and the Buddhist values embedded within this larger corporation. By understanding the day-to-day organization of the monastery it becomes easier to answer fundamental questions such as whether monasteries actually forced laypeople to work for them or whether it was seen as a meritorious exchange. It also helps to comprehend the rights and duties ascribed to laypeople and monks, both materially and religiously. By understanding the underlying Buddhist frameworks, combined with the way in which the monasteries were organized, it becomes possible to gain a more nuanced picture of the extent and nature of social responsibility among monks and monasteries in traditional Tibet.

# 3

# Entrance to the Monastery

## INTRODUCTION

Tibetan society before 1959 is often seen as highly stratified and hierarchical, offering limited opportunities to climb the socioeconomic or sociopolitical ladder.[1] In
the 1920s, Charles Bell estimated that of the 175 monastic government officials at
the Ganden Phodrang government, forty came from (aristocratic) families that
traditionally also supplied the lay officials. The rest of these officials were the sons
of ordinary Tibetans, chosen from the many monks of one of the Three Great
Seats: Drepung, Sera, and Ganden. This, along with other similar examples, is
often seen as evidence that social mobility in Tibet was possible, but that becoming
a monk was a first requirement to move up in life for those from a "working class"
background. Bell further notes: "Among the laity it is wellnigh impossible in this
feudal land for a man of low birth to rise to a high position; but a monk, however
humble his parentage, may attain to almost any eminence."[2] This raises the question of whether the monkhood itself was open to all. And if it was not, what were
the criteria for entering a monastery? This chapter addresses these questions and
explores the limits of this supposed vow-induced social mobility, shedding light
on the opportunities and limitations of ordinary Tibetans in pre-modern times.

   One of the few avenues for climbing the social and political ladder was to join
a powerful monastery. In modern-day Tibetan monasteries in exile, "anyone who
shows the slightest inclination" can become ordained and even the restrictions with
regard to who can or cannot enter the monkhood contained within the Vinaya are
"routinely disregarded."[3] The widespread assumption, perhaps based on this contemporary practice, is that this open-door policy is a historical continuation: that
any male at any given time and place in Tibet could become a monk and make

something of himself.[4] This idea is perhaps strengthened by the popular image of Buddhism as a religion that originally agitated against the caste system and strove toward a more egalitarian society. However, some *katikāvata*s, the monastic guidelines of Sri Lankan monasteries stemming from the twelfth century, state that men of low birth were not allowed to become monks, and elsewhere mention that it was the king who prohibited low castes from entering the order.[5] One *katikāvata* relates that the new monk should be examined according to caste (*jāti* and *gotra*), although it is unclear how this was done.[6] The idealized picture of both Tibetan monasticism and Buddhism in general as promoting equality does not necessarily correspond with historical realities, as we find conflicting information.

## WHO COULD ENTER THE MONASTERY?

Sarat Chandra Das, who visited Tashi Lhunpo monastery toward the end of the nineteenth century, states that "the order of the Lamas is open to all, from the highest noble to the Ragyabas, the lowest in the social constitution of Tibet,"[7] while elsewhere he notes that one from the "lower castes" could not be admitted to Tashi Lhunpo.[8] The latter statement, along with the numerous restrictions that are contained in some of the monastic guidelines, suggests that entry to the monkhood and admission to the monastery were, in certain periods and at certain monasteries, restricted.

The custom of restricting different types of people from joining the Sangha or a monastery was not exclusively a Tibetan phenomenon. To understand what drove Tibetans to such restrictions, we first need to look at the Indic materials. Despite the widely held view that Buddhism does not distinguish people according to their birth, caste, or race, there are ample Buddhist sources that show that one's background often *did* matter. Guṇaprabha's *Vinayasūtra*, which is one of the main Vinaya texts used by all Tibetan Buddhist traditions, states several restrictions in the chapter on ordination, the *Pravrajyāvastu* (*Rab tu byung ba'i gzhi*).

Although the classification is not made in the text itself, we can distinguish (at least) three different types of reasons for excluding someone from becoming a monk. One could be excluded based on one's physical disposition: people who were handicapped, ill, deformed, had one of the five sexual "disabilities,"[9] or who were too young or even too old. Then there were those who were excluded based on their behavior: those who had committed any of the five seriously negative acts (*mtshams med lnga*); monks who had broken any of the root vows;[10] known criminals, and people who generally were deemed to be too troublesome. Lastly, people could be excluded due to their background or social circumstances. Some of these were slaves (*bran*, S. *dāsa*), the king's soldiers, and people without permission from their parents.[11]

So far, excluding the people mentioned above appears quite commonsensical, from a socioeconomic point of view, if nothing else: allowing them to seek refuge in a monastic community could mean ending up on the wrong side of the authorities and society, and thereby depriving the community of its workforce and sons. However, the *Vinayasūtra* also mentions other groups of people: "cobblers, and those of low caste (S. *caṇḍāla, gdol pa*) and 'outcastes' (S. *pukkasa, g.yung po*) may not be ordained."[12] The Sanskrit version contains, but the Tibetan translation omits, chariot-makers from this list.[13] The *Vinayasūtraṭīkā*, attributed to Dharmamitra, gives an explanation for each of the above terms provided in the *Vinayasūtra*:

> A cobbler is someone who works with hides, a *caṇḍāla* is someone of an inferior caste, and a *pukkasa* is a barbarian. These types of people may not be given food and [thus] there also is a prohibition on ordaining them. This should be understood to mean that there is a very strict prohibition against [them becoming] *śrāmaṇeras* and the like.[14]

It is unclear which categories of people *caṇḍāla* and *pukkasa* are referred to here. In this context, the word *caṇḍāla* seems to denote someone who is of low birth, but who exists within the caste system, whereas the word *pukkasa* appears to carry the connotation of an outsider, a foreigner, or simply an outcaste. The explanation seems to suggest that there was no commensality between the givers of the food and the prospective receivers of the food. This may have been the main problem. Although these are important and interesting issues, for the current purpose it is not of crucial importance to understand what Buddhists in early India ultimately meant by the above terms, but rather how Tibetans understood, interpreted, and applied them.

There can be no doubt that the Tibetan society into which Buddhism was introduced was a stratified one, but the Indic notions of caste cannot have been easily adapted, or "culturally translated" by the Tibetans. It is therefore of some interest to look at what the terms "low-caste" (*caṇḍāla/gdol pa*) and "outcaste" (S. *pukkasa, g.yung po*) were taken to mean by Tibetan Buddhists in different times and places. While in some contexts *g.yung* seems to mean "civil" or "civilians" (as opposed to the "military" [*rgod*]), during the time of the Tibetan empire,[15] in some Dunhuang texts, namely Pt 1089 and Pt 1077, the word *g.yung* appears to denote "people of the lowest order, virtually outside the pale of Tibetan society."[16] According to a Tibetan dictionary the word *g.yung po* refers to *caṇḍāla* or *bukkasaḥ*,[17] a low caste in early India. However, the second meaning given is that of a pejorative word for a group of people who eat crabs, frogs, and tadpoles.[18] In the same dictionary, *gdol pa* is also taken to mean *caṇḍāla*, but the word is further explained to mean butcher (*gshan pa*) as well as "a low caste in the society of early India." The phrase *gdol rigs* is said to denote "people who are even lower than the *śūdra* (*dmangs rigs*), the lowest caste of the four *varṇas* in early India, [and they consist of] blacksmiths, butchers, hunters, fishermen, weavers (*thags mkhan*), and bandits (*chom po*), etc."[19] This shows that the terms can denote both Indic and native notions of people at the bottom of society.

The monastic guidelines under examination here deal with these concepts in a similar way, usually displaying an awareness of them being Vinayic stipulations while translating them to the societal sensibilities of Tibetan Buddhists, in different times and different contexts. These notions crop up in the monastic guidelines when the topics of admission to the monastery and entry to the monkhood are raised. The texts state limitations based not just on one's societal background, physical condition, or past conduct, but also on one's economic position, as well as one's place of origin. To a certain extent, however, these limitations are interlinked. In the monastic guidelines, the most common bases on which people are excluded from becoming a monk are (1) one's origins, (2) one's economic position, and (3) one's societal background. *horrible to read, but colleges do this too (you have to explain disciplinary action, have to be able to pay)*

## EXCLUSION BASED ON ONE'S ORIGINS

We know that monasteries in the Tibetan Buddhist world had different functions. Some were small local monasteries that mainly served their direct community with ritual, prayers, and ceremonies. Others were large and had a focus on education, some concerned themselves with retreat and practice, and yet others had a strong administrative function. These different monasteries required and attracted different types of monks. Small village monasteries were usually populated with monks from the immediate surroundings, while certain large, prestigious, and well-positioned monasteries had a more interregional and sometimes even international character.

Because Das accurately noted in 1893 the restrictions with regard to certain people entering the monastery of Tashi Lhunpo, which was both a large educational and administrative institution, he may have seen or known of its *chayik* written in 1876.[20] This work provides a long list of people who were not allowed to enter the monastery as monks.[21] It stipulates that people from the direct surroundings of the monastery could not join Tashi Lhunpo.[22] Sandberg notes that this rule extended to all Geluk monasteries in the Tsang (gTsang) area in Central Tibet: one was not to enter a monastery less than forty miles from home.[23] A similar restriction was in place at the Bon monastery of Menri—local men were discouraged from joining. Most monks living at Menri monastery before 1959 were said to be from the east of Tibet.[24] Cech's informants said that this rule was to guard against the danger of nepotism. We can perhaps then deduce that nepotism was something certain monastic institutions—particularly those that conducted "business" with laypeople in the immediate surroundings—tried to avoid.[25]

The reasons that some larger and more prestigious monasteries did not enroll monks from the neighborhood would therefore seem to be largely pragmatic. Such monasteries were well known for their multi-ethnic makeup. Drepung monastery in the late seventeenth century had monks from almost all of Tibet's neighbors. Its *chayik,* written by the Fifth Dalai Lama in 1682, notes the presence of Indian, Newari, Mongolian, Hor, and Chinese monks.[26] Even though in Drepung the multi-ethnic monastic society was a *fait accompli,* the Fifth Dalai Lama viewed the presence of so many foreigners as a possible security threat, mentioning that this might result in the Barkor (Bar skor) being set on fire.[27] This mistrust of foreign monks may also be implicit in the admission policy of Namgyel Dratsang (rNam rgyal grwa tshang). Although the only extant set of monastic guidelines does not state any restrictions at all,[28] Tupten Yarpel, the current general secretary of the monastery in Dharamsala, India, informed me that its admission policy has historically been very strict. He mentioned that traditionally only "pure" Tibetans (*bod pa gtsang ma*) could become monks there, as Namgyel Dratsang was the Dalai Lama's monastery. It could prove harmful to the Dalai Lama's government if a foreign monk stepped out of line. Tupten Yarpel noted that since the Dalai Lama resigned from his political role in 2011, this policy that effectively excludes "Himalayan peoples"[29]—that is, Tibetan Buddhists who are not Tibetan—has become less relevant. However, the rule of only admitting Tibetans is upheld to this day.[30]

In Sikkim, people were also prevented from entering the monastery on the basis of their origins. According to the "History of Sikkim" (*'Bras ljongs rgyal rabs*) only Tibetan stock was admitted in the Sikkimese "Pemionchi" (Padma yang rtse) monastery,[31] thereby effectively excluding the Lepchas, many of whom practiced Tibetan Buddhism. In the *Gazetteer of Sikkim* it is mentioned that the "novitiate" is questioned by the disciplinarian and chant master with regard to his descent, and if he has "a good strain of Tibetan blood he is let off cheaply and vice versa."[32] As this citation suggests, the entrance fee was not equal for all. Carrasco notes that in Sikkim in the second half of the twentieth century, all new monks had to pay an admission fee, with the notable exception of those belonging to the nobility.[33] This admission fee was formalized at certain monasteries, while at most monasteries the price was not fixed but rather an offering by the parents.[34]

Monasteries were (and are) fundamentally pragmatic: those that were short of monks would invite boys in, for little or no remuneration.[35] It remains likely, however, that certain—possibly more prestigious—monasteries did demand relatively high fees from monks-to-be and that this fee was higher for certain groups of people. Theoretically, therefore, in some cases the poorest families would have been unable to afford to send their sons to the monastery, suggesting that another factor that limited access to the monastery was an individual's economic situation.

## EXCLUSION BASED ON ONE'S ECONOMIC SITUATION

It appears that in pre-modern Central Tibet, an ordinary family had to ask their landlord for permission to send a son to the monastery. Surkhang notes that this permission had to come from the district officer,[36] and that if permission were granted, one would be presented with an official document called a "seal of release."[37] Dargyay, who bases her research on oral accounts, mentions that consent was always given due to social and religious pressure.[38] Even in the unlikely cases that this consent was everywhere and in all instances given, it still does not mean that ordination was always financially possible. A modern Tibetan-language book on Tsurpu (mTshur phu) monastery gives a rather detailed list of what one was expected to donate upon entrance. At least one communal tea to all the monks had to be offered, for which seven round bricks of tea and ten measures of butter were required.[39] This was called the "enrollment tea."[40] The book further provides a long list explaining which quality of ceremonial scarves had to be given to whom by the new monk. This process of providing tea and scarves could then be repeated for the group of monks who shared a home monastery, but only when the monk came from another institution.[41] In Dakpo Shedrup Ling (Dwags po bshad grub gling) during the first half of the twentieth century, monks arriving from other monasteries to study were required to pay one silver coin[42] upon entering and one such coin upon leaving.[43]

In Phiyang monastery (Phyi dbang bkra shis rdzong) in Ladakh the requirements for the enrollment tea were adjusted according to the affluence of the family. I was told that all families could always afford to pay for it.[44] The originally oral version of the monastic guidelines for Sera Je, which now has been written down, also mentions that the entry fee depended on what the individual could afford. For a layman to enter the monastery: "he should offer the master at least a needle and some thread and [if he is well off] a horse or even an elephant."[45] According to Snellgrove and Richardson, however, prospective monks at Drepung, after having made an application with the chief teacher of the monastic house[46] of choice, had to provide a large amount of gifts and offerings just before the start of the Tibetan New Year.[47] The admission fee thus varied greatly over time and among monasteries.

Although it is by no means clear how affordable it was for average-income or poor families to provide such offerings, the above instances show that the monkhood was not as easily accessible as is sometimes imagined. In certain monasteries in Ladakh, a new monk had to have a "monk field."[48] This was a field that was owned and worked by the monk's relatives. The proceeds of the field would go toward the upkeep of the monk.[49] A son of a family that did not hold any land could therefore not become a monk.[50] The so-called monk field was not always provided by the monk's family: Könchok Chönyi, an elderly monk at the Ladakhi Phiyang monastery, was assigned a field by the monastic authorities upon entering the monastery at eight years old in the 1930s. His relatives worked the field for him and he was able to live off the harvests.[51] This meant that in certain monasteries in Ladakh the concept of "monk field" was flexible, and that actual ownership of the land was not a requirement, although it is obvious that one had to have relatives willing and able to work the field one was assigned.

A thirteenth-century *chayik* for the monastery of Drigung Til states that an aspiring monk needed to have provisions that would last him at least a year: it is likely that poorer people would not have this level of resource. This text, one of the earliest works actually (but probably posthumously) called a *chayik*, written by Chennga Drakpa Jungné in the thirteenth century, also asks that monastic officials not ordain people who had not gained permission from their superiors, or those who lacked superiors.[52] This indicates that there were indeed people, perhaps runaway servants, who sought refuge in the monastery, and that their presence was not welcomed. This is in many ways understandable: to allow landowners' servants to become monks would upset the social and economic balance, particularly in Central Tibet, where there tended to be a chronic shortage of laborers.[53] The materials available to me suggest, however, that concerns regarding the entrance to the monastery of "lowly" individuals and fugitives were not simply of an economic nature.

### EXCLUSION BASED ON ONE'S SOCIAL POSITION

Persons whose social position was low, whose position could not be verified, or who were simply destitute, were not always welcomed by the monasteries in Tibet.[54] The author of the guidelines for Drigung Til, mentioned earlier, clearly does not conceive of the monastery as a charitable institution: "Ordaining all beggars and bad people without relatives will bring the Buddha's Teachings to ruin."[55] It is clear from this text that the population at this monastery was growing rapidly at the time of writing. There were too many people, possibly placing too much of a strain on the local population and its resources. Clearly, the author Chennga Drakpa Jungné wanted to put a stop to the unregulated population growth at the monastery: "These people do all kind of things that are not in accordance with the Dharma here in greater Lung (Klungs) in Central Tibet. Because they cause annoyance and bring [us] disgrace, I request that from now on these types of people do not get ordained."[56] It is possible that the author's main reason for not letting beggars and drifters become monks was that certain people had been abusing the system, becoming monks just so that they could acquire food or even enrich themselves. The problem with these types of people may have been that they lacked a support system, a family, which would ensure a level of social control. This does not mean that the author did not also entertain certain notions of class.

Kawaguchi mentions that in the beginning of the twentieth century, people such as blacksmiths who normally would have difficulties gaining access to the monastery sometimes went to places far away and concealed their background upon entering monkhood.[57] It is thus not surprising that a prospective monk who arrived from farther afield and who had no one to vouch for him would often be suspected of belonging to a lower social class. Although in Tibet caste, as understood in the Indian context, was never an issue of much import, this did not mean that *class,* in the broadest sense of the word, did not matter.[58] A late seventeenth-century *chayik* for the monastery of Mindröl Ling (sMin grol gling) states that people desiring to enter the monastery had to be *rigs gtsang*. This can be glossed as being of a pure "type," "class," "background," "lineage," and even "caste," making the phrase very open to interpretation. When I mentioned this term to a monk official from Mindröl Ling in India, he immediately suggested that it refers to people from blacksmith and butcher families.[59]

According to Cassinelli and Ekvall, butchers were not allowed to become monks at Sakya monastery. Men from blacksmith families were also not accepted into the monkhood, "because they disturb the earth gods and make the implements of killing."[60] Kolås cites a propagandist Chinese work, which states that in pre-modern Tibet all lowly types (*rigs dman*) or impure people (*mi btsog pa*) were barred from entering the monastery. These low-ranking people included butchers, blacksmiths, carpenters, leather workers, and corpse-cutters (people who were tasked with cutting up corpses to feed to the vultures as part of the traditional "sky-burial").[61] Spencer Chapman, a mountaineer who visited Lhasa in the early twentieth century, despite being rather ignorant of Tibetan culture, writes that those whose line of work had to do with taking life were excluded from becoming a monk. He names tanners, butchers, gunsmiths, body-cutters, and leather workers.[62]

The nineteenth-century guidelines for Tashi Lhunpo, in addition to excluding would-be monks on the basis of their place of origin, also add further restrictions to do with social background: "[Those not allowed are] outcastes (*gdol pa'i rigs*) who deal with killing, such as butchers, fishermen, hunters, and those who are here in Tibet considered a bad 'class,' namely blacksmiths and tanners, as well as villagers who are after sustenance and clothing, or those who have no land."[63] This demonstrates that the author of this *chayik* was well aware of the Vinaya rules, as he refers to outcastes, but he also includes a local angle by stating "'here in Tibet,'" which shows his awareness that certain restrictions had to do with indigenous sensibilities. One set of monastic guidelines, written by the Seventh Dalai Lama (1708–1757) for Sera Je, stipulates that "black people[64] such as blacksmiths, cobblers, beggars, and the like may not be allowed to become estate residents (*gzhis sdod*)."[65] Unfortunately, it is not clear whether this refers to monks who do not have "resident" status or to all people living on grounds owned or managed by the monastery. However, earlier on, the text mentions that people from Kham and Mongolia who already belonged to a subsidiary monastery (*gzhis dgon*) may not become residents (*gzhis pa*).[66] This suggests that the restriction in place against blacksmiths, cobblers, and beggars becoming estate dwellers might not necessarily have meant that their admission was refused outright but that, if they were admitted at all, they would maintain an outsider status.

Smiths—and blacksmiths in particular—were traditionally considered to be very low on the societal ladder and to be of a "polluted" or unclean type (*rigs btsog pa / rigs mi gtsang ma*). The reason for this pollution is interpreted by some as due to blacksmiths making implements of killing, thereby implying that the justification for their low status is based on Buddhist ethics.[67] Other Tibetans simply state that smiths are despised because they have always been despised. However, when pressed to give reasons, they commonly replied that the work is dirty and dishonest, that they make weapons—the tools of killing—and that they work metal, the mining of which was prohibited because it was perceived to disturb the spirits, which in turn would bring ill fortune.[68]

The notion of pollution is not just a thing of the past—in certain Tibetan and Himalayan communities it is still very much a feature of everyday life, and similarly the exclusion of people from entering the monkhood due to their birth is something that was, until very recently, a commonly accepted occurrence among some communities of Tibetan Buddhists. In Spiti, boys from the lower classes were not allowed to become monks at the local monasteries. Traditionally only sons of the land-owning and thus tax-paying class could become monks, while the blacksmiths (*bzo ba*) and musicians (*bedas*) were excluded. In 2006, sixteen blacksmith boys from Spiti were admitted into Ganden Shartse (dGa' ldan shar rtse) monastery in South India. The rest of the community summoned them to return to Spiti and punished the boys' families by banning their access to water and fire,[69] amounting to social ostracism.[70] This ban was only lifted in 2009 after letters of support by the head lama of the local monastery and the Dalai Lama were sent. The community still maintained that the boys of lower backgrounds should only become monks in monasteries outside of the Spiti area.[71] It is important to note here that the resistance to admitting people of "blacksmith" background originated at the community level, not the monastery level, showing the influence a lay community could have on monastic organization.

It can be surmised from the various examples given above that the exclusion of people on the basis of their societal status occurred throughout the ages, in monasteries of all different schools and in a variety of areas. It has been argued that in Tibet "social inequality was based mainly on economic and political criteria"[72] and that the perception of pollution and the resulting "outcaste" status is grounded in the present or original socioeconomic status of these groups of people.[73] However, it may be more complex than that.

## REASONS FOR EXCLUDING ENTRY INTO THE MONASTERY

It is rare for monastic guidelines to give explanations or justifications as to why a certain rule is made, aside from citing certain authoritative Buddhist texts. This in itself is telling of both authors and audiences of this genre of texts. It implies the assumption on the part of the author that his moral authority will not be questioned and that the justifications are already known by the audience. Thus, the mere absence of explicit reasoning as to why certain individuals could not become monks does not mean that this policy always grew out of socioeconomic concerns alone. It is imaginable that specific restrictions were imposed in certain areas so as not to upset the precarious equilibrium of labor and to prevent the monasteries from becoming tax havens and shelters for runaway peasants. We also can see quite clearly that monasteries tended to act in accordance with the ruling societal norms, because they had to be careful not to upset society in general. However, by making rules and regulations that reiterated these societal norms, the monasteries further solidified existing inequalities. This is in line with how the *Mūlasarvāstivāda vinaya* positions the Sangha in society:

> The Buddhist rule that *dāsa*s ["slaves"], *āhṛtakas*, etc., could not become Buddhist monks or nuns does not seem simply to accept the larger cultural and legal fact that such individuals had no independence or freedom of action (*svatantra*) and were a type of property; it seems to actively reinforce it. There is in any case no hint of protest or reform.[74]

From a purely pragmatic point of view, it made sense to exclude certain people: Who in pre-modern Tibetan society would have been willing to make donations to, or to have prayers and rituals carried out by, a monastery filled with beggars and outcasts?[75] It is tempting to look toward the doctrine of karma to explain why people of low birth, and who thus had accumulated less good karma, were not seen fit to become monks. This is, however, an argument that I have never come across reading pre-modern Tibetan texts.[76] I suspect that the aspect of pollution plays a larger role than previously acknowledged.

This notion of impurity existed both inside and outside the monastery. The ideas of pollution continued into the monastic institutions not just because they had to accommodate the sensibilities of laypeople, who may have been unwilling to have monks from, for example, the blacksmith class perform the death rites for their loved ones. In addition to societal concerns, there are reasons to believe that these "polluted" people were also excluded due to apprehension related to the presence of local spirits, which were often transformed into protector deities,[77] connected to a religious institution.

One of the earliest works actually called a *chayik* gives an indication of the problem the presence of impure people could present for the deities living within the physical compound of the community. This short text by Rongzom Chözang (Rong zom chos bzang, 1012–1088) was not written for a monastery but for a community of tantric practitioners, who were, in this case, preferably celibate but not (necessarily) ordained as monks. It names fives types of people who should not receive tantric vows (*dam tshig*, S. *samaya*): butchers, hunters, thieves, robbers, and prostitutes. These people are classified as sinful (*sdig can*), but it is further mentioned that one should not sleep alongside persons who are impure (*mi gtsang ma*). The text names nine problems that may occur if these people "and tantric vows are mixed." One problem is that allowing such people to receive vows will upset the protectors and the unpolluted *vajra-ḍākiṇis*, and from that will arise unfavorable conditions and obstacles. The text then further explains how these unfavorable conditions would affect people's religious progress and how this in turn would debase the Teachings, and that the end result would be strife and disharmony in the community.[78]

There is further evidence to suggest that the behavior and "purity" of the religious practitioners and the benevolence of the protectors were seen to be intimately related. The set of monastic guidelines for Mindröl Ling concludes by stating that those who go against the rules stipulated in the text will be punished by the protectors and their retinue. The author Terdak Lingpa (gTer bdag gling pa) calls for the monks to behave well for that reason.[79] Another *chayik* in fact does not connect the mere keeping of the vows and behaving correctly to the munificence of the protectors, but suggests that if one does not perform certain rituals or even the style of incantation of prayers according to one's own religious tradition, the wrath of the protectors might be invoked. The text in question is a set of monastic guidelines for one part of Samyé monastery, called Chokdra (lCog grwa), where the mediums of the oracles[80] and the monks who were charged with performing the necessary rituals were based.

These guidelines, written by the Sakya master Kunga Lodrö (Kun dga' blo gros, 1729–1783), suggest that even though Samyé was at that time affiliated to the Sakya school, at some point monks started to carry out certain rituals, in particular those that had to do with the oracles entering the bodies of the mediums, that were derived from other religious traditions. This change, according to the work, upset the oracles, which caused upheaval among the people living in the immediate surroundings. This text, in fact, is primarily an admonition asking the monks to keep to the Sakya tradition. The author mentions that he had asked the Dalai Lama[81] for advice on the situation at Samyé and that the latter replied: "It is not only at Chok (lCog) but in any monastic situation one should adhere steadfastly to one's own original religious tradition—whichever that may be—so that no enmity damages the tantric vows [linking one] to one's deities and teachers, and the wrath of the Dharma protectors is not provoked."[82] It thus appears that protector-deities were not well disposed to change. The monastery then also had to negotiate the local protectors, who were naturally conservative, in addition to maintaining a balanced socioeconomic relationship with the local laypeople and benefactors.[83] The monastic guidelines were witness to this process of negotiating the changing times and socioeconomic and political contexts, while the overall objective was to maintain the status quo.

The adherence to the status quo by Tibetan monastics has often been commented upon by outside observers. Here the hypothesis is that this conservative attitude, in part, has to do with the main self-proclaimed objective of the Sangha as a whole—though not necessarily that of the individual monk: namely, to maintain, preserve, and continue the Buddhist Teachings. Another major factor in the Tibetan monastics' rejection of most types of change, as alluded to above, is not grounded solely in the mere fear of change but also in the fear of the local deities' reaction. Their wrath would not necessarily be limited to the monastic compound but would also affect surrounding lay communities and their harvest.

While the monastic communities saw the preservation of the Teachings as their primary *raison d'être*, the lay population was probably—and understandably— more concerned with the effect that preservation would have on the disposition of local deities. This may have been the perceived fundamental purpose of the presence of the monastery and its monks in the first place—at least, for the local lay population. This demonstrates the rather fluid relationship between laypeople and monastics, which was—in contrast to what is commonly thought—not merely a benefactor-recipient or patron-priest alliance, nor simply a hegemonic relationship, but rather a mutual dependency in which both parties had an obligation to care for each other's livelihood and continuance. The adherence to the status quo was too firmly grounded in concerns regarding the continuity of Buddhism and the sensitivities of the deities for any significant societal change to take place.[84] When changes were implemented in traditional Tibetan society, they most commonly were initiated or authorized by people of high religious standing—exactly those people who were seen to have more control or power over the local deities.[85]

## SOCIAL MOBILITY AND CHANGE

While one of the few possibilities for social mobility in traditional Tibet was entrance into the monkhood, specific groups of people at certain points in time and in certain areas did not have that option. This gives us a rough idea of the layers of Tibetan society for which social mobility seems to have been severely restricted.[86] It had an impact on more than just social mobility—in pre-modern Tibet, education most commonly was only available in a monastic context, and it is probable that those who were excluded from becoming monks were also usually excluded from formal education.[87] Later nonmonastic educational institutions largely followed the organizational patterns of the monasteries, with admission restricted to the children of aristocrats and government officials.[88]

It should be noted that most of the monasteries mentioned here that excluded certain types of people were in one way or another prestigious and important. This makes it likely that these monasteries, at the time their monastic guidelines were written, could in fact *afford* to turn away such types of people. It is furthermore noteworthy that no monastic guidelines written for monasteries in Amdo and Kham—at least that I have come across—contain restrictions on the basis of an individual's social background. This may then confirm the suggestion that historically the east of Tibet had a more egalitarian society,[89] but for now, this is a mere argument from silence.

In sum, there were three grounds upon which a person could be denied entry to the monastery: a person's birthplace (for fear of nepotism); a person's economic situation (for fear of profiteering); and a person's social background (for fear of pollution and social concerns). Some of these prohibitions can be traced to the Vinaya, although the categories found in Vinayic material often underwent a process of cultural translation in order to bring them in line with Tibetan social norms. These social norms were not based only on concerns of a purely pragmatic nature but also on notions of pollution and purity. I hypothesize that these notions of pollution, in turn, were closely related to the perceived presence of local deities and protectors, at monasteries and elsewhere. This perceived presence might have contributed—in part—to the aversion to change, regularly commented upon by outside observers of pre-modern Tibetan society. A proverb from Sakya echoes this general attitude: "No progress could be made unless the gods were offended."[90] Although the local deities were clearly not advocates for change, they presented lay and monastic Buddhists with a common cause: to appease these supernatural yet worldly beings.

# 4

---

# Monastic Organization

INTRODUCTION

In most Buddhist monastic societies, a well-developed organizational structure was in place. Nonetheless the Vinaya texts do not provide "an administrative structure or hierarchy beyond that of seniority."[1] For the Tibetan context, the structure of monastic organization is most evident in the monastic guidelines. Little is known of the Tibetan monastic organization from the ninth to twelfth centuries. It appears, however, that monasteries expanded during and after the twelfth century. It was during this time that the first *chayik*-like prototypes emerged. This may have been because larger monasteries were seen to be in need of a more streamlined organizational structure. The *chayik* then can possibly be seen as a benchmark for the institutionalization of monasticism in Tibet. A similar argument is made in the discussion of the relative late emergence of summaries of Guṇaprabha's *Vinayasūtra* in Tibet, which may also be seen as indicators of increased monastic institutionalization.[2]

In the case of the monastic guidelines, it is difficult to confirm this hypothesis because a significant number of texts have been destroyed. Looking at the texts that were preserved, we see that the genre emerges only during the twelfth century and that a surge in new *chayik* occurred after the establishment of the Ganden Phodrang in 1642, indeed when many monasteries were forced—or volunteered—to "reorganize." This at least indicates that the guidelines were written when an improved or new monastic organization was felt to be necessary.

## HIERARCHY AND EQUALITY IN THE MONASTERY

Equality and hierarchy are often seen as dichotomies.[3] Some argue that hierarchy can coexist with notions or practices of egalitarian behavior, albeit in a somewhat contradictory fashion.[4] In many Asian countries hierarchy is more highly valued than it is in the West, and Tibet has been no exception.[5] There is no doubt that the Tibetan monastery was hierarchical, much like Tibetan society itself. Nonetheless, certain elements in the monastic organization, many of which can also be detected in the Vinayic literature, suggest a sense of egalitarianism. The importance of hierarchy in the monastery becomes very clear when looking at the emphasis the *chayik* place on the correct seating arrangements of the monks (*grwa gral*) during the assembly (*tshogs*). While one would perhaps assume that monastic seniority is the decisive factor here,[6] in the case of Tibetan monasteries, the arrangements were much more complex.

In Tashi Lhunpo monastery there even existed a *chayik*—no longer extant—that dealt specifically with the seating arrangements during the assembly.[7] More generally, the seating was not only according to seniority and the level of vows taken but also involved a number of other factors. One *chayik* from 1802 notes that when arranging the seating "one should listen to the two disciplinarians, and not be pushy with regard to one's seniority, saying, 'I am older, I was here first.'"[8] In the heavily populated Drepung monastery not everyone began with a seat in the assembly. In 1682, the Fifth Dalai Lama encouraged the monastery to restrict certain people's entry to the assembly hall. Here the author takes both seniority and level of education into account. In addition, he talks of the "riffraff" who want to use "the possessions of the Sangha" (*dkor*).[9] It appears that to deny the "riffraff" entry to the assembly hall was not directly motivated by a sense of hierarchy; instead, it was paramount to denying these people a means of income, in that wages, tea, and offerings were usually distributed during the assembly.

This policy served to disincentivize the less sincere renunciates from crowding the already overpopulated monastery. The *chayik* reasons as follows:

> Nowadays, if all are allowed in, then the junior monks who are involved in study will not be able to enter [the assembly hall]. Therefore, of course not all monks [can enter], and the riffraff who have not been present for longer than eight years or those who have not passed the five higher exams should not be let in.[10]

In some cases, authors of monastic guidelines felt that the level of education should take precedence over seniority. The *chayik* written in 1909 for all Sikkimese monasteries reflects this sentiment:

> Well-behaved monks, both *dge tshul* and *dge slong*, get—in addition to general admiration—a seat and a table, even when they are young. They also get a double share (*skal*: i.e., wages), the same as the chant master and the disciplinarian. With the monastery's monetary allowance they should be given rewards annually, taking into account their particular conduct.[11]

To a certain extent, this is a departure from the norm, for it was common that status was conferred on the basis of seniority and official appointment alone. The author, known by his Western contemporaries as Sidkeong Tulku (Srid skyong sprul sku, 1879–1914), here values behavior over the traditional sense of hierarchy.

On some occasions, laypeople participated in major rituals at certain monasteries. One early twentieth-century text that is only concerned with the correct execution of a commemorative ritual[12] also notes that the attending laypeople should be seated according to their (ritual) training, while always behind the monks.[13] In fact, the Bhutanese seating-arrangement ritual, initiated in the mid-seventeenth century, in which both lay and monk participants were carefully seated according to their religious, political, and social status, is said to replicate the seating order of the monastery, which was based on both seniority and learning. The ritual was praised as creating hierarchy and order in a society where these aspects were seen to be lacking.[14]

As reflected in the above-mentioned Sikkimese example, monks with official positions (such as disciplinarian or chant master) are also found higher up in the hierarchy, and while most *chayik* do not explicitly mention this, reincarnations would also have a better seat in the assembly. In the guidelines for Drepung, for example, the Fifth Dalai Lama stipulates that the elder monks sit at the front according to seniority, the intermediate ones sit in the middle, while the "riff-raff that is after the possessions of the Sangha" sits at the back.[15] In addition to the level of education, monastic seniority, and official position there appears to have existed another benchmark that determined an individual's place in the assembly:

> From now on, the purity of the *samāya* and the vows shall be examined on a yearly basis. And when impurities do occur, the individuals, whether they are high or low, up until the level of lamas and incarnations (*sprul sku*), are not to enter the great assembly. Judgment will be made, commensurate to the severity and the number of the impurities, as to whether individuals entirely forfeit their entitlement to inclusion in the assembly row, or whether they retain [a place] in the side assembly (*zur tshogs*).[16]

The level of monastic purity thus could also decide where or even whether a monk could sit in the assembly hall.[17] All in all, we can surmise from this that the (spatial) hierarchy is dependent on the level of perceived qualities of the monks and that these were specified in various ways throughout time and in different monasteries. While this emphasis on the correct order of seating is found everywhere in Tibetan society,[18] the ordering on the basis of the individual monk's qualities is likely to be connected to the Buddhist idea that the worthier the recipient of offerings (*mchod gnas*), the more merit is gained by the donor (S. *dānapati, yon bdag / sbyin bdag*). Thus, in the monastery, those who sit in a prominent place are served first and monks in the front row are also likely to receive larger and better shares of offerings.[19]

According to Gombo's experience, for the—mostly married—lamas in the Nyingma religious institution in his village, the seating arrangement was meant to be according to learning, age, and seniority: "in practice, however, their seating positions reflected their social backgrounds."[20] In Chinese Chan monasteries, the rector (*wei na* 維那), which may be equivalent or similar to the Indic *karmadāna* or *vihārapāla*,[21] was in charge of overseeing the hierarchy and seniority at the monastery, which in practice meant that he needed to know the correct seating order.[22] While I am not aware of a particular office in the Tibetan context that is similar to this, overseeing the seating arrangements was generally the task of the disciplinarian and his assistants. The importance attached to the correct order of seating demonstrates that it reflected a particular value system that is shared with other types of Buddhist monastic communities throughout Asia.

While the makeup of the monastery is thus thoroughly hierarchical, at the same time there is a sense of egalitarianism in that important positions, such as that of the disciplinarian, were chosen by means of voting. The apparent presence of elections within the Vinaya is regularly commented upon: when the Sangha met, a chairman had to be elected. This post was valid only until the end of the meeting. All *bhikṣu*s had an equal right to vote.[23] In Tibet, candidates (*'os mi*) for an official position would be selected by the general monastic office (*bla spyi*). However, voting was not open to all. In some cases, only educated monks could cast their vote, and in others, only those who had been living in the monastery for at least ten years were able to do so. While in the Vinaya having the status of *bhikṣu* appears to have been a prerequisite for voting, ordination status does not seem to have played a significant role in the Tibetan context.[24] That the voting process did not always take place in an honest fashion is suggested by the stipulation regarding the collection of nominations of candidates or actual "absentee ballots," given in the nineteenth-century *chayik* for Tashi Lhunpo:

> The tantric lamas who hold office need to appoint new functionaries. And when the lists of nominations of those lamas who had to go to faraway places in China, Mongolia, Kham or Tibet are collected, they [the appointing lamas] need to be honest and collect them, having taken the Three Jewels as a witness. They may not, out of partiality, do things that will harm or help individuals.[25]

In the case of Ganden monastery, the office of disciplinarian is now elected by the general office alone. Previously, the Tibetan government had the authority to appoint monks to this post.[26] Goldstein mentions that the government also chose the abbots of the Three Great Seats from a number of candidates who were preselected by the monasteries.[27] Positions of any consequence were almost always temporary, however, which meant that the governing class fluctuated frequently.

SOCIAL STRATIFICATION WITHIN THE MONASTERY:
THE *CHOS MDZAD* AND OTHER CASES

The privilege of sitting in the front row was not always "earned" by being educated, serving the monastery, or being an incarnation of some variety. This
privilege could, in some cases, also be bought or obtained through other means.
As indicated in the previous chapter, while the view is widespread that entering a monastery would do away with one's previously held status in lay society,[28]
there are indications that in Tibet socioeconomic stratification persisted among
the monks. Stein notes, casually and without providing any sources, that "social
classes are maintained in the monasteries."[29] Even though it is very likely that
merely entering the monastery would not do away with preexisting class differences, not much research on the social dynamics within the monasteries has been
conducted to date.

In the previous chapter, the need to pay "fees" to enter the monastery was
briefly discussed. Alternatively, the family of a prospective monk could pay
additional fees, taking the shape of offerings made to the whole community
of monks, thereby buying their son certain privileges. The monks entering the
monastery in that way were sometimes called *chos mdzad,* which translates as
"practitioners of the dharma." In the Geluk school, these "monk-sponsors,"
as Dreyfus calls them, often came from aristocratic families and were usually
housed in the more influential monastic residencies (*bla brang*), "which were
like small dynasties of monastic administration."[30] While these monks tended to
be aristocrats, they were not always noblemen: often they were simply wealthy.
In Sera Je they were, like the incarnations, also allowed to wear fine wool on the
backs of their garments.[31] The main privilege granted to these monks was the
exemption from menial tasks,[32] such as sweeping and fetching water, that junior
monks had to carry out for one or two years. While it does not use the term
*chos mdzad,* a modern history of Tsurpu monastery describes how relatives of
a newly enrolled monk, in order to prevent him from having to perform these
menial tasks, made offerings to the monks during the assembly. This involved
giving an "enrollment tea" (*sgrig ja*) and handing out some money to each member of the Sangha.[33]

In theory, this could be seen as a way to allow these monks to spend more time
studying, but this suggestion was vehemently rejected by my monk informants,
who were generally dismissive of the *chos mdzad.* Rendo Senggé explains:

> The *chos mdzad* was a position in the monastery that could be bought; it had nothing
> to do with the level of education. It was for the rich. The advantage was that one had
> more rights: one did not have to work and one would get a prominent place in the
> monk rows. It was not for incarnations, except for the very minor ones, who would
> not get a good place in the rows to begin with.[34]

Lobzang Döndrup lived in Drepung monastery for five years until he was forced to leave and return to his native Ladakh in 1959. His description of the *chos mdzad* concurs with the above, while it also suggests that a prominent place in the rows was only allotted to the *chos mdzad* in the monastic houses,[35] but not in the main assembly:

> They were often of aristocratic background. Their quarters were much nicer. The physical space was the same, but they had the means to furnish the rooms nicely. They did not have to do chores: they were not used to working hard. There were other exemptions as well; they did not have to go to the assembly—well . . . maybe except when there was a major assembly. They also did not have to go to the debate ground: they could just hang out. When a communal tea[36] was served at the monastic house they could sit at the head of the row. But this was not the case at the college level (*grwa tshang*). There, the senior monks got to sit at the head. Their special treatment often did not do much good for their studies. The poorer monks usually turned out to be the better students: they worked much harder. The life of the *chos mdzad* was just easier, not better.[37]

While the term *chos mdzad* is not employed by Cech, she notes that a lama (here: a monk) could "buy off" his duties by providing tea for each monk in the Bon Menri monastery. Thus, in the case of two monks who had taken their vows on the same day, the one who had the financial means to offer a communal tea-round achieved seniority over the one who had not.[38]

Actual references to the *chos mdzad* are rare in the monastic guidelines. In fact, the guidelines for Tashi Lhunpo appear to be the only set of monastic guidelines, apart from the *Tshogs gtam chen mo*, that explicitly mentions the term. Das states that monks in Tashi Lhunpo bore titles reflecting their social status. He writes that when the boys who were to be ordained took the vows, the "Grand Lama" (i.e., *Ta bla ma*) added certain titles of aristocratic distinction to the names of those from the upper classes: old nobility and descendants of earlier tantric families were given the title of "shab-dung" [*zhabs drung*] and sons of landholders and high officials[39] were called "je drung" [*rje drung*], the class of gentlemen, and the "sha-ngo" [*zhal ngo*] family[40] were called "choi-je" [*chos mdzad*].[41] Although not stated, Das appears to have taken this information directly from the guidelines for Tashi Lhunpo.[42]

The author of these guidelines singles out the titles that are given to certain people on the basis of their birth,[43] while specifying that other titles, and in particular academic ones, should be bestowed with the utmost care. He goes on to say that only those who are genuine aristocrats or from Kham or Mongolia—in other words, the incarnations and the others, mentioned above—may hold an aristocratic enrollment ceremony.[44] This ceremony may indeed refer to the price (in the guise of gifts to the Sangha) that was paid so that monks of good families and those from areas such as Kham and Mongolia could obtain a position of privilege. Again, the author states how certain privileges could be bought, whereas others could only be earned; he explicitly rules that titles that were earned through passing exams could no longer be bought.[45] This suggests that in the Tashi Lhunpo of the late nineteenth century, the attempt to move up in the monastic hierarchy by offering financial incentives was persistent and occurred with some regularity. Buying a title, as described above for the *chos mdzad*, was often simply a way to get an easier life in the monastery.

Having such a title was not always merely ceremonial, however. In the early twentieth century the *drung dkyus*, a type of middle-rank government official, was drafted as a sort of tax from the Three Great Seats by the Ganden Phodrang government. It appears that these officials were chosen from among the *chos mdzad* monks. It was reasoned that the position was unpaid and these wealthier monks could be supported by their families. As a *drung dkyus* one could rise to higher positions within the government,[46] which allowed the nobility to get an even stronger foothold in the political arena. While Goldstein does not link the two, it cannot be a coincidence that at that time some aristocratic families were made to send an unspecified number of sons to the Three Great Seats so that they could become monk officials there.[47] The same families presumably were rewarded for their contribution through their sons being given the opportunity to exert influence on a state level.

Gombo argues that while one's family's socioeconomic background did, to a large extent, determine one's position in the monastic institution, this was less pronounced in the larger monasteries that had a strong focus on learning.[48] Although it is difficult, if not impossible, to gauge the extent of this type of monastic social stratification within the smaller monasteries, examples given above demonstrate that—while it is possible that this type of class disparity was less prominent there—a lot could be gained by entering one of the larger monastic institutions as a member of the higher strata of society.

The history of Buddhist monasticism in, for example, Thailand shows that the monastic life was at a certain point in time only attractive to the poor: the permanent monks were (and are) almost invariably the sons of farmers or underprivileged city dwellers.[49] As we have seen in the previous chapter, to have a monastery consisting of just the poor and needy was seen in Tibetan societies as detrimental to the continuation of the Sangha. In order to attract sponsors, it needed to have not just good but also well-connected monks. The position of *chos mdzad* made becoming a monk for those accustomed to a life of relative luxury less unattractive. By incentivizing the entry of wealthier and aristocratic monks, the monastery opened itself up to ties with their affluent lay relatives and friends. In a way, the incentives offered by monasteries to encourage certain people to join were balanced against the disincentives developed to ward off the less influential and affluent. This policy clearly did nothing to improve education or discipline but did strengthen the bonds between the monastery and well-to-do laypeople. Having an ongoing connection with high society could ensure the survival of the monastery. A degree of inequality along with the contempt many ordinary monks clearly felt toward these *chos mdzad* may have been seen by the monastic administrators as a small price to pay.

## THE SIZE OF THE MONASTERY, DISCIPLINE, AND SOCIAL CONTROL

*But do not take as important for there to be many monks. . . . Leading a large assembly of monks but being outside the Way is completely wrong.*
—DŌGEN (1200–1253) 1996: 156

In secondary literature, there seems to exist contradictory information with regard to the monastery's social organization and the position of the individual monk therein. Some argue that the family situation is replicated within a monastery,[50] while others opine that a Tibetan monk is often seen as a person with a high level of individuality (in particular when compared to laypeople with comparable social backgrounds) and even that Tibetan Buddhism itself affords a "high degree of individualism."[51] The level of individuality and group identity was no doubt also dependent on the size and the level of control at the monastery. From Welch's research one can generally conclude that in China in the early twentieth century, the bigger monasteries had more control and kept strict discipline, whereas the smaller temples had a more relaxed attitude.[52] The observance of the rules was heavily dependent on contact with laypeople and the economic situation of the monastery.

In the case of Tibet, there exist two divergent views on the correlation between a monastery's size and the level of monastic discipline. The one currently held by many (lay) Tibetans in exile is that discipline is (and was) better in the larger monasteries,[53] whereas at the beginning of the twentieth century, Bell observes the exact opposite.[54] This may be because Bell was in Tibet during a particularly tumultuous time when the larger monasteries were asserting their political influence. Miller connects the position of the monastery within society to the level of discipline. Discipline then was a way for the institution to "enforce its demands and obtain the support needed for large numbers of non-productive residents." She also notes that the small monasteries have relied more on the communities in their immediate surroundings and were more likely to show a relaxation of "orthodox dGe lugs pa practices." She connects this relaxation of the rules to the economic needs of monks in local (read: poorer) monasteries, which necessitated that some monks do farmwork or engage in trade.[55]

Goldstein reports that the large monasteries neither placed severe restrictions on comportment nor demanded educational achievements.[56] Presumably there was simply less social control in bigger communities. One abbot told me that while his moderately sized nunnery did not need a *chayik*, his home monastery Sera Je in South India did, because "it is a very big place."[57] The guidelines for Drepung are witness to the problems caused by overpopulation in what was arguably once the largest monastery in the world. Drepung's massive monastic population may have been a contributing factor to the challenges the monastery faced when its guidelines were written, such as the members of monastic houses and the smaller compartments therein fighting with each other.[58] The guidelines that the author, the Fifth Dalai Lama, composed are clearly geared toward curbing the unbridled growth at the monastery during the late seventeenth century. The uncontrolled nature of the increase in monks was seen to be the root of the problem, though not the size itself.[59] The Eighth Panchen Lama (bsTan pa'i dbang phyug, 1855–1882) notes that in the smaller monasteries affiliated with Tashi Lhunpo discipline was much more relaxed.[60] He observes that certain practices, such as openly drinking alcohol and accepting livestock, presumably to be slaughtered on behalf of the monastery, were not uncommon in the smaller monasteries.

The greatest differences in discipline between monasteries are perhaps most pronounced not when it comes to size but where the overall orientation of the monastery is concerned. Smaller monasteries that were related to larger institutions often saw the brightest and most ambitious monks leave to further their studies. This was more than a brain drain; it also left the local monastery with those people who were less motivated to be good monks.[61] The discipline at monasteries that mainly ritually served the local lay population were often more in danger of slipping, perhaps exactly because of their closer ties to the lay community, but possibly also because educational standards were lower. Many *chayik* demonstrate the corruptive force that laypeople could present, while the same texts also call on the importance of maintaining a good reputation and a harmonious relationship with the lay population. The correlation between the level of discipline and the contact with laypeople on the one hand and that of discipline and the monastic economic situation on the other is important to examine, for it shows the degree of dependency between the unordained and the ordained.[62]

## THE MANAGERIAL MONKS
### AND THEIR QUALIFICATIONS

The terminology denoting the people who hold official positions in the monastery varies. Colloquially, among monks in exile, perhaps the most commonly used term is simply *las byed*,[63] a word that is also used for those (laypeople or monks) who hold any kind of government job. In the monastic guidelines the terms *las tshan pa*,[64] *las sne*,[65] *las thog pa*,[66] *las 'dzin*,[67] and *mkhan slob*[68] all occur, each having a slightly different connotation. In the Tashi Lhunpo of the nineteenth century the monks in office were called *rtse drung*, whereas those in a lower position were called *las tshan pa*.[69] We see that particularly the earlier *chayik* contain idiosyncratic, and now obsolete, titles.[70] Later, specifically after the seventeenth century, a more standardized and homogenous set of titles developed. This may also have had to do with the fact that later (post-seventeenth-century) guidelines are often primarily directed toward the officials, whereas the earlier ones speak more directly to the general monk population. The growth of monks in the seventeenth century may also have had something to do with this development. It is furthermore safe to assume that by this time the guidelines for the bigger monasteries served as something of a template for the smaller monasteries of the same school.

Some *chayik* contain detailed information on the selection criteria for monks in official positions, others only address this when the officials were known to have behaved badly in the past, and yet others do not contain any job descriptions. The fact that many of these texts direct their attention to these roles reflects how important these "managers" were for the monastery and the maintenance of its rules. The selection criteria vary: in some cases, the monk had to have reached a level of education,[71] while in others the monk needed a certain level of economic independence. Dungkar Lopzang Trinlé (Dung dkar blo bzang 'phrin las, 1927–1997) remarks that in the Indian context there was a strict system of economy in place in which the managers of the general possessions (*spyi rdzas*) then could only be a *śrāmaṇera* (*dge tshul*) or an *upāsaka* (*dge bsnyen*), but never a *bhikṣu* (*dge slong*).[72] Dagyab mentions that it was unusual for highly educated monks to be appointed to managerial positions.[73] However, in Sakya the *zhabs pad*, who had the most actual power, had to have reached the level of "doctor of theology" before he assumed the position.[74] The general character and reputation of the candidate was also taken into account.[75]

In other cases, the only requirement was that the officials remained impartial and honest. The importance of an unbiased attitude is regularly stressed, which gives the impression that monks in these managerial positions *may* occasionally have tended to enrich themselves by having others (both monastic and lay) pay in exchange for favors, or that people in these positions simply had a tendency to favor their own friends or kinsmen. Monk officials also were required to be decisive and could not let bad behavior go unpunished.[76] The guidelines for Drigung Jangchub Ling state, for example, that in the case of someone breaking the rules, "the two disciplinarians should not turn a blind eye but should give a fitting punishment."[77] Both favoring certain individuals and being lax in enforcing the rules were apparently not uncommon among functionaries. So much so that some *chayik* stipulate punishments for those officials who let monks get off scot-free or displayed a bias toward a certain group. Several sources mention that monks born in the vicinity of the monastery could not be appointed to official positions out of fear of bias, or accusations thereof.[78]

The guidelines for Drigung Jangchub Ling note that if a *pārājika* offense went unpunished, those in charge of punishing the manager needed to prostrate themselves five hundred times; when the disciplinarian and the chant master were found guilty of letting misbehaving monks go unpunished, they would have to do a thousand prostrations each.[79] Although most *chayik* are clearly not intended to function as monastic management self-help books, the guidelines for Mindröl Ling monastery provides a mission statement for all monks in a management position: "In short, all those burdened with managerial positions, by providing for the livelihood of this place, protect the tradition of liberation of those who are wise, disciplined and good."[80] The monk officials at Sakya had equally high expectations to live up to. The guidelines remind them of the workings of karma and ask them to sacrifice their lives for the monastery:

> Therefore, once one has been assigned a duty, one shall—for the sake of the very integrity of the religion and politics of the glorious Sakya—have the courage to be able to give up one's body, life, and possessions without reservation, and one shall have the perseverance to be able to serve the higher lamas, the lineage, and the religious community ceaselessly, and one shall hold a sincere wish for the subjects of the monastery to expand, prosper, and remain for a long time.[81]

Here, working for the monastery is presented as virtuous and, in line with sentiments held by monk officials today, there is no sense of incongruity with regard to the monks filling managerial positions "taking them from their life of meditation and religious observance and putting them in charge of secular matters."[82]

## THE MANAGEMENT TEAM AND MONASTERY OFFICIALS

Particularly in modern times the "management team" is very important for the organization of the monastery. This committee, depending on the size of the institution, may decide on internal issues, such as the education program, as well as on external issues that have to do with financial matters, for instance. This team or council is sometimes referred to as the *lhan rgyas* and can consist of the abbot, the disciplinarian(s), the chant master, and the secretary.[83] According to Nornang, the monastery of Dakpo Shedrup Ling counted three "offices": the *gnyer tshang*, the *spyi bso*, and the *lhan rgyas*. The former two dealt largely with financial and external matters, whereas the latter appointed its members to those two offices and was primarily concerned with the general monk population.[84] The most important member of this *lhan rgyas* was the *zhal ta pa*, an educated monk who was in charge of supervising the kitchen and its staff. He and the chant master were the only ones to have access to the boxes in which the official monastic documents were kept.[85]

In Sera Je, during the eighteenth century, the term *spyi so* denoted the committee that gave out the wages (*phogs*) to the monks at certain times.[86] In other textual materials we often see the word *bla spyi*: the monastery committee,[87] which is similar, if not the same, as *spyi so/ bso/sa*.[88] Miller explains that *spyi sa* refers either to a place where goods are stored, to goods donated for a particular purpose, or to funds from which interest is drawn to pay for monastic rituals.[89] In many ways, this office served as the treasury for the general populace of monks. To confuse matters further, the term *spyi bso* refers in some cases to an individual rather than to a team of monks.[90] The same is true for *bla spyi*.[91] The most generic and widespread name, however, is *dgon pa/pa'i gzhung*:[92] "the monastic authorities."[93] In the large monastery of Drepung during the first half of the twentieth century, the committee for the management of an individual college (*grwa tshang*), called *phyag sbug,* consisted of four or five members. This committee was responsible, on a lower level, for the distribution of certain goods, such as tea, food, and money that came to the monastery, to the members of that college.[94]

The above names and titles serve to demonstrate that there was no single system of monastic organization in Tibet. For the current purpose, we are interested in how the people in charge of maintaining the monastery behaved and were expected to behave. The guidelines are very informative on the subject of monastic job descriptions and general management. Some of these monastic guidelines in fact solely address those monks with an official position.[95] They thus convey the monk officials' status, background, remuneration, and duties toward monks and laypeople. It is important to understand that, in much the same way as in Buddhist India, monks did not have as their main vocation administration or management.[96] It is thus not necessarily the case that, as Michael has argued, monks of all schools in Tibet "were trained for the management of human affairs as well as for religious service."[97] Most offices were temporary and tenure was rare. The posts most commonly described in the *chayik* are those of disciplinarian,[98] chant master,[99] and steward,[100] whereas the positions of treasurer[101] and the various types of maintenance personnel[102] are referred to occasionally.[103] Notoriously absent from this list is the abbot,[104] the head of a monastery or college. This important role that carries with it "not just responsibility, but real power and prestige,"[105] is hardly commented upon in the monastic guidelines. This is, in part, because the abbots were often the authors of the *chayik* or those who informed the authors, but also because they may have been regarded as having a distinct (religious) status that set them apart from the rest of the monks.[106]

Generally speaking, the members of the committee and the others who held official posts were monks. This is by no means standard Buddhist practice. In Thailand, the monastery committee (*kammakan wat*) consists of the abbot, one or more junior *bhikkhu*s, and several laymen.[107] The lay presence in monastic organizations is widespread throughout the Buddhist world.[108] However, Welch maintains that in China laymen, generally speaking, "played no role whatever in the internal administration of monasteries."[109] While Tibetan monasteries do not advertise the involvement of laypeople, the *chayik* convey their presence occasionally. In the sections that follow, the various offices and their roles are discussed in more detail.

While with regard to Buddhist terminology the Tibetans have been consistent and meticulous in translating and employing Indic terms, this practice has been not extended to titles that denote monastic offices. Most Tibetan official titles appear to be native ones, perhaps with the notable exception of the terms *dge skos* (disciplinarian) and *zhal ta pa* (manager), which have been briefly mentioned earlier. Many of these words, however, turn out to be used in a wide variety of ways in different monasteries and at different times. Not infrequently these terms have lay-world counterparts. This leaves one to wonder whether the monks emulated the laypeople or vice versa.[110] The treatment of various monastic official terms and roles below is merely an initial—and necessarily incomplete—venture into a territory that demands further elaboration.

## THE DISCIPLINARIAN

*I never saw a master of discipline in the lamaseries wearing a delightful smile. More often they seemed to be the type of tormentors that might step out of a picture of the Eighteen Buddhist Hells.*
—SCHRAM [1954] 2006: 374

The word *dge skos*[111] occurs in the *Kṣudrakavastu* of the *Mūlasarvāstivāda vinaya,* the *Vinayasūtra,* and the *Mahāvyutpatti* as a translation for the Sanskrit *upadhivārika.*[112] The Tibetan term, which is not a literal translation from the Sanskrit, may be short for *dge bar skos pa*: he who establishes [others] in virtue, or he who is established in virtue. In the Indic context, the term is translated as "supervisor" or "provost" of the monastery. He is in charge of the material possessions of the Sangha, and in the *Kṣudrakavastu* his task is to beat the dust from cloth seats.[113] In Tibetan-ruled Dunhuang, the *dge skos* appears to have been in charge of loaning out grains from the temple granary against interest.[114]

The connection of the *dge skos* to the maintenance of discipline appears exclusively in later Tibetan sources. He is a supervisor of the standards of discipline, but he does not have a consultative role,[115] solving problems according to Vinaya scripture.[116] Rather, his is an executive role, and he is to punish those who are in breach of the rules. His judiciary arm was said to stretch beyond the monks in the monastery itself, as a recent work on Tibetan monasteries notes: "The disciplinarian has the authority to take charge of things related to the discipline of the general monk populace. Previously, he could also take charge of the judiciary issues of the laypeople and monks at the monastic estate."[117]

While the word *dge skos* has older Indic precedents, the earliest extant *chayik* do not mention the term. Discipline in Drigung Til in the first part of the thirteenth century was kept in the following way: "In order for the new monks to listen to the honorable preceptor (*slob dpon,* S. *ācārya*) who holds the vinaya (*'dul ba 'dzin pa,* S. *vinayadhara*), you, supervising monks (*ban gnyer ba*), must encourage them. Unfamiliarity with the trainings and the precepts will cause annoyance to all."[118]

Some of the available sources state that the disciplinarian required a certain level of education, whereas others stipulate a preference for non-intellectuals. Nornang, for example, notes that in his monastery before the 1950s the disciplinarians were appointed from among the monks who did not study logic.[119] The colleges of Drepung monastery found middle ground by choosing their disciplinarians during the summer period from among the scholars and those who would serve in the winter from among "the lay brethren."[120] Per college two disciplinarians thus served terms of six months at a time.[121] This half-year term was the same for Mindröl Ling monastery in the late seventeenth century.[122] Its *chayik* explains the ideal disciplinarian as someone who has good intentions, is strict, and is incorruptible.[123]

The disciplinarian is in charge of the day-to-day maintenance of discipline: his permission must be gained before leaving the monastery grounds; he makes sure all dress appropriately; and he is responsible for the comportment of the monks, during assembly, but also outside of it.[124] He confiscates improper attire or forbidden objects, such as weapons, but also divides the shares of donations to the Sangha among the various monks.[125] He furthermore is responsible for keeping the register of the total monk population.[126] In Drepung monastery during the late seventeenth century, the disciplinarian was also charged with handing out degrees. According to the Fifth Dalai Lama the disciplinarian did not always remain an impartial judge: "It is well known that when taking the *gling bsre* [exam],[127] one would be let off the hook without having one's level of education examined, if the disciplinarian had received a present (or bribe: *rngan pa*)."[128]

The guidelines for Tashi Lhunpo monastery describe its ideal candidate as someone who is not just well educated, but also affluent, from a reliable background,[129] and with a physically imposing appearance.[130] The text then states that suitable candidates should not try to get off the short list, and that those not on the list should not try to get on it. The monk selected for the job would be given a seal or contract,[131] which lists his responsibilities, and from that moment on he was not to go back on his word.[132] While describing the procedure, the text then warns that no one should try to give orders to those who exercise the general law, such as the disciplinarian.[133]

The above selection procedure for Tashi Lhunpo was for the position of "great disciplinarian."[134] This position is similar to that of *zhal ngo* in Drepung, Sera, and Ganden. This is a disciplinarian who oversees the great assembly and has a position of considerable power. The word *zhal ngo,* literally meaning "presence," is also used in the secular world. Aside from referring to "someone who does the Sangha's work" the term is also simply explained to mean "manager."[135] In Bhutan, *zhal ngo* are the "hereditary chiefs," i.e., the leaders of the clans.[136] The sense of an exalted social status in the secular world is also affirmed in the guidelines for Tashi Lhunpo, which mention that the *chos mdzad* have come from a lineage of *zhal ngo.*[137] In the early twentieth century, the word referred to a low ranking military officer.[138] Although there is no clear evidence for this, it seems unlikely that the monastic institution borrowed this term from the "secular world" or vice versa. The term in all cases appears to imply a certain natural authority that the *zhal ngo* possessed.

In Tashi Lhunpo, the disciplinarians for the individual colleges were called *chos khrims pa.* These disciplinarians exercised their own set of rules with the help of their own guidelines:

The disciplinarian is one who, without hypocrisy, enforces the rules with regard to the duties allotted to each tantric functionary. By praising the good and putting an end to the bad and by taking the contents of tantric college's own *chayik* as his starting point, he enforces the rules and guards their upholdance.[139]

A large monastery could thus house a sizeable number of disciplinarians, whereas in smaller monasteries there was often just one.[140] While the role of the disciplinarian was seen by some monks as a burden or a distraction, within the Geluk school in particular it was an important stepping-stone. For the selection of the position of Ganden Tripa (the head of the Geluk school),[141] one had to have served as a disciplinarian at either Gyütö or Gyümè (rGyud smad).[142]

It can be surmised from the above that the disciplinarian, as the enforcer of unspoken rules and the monastic guidelines, was not required, generally speaking, to have an in-depth knowledge of Vinayic literature, whereas a thorough understanding of the local monastic rules was pivotal. He had high levels of responsibility and power and was therefore corruptible. This is perhaps one reason that the Bon monastery Jatilo (Bya ti lo) in Lithang (Kham) only replaces its disciplinarian yearly, leaving all of the other administrative monks in place.[143] While, as shall become apparent from the discussion below, the disciplinarians did not stand alone in maintaining discipline in the monastery, the day-to-day activities depended greatly on the moral standing of these monks.

## THE CHANT MASTER

In many guidelines the chant master and the disciplinarian are mentioned together as *dbu chos,* a contraction of *dbu mdzad* and *chos khrims pa.* This indicates that these two offices were seen to be of similar status. The Fifth Dalai Lama, however, allots the disciplinarian six shares, while the chant master receives only five shares.[144] The guidelines for Tashi Lhunpo describe the duties of the chant master in the tantric college, noting that he needs to make sure that the intonation, pace, and "melody"[145] of the prayers that are recited during the various rituals are carried out exactly in accordance with tradition.[146] This is obviously not the chant master's only job, as he was often also part of the administration.

As with the disciplinarian, for bigger monasteries such as Tashi Lhunpo, there also were—aside from those for the smaller congregations—one or more chant masters for the great assembly,[147] who were in charge of keeping the traditional ways of reciting and restoring them where necessary.[148] The maintenance of the ritual traditions is also stressed in the *Abbatial History of Pelyul (dPal yul gdan rabs),* in which it is said that the chant master was to make sure that "innovations do not stain them."[149] In Gyütö monastery, a position not dissimilar to that of great assembly chant master exists, which comes with more responsibilities. There the one who serves as "great chant master" (*bla ma dbu mdzad,* a position higher than that of *dbu mdzad*) keeps the monastic guidelines in a box[150] to which only he has access. This position can only be obtained by a monk with the highest educational degree who has finished the three-year tantric exam.[151] The other monks of similar stature can vote in a new great chant master. Only those who have served in such a capacity can become the abbot of the monastery, and only those are eligible to become Ganden Tripa.[152] Despite the fact that leading prayers is still an important part of the job, the great chant master's position is significantly distinct from the normal chant master post. It even gets translated as "assistant abbot."[153] The post of "chant master" is not always an exalted position, however. In Drepung, the *lag bde dbu mdzad* appears to have been the supervisor of the kitchen staff and was paid—on par with the scholar monks—one share of the offerings.[154]

The term *dbu mdzad* does not appear in canonical texts. It may simply be the honorific for leader (e.g., 'go byed), a term used to denote the head of a lay organization. A variant of the title is found in the 1845 *chayik* for Rinchen Gang, one of the very few extant sets of monastic guidelines for a nunnery. There the nun in charge of leading the assembly is called *dbu byed*.[155] While it is tempting to surmise from this that authors felt less need to use honorifics when addressing female clergy members, it actually appears that the term is used to denote a chant master in the Sakya school, regardless of gender.[156] Another word that denotes the same position is *byang 'dren pa*, literally "the one who begins" (in this case the prayers or rituals). According to the *Abbatial History of Pelyul*, this person is in the best case a lama, but if education, voice, and behavior are all adequate it can also be a practitioner monk who has completed retreats.[157] Aside from having a good character and voice, he also needs to be able-bodied.[158] While the position of chant master is presented as a temporary one in most sources, Nornang reports that in his monastery it was a lifelong position. The chant master, together with the *zhal ta pa*, had sole access to the boxes that contained official documents.[159]

## MANAGER OR SERVANT? THE *ZHAL TA PA*

This official title was mentioned briefly above as a translation of the Sanskrit *vaiyāpṛtyakara*,[160] and is equated with a Tibetan word that denotes manager.[161] The tasks covered by this person in the Indic context range from doing domestic jobs to making important financial and managerial decisions. While the term *zhal ta pa*[162] appears to be obsolete in contemporary Tibetan monasteries, older Tibetan sources suggest a range of meanings comparable to those found in Buddhist texts from India. The initial connotation of the word is someone who serves, derived from the verb *zhal ta byed pa*: to do service.[163] The seventeenth-century *chayik* for Mindröl Ling gives the prerequisites for the *zhal ta pa* as follows:

> A suitable candidate should be appointed with care, as the *zhal ta* needs to be of middling vows,[164] intelligent, and good at handling the stove. He has a sound sense of responsibility with regard to the welfare of the community and good hygiene. He

does not discard supplies or allow them to go to waste. . . . Doing these things will become a cause for himself and others to accumulate merit. Furthermore, he is not to manage matters privately, by loaning out and giving away water, wood, and kitchen appliances.[165]

This suggests a post for someone who is not a *dge slong* and who is involved in kitchen work. After serving as a *zhal ta,* one could become the "seat steward,"[166] someone who manages the laying out and clearing away of seats during the assembly.[167] The fact that this position gets full mention in the text suggests that it is of some import. A person doing kitchen work had access to both food and (costly) pots and pans that needed to be managed carefully.[168] Here the author also connects the *zhal ta's* role to a larger issue: by guarding the contents of the kitchen carefully, one would thereby ensure that offerings given by the faithful would not be wasted, thereby allowing the donors to accumulate maximal merit.

The *chayik* written for Sera Je by the Seventh Dalai Lama lists the kitchen staff required to provide all the monks with tea. The kitchen needed one supervisor, three tea-makers, two people in charge of the fire, two people to fetch water, and finally two *zhal ta pa.*[169] The suggestion here is that in Sera Je in the eighteenth century the *zhal ta pa* were servants doing odd jobs. Another *chayik* states that the two horn blowers,[170] the clean-handed *zhal ta ba,*[171] the shrine-keeper,[172] and the disciplinarians' assistants[173] needed to be chosen from among the young monks. This suggests that all these posts are junior positions.[174] Equally, the guidelines for Tengpoche monastery in Nepal from 1918 note that the junior workers—the tea server,[175] the shrine-keeper, and the *zhal ta ba*—should not be lazy in carrying out their tasks.[176]

The fourteenth-century *chayik* written by Tsongkhapa mentions the *zhal ta pa* a number of times. He is named together with the disciplinarian as having a position in which one was exempt from certain rules, such as having to ask for permission to leave the monastic grounds and so on. Here, this title refers unquestionably to a post equal to that of the disciplinarian, and the task of managing the monastery is clearly part of his duties.[177] Similarly, in Tsurpu monastery in the sixteenth century, the "Sangha's" *zhal ta pa*[178] was responsible for investigating those monks who had stayed at laypeople's houses without permission.[179] In Drepung there seems to have been a variant of this title, namely *zhal ta dpon.* This *zhal ta dpon,* together with the disciplinarian, was in charge of examining and enrolling new monks.[180] This task of selecting members of the monastic community appears similar to that of the *vaiyāpṛtyakara bhikṣu*[181] as portrayed in the *Pravrajyāvastu* of the *Mūlasarvāstivāda vinaya.*[182]

It is unclear why this term has not survived the test of time, whereas most other organizational titles have remained unchanged for centuries. The above sources suggest that what a *zhal ta pa* was meant to do varied greatly, ranging from performing menial tasks such as kitchen-corvée to supervising and managing the monks. It is perhaps exactly this range of meanings that made the title unworkable in the modern context, in which—generally speaking—there is a drive toward uniformity among the monasteries, regardless of their affiliation.

## HEAD MONK OR HEAD OF FINANCE?

Earlier, the ambiguity of the term *spyi sa/ bso/so* was briefly discussed. That it could refer to both a group of people and individual monks makes it slightly problematic. The word *spyi pa/ ba,* however, appears to refer solely to a person.[183] The sources at hand suggest, however, that this term may refer to disparate roles. Some texts speak of the *spyi pa* as someone in a supervisory position, while others suggest that this post was strongly linked to monastic moneymaking. Starting with the former, the guidelines for the Sakya nunnery Rinchen Gang appear to ascribe a role to the *spyi pa* that is rather similar to that of disciplinarian in other institutions:

> If one is an enrolled nun, one's own clothing should conform to tradition. One is not allowed to wear clothes the color of which has not been altered, such as [any] light colors. When one goes against the above, then an appropriate punishment will be given. The *spyi pa* should not hold back. The incumbent *spyi pa* has to enforce the religious rules,[184] taking responsibility for [adherence to] the monastery's regulations regarding order.[185]

The text further specifies that "the contribution of the *spyi pa* is to bring those subtle matters of behavior and rules that are not clarified here but that are in line with the old system to the attention of all and to make sure that they are put in practice."[186] Similarly, in Pelri Chödè's (dPal ri chos sde) monastic guidelines, the *spyi pa* is named together with the chant master and the disciplinarian as someone who needs to be contacted should monks misbehave.[187]

In the guidelines for Mindröl Ling it is said that when monks travel as a group the *spyi pa* is to confiscate "unsuitable" items of clothing that monks are found to carry with them. When a crime occurs that falls under the "general law,"[188] the monk in question needs to be brought before the *spyi pa* once he is back at the base.[189] The same text states elsewhere that unless one has been assigned to do so by a *spyi pa* and is accompanied by a monk friend, one is not to wander around the village of Pergya ('Pher brgya) as a guide for one's acquaintances.[190] Clearly, the above-cited instances of the term suggest the *spyi pa* to be someone with authority, but not necessarily someone with financial responsibilities.

It appears to be more common, however, for the term *spyi pa* to refer to a post that is of substantial economic import. Unlike in countries such as Thailand, where a lay bursar called *waiyawachakon* handled all money on behalf of the monastery,[191] there was (and is) no perceived problem with monks being involved in financial matters. Ekvall, speaking largely from the experience he had accumulated by living and working as a missionary in the border areas of Tibet (mainly Amdo), describes this post in great detail. He notes that the monastery's wealth is "administered by a formally and tightly structured organization and is headed by a sPyi Ba (superintendent). Often there are two of these, who are elected or appointed from among the monks and serve terms of two to four years." He goes on to relate that the stewards (*gnyer pa*) aid the *spyi pa*, who may also have assistants.[192] Ekvall's description of the duties of the *spyi pa* merits citation *in extenso*:

> To be successful, the sPyi Ba must combine the talents of good business executives, the acumen of investment bankers, and the special gifts of salesmen. They must be able to plan and manage such business ventures as the dispatch of trade caravans, the management of livestock herding, the cultivation of fields, and various handicrafts activities, building projects, and the general upkeep and maintenance of all the projects. They must know how and to whom to lend wealth at interest to the best advantage, avoiding unprofitable enterprises and defaulters. In addition, they must be effective salesmen, advertising and proffering the religious services of the monastery so as to elicit, if not directly solicit, gifts to the Grwa Tshang [monastic college]. Salesmanship is also required to induce individuals, families, and communities to accept capital funds as an investment from which the Grwa Tshang may be assured of regular income. In Central Tibet, the collection of taxes is one of their principal duties.[193]

The above account is confirmed by the 1938 monastic guidelines for the Central Tibetan Dophü Chökhor Ling (rDo phud chos 'khor gling) monastery. It warns of the temptations that accompany the post of *spyi pa*:

> Those who hold the post of *spyi ba* at the monastic residency[194] are involved, during their service, in efforts to sustain the general good [such as] farmwork, sales and loans, horses and donkeys. They have an exemption, but only up to a certain level. It is not allowed to do more than what's necessary, which would be both contradictory and harmful to the general rules and good behavior.[195]

It appears that they not only involved themselves in business but also that they managed the treasury for the general population of monks. It is said, in the monastic guidelines for Sera Je monastery, that when there were gifts that were unsuitable to divide among the Sangha, they were to be placed in the treasury of the *spyi pa*.[196] In other instances, the *spyi pa* also serves as the liaison for the benefactors who wish to sponsor tea for the monks.[197] Together with the disciplinarians they inform donors on how their money is spent. However, when the sponsors fall short, they may not argue with them about it and put them under pressure.[198]

While previously the word *spyi bso/so* was connected to an institutional office,[199] this term can be equated with that of *spyi pa* in a number of cases, thus referring to an individual post.[200] According to Dakpa, in Drepung the *spyi so*, of which there were two, were responsible for the finances.[201] The same was true for the *spyi bso* at the Kongtö Dungkar (Kong stod dung dkar) monastery in 1943:

> Two people serve as *spyi bso* for a period of three years. They make sure there is no decline by keeping clear account of grains, silver, animals, and household items in the record of income. They also ensure that what needs to be given and offered,

which includes the interest on grains and butter and the income from dairy products, accords with the record of expenses.[202]

This shows that the *spyi bso* had tasks that are similar to that of a modern-day accountant. The big difference is that, in line with Ekvall's description, the *spyi bso* had to make sure that the monastery would not incur any loss, by managing its income and expenses in the ledgers. At some monasteries, the *spyi bso*'s assistants were called "keepers of offerings."[203] Together with the *spyi bso* they enjoyed several exemptions. The monastic guidelines the Thirteenth Dalai Lama wrote for Rongpo Rabten (Rong po rab brtan) monastery in 1930 state that except for the *spyi bso* and the keepers of offerings, no one was ever "allowed to do farmwork, cattle herding, business, and the like."[204] As with other managerial posts, this position was vulnerable to abuse:

> The general office, of which the keepers of offerings are the heads, is [to record] meticulously all that is deducted, invested, reduced and subtracted from what was given by the faithful to the field of merit—the Three Jewels—according to how it is stated in the allowance ledger that has been issued by the government. No selfish unmeritorious evil actions may ever be permitted.[205]

The above statement reveals a number of important issues, aside from the fact that the keepers of offerings were seen to be corruptible. It shows that the things offered by "the faithful" were in some cases not exactly voluntary,[206] for these offerings could be increased or reduced by the keepers of offerings, suggesting that they were susceptible to bias. Further it indicates that the allowance ledger contained rules on how to deal with and record offerings and other types of income. Generally speaking, the allowance ledger[207] stated how much the different classes of monks received.[208] At the same time, this ledger indicates that the monastery was economically accountable to and dependent on the government, which appears to be part of the Thirteenth Dalai Lama's political policies. Presumably, it gave the government the leverage it needed to impose stricter rules regarding "playing favorites" (or simply corruption).

Yet another similar term is *spyi gnyer,* which also may refer to the assistant of the *spyi pa.* In Sera Je there were two of them, and they were allowed to keep up to three horses,[209] something that was forbidden for the ordinary monks. This suggests that they had to venture out of the monastery on a regular basis. In the guidelines for Drigung Til from 1802, the *spyi gnyer* are mentioned together with the disciplinarians.[210] They appear to play an important supervisory role in the monastery. The *spyi gnyer,* as did others who held official positions, had to make sure that their robes were in order, in particular when venturing outside of the monastery.[211] This suggests the *spyi gnyer* had a representative role.

## THE STEWARD OR THE FINANCIAL CARETAKER

While the above terms *zhal ta pa* and *spyi pa* now seem mostly obsolete, the word *gnyer pa* is in active use in contemporary monasteries. It indicates a monk who is in charge of the finances of the monastery—a steward. A monastic institution could have several stewards. Khenpo Chöying Lhundrup, referring to the contemporary situation in Khampa Gar in India, explains that the different sections of the monastery function more or less independently. They have separate economies and they each have a steward. However, the "owner" of the entire monastery (*dgon pa'i bdag po*) is an incarnated lama, Kamtrül Rinpoche (Khams sprul rin po che). When one section faces difficulties, the others help out.[212] Similarly, for Sakya Chökhor Ling (Sa skya chos 'khor gling) in India, the two stewards look after the monks during certain rituals and other religious congregations. They are also responsible for food expenses.[213]

In pre-modern Tibet, the stewards appear to have filled positions often similar if not equivalent to that of the *spyi pa*. The elderly monk Könchok Chönyi, speaking of his time in Yangri Gar[214] in the 1950s, notes that in Tibet certain types of incarnations or the richer monks would fill the position of *gnyer pa*. More generally, the monks who worked in the administration needed to be affluent (*rgyu chen po*). They would travel around, making investments, buying and selling things, and doing business for the monastery. They needed to have some startup capital, so this kind of enterprise was not for the poorer monks.[215] Dagyab notes that, at least in the years prior to 1959, in the case of a deficit, such a monk would have to replace the losses himself, whereas he could assume that, in the case of a surplus, he could keep it.[216] That this post is strongly connected to being both wealthy and business-savvy is highlighted by the fact that in the modern Mongolian language the term "Jisa nyarab" (*\*spyi sa'i gnyer pa*) carries a special meaning, namely "that of a person who has money but is very careful and not willing to use it."[217]

This notion that a person who does business on behalf of the Sangha needs to have money of his own does not occur solely in the Tibetan tradition: the rules in the Theravāda Vinaya state that monks were liable to pay damages when their actions lead to the Sangha incurring a loss. One can therefore deduce that monks tended to own property.[218] In the Tibetan case, this Vinayic concern for illegitimately using the Sangha's possessions translates into a general rule that the people investing those very goods had to be of some means themselves.[219]

The steward may have also held an important position with regard to managing the lands that belonged to the monastery. In Ganden, the steward[220] had two ways to do so: he could let it to others and set up a contract for that purpose, or alternatively, he could appoint a subject of the monastic region to look after the affairs and collect the revenue.[221] In the same monastery, before 1959 the individual monastic houses each had three financial managers[222] in Lhasa, who accepted repayment from debtees and busied themselves with collecting rent. These managers were supported by two "pursuers"[223] who acted as debt collectors.[224] That the steward had to be mobile is apparent in the guidelines for Drepung, where it is stated that while the two disciplinarians were allowed to have just one horse each, the steward of Pendè Lekshé Ling (Phan bde legs bshad gling) college could have five horses and the steward of Deyang (bDe yangs) college could keep two horses and two *dzomo* (*mdzo mo*).[225]

Of those who conducted business that required traveling outside of the monastery, it was not just the steward who had to be of means. This is witnessed by the guidelines for Mindröl Ling, where it is indicated that a *rtsis 'dzin pa*—someone taking account of loans (against interest) and repayments of those loans—had to make up for any loss that would occur:

> All the things that are given as loans, to which the *rtsis 'dzin pa* of the treasury and a suitable assistant are assigned with utmost care, may not be loaned out to others, except for when there is an exceptionally great need. And even if something needs to be used, the official to whose care it was given needs to make sure its value does not decrease. In the case of loss, he needs to replace it. When the loss is great a replacement and a surcharge may be taken. When it is minor, recompense should be made. When there is a recollection of who the persons in question are, then they should be held to account. But when they are not identified, the bookkeeper (*rtsis pa*) himself, as it was explained above, needs to carefully make sure that it is taken care of by offering recompense himself.[226]

It is not clear here whether this person loans to monks or to laypeople—but in light of other accounts,[227] I assume that laypeople would visit the monastery to take out loans. The role of the *rtsis 'dzin pa* might be comparable to the post of steward in other monasteries at other times.[228]

The Bon monastery of Menri also had a different term for the persons managing its finances. There two monks held the title *phan tshun dge rgan*.[229] They were chosen for their abilities and appointed for three years. Each year one of them would go to the Jangthang area (encompassing northern and western Tibet) to collect funds from the nomads there. Wealthy families would then donate thirty to forty yaks and butter. The donations would be transported to Tsang (in Central Tibet) to be sold. With the money this monk official then would buy grain. The other steward had to oversee the production of tsampa (*rtsam pa*). The tsampa was distributed during the daily tea-round[230] in the assembly hall.[231] Another term found for a similar position is *kha 'go ba*.[232] According to Nietupski, in Labrang monastery these representatives were chosen because they were natural leaders and good speakers, bold and publicly aggressive. They had to know "the fundamental corpus of rituals and doctrines" but they were "not scholars or even very pious." They were generally wild and rough and some allegedly renounced their vows temporarily.[233]

The above sources clearly suggest that the financial managers were monks. Other sources are more ambiguous regarding these officials. Könchok Chönyi expressly states that in the monastery in Yangri Gar a steward had to have either *dge tsul* or *dge slong* vows,[234] while Lobzang Döndrup maintains that in Spituk, Ladakh, both the steward and the treasurer were chosen from among the *dge slong.*[235] Partly because the term *gnyer pa* is also used in secular organizations,[236] some confusion remains regarding the identity of this steward. Furthermore, in Ladakh, the families that are financially responsible for certain ceremonies also get called *gnyer pa.*[237] Ekvall, however, in describing the role and function of ex-monks,[238] notes that they "are the doers of secular deeds when the monastery needs them to be done; they have the time and opportunity for economic and political activity; they often hold managerial positions in the monastery, such as the *gnyer pa* and the *spyi ba.*"[239]

In other places it appears that laypeople managed the entire monastery.[240] Likewise, in Samdè Ling (bSam bde gling), in the first half of the twentieth century, the steward was also a layman.[241] Michael further notes that managers of monastic estates were often laypeople and that they could make the monastery rich.[242] These "managers," however, could also be the people contracted by the monk stewards to manage the fields.[243]

In many ways, the *spyi pa* and the *gnyer pa* had very similar functions. In Dakpo Shedrup Ling, the offices that took care of financial matters were split into two: the steward's office[244] controlled the agricultural land and the general department[245] controlled the livestock, grain, cash, and other donations. The steward's office was responsible for paying the monks their allowance and also had to provide them with soup on a regular basis. In the years before the 1950s, the general department fared much better financially, but it was not allowed to help out the steward's office.[246] Naturally, not all monasteries had access to income from both land rent and livestock, so having two distinct departments was unnecessary, which may account for the crossover in the meanings of the terms.

## EX-MONKS AND THE MONASTERY

As briefly alluded to above, ex-monks can still play important roles in certain aspects of the monastery's running. Ekvall, describing the situation he found in Amdo between 1925 and 1941, speaks of the so-called *ban log,* which he translates as "monk rebel."[247] According to him, these were individuals who had been debarred from remaining as monks for having violated the basic rules (i.e., the four root vows). However, for various reasons, they continued to live in their quarters in the monastery, wear the garb of monks, and maintain their high standing outside the monastery. An ex-monk could engage in extensive trading for himself or the community, often using his residency at the monastery as a storage and trading post. He was also able to hold managerial positions such as steward. In some cases, he had a family living outside the monastery.[248] This "rebel monk" thus bought and sold, collected debts, and lent out money. He was particularly important when monasteries went to war and monks became armed mobs or private armies. Such a person, even when he killed during a conflict, would still have a

place in the monastery. Ekvall states that "by his activities he both exercises political power on behalf of the monastery and increases and enhances such power."²⁴⁹
The ex-monks became the "doers of secular deeds" on behalf of the monastery.²⁵⁰

In Sakya too, a former monk could maintain his official position, provided
he made a generous offering to his monastery.²⁵¹ In other words, there was little
correspondence between religious standards and political propriety.²⁵² To house
ex-monks who nonetheless displayed loyalty to the monastery may have been a
practical solution to the limitations posed by holding monastic vows. This was
solved in Sri Lankan Buddhism by employing a *kappiyakāraka* (*rung bar byed
pa*, S. *kalpikāra*): a layperson appointed to procure necessities for the Sangha and
make them allowable.²⁵³ At first glance, the ex-monk that Ekvall describes appears
to be a (Eastern) Tibetan equivalent. However, as the next chapter demonstrates,
the handling of money was comparatively less problematic for Tibetan monks—or
simply for any monk within the *Mūlasarvāstivāda vinaya* tradition.²⁵⁴

While Ekvall's observations on these ex-monks are no doubt accurate, they are
far removed from the ideal scenarios set forth by most of the monastic guidelines.
The authors of these texts appear keen to remove these less desirable presences
from their monastery, or at least to prevent them from partaking in any of the
offerings that were divided among the monks.²⁵⁵ Contrary to what is commonly
thought, it was possible for a monk who had been expelled to retake the vows and
return to the monastery. This return to the ranks was under strict supervision and
with the proviso of certain stipulations.²⁵⁶ Furthermore, according to the monastic
guidelines of Pelyul Darthang monastery, these ex-monks who retook their vows
could not hold positions of ritual importance such as that of religious teacher,
chant master, or teacher of ritual dances.²⁵⁷

While in some Tibetan societies disrobing was seen as the greatest shame,²⁵⁸
it was a common occurrence in others.²⁵⁹ Often the economic outlook for monks
who disrobed was bleak, and this may have been one of the reasons why relatively
few monks returned to lay life. Contrastingly, Dargyay notes that former monks
were in demand to become secretaries in noble households.²⁶⁰ Naturally this only
pertained to educated monks. The elderly Sakya monk Shérap Gyatso explained
what happened to monks who disrobed in his monastery:

> Ex-monks would usually go to Kham: they did not stay around. Life must have been
> difficult for a former monk, because he would not know a lot about work. If you
> would have a good family to fall back on, it would not be that bad. Otherwise it
> would be quite difficult.²⁶¹

The role of ex-monks is underappreciated in current scholarship, mainly because
our sources—the monk authors—are wary to report about them, for obvious reasons. However, the ex-monk's affiliation with the monastery, which was in some
cases an emotional bond, in others a pragmatic and financial one, often remained.
This contributed to the development of informal networks.

## THE ABBOT: FIGUREHEAD OR FRONTMAN?

Like most other offices in the monastery, that of the abbot is not straightforward. As mentioned above, the abbot's position is less regularly commented on in the monastic guidelines, likely because the abbots were often either the authors or the people who requested these rules.[262] Still, the guidelines provide information on the role of the leader of a monastery or college. In the Geluk system *mkhan po* is commonly used to denote the ruling head of a monastic institution, although in some cases the leader was called a "throne-holder,"[263] which usually, but not always, referred to an incarnation instated as head of one or more monasteries. In non-Geluk schools the latter position is more akin to what is called the "owner of the Teachings"[264]—the highest authority possible.[265] The throne-holder of Sakya is called *khri thog pa*. It is tempting to suppose that, in the case of there being both a temporary head (such as a *mkhan po*) and an incarnated leader-for-life (such as the *khri pa* or *bstan bdag*), the latter has the function of acting as religious figurehead, whereas the former is more involved in practical matters. It is not clear-cut, however.

Taking monasticism as it occurs in Ladakh as a starting point, Mills makes a case for ritual authority being extended over both the monastery and the laypeople as the prerogative of the incarnates, and claims that ritual authority often extended into organizational authority.[266] Nietupski shows a similar presupposition, as he casually mentions that the Fourth Jamyang Zhépa (1856–1916) served as throne-holder of several monasteries and that "he was thus no stranger to diplomacy, administration, legal or economic matters."[267] This raises the question of what a throne-holder's duties involved.

Presumably, a successful throne-holder needed to have charisma and religious authority so as to legitimize his exertion of power and diplomacy. The *chayik* of Drigung Til states that its monks, "in order not to destroy oneself and others by means of disrepute and the many grounds for disputes," needed to look to the acting abbots as role models and follow their example.[268] Cassinelli and Ekvall state that in Sakya, the abbots of the monasteries were not meant to concern themselves too much with governmental—and thus managerial—affairs and that often officials (presumably those with a "religious rank" in the monasteries) had less political power than ordinary monks.[269]

It appears that there was—at least at the larger monasteries—a dual system in place, in which a group of monks would effectively run the monastery, dirtying their hands if necessary, without "incriminating" the religious figureheads. This arrangement is comparable to that in place in Thailand where "it is quite common for the real business of running the *wat* [monastery] to be undertaken by the deputy, whilst the abbot preserves his charisma by remaining aloof from these affairs."[270] It can thus be argued that it does not follow that a throne-holder, or any religious figurehead for that matter, was also necessarily assigned a practical, administrative, or managerial role. This dual system may have its parallel in the way most of the Dalai Lamas related to their regents.[271]

It is also possible, however, that in smaller monasteries the abbot, or throne-holder, held dual functions. This would probably be seen as far from ideal because it meant that the position of the "spiritual head" of the monastery could be compromised through (public) involvement in worldly affairs. During the reign of the Thirteenth Dalai Lama, there was a concerted effort under way to keep abbots from participating in governmental affairs.[272] A *chayik* written in 1889 by the Thirteenth Dalai Lama on the occasion of the establishment of an unnamed and unidentified educational college[273] gives the job description of the abbot as follows:

> An abbot mainly needs to manage affairs. The abbot also definitely needs to be a spiritual teacher who is endowed with the qualities of being learned, disciplined, and kind. In the best case, he has already gained higher degrees at one of the big monasteries. If not, he should have completed the studies of the five main subjects.[274]

Naturally, because the monastic institution in question is one that focused on education, the abbot also needs to be knowledgeable. However, here—without going into details—the dual function of the abbot as a "spiritual friend" and a manager is clearly indicated.

While the size and function of the monastery was thus a factor, much also appears to depend on whether the appointment is for life or merely temporary. Schram, describing the Tibetan Buddhist Monguor people at the beginning of the twentieth century, notes that the abbots had in principle the power to address malpractices, but that they declined to do so because they were elected by the intendants and after their three-year term they still had to remain in the monastery. Thus, the abbots were in the words of Schram "practical Orientals" and chose not to introduce reforms. This reduced their powers to "theoretical and honorary dimensions." An abbot furthermore had to be a rich man, for he had to be able to entertain the more highly placed inmates of the monastery with sumptuous banquets several times a year. The poorer monks who were put forward as candidates for the position of abbot often declined for that reason.[275]

In the Nyingma monastery of Pelyul Darthang in Golog, Amdo, during the first half of the twentieth century, the abbot was also responsible, along with the disciplinarian, for the maintenance of discipline.[276] The abbot had a supervisory function (*klad gzigs*), whereas that of the disciplinarian was executive (*do khur*).[277] This suggests that the abbot was the one who held the ultimate responsibility. Indeed, when in the early twentieth century monks from Sera monastery were found to have cashed in debts by forcibly seizing goods from laypeople, the Thirteenth Dalai lama fined the abbot, making him "legally" responsible for the conduct of his monks.[278] In Pelyul in Kham, consulting the head of the monastery was seen as a last resort. Only when other officials such as disciplinarians could not come to a satisfactory solution was he asked for advice. Alternatively, the officials could come together in council and reach a decision after discussing the matter.[279] In the hierarchy of the monastery, the abbot had the highest authority. It was his name and his deeds that would be set down in the monastery's abbatial record.[280]

It is suggested that in both China and Thailand abbots were expected to be on good terms with government officials and lay donors and to regularly meet with them. The monastery was greatly dependent on these relationships for its economic and political survival.[281] While in many regards the Tibetan monastic economy was such that it depended to a lesser extent on sponsors, it is highly likely that the abbot was responsible for the promotion and maintenance of good relations with important players on the outside world. The guidelines I have seen do not discuss this, but if the situation in contemporary Tibetan monasteries is a continuation of the past, then—in particular concerning non-Geluk monasteries—the presence, charisma, and amicability of the abbot is indeed crucial for the reputation, discipline, and finances of a monastic institution.

## MANAGERIAL AND RELIGIOUS OFFICES: A TWO-TIERED INSTITUTION?

*Senatores boni viri, senatus autem mala bestia.*

There is a perceived relationship between the level of discipline and the presence of an important master. Lama Tsültrim complained to me that discipline had deteriorated dramatically in his monastery, and when asked to give a reason, he explained:

> This is because the main spiritual head used to always be present in the monastery, making sure the monks would behave well and that all would go to the assembly. Now both our main lamas travel to the West frequently, and they also have a lot of responsibilities elsewhere. Now there is no one with authority whom the monks will respect. Actually, I think that important lamas need to stay at the monastery to look after its affairs. Previously, the lamas lived here, also because they did not really know English and did not have the opportunity to travel. Now this is all different: they speak English and teach all over the world. The monastery suffers from their absence.[282]

This is also echoed by Mills who, in examining the state of smaller Geluk monasteries in Ladakh, writes that "the monastic discipline of ordinary monks is in some sense linked to, and constituted by, the activities of incarnates."[283] While this may be the case in the smaller Geluk monasteries and in the other schools that have a tradition of assigning important administrative positions to the higher incarnations, we find that according to the examples given above, the abbot is important for the maintenance of discipline, but only for setting an example or being an inspiration. The day-to-day matters were (and usually still are) taken care of by the disciplinarians, the chant masters, and the various types of managers. Thus, while

the abbot has a degree of what could be called "ritual authority" over the monastery's inhabitants, it is important to understand the practical limitations of that
authority. In other words, there appeared to be a two-tiered institution, in which
the abbot was able to maintain the moral high ground, while the managers were
burdened with the upkeep of the monastery and—when push came to shove—
took certain measures, which could be perceived as reprehensible.

It appears that some *chayik* attempted to close the gap between the behavior of
the managerial and symbolical powers. In the opinion of their authors, *all* monks
should behave in an exemplary way. The monastic guidelines thus address this dis-
junction between what authority figures prescribed for a monastery and what the
monks actually did. Therefore, when attempting to understand how monasteries
were actually organized, not too much should be made of this "'ritual authority,"[284]
for the *chayik* demonstrate that often no more than lip service was paid to this
authority.

Another point is that there existed a high degree of authority, embodied by
the offices that have been described in this chapter. This "combined" authority
was hardly ever called into question. When leaders have a lot of authority and
control over resources, the level of organizational flexibility may decrease, as people become unable or unwilling to challenge the organization's leadership.[285] This
lessening of adaptability is, in the case of Tibetan monasteries, clearly visible: the
organizational structures were relatively stable over a number of centuries and any
change was viewed with great suspicion. Similar to the Christian monasteries in
the Middle Ages, which are described as "institutions designed to stem the tide
of change," it seems that their Tibetan counterparts too were "living symbols of
immutability in the midst of flux."[286]

In the context of Tibetan monasticism, the identity of the institution is clearly
distinct from that of the individual monk. This may have further ramifications:
when monks act in the name of their monastery, the ultimate (moral) responsibility lies with the inanimate institution. As long as there was no perceived self-
interest among the monks involved, monks may not have been held accountable
for actions that would have otherwise been seen as "unethical." It would have been
unimaginable to blame "the system," i.e., the Sangha as a whole, for any wrongdoing, as this was (and is) seen as bearing severe karmic consequences. Viewed in
this way, we can understand how the actions of the monastery as a whole were
rarely criticized, whereas individual monks, government representatives, and local
rulers were more easily reproached. This would in turn have maintained the status
quo.[287] The Tibetan system of monastic organization—despite it being in no way
entirely homogenous—was geared toward maintaining the monastery and thereby
the Sangha as a whole. This outlook also had an impact on how the monastic institution and its monks dealt with economic issues, to which we turn next.

# 5

# Monastic Economy and Policy

To date, no in-depth studies of monastic economy in Tibetan areas have been done. Writing in 1961, Miller questions the validity of the depiction of Tibetan monastic economies in which the monastery is portrayed as a centralized and corporate institution, but adds that "[we] need desperately a study of the Tibetan and monastic economies before firm conclusions can be drawn."[1] Dreyfus also notes that "it is quite remarkable that there is still no systematic study of the administrative and financial structures and practices of monasteries, institutions so central to traditional Tibetan culture."[2] One of the most important reasons that a thorough study has not been conducted to date is that sources indispensable for quantitative research are currently not available to researchers.

A study of the place of a monastery and its relation to the broader society should be interested less with the mere factual data of the different administrative systems of Tibetan monasteries and their monastic economies, and more with how these were conceived of by Tibetan monastic authors, who held a certain level of moral authority.[3] Phrased differently, according to Durkheimian theory, there are two circuits of social life: "one, the everyday, is the short-term, individuated and materialistic; the other, the social, is long-term, collective and idealized, even spiritual."[4] To the minds of many, the topic of economics falls under the first circuit, whereas most societies attempt to subordinate this to their own cultural or religious conditions, i.e., the second circuit. This chapter addresses the circuit that consists of the long-term and the idealized, which in this context is the monastic economic policies and the monastic *attitudes* to economic matters as represented by the monastic guidelines.

Attitudes change when circumstances change, such that changing attitudes—as detected in works that contain allusions to monastic economic behavior—have the potential to inform us about certain economic developments among the monasteries. According to Sayer, "economic phenomena both depend on and influence moral/ethical sentiments, norms and behaviors and have ethical implications."[5] When considering these mutual influences, one can see how attitudes regarding economic behavior may inform us about actual economic behavior, both on a macro- and a micro-level.

With an understanding of the conceptual and moral framework of monastic economic policies, one can better comprehend the socioeconomic interrelations between lay and monastic societies. Shakya notes in this regard:

> The Tibetan masses may have resented the wealth and privilege of the lay aristocracy, but the question of the economic power enjoyed by the religious institutions was viewed differently. For non-Tibetans, the economic power of the monastery was simply exploitation and the position of the lamas and the monks parasitic. But for the Tibetans such thoughts were irrelevant: they were willing to accept the special position enjoyed by the religious institutions and in fact much of the wealth of the monasteries was accumulated over centuries from voluntary contributions from the masses.[6]

How then was this privileged position maintained by the monastery and why did laypeople apparently accept and support these religious institutions that held such sway over their lives?

There are many misconceptions about the economic systems of monastic institutions. Particularly in studies that deal with the current state of monasteries in Tibetan areas, ahistorical notions abound. In describing the processes through which contemporary monasteries try to find "alternative" ways of managing financial matters, such as tourism, state funding, or shopkeeping, a comment regularly made is that in the olden days monks did not have to resort to such methods. In one such study the author writes that unlike in "pre-revolutionary times when the monastery supported its clergy through a feudal system of land rents, the new generation of monks had to be self-supporting."[7] Such statements indicate a lack of appreciation for the earlier monastic economic systems.

It is certainly *not* true that historically monasteries (always) supported monks' livelihoods. We know this from oral accounts of monks who lived in various Tibetan areas before the 1950s, but this is also evidenced by both very early and rather late Tibetan texts. Dreyfus further confirms this by remarking that in Tibet the large monasteries did not provide for their monks, except at assemblies during which tea was served, although this was not enough to live on.[8] Only the very determined, the well connected, and the wealthier studying monks would be able to bring their studies to a successful end and not have substantial financial difficulties. This was at least the case at the Three Great Seats. Local monasteries generally tended to be easier places to live in, not least because monks often had their relatives nearby who could support them.[9] One such smaller monastery was the Pabongka hermitage during the late eighteenth or early nineteenth century; according to its guidelines: "During assemblies, generally speaking, every day all are provided with seven rounds of tea and/or soup, without fail."[10] This may mean that monks were relatively well fed there, although the authorities did not necessarily cover other expenses. Another problem with the contention cited above is that not all monasteries upheld a "feudal system of land rents," as there were many that did not have land to rent out.

It is exactly this diversity in monastic economic systems and in Tibetan monasteries in general that makes it hard, and perhaps impossible, to present the economics of the pre-modern Tibetan monastery in a comprehensive manner. However, it is certainly essential to make a distinction between local and central monasteries. The local ones were often small, whereas the central monasteries were training centers attracting monks from affiliated local monasteries. The large central monasteries were often at the heart of a far-reaching network of smaller, local monasteries.[11] The differences with regard to the economic circumstances were not necessarily determined only by the number of inhabitants, but were also dependent on the location, the political circumstances, and the "purpose" of the monastery. A monastery consisting of monks hailing from the vicinity would often have a strong ritual function in the local community. The relative prosperity of the laypeople living in the direct surroundings would have an impact on the economic situation of the monastery, regardless of whether the monasteries owned land, or whether they were involved in trade and other financial transactions.

While monks regularly lived at a subsistence level, there was a tendency for the wealthier monasteries to hoard their resources.[12] As alluded to in the previous chapter, there was a rather strict division between the monastic corporation and the individual monks. This divide was particularly pronounced when it came to economic matters. This was also noted, but not elaborated on, by Stein:

> We must accordingly reckon with a certain difference between the ecclesiastic community and the individual prelate. The former tended to hoard and accumulate wealth and political power. The latter was often a factor in their circulation, in both a centripetal and centrifugal sense.[13]

This chapter, then, attempts to explain the rules and attitudes at the monastic institutions with regard to financial and economic matters, such as commerce, property, inheritance, investment, and the redistribution of wealth.[14]

## INDIVIDUAL ECONOMIC SPHERES VS. THE SANGHA'S ECONOMIC SPHERE

Dungkar Lopzang Trinlé, in describing the developments of Buddhist monastic economy, gives a periodization of its development, starting in India and ending in Tibet. On the monastic economy in India he notes that the monastery had four types of general income.

1.  Offerings made to the body, speech and mind,[15] used to repair the temples and so forth

2.  That which fell under offerings received for teaching the dharma given to those who taught the dharma

3.  That which was not to be divided up, but intended as the general possession of the Sangha

4.  That which was to be divided equally among all, regardless of the amount.

These four types of wealth then were not to be moved from one to the other. Furthermore, to sell the general assets to provide loans, collect interest, assume sureties, and the like were allowed for the sake of the Sangha in general, but not for the individual monk.[16]

The above-outlined rules, which have their origin in the normative Vinaya, indicate that monks were already involved in property law and the like early on in India.[17] While this fourfold schema cannot have been strictly enforced throughout the Buddhist monastic world, it was not just in India where a—theoretical— distinction between different types of property, income, and offerings was upheld.[18] In Tibet, the monastic guidelines demonstrate that the most strictly adhered to division was that between the individual and the Sangha: "An individual should not come to own the general possessions of the Sangha and use them without this being necessary. Not even the smallest piece of grass or wood should be taken and the general welfare should be taken to heart as much as possible."[19]

Sometimes certain general possessions were used by individuals, with or without permission. Of course, what belongs to the Sangha and what is owned by the individual monk is not always clear. Therefore, some sets of monastic guidelines detail how to deal with offerings: what a monk had to pass on to the authorities and what he could keep. The Fifth Dalai Lama writes in his *chayik* for the Nyingma monastery Gongra Ngesang Dorje Ling (Gong ra nges gsang rdo rje gling):

> Whatever kind of payment that resulted from having gone to do home rituals, one may only deposit it with the monastic authorities, one is not to take it oneself. The distributions that have been directly given one can keep for oneself. When there are specific offerings made that serve the general good, then they should be collected as part of the "general offerings."[20]

Terdak Lingpa, the author of the guidelines of Mindröl Ling and a contemporary of the Fifth Dalai Lama, is equally specific in maintaining the separation between what is the Sangha's and what can be divided among the monks: valuable offerings were to be kept as general assets, while others would be divided among the monks who conducted the rituals.[21]

Tsongkhapa in his guidelines for Jampa Ling (Byams pa gling) states that whenever monks got ahold of any goods or money, they needed to pass it or them on to the monastic authorities,[22] suggesting that monks could not keep anything.[23] The rules given above suggest that the individual monk was not to take possession of the Sangha's public property. However, the reverse practice sometimes occurred: "It is customary that the monastery monks' clothing is proper. Aside from that which is proper, one is not to wear anything inappropriate. If one is found wearing [something like] this, it will become [part of the] general assets, once it has been reported to the disciplinarian."[24] The monastic authorities not only confiscated inappropriate goods in the possession of monks, but according to several *chayik* they also regularly took "illegal goods," such as alcohol, away from laypeople when they were caught with them on monastic grounds.[25]

With regard to the individual property of monks, it appears that while to own more than what the Vinaya allowed was tolerated,[26] each individual monastery imposed its own restrictions on those possessions. One problematic type of property that features regularly in the monastic guidelines is that of livestock and horses. The monastic guidelines for Drepung allow certain monk officials to keep a limited number of horses and cattle, whereas ordinary monks are dealt with pragmatically: "if they are offered [such animals] they may take care of them for no longer than two months until they get sold."[27] This statement not only shows that monks were given gifts that were—both theoretically and practically— inappropriate, but also that the recipient of such an offering had the freedom to sell it, at least in the Drepung of the late seventeenth century. This concurs with Vinayic rules which stipulate that monks are not to refuse gifts, but it does not follow the examples given in the *Mūlasarvāstivāda vinaya* in which monks are instructed to find a way to use these inappropriate gifts in a certain manner.[28] Furthermore, the above ruling indicates that trade was not only tolerated, but sometimes also necessary.

As pointed out above, the income that the monastery received as an institution could only be used for certain purposes and was not used for the subsistence of monks.[29] The *chayik* written in 1909 for all of Sikkim's monasteries specifies how this wealth was to be used:

> The yearly monetary allowance for the monastery,[30] the tax income from its monastic estates, as well as the income provided by donors in order to bring about merit for the dead and the living, and so on, need to be written in a ledger, specifying what came from where, instead of getting whittled away as has occurred previously. This [resulting] amount, which is kept in the monastic administration, should be used to restore cracked and aging walls on the inside and outside and to restore the receptacles of body, speech, and mind. . . . The trust funds for the scriptures and other works should be developed without ever letting them deteriorate, by which each and every religious festival can continue.[31]

In Menri monastery in Tibet, the income that the monastic authorities generated with the herds they owned was also spent solely on the upkeep and adornment of the monastery's exterior.[32] While in most cases it could not be spent to sustain the individual monks, we see that the monastery's surplus was meant to be used in a variety of ways. While it was intended to go toward the upkeep and expansion of the physical monastery and toward the financing of religious festivals and rituals,[33] in reality it was also used to make business investments. This latter type of wealth management was under the auspices of the financial caretakers. Ekvall notes that they were required to manage the monastic wealth so that "at the end of their terms of office they may be able to report an increase in holdings and substantial earnings on wealth lent at interest or invested in trade operations."[34] Hovden informs us that in the twentieth century in Limi, Nepal, the monastery there hardly ever used the grain that was collected as levy to feed the monks. Rather, this grain was lent out against interest to villagers in need of seed grain.[35] Regularly, however, some of the surplus was left unused.

As mentioned in the previous chapter, when monasteries consisted of several semi-independent subunits, in most cases distinct economies were kept.[36] In a similar way, the economies of the Sangha and the individual monks were also strictly separate—at least this was the ideal scenario.[37] The reasoning that is implicit in both the Vinayic materials and the monastic guidelines is that the monastery is dependent on the donor's decision concerning how his contribution will be spent.[38] The sixteenth-century guidelines for Tsurpu appear to confirm this reasoning: "the desirous ones, who hear but not think, may not just hungrily consume the general assets of the Sangha. Rather, [the assets are] to be used continuously for whatever [they were] intended to be used for."[39] Some donations that were offered to the monastery with a specific purpose were only meant for investment: the monastery could then only use the profits from that investment for that particular goal, which could be religious ceremonies or rounds of tea for the monks.[40]

### FINANCING AND SPONSORSHIP

> *[T]he ascetic regime of the monk, though intended to remove him from lay society, in fact renders him dependent on that very society for material support.*
> —BUNNAG 1973: 30

In the case of Tibet, monasteries were both economically dependent on and independent from lay society. In Tibet, the Sangha was not the chief exemplar of non-reciprocity, as posited by Tambiah, nor was it a passive symbol of independence, despite its dependence on lay donors.[41] Monasteries would not let their fate be decided by the whims of the laity. In fact, monasteries are regularly described as independent: "Since monasteries are exempt from tax and services they can be regarded as *independent overlords,* for they own land and serfs yielding them taxes and services, and discharge all the functions of authority (justice, etc.)."[42] That said, in particular with respect to locally oriented monasteries, the strict conceptual divide between monastic and lay society was artificial at best.

In parallel to the narrative development of the *Mūlasarvāstivāda vinaya,* the emic Tibetan account of the development of monastic economy tells a tale of monasteries initially being solely dependent on the king and wealthy aristocratic laymen. Eventually they inadvertently amass large estates, rendering them largely independent of outside sponsors. Dungkar Lopzang Trinlé, for example, remarks that during Songtsen Gampo's (569–650 or 617–650) reign "the monks, masters, and disciples were given a yearly allowance from the king's treasury, but other than that they owned nothing like fields, cattle, and pasture lands."[43] Here, the monastics were portrayed as being dependent on the state and not directly on lay society.[44]

Certain scholars who research contemporary Tibetan monasticism regard putting monks on a monastic payroll as something that has come about in part due to the more recent Chinese overhaul of the economic situation of the monasteries and report that monks see this option as preferable to subsisting on the gifts of laypeople.[45] A contemporary Tibetan-language work on monasteries in Central Tibet also notes that these days the more well-to-do monasteries give their monks a "dharma allowance,"[46] so that they do not need to go to the village to beg for alms or perform home rituals. The poorer monasteries cannot afford this, which is why their monks wander around the area to collect money.[47]

The sources at hand suggest, however, that the move away from donation dependency to a steadier income provided by the central monastic authorities (or government) was a trend that started long before the twentieth century. In light of the above citation on monasticism during the early Imperial period, one could even argue that living on a "state" income is one of the earliest, if not the earliest, monastic modes of subsistence for individual monks. Be this as it may, prior to the mid-twentieth century there was a gradual shift from monks being dependent on donations and income from ritual services to receiving allowances.

Earlier (pre–Ganden Phodrang) guidelines tend not to report on allowances, while later works occasionally report management changes concerning payment.[48] In a set of monastic guidelines for the practitioners at the big protectors' chapel in Pelpung (dPal spungs) written in 1825, we read that a certain type of allowances was newly introduced in that same year for the purpose of a stable field of merit,[49] in particular for the recitations dedicated to the protectors.[50] The monastic guidelines for Thekchen Damchö Gatsel ling written in 1898 (possibly by the Thirteenth Dalai Lama, as according to the colophon it was written in the Potala) have the stewards handing out the allowances.[51] This indicates that, at least in this case, the distributed supplies were likely to stem from income derived by the monastic authorities.

These allowances tended to be food, not money, something indicated by the stipulation that "when one has taken one's allowances, one can only consume it inside the compound and not take it elsewhere."[52] In later times, this allowance could be money as well. A *chayik* from 1949 states that a certain *geshé* made a donation to the monastery's office, which appeared to have been struggling, consisting of a "monastic allowance" of twenty-five silver coins[53] for each monk on a yearly basis.[54]

The allowances some monks received should not be equated with stipends, i.e., income that anyone could be given regardless of their status, actions, or behavior. According to the rules on Tibetan monastic economy that can be extrapolated from the guidelines, it appears that there was no such thing as a free lunch. While in Benedictine rule—and in Chan monasteries in China—the adage "he who does not work, does not eat" may perhaps ring true,[55] generally speaking one could say of the Tibetan context that "he who does not *pray*, does not eat." Not only because the authorities felt that allowances had to be earned by performing religious services and the like, but also because in most cases the tea, food, and allowances were handed out during the assembly and there were strict rules against passing these goods on to people who did not go to the assembly.[56] The exceptions to this rule mentioned in many monastic guidelines regard those who are too ill to go, who are in retreat, or who are away performing duties on behalf of the monastery.

Some sources suggest that certain monastic authorities wanted to move away from payment during prayers in favor of rewarding educational efforts. A modern history of Tsurpu monastery suggests that monks serious about their studies had the right to a grain allowance,[57] but only after they had offered another "enrollment tea" upon entering the formal education system.[58] Kvaerne, relying on oral history, describes how in the Bon Menri monastery the head of the "office of education," who was chosen from among the *geshé*s, was in charge of taking care of the monks who were studying debate. He would do this by going to the Jangthang area to collect butter from the monastery's herds. The revenue from this enterprise would also pay for the monks' provisions during the debates in the evenings, five days a week, all year long.[59] Clearly, this type of subsidization was only available to monks who were enrolled in the curriculum.

Sidkeong Tulku, in writing his monastic guidelines for all Sikkimese monasteries in 1909, rules that the monks interested in learning had to be provided for economically. The text says that those who study diligently should always be given tea and soup by the central monastic administration until they complete their studies.[60] The guidelines further state, with regard to those who have had some education: "Unlike before, [they] need to get a position and rewards and relief from tax, corvée duty, transportation duty and so on, commensurate with their achievements."[61]

In a similar attempt to increase scholasticism certain monastic officials at Dre-pung in the 1930s created a new rule in which the payment of "the monastic sala-ries" was shifted to the debate ground instead of the previously favored assembly hall. This led to protests from a number of administrative monks who claimed that to change the rules was paramount to sacrilege. Eventually this resulted in an outburst of monastic violence. The Thirteenth Dalai Lama ended up expelling the ringleaders of both factions.[62] An account by the once rogue monk[63] Tashi Khedrup suggests that in Sera monastery too these changes were eventually imple-mented. He notes that on certain days, food and money were distributed at the debate ground and that some of his fellow ruffians would go and pretend to be involved in a debate, just to receive a share of the donations.[64]

It is clear that what the monks received as allowances was not always sufficient to live on, as evidenced by both oral history and textual materials. Monks supple-mented this allowance with the distribution of alms they received, income from their own efforts (which could be ritual services, farming, or commerce), family support; therefore, in all, four types of income.[65] Shérap Gyatso, an elderly monk who lived in Sakya monastery before the 1950s, notes with regard to the living standards then:

> We monks were given allowances every year, which consisted of grain. With this we could do what we liked: we could make tsampa or something else. It was enough for a year, but it was not easy to live off just that. Some had help from outside, whereas others had absolutely nothing.[66]

Another monk who used to live in Yangri Gar in the 1950s describes what monks received from the monastery:

> All monks would get allowances consisting of grains. We would mostly eat tsampa-paste.[67] It was not much but enough to get by. We would go to do rituals[68] and we could get some extra money and food. From that we could get butter and other things. At the assembly we would get tea and whatever sponsors would give us. We lived from hand to mouth. Some monks also had relatives to sponsor them, but my home was too far away. On a daily basis we would get tea four times a day, sometimes soup or rice gruel. Nothing nice like what you get these days.[69]

Elderly monks at Khampa Gar (Khams pa sgar) monastery in Eastern Tibet told one of my monk informants how they used to survive in Tibet. They bought butter and cheese from the nomads in a certain season and sold this later to the farmers for profit. They would also go to collect salt and sell it.[70] This informant, Khenpo Chöying Lhundrup, does not think that this monastery used to have fields or rich sponsors. Monks needed to take care of their own food; this was the case even when he himself lived in Tibet during the 1980s and 1990s and, he adds, is still the case. When he lived at the monastery sometimes food was handed out during the assembly, but not all the meals were provided. He reasoned that it was because the monastery was too poor to feed the monks.[71] This may well have been the case, but Sönam Chögyel, a junior secretary at Sakya in India, states that in the comparatively wealthy Sakya monastery in Tibet there was no communal kitchen at the monastery, meaning that the monks had to cook themselves. He supposed that it was just the custom (*lugs srol*) to do it that way: it was not on account of the monastery being poor.[72] While not all monks are aware of it, this custom is likely to stem from the separation between communal and private income and property.

A *chayik* written in 1934 by the Reting regent for Kunpel Ling (Kun 'phel gling) notes that on top of the allowances they received, prospective monks had to have secured their parental home's financial support.[73] In Ladakh and Spiti, many monks were partially supported by means of so-called "monk fields."[74] These fields were allotted by the monk's family upon entry to the monastery. The field would be managed by the family or by someone hired by the family. In Spiti, the monk had to provide the seeds but also received all of the harvest.[75] In Ladakh, however, the monk was given a sufficient amount of grain, while the families retained the surplus.[76] According to Carrasco, after the death of a monk, the field would be given back to his relatives.[77]

It is not the case, however, that all monasteries in Ladakh had this system of monk fields. Lobzang Döndrup, an elderly monk at Samkar (bSam dkar) monastery, informs us that such a system existed neither in Spituk nor in Samkar, whereas Hemis and Thiksey were well known for their monk fields. This suggests that there may be a difference in schools: the former two monasteries are Geluk, the latter two of the Drigung Kagyü ('Bri gung bka' brgyud) school. Spituk did own religious estates, although the revenue of those fields did not go directly toward the sustenance of the monks.[78] This issue requires further investigation.

It can be safely assumed that these monk fields were not taxed. Particularly in the case where the family kept what the monk relative did not need, this system may have been a (rather modest) type of tax avoidance. This would further incentivize landholding families to make one of their sons a monk: not only, in the case of many sons, would the land not be divided up, but well-to-do farmers might gain a slight tax break. At the same time, one could argue that this arrangement maintained the ties between the household and the monk.[79]

A further implication is that only those boys whose parents owned land could become monks at monasteries in which this system was upheld. However, the term "monk field" may also refer to an arrangement of a rather different nature. Könchok Chönyi was made a monk at Phiyang monastery in Ladakh when he was eight years old. His father had died long before and his mother did farmwork. When he entered the monastery, he was given a monk field by the monastery's authorities. His relatives worked on it for him, something that he asserted was prohibited for monks. He was allowed to keep the harvest on the basis of which he was able to sustain himself.[80] It seems that this system was not in place in Tibetan areas.[81] This may in part be due to the nature of the ownership of land: people never actually owned land, they merely used it, since—at least nominally—everything belonged to the Dalai Lama.

Other information retrieved via oral history methods suggests that monks belonging to the larger Geluk monasteries in Central Tibet—during roughly the same time frame, the 1930s to the 1950s—did not have to worry:

> Monks do not have material concerns about the future, about food or money, about taxes, about droughts or floods, for the monastery takes care of their basic needs. Monks get an allowance in kind and money, partly from the monastery and partly from the trust funds set up by laymen for the monks in a particular monastery.[82]

It may have been the case that monks in the Three Great Seats were given higher allowances also because of their close relationship to the government.[83] Furthermore, the system of handing out these allowances could be seen as an attempt to gain greater control over the inhabitants of these massive monasteries. In the same way that, according to Carrasco, it was feared that Ladakhi monks would neglect to look after the welfare of the local population if they gained economic independence,[84] the government may have tried to prevent the masses of monks, of whom the majority were not native to Central Tibet, from securing financial freedom.

## ON THE PAYROLL

In connection to the allowances that monks received at certain monasteries, we come across an interesting phenomenon, the "allowance ledger."[85] This appears to be a document that contained the names of the monks who were entitled to an allowance. It is likely that the amounts that were handed out were also recorded. One *chayik* from 1737 for the Amdo monastery Gonlung Jampa Ling (dGon lung byams pa gling) also contains a reference to an allowance ledger.[86] Here the reform suggested by the monastic guidelines was that allowances were not to be handed out annually but at the end of every Dharma session, i.e., four times a year, to prevent monks from only going back to the monastery every year just to collect what was due to them.

The earliest extant references to this type of record are from the seventeenth century. The Fifth Dalai Lama stipulates who was entitled to this allowance and the order in which people were to receive it:

> When the allowances of the monastic main office are given out, then liaising with a government representative, one gives, according to the seal-bearing allowance ledger, first to the colleges and their studying monks, secondly to the unaffiliated residents and those from Gepel (dGe 'phel)[87] and Ngülchu Chödzong (dNgul chu chos rdzong),[88] thirdly, to the rest of the crowd who are in one way or the other affiliated, consisting of the riffraff, such as the kitchen aides. Those who have not gone through three debate classes, those who now study medicine and astrology, and the resident servants of the aristocratic monks are not included in the allowance ledger of the monastic main office.[89]

The above indicates who, according to the author, was deserving of financial aid. It perhaps comes as a surprise that the lower stratum of inhabitants, of whom the Fifth Dalai Lama was dismissive earlier in the text, was included among the beneficiaries while the students of medicine were not. Here, the allowances probably functioned to support the most disadvantaged: those who did not have the opportunity to do some business on the side. People who practiced astrology, medicine, or served an aristocratic monk already received an income and were thus excluded from receiving these allowances.

In 1876, Tashi Lhunpo too appears to have had one of these ledgers, called the *Allowance Ledger of the Great Assembly*.[90] This document is mentioned in the context of how monks who served at other monasteries reintegrated back into the "mother" monastery after their term had ended. The text notes that upon leaving they were removed from this allowance ledger and explains what needed to be done to get back on it.[91]

In the guidelines written by the Thirteenth Dalai Lama for Thobgyel Rabgyé Ling (Thob rgyal rab rgyas gling) in 1913, it says that one was not to go against the main directives found in the allowance ledger and the rulebook regarding the distributions and the like, without a reason.[92] The same author again refers to such a ledger in another *chayik* for Rongpo Rabten monastery in 1930. The relevant passage demonstrates that this allowance ledger was used by the managers of the offerings, to make sure that all donations ended up where they were intended to go. The presence of an allowance ledger suggests government involvement of some kind. While references to these ledgers are not uncommon, it is worth noting that none of the monastic allowance ledgers are currently accessible for research.[93] They would make invaluable additions to our knowledge of the economy, the political relations, and the internal hierarchy of the Tibetan monastery.

The likely scenario is that the monasteries mentioned above, which are all Geluk, received state support, and were therefore obliged to keep a record of their income and expenses.[94] This government involvement is also apparent in the monastic guidelines for Sera Je written in the first half of the eighteenth century. This text suggests that when the monastic authorities handed out allowances to the debating monks, which was a process supervised by stewards and disciplinarians, there also was a government representative present.[95]

## MONASTIC SPONSORSHIP THROUGH RITUALS

The strict rules regarding the monastery's economic policy meant that not only was it theoretically forbidden for individual monks to use what belonged to the Sangha, but subunits within, or branches of, a monastery could not help each other out: a donation, as already mentioned, needed to be spent according to the donor's wishes. The large-scale sponsorship of certain festivals may have been not only a way to generate merit but also a way to distribute wealth more evenly. It is well known that the Ganden Phodrang paid for the performance of rituals that were seen to support the state (such as the Great Prayer Festival), but larger monasteries sometimes also paid their branches to undertake certain religious practices. An example of this is the nunnery of Rinchen Gang, which was a subsidiary of Sakya monastery. Its monastic guidelines suggest that this nunnery was financially not well off. Not only did some of the nuns have to go out to collect alms, they are also depicted as having to go out to weave and to work in the fields. Interestingly, nuns involved in doing certain rituals were remunerated by the (presumably Sakya) monastic authorities for their activities.[96] This may have been a way of legitimizing Sakya's sponsorship of the struggling nunnery.

The *chayik* names the amounts that had to be given to the nuns during or after events specified on the ritual calendar, such as the *maṇi* retreat, the monthly Tārā memorial service,[97] and the ritual fast.[98] The text specifies exactly what had to be provided by whom. In some cases, it was the monastic authorities and in others it was the lay headmen.[99] This text then not only contains guidelines for the nuns to abide by, but also serves as a kind of contract in which the economic survival of the nuns was safeguarded. Interestingly, it also involves the cooperation of a headman, who was burdened with soliciting donations from his constituents. It is noteworthy that—as indicated above—none of the contributions the nuns received were given out without there being some kind of religious reciprocation. In many respects, this particular *chayik* resembles documents that contain endowments of funds[100] for particular monasteries. Another set of guidelines, written in 1728 by Rigdzin Tsewang Norbu (Rig 'dzin tshe dbang nor bu, 1698–1755), details not only with what the lay donor endowed the monastery in question, but also what kind of rituals he expected the monks to perform in return for the donation.[101] This indicates that occasionally the *chayik* also functioned as a contract between the donor and the recipient, containing the exact stipulations of the terms and conditions of the endowment.

## THE LAMA'S RESIDENCY AND ESTATE

No discussion of Tibetan monastic economy would be complete without referring to the institution of *bla brang*. In Chapter 3 I pointed out that this term does not always refer to the autonomous units affiliated to a monastery but owned by an incarnation; it also can simply refer to the monastic office in charge of (economic) management. The residencies that were headed by incarnate lamas usually maintained independent economies. However, most of these were neither very big nor wealthy. The smaller residencies did not hold any estates.[102] The incarnated lamas who had a good reputation often won sponsors. They then built their own residences and sometimes even entire monasteries or hermitages, "all of which were under the direct control of the Lama," not the affiliated monastery.[103]

A major source of income for Tibetan monasteries was—and perhaps is even more so today—the presence of one or more incarnations. Religious figures of a certain standing often were an object of veneration for the general populace, thereby generating donations on a large scale. After the death of a prominent incarnation, the monastery not only lost a religious leader but also a significant source of revenue. This appears to have also been the case in Chinese monasteries during the Song dynasty, despite the obvious absence of the incarnation system. According to Walsh, monks who possessed religious authority, usually the abbots, attracted large sums of donations that they in turn would donate to the monastery.[104]

While the estates of the wealthier residencies were occasionally the topic of certain political altercations, we can deduce from the—admittedly scarce—available information that the presence of a lama who managed to attract wealth can be seen as providing flexibility in a monastic economic system that was resolutely rigid. A lama's wealth could be spent where and when he deemed it most appropriate.[105] Stein also notes this feature but only connects it to more recent times (i.e., post-1950): "In the modern period . . . the 'living buddhas' (incarnate lamas in Chinese parlance), as opposed to the monasteries, regularly made distributions of alms, once a year, amounting sometimes to half their capital, and contributed to the costs of the religious ceremonies of their monastery and the state."[106] Thus, while one branch was "legally" not able to give financial aid to another belonging to the same monastery, a lama was at liberty to help out struggling subunits, in order to help the monastery to which he felt an allegiance.

## MONASTIC LANDLORDISM

The *Rules for Sera Tekchen Ling* (*Se ra theg chen gling rtsa tshig*) was probably written in 1820.[107] It was meant for the whole of Sera monastery and authored by the second Tsemön Gyaltok (Tshe smon rgyal thog)—the then-regent of Tibet. The work directs itself only to the monastic officials.[108] It speaks of how the managers of the subjects on the monastic estates have misbehaved:

> To let all the leading positions, such as that of estate manager,[109] be filled by those who are close to oneself and law-abiding, would mean an instatement that is both wise and encouraging, [thereby avoiding] the oppression that has so far been a cause for the monastic estate's subjects to become scattered. One needs to encourage [them] to manage the lands with good motivation, making sure that the Sangha's income and provisions not deteriorate. There were a couple of general managers and treasurers with bad habits who were involved in private enterprises and many other things. Having caused many monastic estate subject families to abscond, they took hold of their lands and made servants out of the few remaining scattered and destitute subjects. When these people, who just did as they pleased without any regard for the two systems,[110] were found out, the only appropriate option was to banish them to a faraway place.[111]

This passage demonstrates that the managerial strategies that Sera monastery maintained were much like those of the lay landlords. It appears that in particular in the nineteenth and twentieth centuries, agricultural laborers were a scarce commodity in Central Tibet. Thus, one had to treat them relatively well, if only to prevent them from running away. These monastic guidelines suggest that previous estate managers had abused their position, ultimately leading to financial losses for the monastery. As punishment they were exiled, not expelled, which may be an indication that the perpetrators were laymen. Be that as it may, the ultimate responsibility lay with the monks who appointed them, which can be gleaned from the advice given on how to select these estate managers.

The text continues, suggesting that this was not just an isolated incident, but an ongoing problem: "Those who send out the provisions let the surplus of the harvest and the profits go toward [their] allowance and good tea, and do not send any to the Sangha: they hoard by expanding and collecting it. There seems to be rather a lot of people who do this."[112] The work goes on to suggest that certain monk officials were involved in accepting bribes, which then is thought to make the general discipline of the Sangha impure. The author exhorts the readers to keep to precedent: "One is definitely not allowed to deviate from the old to the new and be greedy and belligerent and so on, which will become causes for disharmony, rifts, and fights among members of the Sangha."[113] The emphasis on precedent is striking here. While the author of these guidelines in effect encourages change, the change is geared toward reestablishing the previously agreed rules. More generally, the author's primary concern is not the direct welfare of the subjects, who were obviously mistreated by the estate managers, but the long-term income of the monastic community of Sera.

## PROPERTY AND INHERITANCE

It is remarkable that the *chayik* that I have come across do not report on issues of inheritance. This could indicate that when an ordinary monk died, there tended to be no noteworthy problems with regard to dividing his property.[114] This leaves us largely dependent on eyewitness accounts. In the *Mūlasarvāstivāda vinaya* specific rules were made to keep monastic property "in the family, to prevent it from falling into lay hands or the state."[115] Similarly, according to the *katikāvatas*, in Sri Lanka, a monk's property would become the Sangha's after death or giving up robes.[116] In more recent times, in Thailand, it is said that according to state law, upon the death of a *bhikkhu*—unless he has set up a testament of sorts—all his possessions go to the monastery, as it is seen as his home.[117] The willing of one's property to laypeople does not seem to have been an option in the *Mūlasarvāstivāda vinaya*, but a monk's things could go to a layman when there was a "fiduciary deposit,"[118] which I take to mean a fund, owned by the monk, but managed by a layperson. In the Chinese twelfth-century Chan monastic rulebook, the *Chanyuan qinggui* 禪苑清規, it says that the dead monk's possessions were auctioned (presumably among the monks). The profits were then used for funeral and religious practices for his benefit, such as sūtra readings. The text stipulates that a monk should not have too many things—which would make the auction tedious—nor too few, to avoid his funeral having to be paid for by others.[119]

In the Tibetan case, again there does not appear to be a single ruling on what to do with the inheritance of a deceased monk.[120] In Sakya monastery, monks could will their property, and in absence of a will their families could claim the monk's possessions.[121] Shérap Gyatso, who used to live there, further specifies this and indicates that the family was indeed involved but that they would usually not keep the things for themselves:

> If an old monk would die his relatives would sell his things and often spend the proceedings on the funeral costs and rituals, and so on. If he had no relatives the monastery would do this. There were very few monks who really owned something; most did not have a lot, much unlike monks these days.[122]

Similarly, a report on Spiti from 1897 informs us that when a monk died, his property did not go to the monastery but back to his family. The first recipient would be another monk in that same household, but in the absence of someone like this, it would go to the head of the household.[123] In many cases a monk had to "buy" living quarters at the monastery, and a younger monk—often his relative—would oftentimes join him there.[124] Regularly when the older monks died, these younger monks would inherit this "household."[125] With regard to monasteries in Eastern Tibet, Ekvall states that a monk's possessions would become the community's after his death.[126] Khedrup recalls that in Sera Je, when a member of the society of "rogue monks"[127] died, one share went to that society, some was used to pay for funerary costs, and the rest was given to the college to which he belonged.[128]

Due to lack of primary (and secondary) sources, we cannot be conclusive about what happened when ordinary monks died. It can be gathered from the above accounts that the average monk did not own much, at least not enough so as to anticipate serious complications with regard to his inheritance. What the monk left behind was—much like in today's Tibetan communities—used for the performance of the necessary death rituals. Thus, regardless of whether it was the family or the monastery spending the money, eventually all flowed back to the monastic community, whether it be into the pockets of the monks or the coffers of the monastic government.

Naturally, inheritance also worked the other way around. That is to say, monks also inherited.[129] Or did they? Again, this is not entirely straightforward. According to some, monks were not allowed to inherit land.[130] French states that monks and nuns could inherit land, but never the primary family land.[131] According to Cassinelli and Ekvall, monks had the same rights as laymen over "movable possessions"– which is to say, anything but land.[132] In any case, living off one's parents' inheritance was not a common method of subsistence.

## BUSINESS AND TRADE IN AND AROUND
## THE MONASTERY

Tibetan monks and monasteries have probably always been involved in trade. Monks and merchants made natural bedfellows: neither was inextricably tied to land or locality. They were not bound to stay in one place, as the farmers were. Moreover, monks and traders regularly traveled together for safety reasons,[133] and often pilgrimage and business went hand in hand. Due to their monastic affiliation, monks could have networks that were far-reaching, facilitating trade across the board. Chen, speaking on Kham, supposes that the economics of "the lamasery" was "not so much based on land as on trade and usury."[134] Michael estimates that thirty percent of the (Central Tibetan) monastery's income came from "trade, business and banking activities, such as money lending and investment."[135] This involvement in trade is seen by many as a transgression of monastic vows, as all the different *prātimokṣa*s have a ruling against buying and selling.[136] But was commerce really forbidden? At the beginning of the eighteenth century Desideri remarks:

> According to their rule monks are absolutely forbidden to engage in trade or commerce. Nevertheless, this rule is commonly—or rather almost universally—disregarded. They are very active and interested in business dealings, and for that purpose they obtain leave from time to time to go on journeys and to absent themselves from the monastery for a certain period.[137]

While this missionary's observations are normally rather well informed, the perceived strict taboo on trade in (Tibetan) Buddhism rests on a misunderstanding or a misinterpretation. Nonetheless, this distorted view on monastic trade has pervaded the thoughts and minds of scholars and nonscholars alike to this day. This notion added to the—once pervasive—view that Tibetan (monastic) Buddhist practices are diluted or debased versions of what was once current in Buddhist India.

That Tibetan monks obviously engaged in trade does not mean that Indian monks did not. The *Mūlasarvāstivāda vinaya,* for example, depicts monks storing rice and selling it when it became scarcer.[138] According to the same corpus—being arguably the most lenient of the Vinayas with regard to financial matters—buying and selling is fine, provided one does not seek gain.[139] The relevant passage from the *Vinayavibhaṅga* can be translated as follows: "There is no transgression [regarding] a *bhikṣu* both selling without seeking gain as well as him buying without seeking gain."[140]

The monastic guidelines demonstrate a diverse range of attitudes toward trade. Sometimes, the Tibetan texts reiterate the Vinaya rules and at other times they diverge considerably. One of the earliest texts in this genre mentioning trade was written by Chennga Drakpa Jungné (1175–1255). He was the fourth abbot of Drigung Til, for which this *chayik* was composed. The author held that post from

1235 to 1255, suggesting that this text is likely to have been composed within this time frame. Concerning monks' business, he writes: "Those monks who, under the false pretext of going to Kyishö (sKyi shod) and Yorpo (g.Yor po) and other places for business or on an alms-round, are found to drink alcohol, should be punished, for they are the enemies of the Teachings. They are not allowed back to Til."[141] This section is significant for a number of reasons. Going to do business is mentioned together with collecting alms.[142] It is a casual reference: there is nothing wrong with being involved in trade. The problem here is drinking alcohol, not doing business.[143] Generally speaking, the monastic organization in this earlier period was demonstrably looser and monks were more likely to be self-financed. Often, they were also not necessarily attached to a single monastery.

Later *chayik* demonstrate a less casual attitude toward trade. The monastic guidelines for Sera Je, written in the 1737, note that when one is healthy and intelligent, "it is not permissible to live a life of ease and do business for profit or to give out loans of barley."[144] This statement suggests that the mind is a terrible thing to waste, in particular on something as frivolous as business. It also does not categorically forbid trade and providing loans—activities that perhaps would be more permissible for dull-witted monks.

In a similar vein, it is reported that at the Sakya branch monastery of Dongga Chödè (gDong dga' chos sde), ordinary monks were allowed to do business, whereas monks of "the highest order" were forbidden to engage in these mundane affairs.[145] The detrimental effect of commerce on the mind is also noted by Patrul Rinpoche in the early twentieth century, who complains: "Lamas and monks these days see no harm or wrong in doing business; indeed, they spend their whole lives at it, and feel rather proud of their prowess. However, nothing debilitates a lama['s] or monk's mind more than business."[146] Not only was trade seen as debilitating, but by being involved in commerce one also puts oneself on a par with laypeople. The Eighth Panchen Lama remarks: "These days there are many who—under the impression that they are following in the footsteps of Śākyamuni Buddha—despite having been freed from the household, still have not been freed from householders' activities and thus do much trading for profit."[147]

Interestingly, during the first half of the twentieth century, the polymath Gendün Chöpel (dGe 'dun chos 'phel, 1903–1951) linked the recent rise in monastic commercial activities in Amdo with the inability to keep the vows of celibacy correctly.[148] The monastic guidelines for Drepung by the Fifth Dalai Lama—on which the above-cited Sera Je *chayik* is based and from which certain sections are taken nearly verbatim—give another ruling on trade. This text conveys similar sentiments, but from a slightly different angle: "It is not allowed to pretend to be a debating monk, and while being healthy and intelligent, to not study but [instead] to do business for profit and make loans of barley."[149] Here it is important to note that the reason why the Fifth Dalai Lama had a problem with debating monks doing business is not just because it would be a waste of their talent, but because earlier on in the text he ruled that registered debating monks were to receive an allowance from the monastic authorities. This means that if they would involve themselves in trade and not study, they would be receiving that "salary" illegally and in addition to the returns of their business enterprise.

A set of monastic guidelines from 1900 states that one needed to be given permission to trade: "Whether the trade is on a big or a small-scale, one is not to engage in trade without asking the monastic authorities or the disciplinarian. Do not use bad weights and measures."[150] Again, what we see here is not that trade—buying and selling—was forbidden outright; it simply needed to be regulated. Ideally, it was to serve a purpose other than greed.

## COMMERCE: THE INDIVIDUAL VERSUS THE WIDER MONASTIC COMMUNITY

In the *chayik,* when restrictions with regard to business are imposed, they are always directed toward individual monks, never toward those who accumulate wealth on behalf of the monastery. As mentioned above, this distinction between the individual personal livelihood and the larger corporation of the monastery is generally very pronounced. This distinction has its roots in the Vinaya.[151] Gernet, who studied the *Mūlasarvāstivāda vinaya* in Chinese, remarks that "commerce is . . . prohibited to the monks but recommended to the Sangha."[152] In the monastic guidelines this separation of the corporate and the individual is pronounced when treating how to divide donations, but also when it comes to rules on trade and other "'work." The *chayik* for Ramoche monastery, which was written in the 1740s, states: "Except for the benefit of the monastery and the monastic official lamas' fields, the monks are not to conduct trade, work in the fields, or give out loans and so on."[153]

A similar sentiment is expressed in the set of monastic guidelines for Pabongka hermitage: "Except for the officials who work for the general Sangha, no one else, whether high or low, may keep horses and cattle, do business and give out loans against interest, interfere in the matters of laypeople that are inappropriate, and carelessly wander about, and so on."[154] Similarly, the *chayik* for Ochu Gon ('O chu dgon) from 1918 states: "Except for the managers, it is not allowed for the general monk populace to do business and make loans against profit. It has been said by the Victor(s) that it is impossible for those who have gone forth to be lacking in sustenance. Therefore, do not do things that go against the rules."[155] This is reminiscent of a Bhutanese saying: "Monks sustain themselves by means of rules."[156] This proverb reflects the very widespread (and still current) notion that as long as one lives a virtuous life, one need not worry about one's livelihood. A similar sentiment is reflected in the sixteenth-century monastic guidelines for Tsurpu:

In particular, one needs to give up on fearful thoughts that one will be overlooked, thinking: "what will happen when I run out of food and clothing?" According to many texts, excessive attachment and craving need to be abandoned, as the books state that when one relies on the continuity of the Dharma, shortages will be impossible.[157]

Sometimes, the line between the monastery's affairs and the individual monk's business became (intentionally) blurred. The Drepung monastic guidelines report that on occasion there had been:

> some greedy teachers, who would go to Lhasa on official business, not hiding the fact that they were Geluk, and pretended that what they received went solely to their college. They would put a seal on the goods and their own living quarters would be full of them. Those items have now turned up and it is obvious that they should wholly go to the big colleges. These actions are a total embarrassment and should thus not be done.[158]

Similarly, the monastic guidelines for Tashi Lhunpo first mention the monks who were trusted to conduct the monastery's business and then state:

> Also, others who are astute will mingle with this crowd [of business monks] and involve themselves in making profits through trade and give out loans of money and grains against interest on a large scale. Furthermore, some creditors, in dealing with people who shamelessly default on their loans and interest, pretend that the investment capital of the monastic office is involved. To pursue them aggressively and the like is to be on the verge of [committing] many wrongdoings.[159]

Again, the problem that the Eighth Panchen Lama, the author of these guidelines written in 1876, articulates is that monks doing business for themselves may become indistinguishable from monk officials. When pursuing debt defaulters, one could profit from being perceived as a monk official—only then could one apply pressure by making the debtors believe the money owed was actually the monastery's investment capital. Obviously, people were more inclined to pay back money that belonged to the Sangha than to an individual monk. The same author is also rather strict about business carried out by individual monks:

> While the elders and their assistants at the college may use the monastic office's investment capital to give out loans against interest, none of the ordinary monks, whether old or young, may ever be involved in such things as loaning out grains and money against interest or do things that fall under doing business and making loans for profit, such as hoarding, horse-trade, donkey-trade, or things like managing acquired fields. Rather, they should prioritize the practice of the various stages of Dharma: study, contemplation, and meditation.[160]

Here the author strongly opposes any business conducted on an individual level. Elsewhere in the same text he demonstrates his aversion to the "worldly" behavior of his monastery's monks: "One should never manage fields, use cattle, hoard, give out loans and so on. This is turning one's back on what a monk is meant to do."[161]

This is in many ways similar to the rules on trade in Menri monastery: "Activities that lead one to the worldly life: trading in order to obtain profit, lending money for interest, deceit in making weights and measures and breaking sworn oaths. It is acceptable to make an honest living by petty trade, following the rules of the state."[162]

We thus find that the guidelines stipulate rules on *who* could do business as well as on *how* it was to be conducted. As some of the texts cited above suggest, commercial activities could also give rise to dishonesty, in particular with regard to the measures and weights used. Again, the guidelines for Tashi Lhunpo state:

> Considering that the Dharmarāja Songtsen Gampo has prohibited fraud to do with weights and measures for laypeople, does it need mention that we, who have gone forth, should also not be doing this? Previously, from within the ranks of the monks enrolled here, there have been cases of people swindling others by means of incorrect weights. Obviously, this brings about very heavy negative karma! Taking into consideration that this is a disgrace to both the general and the specific Teachings, as well as to the community of the Sangha, no one—be they young or old—may do this from now on. If there are people who have done this, they need to be punished severely after the faults have been established on the basis of investigation by the 'religious rules office.'[163] It is said in the collected works of the Kadam masters that: "Even in the ocean-like community of those who have been instructed, if the rules are relaxed only slightly, hooved and fanged beasts with faulty discipline will appear."[164]

It is telling that here the author refers to what can be translated as "secular laws,"[165] namely those that are purported to have been established by Songtsen Gampo in the eighth century. His laws were thus seen as applicable to the whole of the population in Tibet, and not just to laypeople. Another text also comments on *where* commercial activities should take place:

> A lot of unnecessary trading should not be done. When it is done, the price should be according to what is current; one should not go higher or lower than the current rate. One should not be obsessively attached toward business that has not yet been finalized.[166] Trading should be done outside the gate and nowhere else.[167]

Schram also notes that when business deals were made by monks, they were not to be made too ostentatiously.[168] Similar rules can be found for the Japanese Zen monastic context in Dōgen's (1200–1253) *Eihei Shingi,* in the section entitled "Regulations for the Study Hall." Here it is said that monks were not to talk to tradesmen in the study hall, but to do this elsewhere.[169] This suggests that trade by monks was both conducted and tolerated, but not in a place reserved for the study of the Dharma.[170]

Because the *chayik* indicate that trade by individuals was sometimes seen as a problem and sometimes as being in need of regulation, one may conclude that business was conducted by many monks throughout the Tibetan Buddhist world (and beyond). However, Miller, who did fieldwork in the 1950s in the Himalayas, reports that the Bhutanese saw trade by monks and monasteries as something typical of Tibet. The Bhutanese themselves deny that their monasteries were ever involved in trade.[171]

While, as noted above, some monks managed to exchange butter for grains and made a small profit from such exchange, for extensive trade one needed startup capital.[172] According to Shérap Gyatso, most monks did not really do business for this reason. He adds that to be successful one needed to be business-savvy, which most were not. Monks who had both the capital and the financial know-how were—in his experience—rare indeed.[173]

Overall, when reading these monastic guidelines through a wide lens, both diachronically and synchronically, we can see a shift from a reasonable tolerance with regard to trade to a less understanding attitude. This decreasing tolerance toward commercial activities is, I believe, strongly related to the gradual change in the economic policies of many monasteries. The Ganden Phodrang government greatly increased the state sponsorship of certain monasteries.[174] Therefore, from the late seventeenth century onward there appears to have been a greater push, incentivized by the government, toward providing individual monks with their upkeep, at least partially.[175] In particular in the twentieth century there were multiple attempts to provide monks with an income, but only in exchange for an interest in education, good behavior, and allegiance to the Dalai Lama.

At the same time, when we view the rulings on trade in context, it appears that the choice of individual monasteries to either restrict or to (tacitly) allow trade also had to do with the specific circumstances they found themselves in. In the case of Tashi Lhunpo in the late nineteenth century, we learn by reading the monastic guidelines that it was an institution that held great prestige and had no problem with its monk enrollments. This text contains policies geared toward curbing monastic growth by being selective. To categorically forbid commercial activities can also be seen as one of those policies, for one would only attract those monks who were not dependent on trade to begin with. For smaller monasteries, it was simply not feasible to prohibit trade: the only thing that they could do was to regulate it.

## SERVICING LOANS AND LOANSHARKING

As has been shown above, trade and giving out loans against interest are often mentioned in the same breath in the monastic guidelines. It has often been remarked upon that in old Tibet the monasteries were the biggest "money" lenders.[176] From a financial perspective, this is a logical process as (the monastic) trade provided a surplus that could subsequently be invested.[177] The rules applying to loans were very similar to those applying to trade: individual monks were often discouraged from giving out loans, whereas monasteries often functioned almost as modern-day banks, making investments and giving credit, without monastic authors ever expressing their dismay over these "usurious" practices. It can even be argued that, when one considers the financial relationships between donor and recipient as portrayed (among others) in the Vinaya, giving out credit is a more reasonable and more widely acceptable method of sustaining the monastery's financial health than trade. Before turning to the above-outlined issue, the role of individual monks as creditors should be briefly discussed.

Among the reasons monks are discouraged or even forbidden from being involved in giving out loans is that, at a certain point in time, these loans along with their interest need to be retrieved. There is then a danger of monks exercising force in the process.[178] In one of the earliest sets of monastic guidelines, the issue of monks (aggressively) pursuing payments due is already noted as a problem. The *chayik* for the community at Densa Til (gDan sa mthil) was written by Jigten Sumgön (1143–1217) during or directly after a period of famine.[179] The relative poverty of both the lay population and the monks is pronounced. He therefore warns monks not "to pursue traders for old debts; not to ally oneself with 'strongmen' from among the destitute country folk and then to chase people who have long-standing debts; and not to pursue them one by one, come what may."[180] While the language of this text is abstruse, there can be no doubt that this author felt that monks were attempting to retrieve their outstanding loans at a time of great scarcity, and he chastised them for doing so.

A somewhat later *chayik* by the Eighth Karmapa (Mi bskyod rdo rje, 1507–1554) connects debt, whether on the part of the creditor or the debtor, to deceit and theft: "Furthermore, tying [someone else] up in a loan, not repaying one's debts, and being deceitful when it comes to selling foodstuffs must be abandoned in every way. Then one can prevent the causes that lead to the downfall (*pārājika*) of stealing."[181]

The individual enterprise of both lending and borrowing was, according to Cassinelli and Ekvall, not restricted by Sakya monastery in the first half of the twentieth century. Rather, when engaging in these types of practices the monks operated under "royal law."[182] This certainly was not always the case, for in Mindröl Ling monastery during the late seventeenth century, for example, a monk caught privately lending against interest would risk losing that which he had loaned out:

> The giving out of loans by individuals should not be done, because it is a distraction and it is unstable, and because it is a cause for becoming degenerate, without ever being satisfied. If you do this, then the thing that one has loaned out will become communal property. However, this is not forbidden if one loans out something to those in need, without getting a profit out of it, as long as it is not an excessive amount.[183]

Contrasting the restrictions individual monks experienced with regard to giving out loans, it was mostly unproblematic for the monastery to lend out property on behalf of the Sangha. The *Vinayavibhaṅga,* to which the Tibetans had access, appears not just to tolerate monastic communities collecting interest but to encourage it: "The Bhagavan decreed that the goods in perpetuity[184] [given] to the Buddha, Dharma, and Sangha should be given out on loan.[185] The resulting interest needs to be offered to the Buddha, Dharma, and Sangha."[186] As to be expected, here a proviso with respect to lending against interest is given, namely that the profit needed to be offered to—or "reinvested in"—the Three Jewels. We see this "rule" on giving out loans adhered to in the Tibetan context. In essence it means that all profits from monastic enterprise (be it interest from loans or investment) would flow straight back to the monasteries, but in what form is not entirely clear. In other words, we do not know exactly what the revenue was eventually spent on. Was it to be spent on the monks, to go toward the monastery's upkeep, did it go straight into the monastic coffers, or was it used to make extensive offerings?

The *Kṣudrakavastu* offers a narrative in which a merchant pledges to the monks a certain amount of venture capital. The merchant then proceeds to invest the capital on the monks' behalf, and any profit made from the capital he then distributes to the monks, who also continue to own the capital.[187] In this instance, then, it is the individual monks, albeit as the Sangha, who profit. From the sources under consideration here it can be gleaned that Tibetan monks usually did not directly profit from the monastery's entrepreneurship. However, there were certain ways to circumvent this, other than by spending it on specific rituals.[188] The *chayik* for Chamdo Ganden Thekchen Jampa Ling (Chab mdo dga' ldan theg chen byams pa gling), written in 1933 by the Thirteenth Dalai Lama, gives us a glimpse of this process:

> The monastic authorities, represented by the managers of the private and collective offerings,[189] need to give out loans and make business investments and the like using the older offerings for investment or newly received wealth, in a careful and considered manner. One is to increase and not to let decline [this money] without any changes in the procedures. The distributions, whatever they are, need to be given out when the recipients of the offerings are thought to be the largest number. One should not allow the continuity of offerings to decline and be neglected, letting the gifts deteriorate.[190]

Here the managers are encouraged to invest the wealth and distribute the profits from these investments at a time when most monks would be able to benefit. The alternative was to let the offerings go to waste. That the Thirteenth Dalai Lama felt the need to point this out, however, in fact suggests that the reality was otherwise: that, indeed as several other accounts suggest, many monasteries tended to hoard goods, rather than to use or invest them wisely. The above process is confirmed by an account—based on oral history—which suggests that in the first half of the twentieth century the profit from investments was regularly used to buy perishable goods, such as grain and butter. These products, subject to decay, were thought of as unsuitable to invest further.[191] Presumably, this was a way to actually use the profit. This was not the norm, however: Tibetan monasteries had a tendency to hoard goods—I suspect exactly because of the Vinayic restrictions given above—while the monks present at the same monastery regularly experienced relative economic hardship.

The interest rate on monastic loans is reported to have been rather high—the highest interest rate was about twenty-five percent per year.[192] Chen states that, much the same as in contemporary finance, larger loans carried lower interest rates whereas smaller loans had higher interest rates. The rates on grain loans were higher than those on cash loans. The interest paid per annum on cash loans was around fifteen percent.[193] In fact, it is claimed that the monasteries tended to charge interest that was higher than that of the government. In Ganden, for example, one would borrow four measures of grain and eventually pay back five measures. But to borrow with the government was to borrow ten measures and to pay back eleven.[194] It is not that the prospective monk lenders would get lower rates than laypeople, however. A loan contract from an earth dog (sa khyi) year[195] suggests that a monastic house at Drepung Loseling (Blo gsal gling) loaned five hundred silver coins[196] against a yearly interest of eighteen percent.[197]

Unsurprisingly, loans were not accessible to all. Monasteries often would not deal directly with the poorer households, possibly because this was seen as too risky—a loss made with offerings of the faithful would amount to squandering the Sangha's possessions. Regularly, the debtors of the monastery were the well-to-do families who occasionally passed on smaller segments of the loans to the less affluent.[198]

That monasteries gave out loans and became de facto debt collectors must have added to tensions between the monastic and lay populations—particularly the higher strata of society. Above we saw that collecting the interest or the debt posed a threat of violence. The debt collectors of Ganden in the first half of the twentieth century were not permitted to use physical violence. They would visit the families of those in debt to ask them to help with repaying the money. Here then the method was social pressure rather than threatening punitive action.[199] In Chinese monasteries during the same period, the last resort when dealing with people defaulting on their debts was to hire a couple of ruffians to dismantle the door and take away the furniture. Another option was to take them to court, but this was less common.[200] Similar practices were also employed in the Tibetan monasteries—with the ruffians often being monks.[201] That this occurred did not mean that it was acceptable behavior. In Tibet in the 1930s, monks from Sera monastery had resolved debts by seizing goods. The Thirteenth Dalai Lama ended up fining Sera's abbot for this, implying that the abbot was held legally responsible for the conduct of his monks.[202]

In contemporary Tibetan monasteries loans and business investments are still made by the monastic management. Until recently the larger monasteries in exile in South India loaned money to Tibetan sweater-sellers so the latter could buy their materials. When one year the sellers defaulted on their loans, the monks—not willing, or able, to take their fellow countrymen to court—took no action. The monasteries ended up losing a lot of money.[203] Some monasteries in the PRC still loan grain out to those families who need it, but without any interest or deposit. Again, no measures, legal or otherwise, can be taken when it is not paid back.[204] Contrasted with the manner in which the monastic authorities dealt with debt collecting prior to the 1950s, this is clearly indicative of the changed power relations between the lay populations and the monastery.

## USURERS OR BANKS: MONASTICISM AS AN ECONOMIC MODEL?

*Perhaps Buddhist monasteries . . . acted as agents of economic development in much the same way as the monastic foundations of medieval Europe.*
—STRENSKI 1983: 474

I now return to an issue alluded to above, namely that providing loans and making investments were methods of wealth accumulation that were less problematic for the monastic agents than, for example, trade or owning fields. When reading theoretical works on the ethics of commerce and finance that have a strong focus on Western religious and philosophical discourses, we are informed that, generally speaking, trade is inevitably good, for it is a simple exchange, whereas moneylending is morally reprehensible. This is regularly presented as a universal truth. The practice of lending money and charging interest is equivalent to the more archaic usage of the word usury.[205] In Christianity, usury has traditionally been seen as a grave sin. It has been described as either theft from people or from God. Thomas Aquinas saw it to be a sin against justice, a notion probably inspired by ancient Greek thought, according to which usury was seen as something despicable.[206] Aristotle contends the following: "The most hated sort, and with the greatest reason, is usury, which makes a gain out of money itself. For money was intended to be used in exchange, but not to increase at interest. . . . That is why of all modes of getting wealth this is the most unnatural."[207]

In Tibetan Buddhist societies, when considering the sources at hand, on the whole commerce is never described as preferable to moneylending: they are seen as equally bad (or good). Moreover, when the Sangha is the moneylender, it is even encouraged. As has been demonstrated above, according to the *Mūlasarvāstivāda vinaya,* the Sangha is to use money (or otherwise) in a manner that is *exactly contrary* to Aristotle's views: the Sangha preferred *not* to use the offerings of the faithful in exchange, and instead tried to increase the offerings through interest. The Buddhist rationale: as the interest accrues, so does the merit of the original donor.

Even though they are part of a slightly different argument, Walsh's remarks on Chinese monastic matters of economy during the Song Dynasty ring true with regard to the issues at hand, namely that "monks and nuns . . . did not engage in socioeconomic practices *in spite* of their salvational or devotional dispositions; they engaged in such practices *because* of them."[208] As far as I am aware, there was no linkage of usury with "sinfulness" among Tibetan Buddhists—or Indian Buddhists for that matter. This disproves the widespread notion that money-lenders were *universally* despised. In fact, Graeber, in his work that considers the morality of debt in time and place, points out that Buddhism "is one of the few of the great world religions that has never formally condemned usury."[209] The proviso here is that the Sangha as the creditor is never faulted: the individual monk does get criticized for extracting interest on loans.

Naturally, there is no way of knowing how the debtors felt about their monastic creditors, but we do know that moneylending was generally not seen as morally reprehensible by ordinary Tibetans. Caple writes that, when researching the monastic economy in contemporary Rebkong in Amdo, she was told that local people who were relatively poor saw borrowing from the monastery and giving back interest as a form of giving to the monastery.[210] Dagyab reports an instance in which Tibetans complied or even agreed with the economic policy of the monasteries: Ganden monastery, before 1959, both bought and sold grain. The monks in charge of this business had two sets of scales: one for buying and one for selling the wares. The local population was well aware that the scales had been tampered with so that the scales always tipped in favor of the monastery, but—at least according to oral history—people still preferred to do business with the monastery because of the merit involved. It was even perceived by some as a donation.[211]

It has been argued that the relatively good economic position of the monasteries before 1959 made it possible to help out the local population in difficult times with credit, and that in particular in areas where the infrastructure was poor, the monastery was an important giver of credit.[212] However, as has been noted above, often only the wealthier people were eligible to do business with the monastery: the monastic corporation did not give out small loans to "the little people." The wealthier families pass on their loans to the poorer families, although they may also have been served with loans by the individual monks, thereby filling a niche in the market, albeit one that was not always legal, "Vinayically" speaking.

The alternative to seeing the monastery's commercial enterprises as usurious practices is to view them as a service, not that of a charitable institution, but that of, for example, a bank. Gernet, relying on various Vinayas, remarks that prior to the spread of Buddhism there were no lending banks, and that thus "Buddhist communities must be credited with their creation."[213] Banks, in turn, are often recognized as catalysts of wider economic growth. The same parallel is drawn by Ekvall:

> It is the Grwa tshang, or college, however, which, in the office and operations of
> the Spyi ba, or manager, corresponds most closely to the organization and function

of the investment banking in other parts of the world. The analogy, though close, does not hold good in every respect. Although it operates like an investment banker, the monastery bank derives its capital from gifts and not from deposits on which it would have to pay interest or other financial outlay. The self-sacrifice of those who give, in terms of satisfaction derived, has not been ruinously or appallingly great. Nor have the sPyi Ba and others imposed altogether unreasonable interest rates or altogether stifled economic development. The sacrifice expressed in offering and the management of wealth together represent an economic contribution to the culture of Tibet.[214]

The real impact of the monasteries on the economy of pre-modern Tibet often gets ignored by scholars more concerned with issues of political or religious history. Alternatively, it is described as a burden on the ordinary people, a mode of exploitation of serfs, and an obstacle to economic development. The economic surplus is often portrayed as being solely used up for religious purposes. This understanding is countered when one views Tibetan monastic economic practices from a different perspective, namely as an economic "model" that was seen by Tibetans as a stable alternative to the hegemony of feuding aristocratic families[215] and the decentralized government, which actively stimulated local-level governance. When placed in the historical context of Tibetan political history, the monastic economic model may have been the most viable option. Needless to say, this model has developed organically and gradually from the introduction of monastic Buddhism in Tibet onward and should not be seen as a model that has been deliberately created or adopted at a certain point in time.

To assert that the monastery performed the functions of a bank and that this institution as a main center of trade was seen as a better alternative is not the same as defending the economic practices in pre-modern Tibet (in particular from the point of view of the Western discourse on morality). However, it does contradict the notion that the reason a large part of the economic power was placed in the hands of the monasteries was due to the blind faith of the uneducated Tibetans, as certain apologists of the PRC's policies toward Tibet would have it.[216] Tibetans, not unlike most people, were—and are—pragmatists at heart. However, as has been demonstrated time and again, pragmatism and religiosity are not mutually exclusive. This is not to say that the opposite is true either. While there are obvious parallels, a distinct difference between Buddhist (monastic) agents in financial issues and their medieval Christian counterparts is that among the latter the price of goods and money in general was continuously seen as an ethical issue: "they perceived justice rather than efficiency as an appropriate goal of economic policy."[217] It has been argued that this Christian ideology concerning finance (which includes usury) halted or delayed the development of "a new economic system."[218]

The fact that Buddhist monks were committed to certain shared rules as well as to the rule of law, coupled with the fact that monasteries were perceived to be, as

well as *devised* to be, stable institutions in what was often a largely unstable political setting, meant that the monastery's management of the local economy was, in
the eyes of Tibetans, not undesirable.[219]

## CHALLENGING THE PARADOX OF MONASTIC PROPERTY

While it has been argued that "profit taking was perfectly compatible with Buddhist philosophy,"[220] the combination of wealth accumulation and religious practice is more often than not seen as a paradox. Weber, for example, notes that: "The
paradox of all rational asceticism, which in an identical manner has made monks
in all ages stumble, is that rational asceticism itself has created the very wealth
it rejected. Temples and monasteries have everywhere become the very loci of
all rational economies."[221] Reflecting on the contemporary economic practices of
monasteries in Amdo, Caple views the idea that monasteries must improve and
even compete "with the economic standards of secular life is in tension with the
ideal of the 'simple monk.'" This increasing material well-being of monks and their
engagement with modern life is then seen in contemporary narratives as an element of moral decline.[222] Here it is important to realize that, even though some
monks maintain the attitude that hardship is good practice,[223] historically, monks'
living standards were on average higher than those of ordinary laypeople.

Whereas hardship among monks was occasionally espoused, large-scale des-
titution was never encouraged. Dungkar Lopzang Trinlé makes the link between
poverty and discipline. He describes that in the time between the passing of the
Fifth Dalai Lama up until 1958, certain monasteries that had autonomy, religious
estates, workers, and a substantial (government) stipend were successful in maintaining and even increasing monk numbers, whereas the monasteries that relied
only on wages and alms-begging saw their numbers drop no matter what they did.
This, Dungkar Lopzang Trinlé asserts, resulted in the monks housed there not
being able to sustain proper religious discipline.[224]

Despite perceived dichotomies, both in terms of ideology and practice, neither
Tibetan monasteries nor Tibetan monks ever rejected wealth *an sich*. This is entirely
in line with the Vinaya they adopted. The common overall principle is the nonat-
tachment to wealth, which can be found in most Buddhist traditions.[225] At first
glance, there appears to be a conflict between rules on not having property beyond
the stipulated items (on which, even in the *Mūlasarvāstivāda vinaya* itself, the rules
seem quite flexible) and the prohibition to refuse donations given to the Sangha
(which would mean to deny the layman the accumulation of merit).[226] However,
it can be gleaned from the examples of the guidelines given earlier that concerns
about not wasting the offerings given by the faithful and ensuring that they are used
in the right way was prioritized over the simple lifestyle of individual monks.

In many ways, the pivotal role of the Tibetan monastery in commercial enterprise was justified in terms of the Vinaya. Additionally, there are also various indications that ordinary people preferred doing business with monks and monasteries on account of the merit involved and the (financial) stability of the monastic institution. Walsh argues that, in medieval China, merit was the most powerful material religio-economic commodity monks produced and disseminated.[227] In the context of pre-modern Tibet, it seems, stability vies with merit for being the most formidable monastic "product."

In this chapter a recurrent leitmotif has been the separation between the individual and the communal. The Sangha, as a corporation, has had almost no restrictions when it comes to accruing wealth, whereas the spending of that wealth is deemed more problematic. One could argue that Tibetan monasteries' economic policies were thus motivated by the freedoms *and* limitations, originally informed by the Indian Vinaya. At the same time, they were also heavily colored by the political situations, the Zeitgeist, and geographical limitations. It needs to be noted here that, for practical purposes, economic policy has been—at least nominally— separated from social policy. Ultimately speaking, however, economic policy and social policy amount to the same thing.[228] This may even be extended to religious policy. Gernet notes that there were two types of relationships between the laypeople and the monastery in medieval Buddhist China: one was religious and the other economic. He argues that people did not see these relationships as differing radically from one another.[229] The next chapter deals with these social and religious policies executed by the monasteries—in particular those that concerned laypeople.

6

# Relations with the Laity

## The Roles of the Monastery in Society

INTRODUCTION

*Put homeleavers first and householders after.*
— DŌGEN (1200–1253) 1996: 159

Monastics throughout the ages—Buddhist and otherwise—have sought to actively distinguish and distance themselves from the lay population. In this respect one can say that monkhood is "an alternative culture."[1] At the same time, the high percentage of the male population devoted to monastic life meant that an overwhelming majority of families in Tibetan society was linked to the monastery as a social group and an institution, making laypeople socially and emotionally involved in the support and perpetuation of the monastery.[2] This is reiterated by Gyatso, who comments: "So thoroughly are the monks and the idea of monk-hood integrated into the wider society that they are not seen as a separate block, constantly vying with the lay authorities."[3] Some see the presence of the large number of monks in Tibet as due to the fact that they were perceived to be in a better position to accumulate merit than the laity. According to Kapstein, they were then—by extension—seen to contribute to the merit of society as a whole.[4]

Many monastic guidelines demonstrate great concern for the general standing and reputation that the monks enjoyed in wider society.[5] The reasoning often given for creating certain rules is that if the monks did not behave properly, the laypeople would lose faith in the community of monks and thereby in the Sangha, part of the Three Jewels. Similar arguments are common in Vinayic literature. Due to the position of political, judicial, and economic power maintained by the larger monasteries in pre-modern Tibet, relationships between donor and recipient, between layperson and monk, were multilayered and varied according to time and place. By reading the guidelines one can get a glimpse of the balancing act that took place between monks and lay society. All had happiness, stability, and continuity as shared goals. The methods to achieve these goals, however, occasionally differed.

Miller, providing a sociological perspective on Tibetan monasticism, stresses the interrelatedness of the Tibetan monasteries. Commenting on all of Tibet, she paints a picture of "[a]n area rent by political divisions, sectarianism, and regional conflicts, where some isolated monasteries are independent and powerful and the vast majority of monastics must depend either on the favor of the lay authorities or on the poverty, backwardness, and superstition of the population."[6] Although it is true that there were great divergences between the "landed monasteries" and the landless ones, it cannot be said that the vast majority of monasteries had no say whatsoever in their own lot, as Miller seems to suggest. At the same time, recent scholarship on more peripheral Tibetan Buddhist communities demonstrates that the paradigm of the powerful monastery was by no means all-pervasive.[7] Indeed, there were not many monasteries that were actually powerful and reasonably independent. Monasteries that had to negotiate power and services were the norm. Numerically, monastic institutions that stood in the service of the direct community were in the majority. This means that even in "theocratic" Tibet, just like in other Buddhist countries, more often than not "the focus of the structure of village life" was the relation between the monastic community and the village population.[8] This relationship was not without tensions.

Many monastic guidelines contain—implicitly or explicitly—views on the presence of laypeople. A balance had to be struck with regard to the laity's access to the physical space of the monastery. That the guidelines often place restrictions on laypeople entering the monastic compound is indicative of the societal role of the monastery. Related to this is that pastoral services—in the West associated with the duties of ordained members of organized religions—were not part of the responsibilities of the monks or the monastic institution. Closely connected to the role of the Sangha in society is the issue of identity, a decisive factor when it comes to understanding societal interactions.

## MONASTIC IDENTITY AND MONASTIC BOUNDARIES

*Social identity lies in difference, and difference is asserted against what is closest, which represents the greatest threat.*
—BOURDIEU 1984: 479

Representing oneself as "other" appears to be essential for the survival of monastic Buddhism. It is well known that monks, from the time of the Buddha onward, actively distinguished themselves from laypeople. Goldstein and Tsarong make a strict distinction between the identities of laypeople and the clergy:

Lay people existed to serve monasticism by producing sons and surplus. Tibetan monasticism, therefore, attempts to socialize recruits into an alternative set of norms, values, and standards for perceiving and evaluating the world: a cultural template in which love, desire, and wealth were renounced as the source of misery and suffering.[9]

One can wonder whether such an "alternative set of norms" exists and to what extent it differed from laypeople's norms. Furthermore, to present laypeople as merely existing to serve the monkhood is to deny the complex interactions that took place. While there may or may not have been an alternative set of norms, there indeed was an alternative set of *rules* that monks had to abide by.

Certain rules in the Vinaya can be explained on the basis of their intention to distinguish the Sangha from the lay community. These are, for example, not moving one's arms back and forth while walking and not eating noisily.[10] Developing a separate identity from laypeople was essential for the continuation of the Sangha as a distinct entity. The monastic guidelines can be read as expressions of this identity, this *esprit de corps*. They serve to remind monks of their behavior: to adhere to a relatively strict code of conduct, to remain celibate, and to abstain from drinking alcohol. They make monks mindful of their attire: they could not wear lay clothing, and the correct manner of wearing the robes is emphasized throughout the texts. The texts also stress the importance of the kind of daily activities acceptable for monks, namely, to perform religious ceremonies, to study, and to recite prayers and texts.[11]

One of the other ways to keep the Sangha from becoming indistinguishable from the laity was to impose restrictions on the physical movements of monks and laypeople alike.[12] Most monastic compounds had clearly delineated physical boundaries,[13] and the *chayik* comment regularly on both monks and laity crossing them. For the monks, this often had to do with asking permission to leave the monastery's premises, whereas for laypeople entry in some cases was not given at all. The monastic guidelines for Mindröl Ling acknowledge that monks sometimes could leave the compound, provided they had gained permission and were accompanied by another monk:

> Monks are not allowed to go outside of the boundary markers without permission, however important their reason is. In short, if one does need to go out, by way of exception, such as in order to roast and grind [barley], one is not to go without a monk companion.[14] If one does go to town without company, one needs to offer a butterlamp of seven measures,[15] and if one has crossed the boundaries one offers a butterlamp of three measures. Depending on the situation one should make somewhere between twenty and a hundred prostrations, making one's fault public in the assembly.[16]

The disciplinarian granted the permission and punished those who left without authorization. These regulations were deemed necessary to restrict inappropriate interaction between laypeople and monks. In a similar way, a Sri Lankan *katikāvata* from the twelfth century does not forbid leaving the monastery, but limits the entry to the village between dusk and dawn, unless it was to help one's parents and widowed sisters or in the case of needing to get medical help for a fellow monk.[17] The rules in Tibetan monasteries were tightened during the yearly retreats, when any movement (and thus social interaction) was limited, even between monk residencies.[18]

The laity's movement across the monasteries' boundary markers was also regularly restricted. A *chayik* for the Bon Menri monastery states that no laypeople could enter the monastery except those who served the monastic estate and those who looked after the animals or brought in the firewood.[19] This indicates that lay workers were employed at the monastery, but also that this monastery was not seen to have a direct "pastoral" function, and as was suggested earlier this was the case for Tibetan monasteries in general. The monastic guidelines of some other monasteries show that laypeople were welcome, provided that their purpose was religious. This was particularly the case when female visitors were involved.[20] Other monasteries had to make rules in order to avoid "exploitation" by laypeople posing as pilgrims: "From the end of summer until the beginning of winter, only those pilgrims who take refuge without their sheep and goats are allowed to stay in the surroundings of the monastery."[21] These guidelines were written in the late nineteenth or early twentieth century for Pelyul Darthang monastery in Amdo, which was situated in a nomadic area. It seems likely that in the past laypeople had been using their visit to the monastery as a pretext to graze their animals on its pastures, which explains why in the autumn people were only allowed to visit without their flock.

The Jesuit missionary de Andrade, who traveled around Western Tibet in 1626, also notes that common people did not tend to frequent the temples, which were nearly always closed. He writes that they visited them only on two days of the year to attend religious festivals.[22] The above examples serve to point out that in an ideal monastic world contact between laypeople and the Sangha was to be restricted. We know, however, that not all monasteries were created equal. Some monasteries had a function that could be compared to that of Christian churches that encourage believers to visit, whereas others limited contact with the outside world.

Currently, certain monasteries encourage pilgrimage, resulting in laypeople passing through the premises, while others strongly discourage or even forbid it.[23] The guidelines also record such rules, allowing us to identify the kind of monasteries that restricted contact with laypeople. Unlike the function of the (modern) Christian churches, the Tibetan monasteries—and their temples—were not places where people in need of spiritual guidance were expected to seek refuge. Interaction was usually only encouraged for religious purpose and services.

## GENEROSITY AND CHARITY

The most commented-upon relationship between the Sangha and the laity is undoubtedly that of recipient and donor of offerings, respectively. In this inter-action, the monks are assigned a passive role, as Strenski—in commenting on Theravāda Buddhist giving—remarks: "ritual giving sits squarely in the center of the relation between the Sangha and lay society. The monks are always receivers, the laity always givers."[24] Similarly, it has been asserted that the clergy is "the paradigm of non-reciprocity."[25] This type of generosity is well supported in Buddhist doctrine and takes up a prominent position in most Buddhist cultures. Its prominence has had, according to some scholars, important repercussions for Buddhist societies. For Spiro, writing on Burma, the fact that all acts of generosity involved monks meant that "nonreligious charity" was not supported, because it was seen as less meritorious. He argues that this translated to less social action, and that this phenomenon was shared with other Theravāda countries.[26]

The phenomenon of giving to the Sangha then could be seen as resulting in less social action on the part of the laity, but what were the monks expected to do with what they received? Christian clergy is often reported to have used its resources to aid those in need. Taken on the whole, this is less apparent among Buddhist monks,[27] and this has, in part, to do with the Vinaya rules. First of all, a monk was meant to use what he was given, even when it was of no direct use to the Sangha. Only when the gift is used does the act of giving generate merit for its donor. For the monks, accepting offerings was not merely a privilege, it was a duty, as Scho-pen describes the role of the Sangha as portrayed in the Vinaya: "A monk here is one who accepts gifts so others can make merit, and he is *obligated* to do so by the authority of the Buddha."[28] In fact, the monks—according to the *Mūlasarvāstivāda vinaya*—were also under the obligation to *use* what was given to them: this was "their obligation to make merit for their donors."[29] Secondly, only members of the Sangha were meant to use the offerings, and no one else. The Buddha is reported to have said: "Monks, you must not give to others what was given to you for your own use."[30]

Thus, the Sangha was obliged to accept most offerings, to use what it was given, and it could not pass on these gifts to the laity. Tensions, ensuing from these rules regarding charity, can be perceived throughout the Buddhist world. Not being able to refuse a gift could be a reason or justification, for example, for monasteries coming to own lands and even people. While slavery, in the most common sense of the word, was not a feature of Tibetan society, it did occur that a rich donor "gave" people to a monastery. An example of this is the gift of eighty Amdo families to Labrang monastery in 1712 by the Mongolian prince Erdeni Jinong.[31] Even though the primary sources may state that "families were donated," this act sounds more inhumane than it actually was. In practical terms, this simply meant that the tax, in labor and in kind, which the donor previously received from a number of families would from then on be paid to the monastery. There is unlikely to have been any noticeable change in the circumstances of those so "gifted": they were not displaced, nor was there any significant upheaval of the social structure of these communities. While the guidelines do not tend to comment on such transactions, the above-outlined issues regarding charity are regularly discussed.

## CHARITY FOR LAYPEOPLE

*The beggar beside the road means nothing to the monk.*

Spencer Chapman, who penned the above line ([1938] 1984: 182), visited Tibet in the 1930s and was critical of the position of monks there. However, it was not just Tibetan monastics who were thought not to give to beggars.[32] In China, during roughly the same period, lay beggars were not only kept out of the monastery, but were also refused food. The rationale that Welch's informants gave for this is that monks were meant to be the receivers and not the givers of charity.[33] Similar arguments are made in the Tibetan monastic guidelines. One such text, written in 1820 for the whole of Sera monastery by the then-regent of Tibet, contains a justification for the prohibition on monks allowing entry to beggars or to feed them:

> If there are beggar-wanderers—male or female vagabonds—in the monastery asking for food, quickly protect the compound and turn them out. Particularly when the unceasing flow of communal tea and monastic tea is given to those who are not ordained, there is no difference with giving them boiling molten iron. For that reason, leftovers need to be thrown away.[34]

Here the author implies that by giving beggars food intended for the monk population, one would be doing them a disservice. This is because karmically speaking they would be worse off. The reference to molten iron undoubtedly refers to the results one is said to experience in one of the hells as retribution for using the Sangha's possessions. The citation from the *Vinayavibhaṅga* often given elsewhere does not refer to boiling molten iron but to blazing iron balls: "It is preferable for one who does not have proper vows [or] whose discipline is faulty to eat iron balls that are ablaze with fire than to consume the alms from [people] in the vicinity."[35] This citation is more regularly used, however, to refer to monks with faulty discipline making use of the monastery's amenities (and by extension the laity's donations). Another *chayik* written for Tagdrag (sTag brag) monastery in 1947 gives exactly the same citation in relation to monks whose vows are not pure, but then goes on to state:

> But, as it is worse if householders partake of the Sangha's food, it would be better not to give them anything. However, the ones who work for the Sangha and the like need to be given tea and soup. A daily morning tea and a tea and soup at noon is permitted, but no more. The managerial committee should entertain the more important

sponsors appropriately but is not to do anything that leads to faith in the Sangha becoming perverted.[36]

Thus, according to this text, the random giving of food to the laity should be avoided, although qualified exceptions are made for workers and significant sponsors.[37] There is the suggestion here that if the benefactors were to learn about laypeople receiving food from the monks, they would not be pleased.

In a rather similar way, the Fifth Dalai Lama also comments on this problem in Drepung monastery:

> These days it is increasingly the habit of the monastic houses or the teachers, when they have obtained their share of allowances, to give handouts to all kinds of lowly drifters. Even the benefactors were dismayed that the communal tea and the donations would not get to each of the colleges and that they would go unrecorded. This is a very great wrong amounting to depriving the general Sangha of income.[38]

The set phrase that the Fifth Dalai Lama uses here, namely "depriving the general Sangha of income,"[39] is one of the five secondary acts of immediate consequence.[40] This served to highlight the gravity of the matter. It appears that monks in Drepung were giving away their donations rather randomly. This seems to have angered the donors, but it also went against certain rules. Whereas in the previous example the direct karmic consequences of giving away donations to people who do not deserve them are suffered by the recipients of the donation, the beggars, in this instance the monks who give the food to the lowly drifters, bear the karmic brunt of "depriving the general Sangha of income."

In line with the rules for Sera monastery, the Fifth Dalai Lama also warns that if the monastic community had too much tea and soup, the leftovers needed to be used as fodder and nothing else.[41] Presumably this means that the food scraps could not be given to beggars and other needy people in the surroundings. Again, the reason for this restriction is likely to be a "Vinayic" one: what is intended for the Sangha should not end up in the hands of "undeserving" laypeople.

Interestingly, this is not entirely in line with the view expressed by Tsongkhapa, one of whose monastic guidelines is paraphrased by the author of the above-cited text.[42] In his *chayik* for Jampa Ling monastery, probably written in 1417, Tsongkhapa takes a clear stance on the issue of redistributing goods beyond the monastic community. He instructs the monks not to let beggars and people who have come to do petty trade into the monastic compounds, but instead to leave them waiting at the boundary marker. Food could then be given to them there by an *upāsaka* (*dge bsnyen*).[43] A later *chayik*, written in 1943 by the Tagdrag regent, for Kongtö Dungkar monastery, echoes Tsongkhapa's ruling: "Dogs and beggars are not to be let in the monastic compound, but food and drink is to be given outside to individuals."[44] The *chayik* for Mindröl Ling from 1698 also demonstrates close parallels to Tsongkhapa's guidelines: vagabonds and beggars should not be allowed in the monastery grounds but instead should be given food outside the gate.[45] Elsewhere in the text, however, it mentions that the Sangha's gifts should not be distributed to the laity: "It is said that the gifts for the Sangha are not to be given to laypeople. Therefore, during the communal tea-round, one is not allowed to give anything away without permission from the disciplinarian."[46]

It is clear that a balance had to be struck among keeping to the rules of the Vinaya, the maintenance of the monastery, and the care for other beings. For a monastery to be excessively generous would send out the wrong message and attract unwanted elements, which in turn would put off existing or potential donors. In addition, we can see the importance attached to maintaining a strict separation between beggars and monks: for them to mix would upset the equilibrium of the religious community. An eleventh-century *chayik* for a community consisting of both monk and lay tantric practitioners gives very specific instructions on how to treat the destitute, while also keeping them at a distance:

> If there are people who are poor, who out of destitution look for food and things, or if persons are not able to rid themselves of suffering, then all should give [them something]. They should be treated like outsiders without [further] contempt or respect, but they should not be allowed into the community.[47] They should be considered as mere "outsider friends."[48]

It is clear that there existed different ways to deal with the problem of helping those in need, while keeping to Vinaya rules and maintaining an autonomous community. The perhaps expected tension between the Vinayic limitations on monks' giving and the "universal" Buddhist values of love and compassion and giving[49] as the first of the six *pāramitās* are nowhere discussed in the texts, but the above passages show that giving to the needy was an issue that demanded regulation, implying that monks showed an inclination toward charity and that this occasionally posed challenges.[50]

## THE EMPLOYMENT OF LAYPEOPLE AND CORVÉE DUTY

Related to the act of giving to the laity is the employment of laypeople by monks. Not just accepting help from the laity but remunerating or compensating them for their help was common in most Buddhist monastic societies. The *Mūlasarvāstivāda vinaya* shows that those who worked for the monks were given food and clothing and that sick workers were to be given food, clothing, and medical attention.[51] However, it should also be mentioned that more generally "Buddhist monastic institutions almost certainly did employ forced labor, and very probably also slave labor."[52] In the Tibetan context, the question of whether the system in which certain monasteries called on people of the surrounding areas to perform corvée labor[53] constituted forced labor is a contentious issue. It is clear, however, that at least during the first half of the twentieth century the monasteries employed lay-people as staff,[54] but drew in others only on special occasions. An example of this is given by a corvée-worker[55] of Dargyé Ling (Dar rgyas gling) monastery in Central Tibet who recalls her corvée duty: "In the Fifth Month all of us were called to the Dar gling monastery and fed there for three days. We would be given whatever offering the monks received at that time."[56] On other occasions, when working for the monastery, people would be provided with meals.[57] The elderly monk Lobzang Döndrup of Spituk monastery in Ladakh describes labor relations with the local people, then and now:

> The people had to perform corvée services and worked the many fields the monas-tery owned. Before, the sponsors gave the workers a salary on behalf of the monastic estate. Also, when repairs had to be done or if there was another major work one could call on the people to help, and they would take turns. If it was your turn you could pay someone to be your replacement. Nowadays, if you do not pay them they will not come. The fields are still there but now the monastery pays the people who work on them.[58]

Both the guidelines and eyewitness accounts confirm that, in many cases, the "compulsory labor" was regularly remunerated to a certain extent. Nornang notes that the managerial office was obliged to provide one bowl of soup and three rounds of tea or Tibetan beer (chang) per day at times when laypeople came to perform corvée for the monastery of Dakpo Shedrup Ling.[59] The provision of alcohol "as compensation" to the workers at the monastery is also attested in the Fifth Dalai Lama's chayik for Gongra Ngesang Dorje Ling. One section stipulates that the use of alcohol is only permitted for ritual purposes and then only in very small amounts, but that permission should be asked when it is used as a base for medicine or as compensation for masonry or construction work.[60] Apparently construction work was then paid for with alcohol. Masonry and construction in particular were jobs that, ideally, were handled by laymen and women. In Sakya in the first half of the twentieth century, for example, when a considerable part of the monastery collapsed, the abbot wanted to levy labor from the subjects to restore it.[61]

Tsongkhapa forbids monks from initiating construction work and recommends that they ask the permission of the disciplinarian or the manager if an urgent need for it were to occur.[62] This is not to say that all monasteries were in a position to hand such jobs over to the local population, as some institutions did not have the necessary economic infrastructure. The early twentieth-century chayik for Pelyul Darthang monastery in Amdo, for example, demonstrates that monks did many things themselves: "One only gets permission to [not wear] one's robes when the individual monastic colleges need to have work done, such as getting earth to seal the roofs, painting, and making the floor."[63]

It appears that compulsory labor was a feature of politically powerful monasteries and their branches and that at other places—particularly in the monasteries in Nepal—monks either did most types of work (including farming) themselves or the works were undertaken as a (noncorvée) lay community effort.[64] While clearly corvée duty was by no means voluntary, we cannot know whether laypeople deemed the remuneration they received to be sufficient. Nietupski notes that among the communities surrounding Labrang monastery in the eighteenth century: "Many, even most sources reported that mandatory labor was not oppressive, simply a fact of community life." It is furthermore suggested that this mandatory labor was "broadly publicized as a religious merit-generating activity."[65] A parallel to this sentiment is given by Welch, who writes that in pre–Communist China, laymen who worked in the monastery were all fed by the monastery and sometimes accepted wages lower than the going rate, on account of the merit gained. The difference here is of course the fact that in China compulsory service to the monastery was not in place at that time. When laypeople volunteered to work for the monastery, the phrase used was "to ask for happiness."[66]

Dargyay reports on the situation of laypeople who lived at a monastic estate (*mchod gzhis*) in Central Tibet in the first half of the twentieth century and notes that their behavior toward the estate was "to a great extent unemotional, objective and practical" and that "the submissive demeanor worn by subjects of the nobility was strange to them." She notes that relationships were cordial toward the individual monks, "bearers of the Buddhist religion," but that the administration of the monastic estate was viewed skeptically.[67] There is no mention of laypeople viewing their work for the monastery as religiously gratifying, however. Lobzang Döndrup describes the relationship in the context of duties toward the monastery more as a *quid pro quo*:

> The relations between the people and the monastery have always been very good. They would work for the monastery and the monks would do religious services for them. These days if there is a special job to be done, for example during religious festivals, they come and help. When an important lama is coming, and when a lot of people are expected, we ask the laypeople to bring mats to sit on.[68]

The previously cited corvée-worker at Dargyé Ling monastery notes that she never saw monks treating the laypeople badly.[69] The monastic guidelines are largely silent about how to treat those employed by monks. One of the few exceptions is the *chayik* for Mindröl Ling, which contains rather lengthy regulations on how to behave when traveling.[70]

> All that which is to be adopted and that which is to be abandoned, such as treating the valets and servants continuously gently and honestly, without being pushy and aggressive and without addressing them harshly, is the responsibility of a protector of beings.[71] Thus [the punishment is] a butterlamp of one measure when one

makes the load too heavy or when one, out of disregard, sends [them] to and fro on the way.[72]

This passage suggests that individual monks could indeed be forceful at times. The two-tiered system of the monastery and the individual monk, as discussed in Chapter 4, appears to also have been in place with regard to putting laypeople to work: corvée as a sort of tax was seen as unproblematic, whereas when individual monks applied a similar level of force, there would be implications. Tsongkhapa states this in no uncertain terms: "Those ordained, who have the wish to stay to receive teachings and [for that purpose] order the people from Zangri (Zangs ri) and beyond to do corvée duty, will accumulate grave negative karma.[73] This should therefore be avoided."[74]

## SPONSORS AND THE "COSTS" OF OFFERINGS AND RELIGIOUS SERVICES

Laypeople worked to maintain the monasteries and their inhabitants, but the service that monks performed for laypeople was theoretically of a religious nature. People were usually expected to make a contribution in lieu of provided services. The transactions were not solely of an economic nature, nor were they mere favors done out of Buddhist benevolence. The negotiation of these transactions is illustrated by rules in the monastic guidelines on religious services, accepting offerings, providing estimates of the cost of services, selling Buddhist images, and so on.

In some cases, the prices of certain offerings were very clearly stated. The Fifth Dalai Lama, for example, even sets lower and upper limits for the sponsors of particular types of offerings. The minimum was paying for soup and tea served six times a day for thirteen days; the maximum was to do the same for twenty-three days.[75] The cost of offerings was often seen as a possible reason for disagreements, and therefore rather complex calculations needed to be communicated to the prospective sponsor of a ritual or a communal tea-round. In Sera Je in the eighteenth century, the possibility of upsetting laypeople by naming different prices at different occasions was taken into account, which is why fixed prices had to be established:

> [F]or 3,000 monks one needs at least sixty measures of tea[76] and three times that for the butter. The sponsor needs to be honestly informed of the three levels of quality, so that he can make a decision in accord with his wishes and his resources. Do not take more than this. Similarly, with regard to the three greater and the eight smaller offerings and arrangements and scarves for the protectors' chapel, there should not even be a hint of dispute about the costs of the offerings.[77]

The point made here is that by setting a clear and honest price of the offering or religious service to be rendered, misunderstandings and arguments could be avoided. The author of the above-cited text, the Seventh Dalai Lama, makes a similar point in his guidelines for the monastic community of Ramoché:

> The disciplinarian and the managers together explain to the sponsor what they need and make sure that the things are given to the right recipients. They may not push for them to give more than they can. The sponsors for the communal tea-round may only be encouraged by the managers and not just by any other official.[78]

It appears then that clear rules were seen to be a desideratum when it came to negotiating the price and the types of offerings. As is the case elsewhere, the job is assigned to the disciplinarian and the manager, possibly to prevent potential donors from receiving contradictory information. Again, bias might also have played a part here, as the *chayik* for Pabongka monastery suggests:

> One is to follow the established traditions when it comes to [stating] the costs of rituals, such as village rituals[79] and the like, be they private or public. One is definitely not to do something that becomes a cause for discord within the Sangha, such as being biased toward one's near and dear ones.[80]

Such statements seem to have been intended to counter a perceived bias with regard to friends and family and to wealthy donors. A set of monastic guidelines for Thekchen Damchö Gatsel Ling from 1848 also warns against treating benefactors differently, presumably on the basis of their wealth.[81] As mentioned before, goods that were being offered were often carefully recorded along with their value. In Pelyul Darthang the disciplinarian and the manager were charged with providing an estimate of the cost of the requested ritual and with recording it and dividing some of the proceedings among the reciting monks.[82] There were monks who were assigned to make an assessment of the value of the things given. Again, this was potentially problematic, as the guidelines state: "Even though there are people who ascertain the relative quality of goods, the basic value is handed over to the authorities—it is not allowed to haggle over it."[83]

Another occasion at which one could expect arguments is during the "buying and selling"[84] of religious statues, images, and books. In pre-modern Tibet, there were no shops in which one could purchase Buddhist texts and paraphernalia. Rather, these items were made to order, often by monks. Cassinelli and Ekvall note, somewhat puzzlingly, that Sakya monks were only allowed to do printing and painting for outsiders and they were not to receive payment.[85]

In Mindröl Ling in the seventeenth century, some kind of payment or remuneration was involved, however:

> With regard to printed images of the enlightened body, speech, and mind, the original should not go to waste, but be kept in accordance with one's own wishes.[86] One should not argue and ask for more than the agreed-upon price for the prints. Half of the remaining offerings and the materials that were part of the printing price should be contributed toward replacing the butterlamps,[87] the canopies, tassels, and door-hangings in the many shrines.[88]

Here we learn that monks in this monastery made prints to order. Presumably, the people who made the prints were allowed to keep the other half of the "offerings," whereas the rest was to pay for the upkeep of the shrines at the monastery, thus contributing toward the "greater good."

The monastic guidelines confirm that prospective benefactors were sometimes given several options, taking into account their relative wealth. However, it is clear that one only got what one paid for. This is in contrast with the medieval Christian Church, which calculated religious penalties on the basis of "weighed incomes": richer "penitents" usually bore a heavier penalty than poorer ones, so that the variation in practice was akin to a discriminatory tax.[89] The guidelines that report on the interaction with the sponsors make it very clear that religious services were expected to be paid for. They also exhort the monks to be straightforward and honest about the prices of the offerings or services and not to put any type of pressure on the laypeople requesting them.

## COLLECTING ALMS AND SOCIAL PRESSURE

*As a community of "beggars of alms," the Sangha must physically be located within secular society.*
—ISHII 1986: 6

A number of sources convey that collecting donations was often viewed as problematic by Tibetan authors. Various *chayik* stipulate the circumstances under which money for the monastery had to be amassed. Force is emphatically discouraged and so is begging for alms without permission from the authorities.[90] In the area under the administration of Sakya, individual monasteries had to request special permission from the Sakya government to ask the laity for donations.[91] Similarly, the Bhutanese law code[92] of 1729 notes: "lamas of the monasteries and the representatives of the *dzong* (*rdzongs*)[93] who ask the benefactors for alms destroy villages. From now on, they should be stopped."[94]

These begging-rounds, occasionally carried out by monks on behalf of the monastery, may have presented a financial burden to ordinary people, partly also due to social pressure and one-upmanship. It is not difficult to imagine that this occasionally irritated laypeople. The *Gazetteer of the Kangra District* from 1897 describes the way in which this type of begging occurred in Spiti at that time, namely that after the harvest, the monasteries sent out five or six monks "on begging expeditions":

> They go round from house to house in full dress, and standing in a row, they chant certain verses, the burden of which is—"we are men who have given up the world, give us, in charity, the means of life; by doing so you please God whose servants we are." The receipts are considerable, as each house gives something to every party.[95]

French describes a legal case reported to her by a former employee at the Lhasa courthouse that concerned the murder of two monks. These monks were part of a group traveling from Kham to Ngor monastery in Central Tibet to receive teachings, and along the way they begged for food from the locals. A man reportedly got very angry with the two monks and murdered them—possibly on account of their forceful methods of "begging."[96] In some cases there seems to have been a fine line between soliciting charity, religious blackmail, and straight-out looting. Bell reports in the beginning of the twentieth century that during the Great Prayer Festival Drepung monks would take over the city of Lhasa and "loot extensively." The wealthier people would flee the city and hide their belongings.[97]

A number of monastic guidelines express concerns about monks pressuring laypeople into giving donations, in particular when the sole beneficiary was the individual monk and not the monastic institution. The restrictions with regard to asking for donations are in tension with the Vinayic ideal of the monk begging for alms: "One of the most important monastic rules is that the monk obtain food and other bare necessities by begging."[98] It seems as though this particular practice, so widespread in Theravāda countries, has never been common or entirely acceptable in Tibet as the sole basis for monks' livelihood. Notable exceptions are the members of the Joden Dézhi (Jo gdan sde bzhi). These monks are understood to have solely lived off alms-begging, in emulation of their Kashmiri master Śākyaśrībhadra (1127/40s-1225), whose epithet was "the Great Almsman."[99] An equally early reference that seems to suggest that the begging for alms by individual monks did occur is found in the guidelines for Drigung Til written in the first half of the thirteenth century.[100] By contrast, the biography of the Zhalu master Trülzhik Tsültrim Gyentsen ('Khrul zhig tshul khrims rgyal mtshan, 1399–1473) reports that he asked his monastic followers to never request donations from sponsors—either directly or indirectly.[101]

Although the points on which monastic guidelines and Vinaya rules potentially clash are almost never explicitly remarked upon, the author of the guidelines for Drepung, the Fifth Dalai Lama, makes an exception:

> Because going on an alms-round in Tibet proper, during for example the autumn, is in accordance with the intent of the Vinaya, there is no need to stop it. Except for people who collect offerings for the general good[102] in China, Mongolia, and Kham, etc., one is not to go to ask for donations on one's own accord—it has to be an exception [on behalf of] the officials and the general good.[103]

Here the author sees the possible conflict and knows he cannot contradict the Vinaya rules directly by forbidding the practice outright. He uses the Vinayic term *bsod snyoms brgyag pa*, literally "to do the alms-round," which he then allows, albeit reluctantly. However, he limits the practice to Tibet and employs a more pejorative term for the forbidden practice of collecting donations elsewhere, which can simply be translated as "to beg."[104] Interestingly, this section was cited almost verbatim by the Seventh Dalai Lama in a set of monastic guidelines for Sera monastery from 1737. In this text, he appears to alter the language somewhat by conspicuously leaving out Kham as a place one cannot go to collect donations.[105] This may have to do with the changed perception of what was seen to be Tibet (*Bod*). In the mind of the Fifth Dalai Lama, Kham perhaps did not belong to Tibet, but some fifty years later it may have done so in the opinion of his incarnation, the Seventh.[106]

The author of the guidelines for the—financially struggling—nunnery Rinchen Gang also provides stipulations for those who did go on an alms-round on behalf of the institution:

> Because those who have to go to collect alms are the representatives of the Teachings, their entire behavior needs to be as good as possible. Mornings and evenings, their meditational deity rituals[107] and the like need to be performed properly. When going for alms, except when it is necessary, do not stay in the areas of one's friends, thinking one will get something [there].[108]

It is clear that going to collect alms here meant that one not only was expected to behave in an exemplary manner but also one's religious practices had to be correct, presumably due to the "karmic weight" that accompanied these received donations.

This tension with regard to soliciting alms still exists today among monastics, for example in contemporary Amdo. Its economy having improved, Dhitsa monastery prohibited "begging" in 2008, as it was no longer seen as necessary.[109] Caple reports that monks at a number of monasteries in Amdo emphasized that the donations they received were *voluntarily* given and that their monastery no longer collected alms.[110]

While it may be the case—particularly in those Tibetan areas currently in the PRC—that all manner of asking for donations is discouraged, evidence from the thirteenth century suggests that the practice was perhaps not common but also not necessarily regulated by the monastic authorities. Earlier guidelines show, however, that pressuring people for gifts for one's own sake was generally disapproved of, but that well-organized, scheduled, and ordered visits on behalf of the monastery to solicit donations was usually both permitted and encouraged. The sixteenth-century monastic guidelines for Tsurpu make this point eloquently: "Aside from alms for the benefit of the Sangha, one should not beg and solicit, and particularly one should not read out the scriptures and the like, to get food and clothing with the offerings intended for the virtue of the dead and the living. Do not sell the Holy Dharma."[111]

Seasonal collective alms-rounds were a common feature of Tibetan monasticism,[112] but the daily ritualized begging for alms by individual monks that is common in Theravāda countries was largely unknown in Tibet. The pressure that seeking alms put on the laity may have been a consideration in regulating these practices.

## ACCOMMODATING LAY SENSIBILITIES

In the corpus of Vinaya texts, the concern for the reputation of the Sangha is regularly expressed. The Sanskrit term that is used in this context is *kuladūṣaka*.[113] Behaving badly in full view of the laity is one of the thirteen *Saṅghāvaśeṣa dharma*s, offenses that require suspension,[114] listed—among others—in the *Prātimokṣasūtra*. In the *Vinayavibhaṅga* the actions that may lead to *kuladūṣaka* are described as eating and drinking from the same vessel as a woman, dancing, picking flowers, singing songs, speaking loudly, making garlands, playing musical instruments, playing games, and a whole range of other behavior deemed inappropriate. It has been suggested that (some of) these acts were regarded as "courting behavior," and therefore out of bounds for monks.[115] An Indian commentary explains this *kuladūṣaka* as something that causes the loss of faith, specifically by interaction with women who "belong" to Brahmans or householders.[116]

While this Vinayic worry over the Sangha's good name is found throughout the Buddhist world, the kind of monk behavior that corrupted laypeople, annoyed them, or caused them to lose faith varied according to time and place. Obviously, public opinion was crucial for those monastic communities that were economically dependent on the laity.[117] But how important was this public opinion in places where monasteries maintained important positions in the local economy? In the previous chapter we have seen that monasteries were sometimes economically largely independent from the local population but also that there always existed a certain degree of dependency—be it on the government, interregional trade routes, or the presence of sufficient farmers to work the fields.

It comes as no surprise that the Tibetan monastic guidelines also echo the Vinaya when it comes to the act of "annoying laypeople."[118] The sources at hand convey the problems that the monks occasionally caused in lay society and how certain figures in authority sought to solve them. This was sometimes aided by reasoning found in Vinayic texts, but also by coming up with solutions of a more pragmatic nature, thus bringing together orthodoxy and orthopraxy. What in fact was believed by the authors of the *chayik* to cause laypeople to become annoyed and subsequently disenchanted with the monkhood varied in time and place.

It is clear that this offense was most feared to occur when monks had to deal directly with laypeople. The guidelines contain ample examples of these interactions. The most common types of interactions in which the perceived danger of "annoying laypeople" are: receiving offerings; giving quotes of the cost of a particular ritual to sponsors; levying donations (or begging for alms); performing rituals at laypeople's houses; taking time off and traveling. The possibility of annoying laypeople was often seen to be more likely when monks found themselves out of the direct sight of the monastery officials, such as during holidays. The guidelines for Namgyel Dratsang from 1727 note this possibility in the context of monks who were allowed a break from their duties: "During those periods one should not do anything that causes laypeople to get annoyed, which will cause the worldly ones to lose faith. If there are people who do this, the disciplinarian will impose restrictions."[119]

The most important and most regularly commented-upon relationship of monks with laypeople is that of recipient and donor. As mentioned earlier, in Tibet, the monks were not mere passive beneficiaries of offerings. Rather, they were often given a donation in return for the performance of specific rituals. These could take place in the monastery itself or at the house of the benefactor, or wherever else a ritual was deemed necessary. Thus, "the gift" was typically more akin to a transaction. This posed difficulties for the monks, for they were emphatically not meant to peddle their "dharma" and to deal with sponsors in an unethical way.[120] A set of monastic guidelines, written in 1888 by the Thirteenth Dalai Lama, notes how monks were not meant to haggle with potential sponsors over the cost of certain rituals:

> Then, even when the sponsor makes a request for any kind of religious service that is commensurate with his level of prosperity, one may by no means argue about it. One is, in accordance with the sponsor's wishes, to reflect on the Three Jewels at lunchtime and purify the donations and so on. Thus, in all manner of behavior one is to be a cause for instilling faith in the sponsor. Other than that, one is not to do things that annoy laypeople.[121]

This "purifying the donations" is a ritualized way of dedicating the merit to the benefit of the donor that includes the recitation of a *dhāraṇī*, which can be found in the liturgies of most schools.[122] Here "to instill faith in the sponsor" can be read as doing all that was required, and monks behaving as laypeople expect them to behave. To do the opposite may have invoked their derision. It is noteworthy that here the sponsor's material circumstances were taken into account: being of limited means was not deemed by the author to be a justification for turning him away, although the fact that this is noted in the monastic guidelines may indicate that this indeed happened on occasion. Other ritual services such as the communal tea-round were meant to have fixed fees, again to avoid upsetting laypeople.

The Seventh Dalai Lama recommends set prices and also gives the exact amounts of butter, tea, and salt to be donated: "When there are many different ways to arrange the offerings for the communal tea-round, it might irritate the sponsors and may also be a cause for annoying laypeople, who then lose faith."[123] He continues to detail the amounts of tea and butter needed to provide the monks with two bowls of tea each. But he also warns that the monks could not take more than the sponsor intended to give and could afford.[124]

In the monastic guidelines for Mindröl Ling monastery, written in the late seventeenth century, arguing with laypeople about donations is represented as being on par with abusing power and pursuing debts:

One is not to bother laypeople by misusing power. This may consist of disputing with the laypeople over monk's shares that are not deserved, [dealing in] loans,[125] or ordering them to perform "corvée tax." If these mistakes are made then a punishment will be imposed of a fine of butterlamps consisting of one to three measures [of butter] and prostrations and the like.[126]

Here what is seen as bothering laypeople is not just arguing over the offerings but also the abuse of power by imposing corvée labor and the like. Later in the text, the author Terdak Lingpa forbids the monks who travel in a group from being too pushy in their interactions with laypeople: "The [monks] who are responsible for the baggage should not make it so that laypeople get annoyed by heavily pursuing [them] and ordering [them] around aggressively."[127] In fact, one would expect that monks "heavily pursuing [them]" and "ordering [them] around aggressively" would always be considered annoying by laypeople, but only this particular *chayik* classes such behavior as "bothering laypeople." More generally speaking, it appears that what caused laypeople to lose faith had mostly to do with decorum and reputation. In other words, the problem was not monastic abuse of power, but monks not behaving and dressing like monks, often in full view of the laity.

As mentioned above, there also was a possibility of monks putting too much pressure on laypeople when they went outside the monastery to ask for contributions. A set of monastic guidelines from 1899 for Taklung Drang Mangthö Samten Ling (sTag lung brang mang thos bsam bstan gling) speaks of the yearly trip used to levy donations:

> When going on the annual alms-round, one needs to behave as well as possible, taking with one the six possessions and one's *paṇḍita*'s hat,[128] one's staff and a *maṇḍala*, without falling in either of the two extremes with regards to clothing. Having given up on resentful arguments with each other and careless behavior—things that cause laypeople to lose faith—one properly observes a mindful attitude and, without wasting anything given by the faithful, be it big or small, one amasses the effective methods that increase both one's own and others' merit.[129]

In Tibetan societies, the practice of begging for alms was—as we have seen—occasionally problematic, and the above section warns the monks to conduct their alms-round in a careful and correct manner. Monks also came under the scrutiny of the laypeople when performing rituals in their homes. As mentioned in the previous chapter, away from the disciplinarian's watchful eye certain types of misbehavior could occur during these types of outings. The *chayik* for Ramoché monastery from the 1740s points out the potential danger:

> The monks, when they go to do village rituals and the like, listen to the advice of the honorable elders and they make sure they behave in an exemplary fashion, being an inspiration to others, and as a field of merit. One is emphatically not to deceive the sponsors who have put their trust in one and do anything careless, which causes laypeople to get annoyed and lose faith.[130]

A similar sentiment is expressed by the Fifth Dalai Lama in 1664, for the monastery Gongra Ngesang Dorje Ling, yet without using the phrase as found in the Vinaya. Here the concern is not to do anything that would give the sponsors reason to lose faith. The Fifth Dalai Lama further demonstrates concerns about the correct performance of rituals.[131] In other cases, as expressed in the set of monastic guidelines for Tashi Lhunpo, the problem lay not so much with the proper way of undertaking these rituals but rather with the monks' behavior and the potential to upset laypeople: "Those who go to do rituals for the dead or the living, other than reciting the prayers they have been given to do, should not do things that will make laypeople annoyed such as drinking alcohol and laughing."[132]

It would have been well known among the audience of these monastic guidelines that drinking alcohol and laughing out loud were not accepted types of behavior for monks. It here appears to be reiterated out of appreciation that this would even further upset people who were often already dealing with bereavement of some sort. Elsewhere, the same author also shows concern regarding the sentiments of laypeople. Monks, he writes, are to avoid going to Kyina (sKyid na)[133] and to a particular religious festival.[134]

> Whoever is there may become a real burden, and when only bad omens[135] occur in succession, there is a great danger that the laypeople get annoyed. Therefore, taking the welfare of sentient beings and the hardship such as the contributions offered by the dependents into account, one needs to go [there] with a motivation that combines compassion and a special intention and recite the various prayers as carefully as possible.[136]

This passage indicates that large groups of monks descending on a relatively small community would pose a significant burden on the resources of the locals. If, in addition, what were called bad omens would occur, the monks could be in danger of being scapegoated. Whether these omens had to do directly with the monks' behavior or whether they referred to naturally occurring phenomena is not clear here. However, as has been noted in Chapter 3, in the minds of many (Tibetan) Buddhist believers the two were intimately linked.

Elsewhere, the same text links the same phrase to issues that have more to do with decorum than with being directly sensitive to the feelings of others, such as growing garlic within the monastery and swimming in medicinal springs.[137] Although it can be conceded that to grow garlic is not in line with Vinayic sentiments and that to swim in medicinal waters can be seen as unacceptable behavior on many counts,[138] unlike the other examples the laypeople are not directly involved.

In particular in Geluk *chayik* the phrase "annoying laypeople" takes on a strong formulaic aspect, which leaves one wondering to what extent these rules pertained to actual monastic behavior. The guidelines enumerate the actions that were seen to annoy laypeople and promise that this type of behavior would receive punishment. The type of punishment is usually not specified.

The monastic guidelines for Jampa Ling in Dranang (Gra nang, Central Tibet) from 1927[139] state: "To jump, to swing one's arms, have them behind your back, to cover one's mouth with one's upper robe: one needs to restrain oneself from doing these types of coarse behavior, which may lead toward the act of annoying laypeople."[140] Some of the activities described here are in fact mentioned in the *Prātimokṣa* (part of the 253 vows), such as jumping, which is the twenty-first *śaikṣa* (*bslab pa*) in the *Mūlasarvāstivāda vinaya*,[141] and swinging one's arms, which is the twenty-fifth.

A *chayik* by the Thirteenth Dalai Lama, written in the same year, mainly connects the potential offense to the monks' attire:

> Even though, in accordance with the time and place, the practice of wearing [items of clothing with] sleeves may be appropriate, it is very important to distinguish oneself from laypeople. Except for those who are exempted, one may not wear an upper garment made of serge and the like. For other items of clothing, aside from those that are suitable, all manner of clothes, which do not feature in the texts and lead to the annoyance of laypeople, are not allowed.[142]

Here it is exceptional that the author allows the monks of the monastery for which the monastic guidelines were written to wear clothing with sleeves in certain cases. This is in sharp contrast with many other *chayik,* which explicitly forbid sleeves. This exemption may have to do with the fact that the monastery in question was in Central Asia (Mongolia or Kalmykia), where monk garments with sleeves were (and still are) rather widespread.[143]

In another *chayik* by the Thirteenth Dalai Lama, clothes with sleeves[144] are deemed to annoy laypeople. This set of monastic guidelines from 1930 was written for Rongpo Rabten monastery, a politically important Geluk monastery in Sogdzong (Sog rdzong, Central Tibet). Like the *chayik* cited above, it connects *kuladūṣaka* to the monks' attire: "The Sangha should wear clothing properly; one is not meant to wear, either out in the open or in private, all manner of items that annoy laypeople, such as clothes with sleeves, all kinds of belts, bowl holders, Chinese shoes, meditation ropes,[145] knives, thumb rings, and other rings."[146] Here what is seen to annoy laypeople the most is monks wearing items that are either worn by the laity or by practitioners of other schools—the meditation rope is a clear indication of the latter issue. The same author uses the phrase "to annoy laypeople" in a different manner when addressing a different monastery. In the guidelines from 1930 for a monastery in the north of Central Tibet the concept is solely connected to behavior:

> For all, be they highly or lowly placed, it is important to always avoid all actions that annoy laypeople as if [such actions] were contagious diseases, by means of behavior that is careful and conscientious. Thus, one is not to engage at all in careless behavior such as fighting, singing, and playing dice and mahjong.[147]

A set of monastic guidelines written by the Reting regent for Kunpel Ling monastery in Central Tibet in 1934 notes the following:

Apart from a few monastic officials, the remainder may not do things, either out in the open or in private, that go against the Sangha's inner rules[148] and that annoy laypeople such as: wearing the insignia of a householder like clothing with sleeves, leaving hair longer than one finger-width, singing songs, playing games such as dice and mahjong, using tobacco, snuff, and cigarettes (*shig ras*), playing musical instruments at inappropriate times, and being noisy and calling each other from afar.[149]

Aside from the fact that this text exempts certain officials from these restrictions, the above section is also interesting because it combines notions that are very obviously Vinayic with more recent rules, such as those regarding smoking cigarettes,[150] for which a phonetic rendering of the English word is given.

A *chayik* from 1938 that also combines the Vinayic with issues that are more local in nature was written for Dophü Chökhor Ling monastery (Central Tibet), by the same author as the one cited above:

Not allowed are things that lead toward the annoyance of laypeople, which may be a contributing factor in others losing faith such as: to shout on top of one's own monks' residence or in the vicinity of the monastery's compound, to make noise, to jump, to throw stones [competitively], to use a slingshot, to sit in a secluded place together with a woman but without one's monk friends, to follow her and go together on the road for more than a *krośa*.[151]

Elsewhere in the text, he uses the phrase again and notes: "All crude behavior that annoys laypeople such as planting apricot and walnut tree seeds, beating guard dogs, wearing 'upturned hats,'[152] and interchanging the upper and the lower robes needs to be avoided."[153]

The issues mentioned here concern monks' attire, decorum, and—on one count—actual interaction with laypeople, namely being alone with women.

As mentioned above, in the *Mūlasarvāstivāda vinaya*, *kuladūṣaka* is considered inappropriate behavior that might suggest courting behavior. Other monastic guidelines also make this connection. The monastic guidelines for Thobgyel Rabgyé Ling from 1913 comment: "The disciplinarian is to impose a fitting punishment to the annoying of laypeople—for example—by needlessly staying the night at the village after performing a personal or public task or a home ritual, or by sitting with a woman at a secluded place without monk friends or by following her."[154] The *chayik* for the Pabongka hermitage written in the early 1800s remarks:

It is not at all allowed to do things that annoy laypeople such as sitting at a secluded, concealed place with a woman but without virtuous monk friends or speaking placating words to a woman. If things like that are done, then there will be a punishment imposed, in accordance with the severity, which ranges from expulsion to confession.[155]

Here we see for the first time that more clearly defined punishments are prescribed. They resonate with the way in which infractions of the trainings are dealt with in the Vinaya materials. It is important to note, however, that none of the mentions of *kuladūṣaka* in the *chayik* are treated according to the Vinaya rules, namely as resulting in temporary expulsion lasting six days and nights.[156] Rather, the phrase—merely loosely associated with the one found in the Vinaya rules— serves to denote a variety of bad behavior, which sometimes also features in the Vinaya.[157] When reading the *chayik* as a genre, the idiom indeed gives a general idea of the way the authors wanted the monks to represent themselves, not just to the outside world but also to each other.

Obviously, some *chayik* show more concern for actual relationships with surrounding communities, whereas others are more worried about their appearance and—by extension—the reputation of the monks among laypeople. On the basis of available sources, we can tentatively speak of a chronological development—from the phrase actually referring to dealing with laypeople, being afraid of burdening them, to using the same phrase in the context of attire and decorum, making sure one looks monkish enough, and not corrupting oneself—and the Sangha as a whole—by associating oneself with laypeople.

It is not the case, however, that a conscious reinterpretation of the Vinaya rules has taken place, but rather that the phrase, originally derived from the Vinaya, has taken on different meanings in a Tibetan context. In summary then, what— according to the *chayik*—is counted as behavior that is, or leads to, *kuladūṣaka* is the following:

· To order laypeople around
· To levy donations (and begging for alms) in an aggressive or dishonest fashion
· To be a financial burden to laypeople
· To improperly perform rituals for laypeople
· To interact with women in secret
· To not behave in a monk-like manner, whether through dress, singing, shouting, jumping, or playing games
· To argue with each other and to be careless or unscrupulous when out among laypeople

It is clear that not all texts will use "Vinayic vocabulary" to convey a similar message. It can be gleaned from the examples provided above that they are predominantly written by Geluk authors. This is, I believe, not merely due to the wider availability of Geluk *chayik*, but also because of the more extensive use of Vinaya-related terms by authors belonging to this school. While the wording in the *chayik* is occasionally formulaic, the accommodation of lay sensibilities was not merely symbolic.

Much of the contents of the *Mūlasarvāstivāda vinaya* seems to have been written in reaction to criticism by laypeople, so that the Sangha was "shown as sensitive to and accommodating toward the norms and values of what they took to be their surrounding community."¹⁵⁸ The wording suggests the redactors of the *Mūlasarvāstivāda vinaya* may not have been truly concerned with what the lay community thought of them. However, we need only remind ourselves of the presumed intended audience of Vinayic works to understand that the concern for a good reputation with nonmonastics must have been genuine, if not largely for reasons of (economic) survival. The same holds true for the Tibetan monastic guidelines.

The authors of the *chayik* show a genuine concern for the sensibilities of laypeople and the reputation that the monastery enjoyed in the area, despite the fact that in some cases their economic well-being was not necessarily dependent on the correct behavior of monks. Still, many monasteries relied on the laypeople's opinion in one way or another. For instance, families had to be prepared to send their son to the monastery; if the institution in question had a bad reputation, they may have been less willing to do so. The prosperity and survival of a monastery were thus not always dependent solely on finances. This dependency and awareness of lay sensibilities demonstrates that—in contrast to what is sometimes argued—the relationship between the Tibetan monastery and society was not simply hegemonic, but one in which it was crucial to reach a consensus.

## MORAL OBLIGATIONS: THE MONK AND THE SPONSOR

Perhaps in Buddhist India "monastic duties were seen as essentially oriented toward the monastic community itself,"¹⁵⁹ but to what extent is this true in the Tibetan context? Naturally, the primary goal of the monastery is to perpetuate itself and rules are made accordingly. However, the laity has an essential role to play in this continuation. As has been indicated above, monastic authors showed considerable concern for maintaining favorable relations with laypeople, although the motivations may have varied. But what were the *duties* monks actually felt they had? Goldstein claims that the monks are perceived to have "a moral obligation to attend to the spiritual needs of the lay people."¹⁶⁰ To a lesser extent this is also asserted by Miller, who claims that the Tibetan Sangha is seen to have "at least some minimal responsibility to the lay community as well as to itself," and that "this responsibility can be thought of as community service."¹⁶¹

Much has been written about the position of Buddhist monks particularly in Theravāda communities.¹⁶² The monk is described as a field of merit and thereby ascribed a somewhat passive role. Solely by keeping his vows properly, he is a source of merit for all who give to him. This notion is found in all Buddhist cultures and is eloquently vocalized by the Seventh Dalai Lama, who concludes his guidelines for Sera Je as follows: "Because the foundation of the Teachings is the purity of the rules of the Holy Vinayadharma, one needs to make sure one becomes a holy field through which merit can be accumulated."[163] This passage was probably intended as a further incentive for monks to behave well. In a similar vein, a *chayik* from 1900 notes: "Because the faithful sponsor is one who definitely can purify *dkor*,[164] one needs to strive to become worthy of offerings."[165]

In Tibet the monk's duty in society was seen as something more than merely being a field of merit. Naturally, monks in lay society are performers of ritual, recipients of offerings, and thereby providers of good karma. But monks have another role that is not often commented upon. The religious practitioner— which includes the monk—was seen as a pacifying force. As briefly mentioned in Chapter 3, this force served to keep in check potentially dangerous local spirits and demons. Just as a number of Buddhist temples were built to pin down the "supine demoness" in Imperial times,[166] the monks were seen to be in a position to keep harmful spirits in check. This was not only achieved by performing rituals, but also by their conduct, their practice of the Dharma, and the maintenance of their vows.

While the monastic guidelines frequently invoke the power and authority of the protector deities, who were often originally "local spirits" converted to Buddhism, they do not spell out what is thought to happen when rules are not adhered to.[167] A legal code for Bhutan from 1729, however, is more explicit:

> By discarding the Dharma rules,[168] the main protectors depart into space.
> They are dispersed into the exhalations of the Samaya-corrupting demon brothers.
> By discarding the human rules,[169] the deities decline.
> The black devils laugh "ha ha."[170]

The belief in the connection regarding adherence to rules—be they religious or not—local spirits, and the general well-being of the population was, no doubt, widespread. This meant that the local people saw themselves as having a vested interest in the general conduct of the monks in their local monastery. This further complicates the relationship between the lay and monk communities. Now, the monks are not mere fields of merit: the purity of their vows affects the local spirits and gods, who control the weather, eventually affecting the harvest. This makes the keeping of vows a matter of life and death.

It may not be entirely correct to label the monks' obligations "moral" per se, but this perceived duty on the side of the monks presumably did have an effect on the moral behavior of the monastics. In the sixteenth-century *chayik* for Pelri Chödè, for example, the initial sponsor and political ruler of Chonggyé ('Phyongs rgyas, where the monastery is located) was Zhabdrung Hor Sönam Dargyépa (Zhab drung Hor bSod nams Dar rgyas pa). The author, Shérab Özer (Shes rab 'od zer, 1518–1584), calls on monks to behave in an exemplary fashion and then lists a large number of ways to achieve such behavior, "in order to bring to perfection the intention of the ruler and to not let the efforts of his son, his relatives, and his ministers go to waste."[171] This would invoke a sense of indebtedness toward the sponsors, and in the likely case of important benefactors also playing some political role, a certain sense of loyalty as well.

The notion of sponsor, *sbyin bdag,* is more complex than is currently appreciated. In the eyes of many today, being a sponsor or donor does not fully *oblige* one to give: one gives out of free choice and religious fervor. The much analyzed "patron-priest relationship" (*mchod yon / mchod sbyin*)—that Tibetans found a favorable construction—may feature the word *sbyin bdag,* which is often explained in the context of political macro-narratives.[172] When operating on a micro-level, however, the connotation of the term appears often very similar. The relationship between a monastery and its sponsors was often not without mutual obligations, nor was "giving" entirely optional. For instance, Kvaerne, who conducted fieldwork among monks from Bon Menri monastery, notes that each college of the monastery used to have a donor, a layperson from the nomadic Jangthang area, who was "elected" by the monks in charge of revenue derived from donations.[173] This "rotating community sponsorship"[174] was also in place at Labrang monastery.[175] The purely "voluntary" nature of being a sponsor then is very much in doubt. Rather, we see a picture emerging of mutual obligations and duties, both in economic and religious terms. The monastic guidelines attempt to negotiate, calibrate, and maintain this fragile relationship.

## FAMILY TIES

The most obvious and ubiquitous relationship between monks and the lay community was the family tie, which—contrary to popular perception—was *not* broken when a person became a monk. Clarke convincingly demonstrates that in Buddhist India a monk maintaining contact with his family was never directly discouraged, and that upon examining the ideals of authors and redactors of the extant Vinayas, "there seems to have been little, if any, expectation that when one left home for the religious life one would either reject one's family or sever all family ties."[176] Rather, "all extant Indian Buddhist monastic laws suggest that monks and nuns could continue to interact with family members both lay and monastic."[177] The *Mūlasarvāstivāda vinaya* even contains rulings that *made* monks look after their parents.[178] The *Uttaragrantha* has the Buddha order "that even a son who has entered the religious life must procure food and clothing for both father and mother." Not to do so is an offense.[179] While, generally speaking, monks were expected to provide service to other monks and not to householders, forsaking one's parents was never a requirement.[180]

In the case of Tibetan monasticism, we can speak of family relationships as mutually beneficial: sometimes monks would help their family, and other times the family would send food and money.[181] In fact, the monk often depended on his family for his upkeep in the monastery, much as would a child sent to boarding school.[182] Nietupski also notes this relationship between the monk and his family, in the context of Labrang monastery. He then extrapolates that monasteries were therefore "fully integrated with lay society,"[183] which makes Labrang "a community-funded and community-integrated institution."[184] This statement is not applicable to all types of monasteries, however, for we know that monasteries actively sought to distance themselves from the lay community and that monasteries often did not rely solely on donations from generous laypeople, but that they also owned fields, had lay dependents (or "subjects"), were engaged in trade, and sometimes were heavily dependent on government funding.

Nevertheless, it should be emphasized that the fact that many families in pre-modern Tibet had sons in a monastery often created a bond that was more than a religious or an economic one. Furthermore, these emotional ties between the lay community and the monastery were frequently translocal. This is to say that monks would regularly join a monastery outside of their locality. As has been demonstrated in Chapter 3 several monastic guidelines even stipulate coming from an area farther away from the monastery as an entrance requirement. The ties thus created show that there was not necessarily an obvious emotional connection of the local community with the local monastery, but that there existed intricate networks of family relations that often were also economic ones, stretching throughout and beyond Tibet.[185] What has not been noted by researchers who work on modern-day Tibetan monasteries in the PRC is that this represents one of the biggest breaks with the past. According to current state regulations, people are only allowed to become monks at monasteries in the region in which they are registered.[186] This has reduced monasteries in Tibetan areas from being interregional and sometimes even international institutions to largely local establishments.[187]

When a person "went forth, from home to homelessness,"[188]—that is, became a monk—he usually was no longer a subject of the estate to which his family belonged; he could no longer lay claim to inheriting his family's agricultural lands and, by extension, could not be held legally responsible for the debts of his family.[189] These changes had legal implications, but were not likely to fundamentally change the sense of responsibility a monk had for his parents. There is no doubt that monastic culture discouraged intense contact with householders, regardless of whether there was a blood relation or not. However, exceptions were always made. An example of this is found in the monastic guidelines for Mindröl Ling monastery:

> Generally speaking, because the regular visiting of other people's houses is a cause for the very bad condition of increasing worldly desire, one should not go. In the exceptional case that one needs to go, such as when parents and relatives and the like are sick and dying, one should return no later than the agreed date of return, when it is not farther than a month's march away.[190]

While relationships with relatives were maintained, they were also reasonably well regulated. As we have seen in previous chapters, monks could not simply leave without permission from the monastic authorities and often could not stay at a layperson's house for more than three nights.[191] Visits by family members to their sons at the monastery were equally restricted. This was particularly the case for female relatives. Mindröl Ling's guidelines are strict when it comes to women entering monastic residencies: "Except for when they come to do masonry or roof repairs in the living quarters, females, even one's mother and sisters, are not allowed."[192] Elsewhere, the same text extends this restriction to all relatives: "Without special permission, monks are not to allow their relatives and the like in the living quarters."[193]

Even more problematic was a monk helping out his kin by working on the land. In some cases, however, monks could assist their family or even fellow countrymen with agricultural work, with the notable exception of plowing. If necessary, they could even give some of their monk's income to their relatives.[194] These types of allowances, however, do not appear to feature in the *chayik*. In many texts all manner of agricultural labor is forbidden, such as in the Fifth Dalai Lama's guidelines for Kumbum Jampa Ling (sKu 'bum byams pa gling): "Because worldly activities, such as harvesting, contradict the holy Dharma and the Vinaya, they should not be done."[195] In his guidelines for Drepung, the same author also forbids monks to work in the fields, but makes an allowance for the monastery's residents who had not taken vows. They could proceed but were required to wear lay clothes while farming.[196] Similarly, the 1729 Bhutanese law code states that monks "who loiter should be engaged in farming work."[197]

While rules that regulate and restrict farmwork by monastics were in place across the board, we know that at least in more recent times these rules were often not adhered to, for a number of eyewitness accounts describe monks as helping their families and communities by providing manual labor—a scarce commodity in most Tibetan and Himalayan regions.[198]

## HEALTHCARE FOR ALL?

As alluded to above, monks often took care of their ailing parents and relatives, an obligation that remained after "leaving the family." The link between the Sangha and medical care is strong in Buddhist narratives. The Buddha is repeatedly shown in the Vinaya nursing people afflicted by illness. Monks, including senior ones, are also described as caring for the ill, who in some cases were laypeople.[199] However, the Vinaya forbids practices that are "not soteriological" such as astrology and medicine.[200] The Sri Lankan *katikāvata*s state that, except for "the five co-religionists"[201] described in the Vinaya, no medical treatment was to be provided to others.[202] The reality, however, seemed to be that throughout Sri Lankan history, monks often practiced astrology and medicine.[203] The *Mūlasarvāstivāda vinaya* states that ill monks needed to be taken care of and that the property of the Sangha should be used to pay for their treatment.[204] At the same time, workers employed by the monastery were also meant to be looked after.[205] This does not necessarily contradict the prohibition on practicing medicine, as it appears to refer to the cost of healthcare.

While access to healthcare was not widely available in pre-modern Tibet and usually restricted to "urban" areas,[206] the study of medicine was promoted throughout the country. Initially, entry to the Chakpori (lCags po ri) medical college built in the late seventeenth century was only possible for monks.[207] In 1696, its founder, Desi Sangyé Gyatso (sDe srid sangs rgyas rgya mtsho), wrote the *chayik* for this college, explicitly modeled on guidelines for actual monasteries.[208] Similarly, a number of monasteries had colleges solely dedicated to the study of (Tibetan) medicine. For example, Labrang monastery in Amdo had a monastic college for medicine,[209] founded in 1784 in order to promote the study and development of Tibetan medicine.[210] Medicines were also often produced at monasteries.[211] While physicians were by no means always monks, in particular after the seventeenth century the monastic institutions and the Tibetan government increasingly staked their claim on the education of doctors and the production of medicine.[212]

It is not the case that healthcare was provided freely and without restrictions. How monastic guidelines deal with the ill is remarkably close to the Vinaya's stipulations regarding the management of the financial aspects of medical care. The most common mention of ill health among monks is in the context of attending the assembly. Sick monks, along with the "very old" monks, are exempted from having to attend, while they still receive their "shares." The 1899 monastic guidelines for Taklung Drang Mangthö Samten Ling explain: "The permanent resident *bhikṣus* who are very old practitioners and the ill, who are known to have no assistance or any capital whatsoever, may only receive handouts based on the agreement from the general Sangha and the monastic administration, but they may not be given a share of 'the continuing tea.'"[213] The 1947 guidelines for Tagdrag monastery give the following ruling: "If there are monks enrolled here who have been ill for a long time and whose finances have been depleted, then—in consultation with the preceptor, the chant master, and the disciplinarian—they need to be given the cost for treatment and the support for their livelihood and so on, from the general assets."[214]

The monastery thus had a duty to take care of chronically ill monks, but *only* if they could not do so themselves. Equally, the Mindröl Ling guidelines report: "When someone gets ill, then he needs to be taken care of untiringly, whether or not he himself has the means [to pay for] a nurse[215] and necessities. If not, he receives all that is necessary, such as a suitable nurse, a physician and healing rituals."[216] Here it is not stipulated who ends up paying for the medical bill, but the point made is that monks who cannot afford care should not be left to fend for themselves. The Pelri Chödè guidelines by Shérab Özer from the late sixteenth century note that monks should not only be cared for in sickness but also in death. The text stipulates what prayers needed to be done and for how long, but it does not mention any sort of remuneration for the received care.[217]

The Fifth Dalai Lama is more informative on this matter in his guidelines for Gongra Ngesang Dorje Ling:

> When a monk without resources becomes ill, the healing rituals need to be done[218] with the assets of the Three Jewels or those of the Sangha. When he recuperates and he has the means, he should repay all. Also, destitute ill people who are not from here should be helped by means of things like food, clothing, medical examination, and instructions.[219]

Interestingly, here—unlike the rulings in the *katikāvatas*—the monks are also to help people who are not (necessarily) monks and who come from elsewhere.

The guidelines for Kongtö Dungkar monastery from 1943 state the following on the topic of illness:

> Someone who is ill and without resources needs to be taken care of by means of the assets of the Sangha and the Three Jewels. Once he has recovered, if there are funds that can be taken from, for example, his own region, then the deficit of the Three Jewels assets can be replaced. But if not, his relatives and countrymen should not be held accountable. People in the vicinity who do not belong to this region, lay or ordained, who are ill, should be helped by means of assistance, food, clothing, medicine, and the like. If you have been to a place where there is a contagious disease, do not go among the general Sangha, as this will be harmful.[220]

This text clearly ascribes an important task to the monastery to take care of ailing laypeople and—if they are truly destitute—to pay for their treatment.

Treatment was not always entirely free, not even for poor monks. The guidelines for Ramoché monastery from the 1740s offer an interesting way to repay the medical debts:

> Some ill people, who have no wealth at all, are looked after by the monastery officials and supported by the monastery. Monks who, after having been provided for by the government and the monastery due to their financial destitution, have not yet settled their debts, should be made to compensate this by doing home rituals.[221]

While there is no justification given, it might be argued that this rule was created in the interest of fairness—that all monks pay equally for their healthcare regardless of their level of wealth. It is more likely, however, that the encouragement to repay the costs has to do with the fact that the wealth used would (in most cases) be drawn from the Sangha's assets. We have seen in the previous chapter that the depletion of these assets was to be avoided at all cost—in the interest of karma, not of fairness.

Monasteries, aside from the medical colleges, do not appear to have made efforts to develop any type of structural healthcare[222] or geriatric care.[223] This stands in contrast with recent efforts by monasteries in exile and in Tibet alike to build public clinics, which often provide very affordable (primary) healthcare to people of all walks of life. While the history of Tibetan medicine currently receives scholarly attention, an investigation into actual medical care (of monks and laypeople) in pre-modern Tibet still remains a desideratum.[224] For now, from the above it can be gleaned that, if monks were generally expected to pay for their treatments themselves, laypeople were too.

## THE MONASTERY AND THE EDUCATION OF LAYPEOPLE

Attitudes toward education in Buddhist countries have varied a great deal throughout the centuries. According to one of the Sinhalese *katikāvatas*, it is maintained that "without intending to ordain them Bhikkhus should not teach the children of laypeople."[225] Still it appears that in Sri Lanka monks were the primary educators, as they taught reading and writing as well as moral values and literature.[226] Spiro states that in pre-modern Burma all education was provided by monks and that children attended only the monastery school. During Spiro's fieldwork in Burma monks continued to serve as schoolmaster in the rural areas.[227] In China, a temple ordinance of 1915 made all Buddhist monasteries and temples open schools that would provide a general and a religious education, but the text does specify that the educators had to be monks and nuns.[228]

In Tibet, the level of literacy has been traditionally comparatively low, and an educational system, comparable to modern times, only started to develop properly in the early twentieth century.[229] Literacy was largely in the hands of the monastics. Kawaguchi notes in this regard that only at religious schools could one obtain even "a comparatively advanced education" and—as has been alluded to in Chapter 3— the doors of those schools were, "of course, shut to those of humble origin."[230] The sons of the nobility and of wealthy subjects either were sent to the monastery to get an education or tutors were hired.[231] These were often "retired monks"— presumably monks who did not reside at a monastery—who would live in the same house or "active monks" who would make house calls.[232] The educational contribution that the monastic institution made was also apparent in Spiti in the nineteenth century. The *Gazetteer of Kangra* reports:

> Nearly the whole of the male population of Spiti receives some education at the monasteries; the heir to the family estate goes when a boy in the winter to the ancestral cell with his younger brothers, who are to spend their life there, and passes two or three winters there under instruction. Consequently, nearly every man can read.[233]

An unstructured educational arrangement as apparently once existed in Spiti could only be maintained when the monastery and the local community were a close-knit society. In Central Tibet, this was often not the case, in particular when it came to the larger monasteries. However, according to Cassinelli and Ekvall, even the poorest in the Sakya principality could get an education at a neighboring monastery. The reason given for this is that "Tibetan Buddhism implied that the extension of literacy was beneficial because it enabled more people to participate in an additional degree of religious observance."[234] Be that as it may, such notions have not resulted in any efforts to set up a well-organized educational system. Another manner in which education could be enjoyed was by sending one's son to the monastery for just a short period of time. This is also noted by Miller, who remarks that many young novices returned to their families after having received a nominal education.[235]

Certain politically significant institutions did set up schools that allowed lay-people to study there. Das mentions the "boarding schools in Tashi Lhunpo" in the late nineteenth century and notes that the monastery maintained a school for the education of the advanced students, both monk and lay.[236] People who wanted to pass the government exams[237] went there; the elementary level was not taught. There were no fees, as the teachers were provided by the state. The school was not open to women, because women were not allowed in the monastery compound. Upon completion, the students were required to serve the government, and those who were unable or unwilling to do so had to pay a large sum to be exempted.[238]

It is important to note here that all types of education available to laymen— women were hardly ever formally educated—were dominated by Tibetan monastic culture. This means that monastic education left a mark on society that went far beyond the direct sphere of influence of the monastery. The contemporary author Rendo Senggé, a monk at Kirti monastery, notes the following: "These monasteries are the foundation on the basis of which Tibetan education, moral behavior, arts and crafts have developed and flourished. Therefore, the Tibetan system of monastic learning within the history of Tibetan education can be compared to a precious jewel rosary bead."[239] While monk authors would naturally be keen to emphasize the importance of monastic education, this point is crucial when trying to understand the impact of monks and monasteries on Tibetan societies through history.[240]

## THE SOCIAL POSITION OF THE MONK IN TIBETAN SOCIETY

*The bhikṣu is the best, the śrāmaṇera is in the middle, and the resident of the household is the lowest.*
—THE FIFTH DALAI LAMA (SEE NOTES)

The social position of monks fluctuated a great deal throughout history, both in Buddhist and Christian contexts.[241] That of the Tibetan monks seems to have been comparatively stable, largely due to the high level of religious homogeneity in Tibet. While monasteries regularly found themselves in a position of power, this did not mean that monks were seen to be infallible or above the law: there are various instances in which people are reported to have protested against the actions of monks. Miller remarks that acute dissatisfaction with the monastery's handling could cause the community to switch to a rival monastery. This meant that the lay community could potentially influence the monastery through its personnel and by granting or withholding funds.[242]

As shown in this chapter, the monastic guidelines make continuous implicit references to the danger of losing the support of the laity. In this regard, the texts function similarly to the Vinaya. Horner's remarks on early Buddhist monasticism ring equally true for the Tibetan context: "Historically, the success of the Early Buddhist experiment in monasticism must be in great part attributed to the wisdom of constantly considering the susceptibilities and criticisms of the laity."[243] At the same time, more mundane types of contact with laypeople were to be discouraged.[244] As identities needed to be kept separate, the layman tended to be portrayed as the opposite of a monk, and vice versa.[245] In reality, however, "the Tibetan monastic world defies both idealistic and cynical expectation: neither do we have here a world of pure spirituality nor of Machiavellian intrigue. It exists not on the community's periphery, but very much in the thick of it."[246]

When examining normative Tibetan works that only implicitly address social welfare, we see that for the authors, the interests of laypeople are taken seriously, without being sentimentalized. In other words, while the monastic institution in pre-modern Tibet was most definitely not a charitable institution, like other religious institutions in Europe and beyond, it had the function of "a social safety net."[247] However, as has been established previously, rules often had to be created only in order to right certain wrongs. Many prescriptive (and indeed proscriptive) pronouncements, often made by figures of religious authority, probably were—to a certain extent—regularly ignored by the managerial "establishment" and individual monks. These particular monks had to be continuously reminded of the laity's importance.

The importance of the monkhood for the laity is—due to lack of sources—less well documented. In this chapter, the ritual role of the Sangha has been mentioned: monks and nuns are needed to perform rituals, in the case of death, sickness, and other important life events. Significantly, the view that for the Buddhist Teachings to survive the Sangha needs to be maintained is common among both lay and ordained Buddhists. Wangchuk provides the rationale for this argument, noting that the Vinaya is part of the Buddhist Teachings and that "without monk- or nun-hood the Vinaya would be dead."[248]

In more recent times, the monks are seen to have been given additional responsibilities toward the laity and toward "Tibetan society" as a whole. The monks interviewed by Schwartz showed a strong sense of being bearers and preservers of tradition, "serving Tibetans by setting an example."[249] With Tibetan traditions under threat, the monks are not just the guardians of religion, but have also become culture heroes of sorts. In addition, with the previously existing power structures having disappeared, the relationship is viewed by many Tibetans in

Tibet as a cooperative and complementary one, "where both people and resources are willingly committed by the community to the monasteries because the benefit is understood in general social terms."[250] On this basis, it could be argued that political developments since the 1950s have strengthened the bond between the laity and the monkhood. In particular, the restrictions regarding religious practices and the PRC's control over monastic affairs are seen by many Tibetans as "directly interfering with the traditional relationship between the monastic community and the laity."[251]

This traditional relationship was bound to restrictions of its own. The legal and judicial aspects of this bond between the laity and the monkhood in pre-modern Tibetan Buddhist society also drastically diverge from the current circumstances. It is this, and more generally the legal position of the monastery, to which I turn next.

# 7

# Justice and the Judicial Role of the Monastery

*Beneficence ... is less essential to the existence of society than justice. Society may subsist, though not in the most comfortable state, without beneficence: but the prevalence of injustice must utterly destroy it.*
—SMITH [1759] 2002 II.II 3.3: 86

The judicial position of the monastery in traditional Tibetan society is not well known. The numerous examples given in previous chapters suggest that indeed the monastic authorities had the power to discipline and punish their resident monks. It has furthermore been noted that "the monastic estate was a legal unit."[1] Unknown, however, is how this legal unit functioned. To what extent were monasteries autonomous in terms of jurisdiction? Speaking of Buddhist monasticism tout court, it has been suggested that "monks are under no authority but their own order"[2] and that "[t]heoretically, the monk is no longer subject to the secular authority and answers only to the Buddhist code of discipline, the Vinaya."[3] However, there is historical evidence that monks in Tibet were occasionally subject to state law.[4] My informants, in answering the question as to how the monastic guidelines relate to the secular law, are unanimous in their understanding that the monastic guidelines—and thus the behavior of monks—need to be in accord with the law of the land. A scholar monk from Kirti, Rendo Senggé, responded in the following way:

> Generally speaking the monastic guidelines fall under the state law: their contents can never be in contradiction with the general law. In old Tibet there was never any such problem. Nowadays it is quite difficult, because we are focused on education, our own system of education. China does not want the monks to study, they want them to stay put and just pray.[5]

The issue referred to here is that of the minimum age set by the Chinese authorities to enter the monastery. It is currently higher than is customary or ideal in Tibetan monasteries and this policy is seen as a serious limitation to the education of monks. This presents a large number of monks in contemporary Tibet with an ethical problem, although on the whole, prioritizing is not difficult: the monastic customs are seen as more important than state policy.

If in pre-modern Tibet monastic estates were indeed legal units, could monasteries try and punish laypeople who committed crimes within their jurisdiction? And, for what "crimes" would a monk be subjected to the secular authorities? How sharp was the distinction between secular and monastic law? These are crucial questions, the answers to which are important to determine the overall position of the monastery, and by extension, monastic Buddhism in Tibetan society.

According to Ellingson, *chayik* were based on "secular" law codes.[6] A preliminary comparison of the monastic guidelines and the extant legal codes of Tibet indeed indicates that—in particular, terminologically and linguistically—there are striking similarities between the two genres. However, it appears more likely that these similarities are due to the fact that the authors of the two types of texts were often one and the same, and because, as indicated in the previous chapter, the educated few were almost always monastically schooled. There are even instances of law codes that were explicitly based on monastic guidelines, the current code of conduct issued by the Bhutanese state a case in point.[7] The question of how exactly monastic guidelines and legal documents are related requires further investigation,[8] but this chapter focuses on the ways in which the *chayik* inform us about monastic legal policies and practices, and the Buddhist sensibilities that may be embedded within.

Such a discussion belies larger issues, such as the relation between Buddhism and the execution of justice. According to French, the two are intimately related: "Mind training and inner morality are also the center of the legal system for Tibetan Buddhists because it is the afflicted mind that creates the conflict and unhappiness that brings about legal disputes."[9] She argues in her anthropological study of the legal system in traditional Tibet that ultimately "[a]ll laws were understood as religious."[10] And following that, all punishment "was meant to promote a return to inner morality."[11] This, whether it concerns secular or monastic legal policies, seems highly questionable.

The many punishments enumerated in the monastic guidelines suggest that the aim of such measures is only to a very limited extent to purify negative karma. Rather—comparable to legal systems all over the world—the primary goal of punitive measures and rules is to keep the peace and maintain a balance. Authors of regulations were not directly concerned with the individual's karma, mind training, or morality, but with protecting the monastery, the Sangha, and thus the Dharma against the threat of lawlessness. The monastic guidelines then, when they note the importance of adhering to the rules, do entreat the monks to heed their vows, but at the same time in the practical application of the rules (or monastic laws), karma, mindfulness, and morality play only a minor role.

## THE JUDICIAL POSITION AND JURISDICTION OF
## MONKS AND MONASTERIES

According to a narrative found in the *Mūlasarvāstivāda vinaya,* the ideal situation is a separation of secular and religious law. The king must acknowledge that lay law does not apply to the monks and that, obviously, monastic law does not apply to the laymen.[12] In the Tibetan case, however, it is obvious that this strict division was seen as neither practical nor desirable. However, clear distinctions *were* made. Early on in the history of Tibetan monasticism, monks were granted a legal status distinct from that of laypeople. The sixteenth-century work "A Scholar's Feast,"[13] citing an edict purported to have been issued by the ruler Tridè Songtsen (Khri lde srong btsan, a.k.a. Sad na legs, r. c.800–815), records this position of privilege: "Those who have gone forth may not be given as slaves to others. They may not be suppressed [by tax]. Having placed them on the protection of householders, they are not subject to lawsuits."[14]

The Changbu (lCang bu) Inscription, issued by Tridè Songtsen's son, Tritsuk Detsen, from the ninth century, chronicles the foundation of the Changbu Temple and displays similar sentiments. The edict states that the gifts given in perpetuity should not be lost and that the great temple and its subjects cannot be taxed or punished.[15] This edict places the judicial authority, over both the Sangha and the laity, firmly in the hands of the monks residing there.

An early law code ascribed to Trisong Detsen, despite having been only poorly preserved in secondary sources, makes a distinction between monks and lay tantric practitioners. It stipulates that people are to venerate and bow to monks and suggests harsh punishments for those who insult or harm them.[16] While they clearly enjoyed a privileged position, monks were not above the law. In fact, legal regulations from Imperial times, as preserved in later historiographical records, show that punishments of crimes against the king were harsher than those committed against the *Triratna,* which of course included the monkhood.[17] By contrast, "The History of Ngari"[18] states that in 988, then-ruler of Western Tibet Lha Lama Yeshé Ö (lHa bla ma ye shes 'od) issued a "religious edict"[19] that prioritized religion over the "secular." The text reports that his whole entourage swore an oath to uphold this, calling upon the protector Pehar as a witness.[20] The (legal) authority of the ruler with regard to the monasteries seems to have been greater in earlier times than later on.[21]

It appears that the privileged legal status of Tibetan monks established early on set the stage for centuries to come. Monasteries, together with their estates, seem to have been "judicial islands": the monastic authorities had the power to try and punish whomever was seen to be in the wrong, be they monks or laypeople. Darg-yay reports that, in the first half of the twentieth century, monastic estates even had two levels of (monastic) judicial authority: The lowest judicial court was headed by the steward of the monastery, the higher one by the manager.[22]

At the same time, monks were supposed to follow the secular state laws as well as regional laws, which were often not more than customs. Many of these customs were already included in the vows and rules to which monks were committed in the first place, such as not to kill and not to steal. The most basic and widespread "secular" legal code is "The Sixteen Pronouncements."[23] A number of variations and adaptations exist, resulting in various numbers of pronouncements, but the text is traditionally attributed to Songtsen Gampo. The colophon of one relatively early variation, "The Thirteen Pronouncements,"[24] mentions king Ādarśamukha[25] as the one making the pronouncements. This person features in the Jātakas as a previous birth of the Buddha, who was known as a just king.[26] The ascription to him thus maintains the secular nature of the code while granting it the authority of the Buddha. This textual genre had a mainly symbolic function, but nonetheless was deeply ingrained in the "legal consciousness" of the Tibetans.[27]

Connected to these pronouncements are the sixteen human rules or norms often attributed to Songtsen Gampo.[28] A relatively late set of monastic guidelines for Ochu Gon from 1918 connects these sixteen rules to upholding monastic discipline and basic ethical behavior: "Because the purity of the Sangha's discipline, the foundation for the well-being of the region, and the practice of the ten virtues is dependent of the sixteen pure 'human rules,' monks and laypeople all need to be mindful and conscientious of not engaging in actions that go against these."[29] Equally, the guidelines for Mindröl Ling note that monks had to adjust their behavior according to the contemporary and contextual "human rules."[30]

When monks committed particularly heinous crimes, such as murder and treason, they tended to be tried under state law.[31] Bell writes that a monk who committed a murder would first be flogged and expelled from the monastery and then handed over to the secular authorities.[32] A similar type of legal ideology is attributed to Emperor Xuanwu (宣武 r. 500–516), who attempted to regulate the Chinese Sangha in an edict:

> Since black and white [monk and lay] are two different things, the laws (法 *fa*) and Vinaya (律 *lu*) are also different. . . . From this moment on, let all Buddhist monks who commit the crime of murder or worse be judged in accordance with secular laws. For all other crimes, let them be judged according to the Vinaya.[33]

While in Tibetan society there occasionally was a rather strict theoretical divide between state and religious justice, in practice, the two were often intertwined. This, of course is also related to the fact that politics and religion were combined,[34] the most notable expression of this being the office of the Dalai Lama. Bell mentions that the Thirteenth Dalai Lama would occasionally try legal cases when he was a novice (probably *śrāmaṇera*) but that he stopped this practice later on,[35] likely when—or because—he became a *bhikṣu*. Within existing Buddhist ideologies, there are many justifications for why a ruler *should* bring a wrongdoer to justice.[36] In the monastic guidelines, the implementation of rules is often portrayed as being crucial to the (social) order. This sentiment is found in the set of monastic guidelines for Sera monastery from 1820: "For the teachers and the disciplinarians and the like not to implement the rules is to undo the Teachings from their base."[37]

## GOLDEN YOKES: RELIGIOUS LAWS AND
## SECULAR LAWS

The secular and religious "law systems" are regularly described as "the golden yoke" and "the silken knot" respectively. In post-Imperial sources the terms were used to describe the government of Trisong Detsen and Tritsuk Detsen. Nyangrel Nyima Özer (1124–1192), in his description of the era of fragmentation,[38] notes that during this time "the silken knot of the rule of the Dharma unraveled and the golden yoke of the rule of the king broke."[39] The most common descriptions attached to this imagery convey that the golden yoke of secular law is heavy and that the silken knot of the religious law is tight,[40] implying that both are tied around and resting upon the necks of citizens.

Interestingly, at least two sets of monastic guidelines have "golden yoke"[41] in their title. The set of guidelines written by the Seventh Dalai Lama for Namgyel is called "The Golden Yoke: The Monastic Guidelines Written for Namgyel Monastery."[42] The *chayik* for Tashi Lhunpo from 1876 also carries this phrase in its title and "explains" it in verse:

> This magnificent golden vajra-yoke
> That evokes joy among many intelligent ones,
> Clamps down on foolish people who behave badly,
> While it strengthens the two good traditions[43] and spreads joy.[44]

Here the phrase "golden vajra-yoke" appears to suggest that both the Dharma and secular authority were represented by this text, and indeed by its author, the Eighth Panchen Lama, whose political position had to be asserted and reasserted so as to prevent the Lhasa government from overpowering the monastery and its significant domains and assets.[45] In other cases, however, the golden yoke only refers to the internal rules of the Sangha, such as in a *chayik* written by the Thirteenth Dalai Lama in 1927: "The internal rules of the Sangha, which are in accord with place and time and which are in fact an abbreviated form of skillful means, are clean like the stem of a lotus and suitable to carry[46] like a golden yoke."[47]

For the Fifth Dalai Lama, the golden yoke belongs to religious imagery, although this does not necessarily exclude a possible secular affiliation. The closing verses of his monastic guidelines for Drepung convey that he sees the combination of the two traditions as leading to the happiness of all, with the Dharma being the primary factor:

> By means of the extremely heavy golden yoke
> Of the Buddhist law [upheld] at the palace that possesses the two traditions
> That rules every single beautiful region of the golden ones,
> May beings be led toward glorious happiness.[48]

The combination of secular and religious traditions was seen by many as the ideal way to rule a country. The legal code for Bhutan from the eighteenth century expresses a similar view, while using different imagery: "By placing the bejeweled parasol of the Buddha's Teachings on the spokes of the wheel of the state law, the field of merit will remain for long."[49]

The picture that emerges from the above examples portrays the need to uphold the law—be it religious or secular—for the sake of the general well-being, in which social order could be said to be implied. This suggests that both types of law implemented punishments for similar reasons and in similar ways.[50] As previously alluded to, this implementation of the rules, as contained in the monastic guidelines, concerned both monks and laypeople. We now turn to the way, and the extent to which, monasteries were involved in laypeople's justice.

## JUSTICE, THE MONKS, AND THE LAITY

A number of monastic guidelines make it clear that the extent of jurisdiction was not necessarily based on the division between laypeople and monks, but rather that it was geographically determined. The moment one found oneself on monastic territory, one needed to abide by the rules belonging to that institution. This is in fact a more general Tibetan notion, as captured in an oft-used proverb: "One should abide by the laws of the land of which one drinks the water."[51]

The Tibetan secular laws appear to have been viewed as "reliable suggestions"[52] rather than records of case law, and it is likely that this was also true with regard to local laws and customs. Many, presumably, were passed on orally. This was in most cases also true for monastery-level jurisdiction: most of the laws or rules would have been understood by the local populations, but were not accessible to them. The monastic guidelines then only address those instances in which the rules were regularly broken, when the rules were seen to be in need of clarification, or when they concerned activities that the monk authors felt particularly strongly about. One example is the killing of animals—either by hunting or slaughter—on monastic territory or within view of the monastic grounds.

The connection between territorial control—in particular with regard to hunting—and the monastic guidelines has been noted by Huber. He discusses the "sealing"[53] of specific areas, which "applied to a generally smaller, well defined unit of territory over which the monastery had rights and control."[54] The descriptions of monastic territory given in the guidelines are sometimes very detailed, while others are vague. The guidelines for Sera Je note that in the areas east of Sera: "One is not to buy or sell alcohol or slaughter animals. One may not burn black things,[55] or keep pigs and chickens. One is not to hunt birds and wildlife in the mountains behind the monastery and in the vicinity."[56]

The monastic guidelines for Pabongka are rather detailed with respect to the area where hunting was not allowed, which then could indicate the boundaries of monastic jurisdiction.[57] Kongtö Dungkar monastery in upper Kongpo forbade hunting and fishing in the hills and valleys up to one *krośa*[58] from the monastery. If these types of activities did take place the area had to be "sealed."[59] While this "territorial seal," according to Huber, became a "legislative act,"[60] it is not known here how exactly this legislation was enforced. In other monastic guidelines, various punishments for killing animals within monastic territory are suggested. Perhaps the most common punishment was "the offering" of a communal tea-round. The monastic guidelines from 1903 for Pelkor Chödè in Gyantse set out this punishment of offering a tea-round when a hunter or trader is found to have killed an animal within the stipulated parameters.[61]

Huber notes a more intriguing punishment, given by the Thirteenth Dalai Lama concerning Rongpo Rabten monastery: "When itinerant game hunters appear, they should be punished by gathering their weapons in the protector's [*sic*] temple and in addition exhorted once again to observe lawfulness."[62] According to Huber, other monastic guidelines mention that hunters and the like should be made to recite religious texts in the protectors' chapel.[63] Oaths even today are regularly sworn by the laity in the presence of the protectors. The chapels tend to be laden with (ancient or now defunct) weaponry, possibly in part for the above reasons. According to the traditional narrative, the protectors at the monastic territory were often the original chthonic inhabitants of the area, who were "converted" to Buddhism—thus to harm their land, and everything on it, would equate to upsetting these spirits.

Punishing laypeople for killing animals within the vicinity of the monastic territory was not simply seen as a prerogative of the monasteries, but as their *duty*. Monks, the guidelines tell us, were even burdened with the responsibility of patrolling the area and catching the lawbreakers. In the case of Phulung monastery[64] in 1947, it even came with extra paperwork:

> When illegal activities are committed by a couple of evil people, the lamas and the monks all need to—by means of starting a vigorous investigation—create a written agreement, in which a promise is made not to reoffend, or else there will be a set punishment, such as three bricks of tea, soup, flags, communal tea-rounds, scarves, and the like.[65]

Monastic grounds—often not agricultural land, and thus without much economic value—were to be protected by the monks. The guidelines for Tashi Lhunpo even note that monastic officials had to guard against animals moving about in the hills nearby, because their presence or their overgrazing could cause landslides, from which the monastery had to be protected.[66]

For the monks of Reting, however, the reasons for protecting the area around the monastery were formulated differently: "The birds and wild animals in this forest of Reting, the essence of enlightenment, and the foundation for the Kadam, are said to be the emanations of bodhisattvas. Therefore, no one—be they Mongolian, Tibetan, Hor, or nomads—may do them any harm, steal or kill them."[67]

Sometimes, the time spent protecting the monastic lands had some perks, either for the monastery as a whole or for the individual monks. The monastic guidelines for Pelyul Darthang describe the boundaries of the monastery and then state:

From where one can see the monastery, inside or outside, there abattoirs may not be maintained. If slaughter takes place, there is the punishment of the price attached to the meat. And if the buyers are still there then the meat *and* the price paid for the meat need to be both taken away.[68]

This means that both the seller and the buyer of the meat would be punished for being complicit in the maintenance of an illegal slaughterhouse. At the same time, of course, both the meat and the money could be confiscated, which may have served as an incentive for the monks to patrol the area. This early twentieth-century *chayik* also suggests a similar type of punishment for the selling of alcohol on monastic grounds: "When people buying and selling alcohol find themselves on monastic grounds, the alcohol and the profit of the alcohol need to be taken away."[69]

In other sets of guidelines it is more common to punish those carrying alcohol to the monastery by actually destroying their wares. The Mindröl Ling *chayik* states: "Even when a layman simply carries a vessel of alcohol beyond the border-marker, he needs to be punished, for example by breaking the vessel."[70] In Tsurpu the situation was similar, but the difference was that there actually needed to be an intention to break the rules: "When local people, pretending to be newly arrived visitors, turn out to be carrying vessels of alcohol back and forth to the residencies within the monastic compound, then the guards of the residencies have to take the discovered alcohol vessels and destroy them without trace."[71] Interesting here is also the mention of guards, who were likely to have been charged with "policing" the monastic compound.

The destruction of wares may have been the lightest of punishments, as a government decree from 1882 specifically intended to tackle the "use" of alcohol and women.[72] This decree, written for all the major Geluk monasteries in the Lhasa area,[73] states: "It is customary that when laymen or alcohol sellers are in any way seen, heard, or suspected of offering[74] alcohol to monks, a punishment according to secular law, which is heavy as a mountain, is given, so as to set an example."[75] In other cases, it was the trespassing itself that had to be punished. Women caught fetching water within the monastic compound had to be given a suitable punishment, such as being required to offer a butterlamp.[76]

It appears that monasteries, when it concerned the wider territory for which they were responsible, exercised their judicial authority regarding laypeople only in the most serious cases (such as killing), but when laws were broken "closer to home" the rules became stricter. It could be said that the laity and monks had to heed the same authority as soon as they found themselves within the gates of the monastery itself. A work on Tsurpu monastery remarks the following: "Once within the gates of the monastery, whether one is lay or ordained, high or low, male or female, young or old, everybody needs to heed the instructions of the three, the disciplinarian, the master and his aides, which is in accord with the contents of the Garchen's monastic guidelines."[77]

In the monastic guidelines for Drepung from 1682, the ordinary laypeople and monks also had to comply with the same basic rules: "Ordinary laypeople and monks may not ride their horses within the monastery. Loud songs and shouting at each other from afar and any loud noises may not be uttered."[78] In Jampa Ling too, the laity was expected to behave more like monks when visiting the monastic compound: "Within the boundaries of the monastery, it is inappropriate even for laypeople to fight, to sing, to smoke, to use snuff, or to play mahjong, and so on. Therefore, those who knowingly make such mistakes should be punished appropriately."[79] Similar kinds of typical lay behavior were also forbidden when people visited the monastery of Tengpoche in Nepal, and it was the disciplinarian who was given the task of making sure that these rules were upheld, so that "outside guests do not do things that are forbidden such as drinking alcohol, fighting, being loud and laughing."[80]

Justifications why laypeople were not allowed to behave in a certain way tend not to be given in the sources at hand. The guidelines from 1913 for Thobgyel Rabgyé Ling by the Thirteenth Dalai Lama lists things that neither the laity nor monks could do in the vicinity of the monastery, such as riding horses, singing, and having hairstyles that incorporate fabric, as these "are things that are disrespectful to the Sangha."[81]

The above selection of examples that show laity being affected by the monastery's rules strongly suggests that many Tibetan monastic institutions—at least from the seventeenth century onward and likely before that as well—held judicial authority over their own territories and were able to punish laypeople for killing animals, trespassing, and treating the monastic grounds as their playground.[82] Not only did rules pertaining to the laity exist, they also appear to have been exercised. The *chayik* are the documents par excellence that indicate these local laws and to whom they pertained. In the context of Tsurpu, this level of jurisdiction is explained succinctly:

> In short, all the monks, high or low, who are part of this monastery, as well as the faithful sponsors who live in the mountains surrounding the monastery, as well as the pilgrims—basically all, monks or lay, man or woman, good or bad—need to take into account the contents of the precious *chayik* that establishes the law of the disciplinarian, the masters, and their assistants.[83]

## MEDIATION, DISPUTES, AND COMMUNAL VIOLENCE

Able monks were often employed as intermediaries, often on a voluntary and individual basis. In particular, highly regarded monks were seen as ideal candidates for the job of "go-between" or mediator.[84] Tibetan historiographical accounts abound with narratives of revered monks preventing battles and other conflicts.[85] In many Buddhist cultures, the "holy man" is often seen to mediate between various social groups.[86] The Vinaya limits the extent of this mediation: the monk is not to act as a matchmaker, nor is he to engage in marriage counseling. For Tibetan monks, mediation of legal or violent disputes was not out of bounds. In Labrang, it seems, people even "preferred adjudication by the monastery."[87]

According to Goldstein, in Central Tibet this type of adjudication was the first resort for civil disputes, and it was only when such adjudication failed that cases were brought to the local leader.[88] This was also the case in other Tibetan Buddhist areas. In Spiti in the nineteenth century, people rarely had "recourse to the law courts, or even to the primitive justice dispensed by their chief the Nono." When someone's word was not trusted, he was made to swear an oath.[89]

Trusted and unbiased men were thus often called upon to intervene in disputes. In areas where monastics had good relations with the local population, these men were often monks. Of course, mediation and adjudication took place both inside and outside the monastery's walls. In some cases, monks are even reported to have pleaded on behalf of certain criminals for a reduction of a punishment that involved mutilation.[90] When monastic guidelines report on monks acting as conciliators, it is often not specified who their "clients" are. The Mindröl Ling guidelines mention that this role was to be taken seriously: "People who are strong in giving council should communicate sincerely and decide matters in accordance with the truth."[91]

For internal monastic matters, the obvious candidate for mediation would be the disciplinarian. The guidelines for Pelyul Darthang indicate that this person was not handed an easy task:

> From now on, the disciplinarian should not, when quarrels and suchlike occur, oversee major or minor disputes—whether internal or external, general or specific, large

or small—that are not relevant. Surely, one needs to continue to treat all the external and internal rules of the Teachings with priority. Therefore, no one should encourage him to act as go-between for others in disputes, whether they be high or low.[92]

From the above can be gleaned that the disciplinarian was asked to adjudicate various, perhaps personal, disputes, but that was not part of his job description. The involvement of the disciplinarian could easily lead to him losing the impartiality that was emphasized by so many *chayik*.

Disputes—the guidelines demonstrate—seem to have been a common feature of monastic life in pre-modern Tibetan societies. Occasionally, these arguments became violent. Precautionary measures had to be taken, such as the ban against any type of weaponry being brought into the monastery. The rules regarding this issue for Pelyul Darthang monastery are like those of many other monasteries: "It is not allowed for anyone to ride a horse, wear a knife, carry guns and the like within the monastic grounds."[93] For this monastery, it cannot have been very unusual for monks to carry arms *and* to use them, for it is stated: "Only those monks who have never used knives and guns may assemble during *poṣadha*[94] and the summer retreat."[95]

A Ladakhi monk who lived in Yangri Gar in Central Tibet before 1959 was able to confirm that monastic fighting was a rather ordinary occurrence: "In Tibet there were punishments for fighting, and there was a fair amount of fighting going on, but not here in Phiyang. If you would fight here, you would get expelled."[96] The most dangerous types of disputes were seen as those involving various groups of monks, pitted against each other, as it could lead to communal violence. One of these clashes is actually mentioned in the Drepung monastic guidelines. Apparently a Mongolian had fired a gun, thereby killing a monk who—to judge from his name—must have been a scholar monk. This episode seems to have occurred in the context of intercollegial feuding, for the text states:

> Even though previously, when the monastic houses fought over people and possessions, arrows and catapults used to be employed, other than the Mongolian Ngödrup Gyatso (dNgos grub rgya mtsho) firing a gun and killing Lubum Jampa (Glu 'bum rab 'byams pa), nothing else has occurred. Still, from now on firearms should not be used.[97]

The author goes on to warn that, in the case of illegal actions such as causing a rift in the Sangha and bringing down the Teachings by, for example, colleges and houses fighting each other, the ringleaders together with their gang were to be punished according to state law.[98]

It was worse when conflicts were not confined to the monastery, but when a third party was invited to participate. The same author of the Drepung monastic guidelines, the Fifth Dalai Lama, also wrote the guidelines for Gongra Ngesang Dorje Ling in 1664. His remarks highlight the volatile situation in which this recently "converted" monastery found itself. He saw it as a breeding ground for communal violence:

> When one has solicited the help of one's close friends or country-mates, who come into the compound as an army and act as accomplices and aides, joining in as avengers, and when the lama, the chant master, and the disciplinarian behave very badly by not considering it important to impose order, then the original ringleader needs to be expelled.[99]

Interestingly, monastics these days are still seen to take the side of their fellow countrymen when arguments arise, which is due to misplaced loyalty causing them to "throw their weight behind someone in a dispute just because he is from their locality, disregarding the right or wrong of the situation."[100]

This strong sense of local loyalty was compounded by the fact that monastic houses were, and still are, usually organized on the basis of regional origins. For monks who were a regional minority, this could result in getting bullied, as the *chayik* for Pelyul Darthang suggests: "No monk of this monastery, whether big or small, high or low, is to disturb the monks who have come from elsewhere by teasing, calling them names, or insulting them."[101] In this regard, the guidelines for Mindröl Ling warn: "Do not start fights that divide the community by slander, out of bias for one's own house."[102]

The Seventh Dalai Lama, as usual very much in agreement with the Fifth, notes in his guidelines for Namgyel Dratsang the following on communal fighting:

> Fights between colleges, regional groups, older and newer [monks], or mass fights with monks are all against the law and constitute "causing a rift in the Sangha"[103] and "bringing down the Teachings."[104] As the ringleader with his gang is punishable under the secular law, there is no need to go into detail here.[105]

Thus, monastic infighting was deemed to be a crime that was to be tried according to secular law, while this also was judged to cause a rift in the Sangha and to bring down the Teachings. This is a clear indication of the interwovenness of religious and secular policies *and* ideologies.

## INTERNAL JUSTICE: CRIME AND PUNISHMENT

Throughout this book we find references to different types of punishment for various monastic misbehavior. The most common one is the "offering" of something. This can be offering prostrations, butter, scarves, or money. Other punishments are doing menial tasks, getting expelled, or getting expelled as well as tried according to secular law.[106] More sporadic are mentions of corporal punishments.[107] It is important to note that the severity of penances varies greatly among the monastic guidelines, and there is thus no overarching understanding of what punishments fit which crimes. Furthermore, the manner in which monks are punished is often left to the discretion of the monk officials (usually the disciplinarian). In some cases, however, the penalties given are rather detailed. The *chayik* for Drigung Til from 1802 has a long section on crimes and punishments. It first addresses communal violence:

> Because this monastery consists of a large area, it would be wholly inappropriate to hold biases toward the upper or the lower part: all need to uphold the same ideals. If there are any quarrels, arguments, or physical fights, then [the punishment is] a communal tea-round, a hundred prostrations, three sets for the lama,[108] and a ceremonial scarf for the manager and the disciplinarian. If implements are used such as stones, sticks, or claws,[109] then [the punishment is] a communal tea-round, three hundred prostrations, pole-flags and scarves, five sets for the lama, and three sets each for the manager and the disciplinarian. If knives are drawn and blood is shed, then [the punishment is] a communal tea-round, a thousand prostrations, pole-flags and scarves, seven sets for the lama, and five sets each for the manager and the disciplinarian.[110]

Here we see a gradual increase in the severity of the punishment, as the harm inflicted on others gets more serious. The punishment is about three times more severe when one inflicts harm with a knife instead of through one's hands or words. The text continues:

> When people drink alcohol or smoke tobacco, then, because it smells bad and falls under intoxicants, or when someone arrives beyond the black pile of stones[111] riding a horse, [the punishment is] a communal tea-round, three thousand prostrations, pole-flags and scarves, nine sets for the lama, and seven sets each for the manager and the disciplinarian.[112]

This means that drinking, smoking, and riding horses into the compound are punished more heavily than stabbing a person with a knife! There may be a number of explanations for this, but it is likely that, while the previous penalties in all likelihood involved only monks, the latter penalty also affected laypeople. Perhaps the general consensus was that they could be fined more heavily than monks. The text goes on to describe "crimes" that could only be committed by monastics:

> If something illegal happens that is an obvious defeat (*pham pa*, S. *pārājika*) such as sexual conduct (S. *abrahmacārya*), then [the punishment is] a communal tea-round, ten thousand prostrations, pole-flags and scarves, ten sets for the lama, and nine sets each for the manager and the disciplinarian. Having offered this, then if he stays in the monastery, he needs to [first] give back the remainder of his vows[113] and if he does not genuinely abide by the trainings he then has retaken, he will be expelled.[114]

It seems here that, contrary to what is often thought, sexual conduct did not necessitate the expulsion of a monk.[115] Rather, the text explains what "reparations" needed to be made, which included the retaking of the monk's vows.

The text concludes its section on punishments: "If one talks back to the lama, or if one physically retaliates against the manager and the disciplinarian, all this person's things need to be neatly collected and he then is expelled."[116] The suggestion here is that answering back to the lama or punching a disciplinarian was potentially punished more heavily than breaking one's root vows, for here the option of staying in the monastery is not given. Possibly, this type of rebellious behavior was seen as more heinous than sex—the most un-monk-like behavior of all. However, in Mindröl Ling in the late seventeenth century, talking back to the disciplinarian was punished according to the severity of the occasion: "When there is backtalk the punishment is [the offering of] butterlamps. . . . If there is physical resistance he is either expelled from the monastery or made to give a communal tea-round, scarves or butterlamps of one measure depending on the gravity of the offense."[117]

In Phulung monastery in 1947, merely verbally retaliating or resisting the disciplinarian was punished relatively lightly: "When someone, while having done all sorts of things, still utters talk such as 'I am important, I am powerful' and—out of disregard for the disciplinarian—talks back to him, [that individual] needs be punished by doing prostrations, ranging from fifteen hundred through twenty-five hundred, depending on the gravity of the offense."[118]

When punishment is mentioned in the monastic guidelines, the flexibility of the rules is often emphasized and, in most cases, the type of punishment is left to the local monastic officials. In Pabongka monastery too, when actions not in accordance with the Vinaya were committed, the severity of the punishment had to fit the misdeeds: this could be the offering of butterlamps, scarves, or a communal tea-round.[119] By contrast, in Thailand in the 1960s, offenses incurred by the monks were punished by making them do domestic chores, such as sweeping the compound or cleaning the latrines.[120]

More in line with the Tibetan way of punishment, in early twentieth-century China, punishments were often physical, but fines of two to ten Chinese dollars were also common. If the offender did not have the money he would be beaten. Expulsion was rare and could only be demanded by the abbot. In the Chinese monasteries where the emphasis on meditation was less strong, penalties were milder. To judge from anecdotal information, at Tibetan monasteries the opposite seems to have been the case. In China, the offending monks were sometimes made to do three prostrations in front of a Buddha image. Monks with no money to pay the fine would have to do a greater number of prostrations. The mildest type of penalty was chanting a sūtra,[121] something I have not come across in the Tibetan context.

While in the Chinese monasteries the emphasis was on monetary punishments, this was relatively unknown in Tibet, partially also due to the relative scarcity of cash money. However, in recent times, it is more and more common for monks to be fined. In 2000, Sera Me monks in India were fined twenty-five rupees every time they skipped a debate session.[122] In the scholastic college of Drigung monastery in India, getting involved in a fight cost three hundred rupees.[123] It is unclear what the "proceeds" of these fines were intended to be spent on.

## A NOTE ON FORCED "OFFERINGS"

All in all, the above-mentioned penalties are relatively light and—at first glance—appear to be allowing a wrongdoer to "pay" for his bad actions by giving him a chance to accumulate merit, perhaps similar to doing penance. The prostrations, also the punishments of choice in sixth-century Chinese Chan monasteries,[124] suggest that this was an opportunity for the individual to generate good karma (although it is *never* reasoned in this way). Additionally, as these prostrations appear to have most frequently occurred in the presence of all the other monks, this punishment could also have been used as a way to put a rebellious monk in his place.[125] It has been noted that "[f]ines in kind were common, but they were always described as 'offerings'."[126] Furthermore, the texts conceptualize punishment very much as punishment (and not necessarily as offerings), since the word "punishment" (*chad pa*) is also employed, often in the same line. Still, butterlamps, scarves, and prostrations are first and foremost thought of as offerings.

The counterintuitive status of these punishments is also remarked upon by Ngawang Peljin:

> The internal rules talk about how first to tell someone he made a mistake, and that when it happens again he needs to do a hundred prostrations or give a hundred butterlamp offerings with his own money. Normally, butterlamps are offered out of faith, but here the person *has* to offer, whether he has faith or not.[127]

The offerings then, while by no means voluntary, were a way to practice generosity—although it can be debated how much merit would be accrued if the giver gave against his will. An important feature of the prostrations is that they were often done during the assembly: all of the monks present would then know that the monk did something wrong. It can also be seen as a way of making amends with a community whose reputation the misbehaving monk had potentially damaged.

The forced offerings that the authors of the monastic guidelines recommend to give as punishments are not primarily focused on the individual's morality or karmic status. However, there may have been an element of these punishments restoring a balance, within the community but also among the deities to whom the offerings were given.

## ON PHYSICAL PUNISHMENT

Monastic punishments were not in all instances easily rationalized from a Buddhist viewpoint. Corporal punishment, according to many eyewitness accounts in Tibetan monasteries, is one such example. The information on physical punishment in Buddhist cultures is diverse. For some, the case is quite clear-cut: "First of all we must note that there was no corporal punishment in monastic Buddhism."[128] Pachow, in a similar vein, comments that the Buddhists "do not inflict upon anybody any corporal punishment nor impose any fine, their punishments are comparatively very light."[129] More nuanced is the observation by Gethin, namely that "the use of physical violence as a punishment for breaking the rules of the monastic code seems nowhere to be endorsed in the early Buddhist vision of monastic life."[130]

While indeed in the Vinaya materials there are no known references to structural physical punishments for monks breaking rules or vows, textual material and oral history from a wide range of Buddhist cultures from different eras suggest that—as was (and is) the case in the domestic sphere—these punishments were not unheard of in monasteries. The British explorer Pereira, who visited Labrang monastery in Amdo in the early twentieth century, describes in some detail the monastic punishments he was told about:

> For discipline, there is a president (Jewa).[131] He has powers of punishment. For grave offenses a sheet of paper is put over the monk's face and he is branded on the forehead with a red-hot key and is then led to a small door and banished from the monastery. Another punishment is cutting off the ears and nose, but this is rarely, if ever, practiced. Another punishment is to suspend a monk by the hands from a tree, either entirely or with his toes just touching the ground, and he is kept suspended for different lengths of time up to two or three days. The commoner punishments are beatings, or else being fined. Even lamas are liable to be punished in these ways, though generally they are given the opportunity of getting away.[132]

Another traveler account is by Schram, who visited the border areas of Amdo and China in the 1920s: "At night, the disciplinarian with some of his lictors, armed with rawhide whips, makes a tour of the lamasery. Lamas found brawling, quarreling, or fighting are brought to the court of the intendant, where penalties are meted out in various brutal forms."[133]

While earlier authors, with their orientalist tendencies, may have been keen to point out the "brutal" punishments Tibetan monks bestowed upon each other, the most common reports are of physical punishments that were not excessive but also no mere slap on the wrist. Rogue monks tended to get punished by having to do prostrations or by getting beaten—neither for a prolonged time nor severely—by switches on the backside.[134] In Tibet, according to one of my informants, often only the young monks would receive these types of punishments; it was not considered an appropriate punishment for monks who were more mature.[135] Lobzang Döndrup, an elderly monk from Ladakh who spent a number of years in Drepung in Tibet in the 1940s and '50s, recounted how discipline was maintained there:

> If you would do something against the rules, the house-teacher would beat you with a stick.[136] There were several people who would keep order in the monastery: the disciplinarian, the abbot, the disciplinarian's assistants: if you would do something bad

they would report you to your house-teacher. He would then beat you or give you some kind of punishment. Prostrations were also a punishment, but it was mostly the stick. We never had to pay monetary fines or anything like that.[137]

In some monasteries, fines rather than offerings were an accepted way to penalize a monk. The *chayik* for the Nyingma monastery Tengpoche in Nepal from 1918 states: "When a small number of evil people are involved in improper things that are a disgrace to the Teachings, disregarding what is right, then by means of investigation, strict punishments that befit the wrongdoings need to be imposed, which may be either physical or material."[138] In some cases, the type of corporal punishment is specified, such as in the guidelines written by the Thirteenth Dalai Lama in 1927 for a Central Asian monastery: "Arguments and fights should be definitely punished relative to the wrongdoings, setting an example. This ranges from offering butterlamps and scarves to the protectors, to doing either a hundred or a thousand prostrations, or even to getting whipped."[139]

According to one informant, elderly monks could often be overheard exchanging "war stories" of their youths spent in the monasteries in pre-1950s Tibet, saying, "I did this and this, for which I got thirty lashes with the whip."[140] Currently, in Tibetan monasteries beating is no longer an acceptable form of discipline: these practices are being gradually phased out.[141] Some monk administrators, however, talk about how the old ways were more effective. Lama Tsültrim, a monk high up in the administration of a large monastery in exile, is highly critical of current-day discipline:

> The monks these days go everywhere. In the old days you needed to ask the disciplinarian for permission before you could go outside of the monastery. If you would get caught you would get fifty strikes on the backside. Now there is no physical punishment any more. Now the monks are all over the settlement and wander about at night.[142]

There are some monastic guidelines that seem to suggest that laypeople too were liable to get punished physically. The guidelines for Tashi Lhunpo, for example, outline the rules with regard to the use of alcohol. This eighteenth-century text states that no one, not even the lay officials, could drink or even carry alcohol in Tashi Lhunpo, and that people caught buying or selling intoxicants would receive a suitable corporal punishment to make them see the error of their ways, and that they would not be allowed the option of a payoff.[143] A later set of monastic guidelines by the Thirteenth Dalai Lama for a monastery in Chamdo[144] from the 1920s also suggests physically punishing anyone who broke the rules, be they lay or monastic: "In accord with various relevant legal decrees, which resulted in hunting being illegal in the [previously] established areas, such as behind and in front of the main monastery and its branches, when people do not uphold this, they need to be physically punished."[145]

Corporal punishment is mentioned only infrequently in the monastic guide-lines. It is important to bear in mind that the Tibetan *chayik,* as other Buddhist monastic guidelines, often merely portray a normative picture: the way procedural justice was imagined by the authors. Oral accounts and the like then show us to what extent these rules were put into practice and whether the general monastic attitude to justice concurred with that found in written sources. With the informa-tion at hand, it is difficult to ascertain the degree and manner of physical punish-ment that took place in the monasteries. A set of monastic guidelines for the Sakya Mangtro (Mang spro) monastery in Ladakh, written by the King Nyima Namgyel (Nyi ma rnam rgyal) in 1711, threatens with physical and even capital punishment, but only as an instrument of state law:

> As it would not be right to become worse than householders, by taking into consid-eration the honor of the Teachings and the beings based on the religious rules and the state law, a lama should not diverge from this path. A doer of great misdeeds is confined to his monk quarters[146] and all that he has is confiscated by the monastic authorities. After careful investigation, he is expelled by the *gaṇḍi* being beaten,[147] thereby preventing any reoccurrence among the pure ones. Afterwards, one is not to aid him. After this, no one, be they high or low, monk or lay, in whatever capacity, is allowed to act as his support or his accomplice. People who innocently disregard this will be penalized heavily by means of punishments of body and life through the secular law. Therefore, it is important for everyone to be very clear about what is right and wrong.[148]

Within the Tibetan secular courts, physical punishments and even the maiming of convicted criminals were not uncommon practices. These types of punishments did pose a challenge to monastics involved in legal issues. French's monk infor-mant who used to work at the courthouse in Lhasa stresses that he "as a monk" was not allowed to have anything to do with such punishments.[149] By contrast, the people who punished the monks in the monasteries must have always been monastics themselves.

### THE PUNISHMENT OF EXPULSION: *PĀRĀJIKA* AND OTHER REASONS

Among the lists of punishments that feature in most *chayik,* expulsion[150] is often given as the last resort, the highest possible penalty. But what crimes deserved such punishment, and what did it actually mean to get expelled? The threat of expul-sion has been alluded to in previous chapters. According to information based on oral history, actual expulsion was rather rare. In most, but not all, cases, people were expelled when one of the four "root vows" was broken. The procedures of expulsion, as described in the monastic guidelines, are rather intricate. The 1947 guidelines for Phulung elaborate on the process:

When it turns out that someone has gone against [any of] the four root vows, he will definitely be expelled from the Sangha. He—whoever it is—should offer a hundred prostrations in the back row during assembly. After that, he kneels and the disciplinarian sternly relates his misdeeds in public. Then, his monastic robes are taken away from him. He is made to wear white clothes[151] and he is justly given two hundred lashes of the whip in order to make him an example for everyone to see. After that, as settled on paper and established in the sūtras, he is expelled.[152]

The Thirteenth Dalai Lama suggests a slightly milder approach and recommends a fine for transgressing monks in Jampa Ling in Chamdo: "Those who have incurred defeats need to first give scarves to the people of their own college and then they give a fine of twenty-five official silver coins.[153] After that, as settled on paper and established in the sūtras, they are turned out."[154] A similar type of rigorous approach was suggested by the monastic guidelines for Menri monastery. Cech translates: "If the four root vows are weakened, then there should be no delay in expelling the monk from the monastery. He should leave naked with ashes thrown on him. He should not settle in the same area."[155]

Even more detailed is the account given in a recently written history of Tsurpu monastery. The author here reconstructs the *chayik* that was in use in his monastery before it went missing:

> If something occurs that necessitates someone being expelled from the monastery's community, the chant master and the disciplinarian report the culprit to the treasury of the monastic residency to which he belongs. The treasury then dresses him in white. It is appropriate that he gets a punishment in front of everyone consisting of two hundred lashes of the whip, without protesting. He then needs to give, as an offering, a communal tea-round for the assembly of monks, which can be elaborate, average, or limited, as well as scarves for the throne. He then is again placed among the ranks of the menial servants,[156] clerks, and taxpayers[157] of the person who was lord when he was a layperson. Whether he is taxed or not is generally decided upon, depending on how he has been punished and the gravity of his offense.[158]

Here the monk who breaks his vows is suitably "laicized," punished physically and financially, and returned as a subject to his previous "lord." The passage that follows elaborates on what vows were broken. The text then discusses what happens to the girl who caused the monk's downfall:

> The girl also needs to give two communal tea-rounds, as a confession to the assembly of monks, either elaborate or limited. According to the earlier *bCa' gsal*,[159] there was a custom of giving the girl two hundred lashings with the whip as a punishment, but after some time this went out of practice and it was substituted by the punishment of offering communal tea-rounds and by giving beautiful and expensive materials for a throne, pillar decorations or offering-materials and the like, acquired by honest means. Withdrawing her from the community[160] also occurred, making an example [of her], regardless of her social status. In the place of each lash of the whip one

kilogram[161] of gathered wood had to be given, and two hundred kilograms of wood then needed to be offered to the general assembly of monks—this is what it said in the monastic guidelines. Having consulted with various guiding materials, things differed according to the specifics of the personal inclinations of the person in charge. The custom was that the treasury decided on either a heavy or a light punishment that was fitting, making sure that it would not reoccur in the future.[162]

Another instance that mentions the female party getting punished can be found in a *chayik* written for another Kagyü monastery. In this *chayik* for the Sikkimese Phodang (Pho ldang) monastery from the eighteenth century, it is suggested that the woman had to be punished by making a confession and giving offerings, similar to those of the monk. She also had to vow not to reoffend. If the monk and the woman continued their practices, they needed to do the same types of confessions and in addition pay twenty-five coppers coins.[163]

Sometimes, even allowing the mere presence of women in the monastery was enough to get expelled—at least, according to the warning given in a text directed to the population of Sera monastery:

> Even if it is one's own mother, she may not obtain permission to stay unless it is during the "Great Giving ceremony."[164] If there are women in the monastery without permission, then the one responsible along with his accomplices will be expelled and the instigators each have to carry out the punishment of one communal tea-round and five hundred prostrations.[165]

Breaking the vow of celibacy is the most commonly mentioned "defeat" in the monastic guidelines.[166] While sometimes monastic guidelines took a more pragmatic approach toward sexual conduct, in particular in Himalayan regions,[167] for a monk to have sex *always* was tantamount to a loss of vows. A monastic community then could decide either to let the person retake his vows or to expel him. It is important to note that many other, and I dare say most, monastic guidelines—if they mention sexual conduct at all—do *not* take a tolerant stance with regard to issues of celibacy. To cite an example from the guidelines for Mindröl Ling monastery, written in 1698: "When someone is suspected of having had intercourse, he needs to be investigated and if it is found to be true, he is to be expelled under the sound of the very loud *gaṇḍi*. Even if his [case] seems to have supporters, it needs to be put an end to, for it has been determined that it was 'the first *pārājika*.'"[168]

A recurring myth, upheld by scholars even today, is that celibacy was only enforced in Geluk monasteries and that the attitudes toward sex in other institutions were more *laissez-faire*.[169] While it is not possible to make claims on the actual practices of these non-Geluk monastic institutions, on the basis of the textual sources at hand it can be stated in no uncertain terms that on the level of monastic *policy and ideology,* sexual conduct was never simply tolerated. In fact, the emphasis on celibacy is found as often in non-Geluk monastic guidelines as it is in the Geluk ones. Thus, the notion that monastic institutions other than Geluk monasteries displayed a general, or even ideological, disregard for upholding the vow of celibacy needs to be put to bed once and for all.

Another set of guidelines for a Nyingma monastery, this time for Tengpoche from 1918, is equally intolerant of vow breakers:

> As soon as a defeat of the four roots has occurred, the person who has broken his promise to his lama is expelled under the sound of the *gaṇḍi*. Not being allowed to leave behind even his boot,[170] he has to survive in the [lay] community himself and in accordance with state law.[171]

The guidelines written in 1938 for Dophü Chökhor Ling give a reason why these monks may no longer stay at the monastery: "A *dge tshul* or *dge slong*, however good he is, who has transgressed the four roots should be expelled, as he can no longer partake in either Dharma or material goods together with the Sangha."[172]

Regularly, the monastic guidelines imply that monks who break their vows may not take their material wealth with them. The South Monastery of Sakya did not allow the expelled monk to take his possessions with him, and his things would be passed on to a monk relative in the same monastery. In other places in the vicinity of Sakya, however, an ex-monk could take his things, provided he admitted his transgression and offered the monk community a communal tea-round. The monk who tried to hide his faults, however, would be entirely dispossessed.[173]

Naturally, it was not just breaking the vow of celibacy that was punished by expulsion. The *chayik* for Jampa Ling from 1927 notes the range of "crimes" that could possibly result in getting sent away:

> When there is someone who has been stained by the faults of the four roots and alcohol, by for example having hurt [another] by stones, knives, and weapons, then the wrongdoer gets expelled without chance for appeal.[174] After an assessment of the severity of the misdeeds he is punished by the lama and the officials with, for example, a communal tea-round by general rule or by being returned to lay life. And when the monastery has done its task for the general benefit independently, the general populace should then take [this] layperson as their responsibility.[175]

As mentioned previously in this chapter, violence was a problem in many monasteries throughout the ages. A teacher at the Drigung monastic college in India acknowledges that sometimes this type of violence still occurs.

> If weapons, like knives, are involved, the monks get expelled. One has to always look at the circumstances, though. If someone gets into trouble again and again and when this is addressed he talks back to the teacher, then sometimes there is no way other than to expel him. Most of the time, however, someone like that leaves before he can get expelled. Once they are expelled they cannot come back.[176]

The *chayik* written by the Fifth Dalai Lama for Gongra Ngesang Dorje Ling lists intercourse, killing a person, stealing something of value, and hurting others as crimes that could lead to expulsion. The text also adds the smoking of tobacco and stealthily using the Sangha's general possessions for oneself.[177] The latter issue of using the monastic community's possessions is also seen by the author of the *chayik* for Dophü Chökhor Ling written in 1938 as a reason to send a monk away: "If it transpires that a person has taken additional donations and salary, he will be expelled."[178]

## REENTERING THE MONASTERY

So far, the technical term "expulsion" has been used to translate the Tibetan *gnas dbyung*. But what did this entail? Was a monk permanently expelled, banned from the monastery, or was there a way to make amends? Clarke has criticized the translation of "expulsion" for the Sanskrit *asaṃvāsa*. He argues that, according to the Vinayas, being no longer in communion—the actual meaning of *asaṃvāsa*—did not equate to expulsion.[179] It is argued that in the Indian case it was not entirely clear what happened to a monk who committed a *pārājika*. The examples given above, however, make it rather clear that in the Tibetan context, *gnas dbyung* meant becoming dislocated, being made to physically leave the monastic grounds rather than simply to no longer be in communion.[180] As far as I am aware, the more Vinayic *gnas par mi bya ba*, which is a translation for *asaṃvāsa*, is not used in the *chayik*. Thus, while it is clear that expulsion was a punishment given to Tibetan monks, what happens after that is not.

Clarke counters the widespread notion that monks who, for example, had sex were "immediately and irrevocably expelled from the Buddhist order."[181] He argues that this equation of sex with permanent expulsion has been created by "modern commentators," but is not supported by Indian Buddhist monastic law codes.[182] In the Tibetan situation, we have seen that the punishment of expulsion, be it for a *pārājika* or otherwise, was not always immediate. Rather, many monastic guidelines recommend a process of careful investigation. Furthermore, in some cases there was a way back to the monastery. While many guidelines state that monks who have been expelled elsewhere may not be allowed into the monastery,[183] the return to monkhood was technically not impossible. This is in line with the fact that all Vinayas, except the Pāli Vinaya, allow men to remain members of the monastic community "if truly remorseful."[184]

An example of a *chayik* in which reentering the monastery appeared possible is the set of monastic guidelines for the Sikkimese Phodang monastery by the Fourteenth Karmapa (Theg mchog rdo rje, 1797–1868?), composed in 1846. In this text, he—possibly taking the specific circumstances of Sikkim into account—mentions inmates of the monastery who have had sex. They can, he states, remain in or perhaps "reenter" the monastery and the monastic group to which they belonged. This can only take place after the person in question has made extensive reparations in the form of offerings to the Three Jewels and the monastic community, has confessed his faults, has made prostrations in the assembly, and has "renewed his seat"[185] in the assembly. What is made clear is that the monk, having had intercourse, effectively loses his monastic vows and therefore has to retake them.[186] However, this does not deny the offender future monkhood. Risley, who may have had direct or indirect access to a *chayik* in use in "Pemiongchi" (Padma yang rtse) monastery in the late nineteenth century, makes a similar observation in his *Gazetteer of Sikhim*:

> The regulation which is most frequently violated is that of celibacy; but in most of the institutions other than Pemiongchi celibacy is not observed. Should it be proved that a Pemiongchi monk consorts with women, he will be expelled by a chapter, unless it be his first offence and he prays publicly for forgiveness, and then is awarded some penance and pays a fine of 180 rupees according to the rules of the lChags-yig [sic: *chayik*].[187] He must also pay over again the entrance fees and presents as before.[188]

Clearly then, the Tibetan monastic guidelines cited above seem to follow Clarke's findings regarding Vinaya, in that they imply that sex does not *necessarily* lead to expulsion, and that retaking the vows was possible. Pelyul Darthang monastery's guidelines show a willingness to allow even murderers back among the ranks:

> Those who have been dismissed from the yellow ranks, such as those who have started a family, have killed a man, who have done things like robbing and deceiving people by, for example, taking their wealth, or otherwise, those who have insulted others by having caused fights, arguments, and strife, when they reenter the assembly, may only do so after having developed the preliminaries, having been engaged in various practice sessions, and having confessed.[189]

As indicated above, the people who reenter are, in terms of their vows, new monks and thus need to take a junior position:

> When they do enter the assembly, they sit in the lowest row, and not in the higher rows without having taken vows. When they enter the assembly they need to have quit their previous bad behavior. If not, then they need to be dismissed from the rows of the assembly and unless they are punished suitably, they may not be allowed back in just like that.[190]

The text furthermore states that these people, even if they are allowed into the assembly, may not be promoted to lama, chant master, or teacher of ritual dance.[191] This effectively means that monks "with a past" could not occupy positions in which they had to fulfill an exemplary or public function.

## STATE INVOLVEMENT IN MONASTIC LEGAL PROCESSES

As we have seen above, the monastic guidelines occasionally recommend handing over a monastic offender to the "secular authorities." Particularly regarding the issue of murder, the case is almost always referred to "secular law"—which may have meant different things at different times, but always indicated a legal authority outside the monastery.[192] In the same way, Goldstein comments that "murder cases were always considered to be under the jurisdiction of the government; the government retained ultimate control over the taking of human life."[193] Thus when rogue monks were involved in fights that ended in death, there would have been both monastic and secular punishment.[194] According to the Mindröl Ling guidelines all crimes that fell under general law needed to be reported to the headman at the estate.[195] It is unfortunately not specified what crimes these were and what was to happen next.

We do know that in the early twentieth century, it was not only murder for which monks were punished under secular law. Bell reports that the Drepung ringleaders who tried to start a rebellion against the Tibetan government were beaten, expelled, and subsequently punished under secular law.[196] Furthermore, a photograph taken during Bell's mission to Lhasa in 1920–21 shows a Drepung monk with his head in stocks. The note accompanying the picture states that this was his punishment for forging currency notes.[197] Naturally, a close relationship between the monastery and the central government made the threat of secular punishments more likely.

A set of guidelines written in 1920 and directed to the whole of Sera monastery— which, of all large monasteries, was physically the closest to the Ganden Phodrang government in Lhasa—attempts to add an extra layer of state control: "People who have the responsibilities of scholars but do not behave accordingly, who disgrace the Dharma or the practitioners of the Dharma, should be suppressed according to secular law, without relenting."[198] Elsewhere in the same text there is a relatively long section on the occurrence of people in the vicinity posing as monks, who were behaving badly.[199] The work states that it was not allowed to count these people among the Sangha:

> And if there are still people who stay on pretending, like summer grass pretends to be a winter worm and a rabbit pretends to be a rock, then the officials who have agreed to let them stay may not act as if they did not know, because they themselves were in charge. After they [the officials] have been expelled, they are punished heavily for this according to secular law, and then they are banished.[200]

Here, it is not just the people who pretend to be monks who get punished according to state law, but also those monastic officials who allow them to stay, in all likelihood accepting bribes in return for this favor. This shows that having these people live in the vicinity was probably seen as a security threat. Sera monastery's great power also meant being responsible for keeping imposters at bay.

The "purification" of the Sangha was thus, contrary to what occurred in, for example, Sri Lanka, Thailand, and occasionally even in Mongolia,[201] not directly

the responsibility of the state but of the monasteries that were guided and, perhaps, goaded by the ruler. This was only the case when this leader was in a position to assert himself, for example during the rule of the Thirteenth Dalai Lama.
In light of the contents of a number of monastic guidelines, the picture of Tibet
as a centralized state ruled by a theocratic government in Lhasa is not convinc-
ing.[202] Monasteries were, for the most part, self-regulating bodies. The threat of
secular law was merely a last resort. This is further exemplified by Jamgön Mipham
(1846–1912), who wrote *A Treatise on Ethics for Kings: An Ornament for Rulers* for
a prince of the kingdom of Dergé:

> However, in this degenerate age,
> There are many monks who are exceedingly unruly.
> When they cannot be disciplined
> Through the sangha council's religious procedures,
> Then the king needs to do this.[203]

Elsewhere in the same work, the author stresses that the ruler should leave the
punishment of monks who have transgressed their vows to the discretion of the
monastic authorities.[204]

More research is needed to establish the relationship between secular and
monastic laws in Tibetan culture, in particular with regard to the influence of
monastic rulings and punishments apparent in governmental regulations. An
interesting example of this is the description of how government officials were
punished for faulty behavior. They were to make prostrations, and if their position
had become untenable, they were made to wear white clothes and driven out of
the premises on a donkey.[205] This is more than vaguely reminiscent of how monks
were expelled from their monasteries according to the descriptions given above.

Another noteworthy issue is that of the legal status of the monastery as a safe
haven for others. In Sri Lanka, in the tenth century, wanted criminals could seek
refuge in the monasteries from where they could not be extradited. During that
time, the king had transferred the judicial authority he previously enjoyed over
the property of the Sangha to the monastery, allowing and requiring the monasteries to manage their own property in all aspects.[206] Several remote monasteries in eighth-century China exercised a similar level of autonomy: they seem to
have regularly sheltered less savory characters.[207] Considering that certain Vinaya
rules, such as that of not allowing wanted criminals to become monks, appear to
have been created to appease the secular authorities, it is puzzling that monasteries
would offer amnesty to these people, to say the least.

One does not expect the Tibetan monastic guidelines to offer wanted criminals
an escape from justice, but the monastic guidelines for Gongra Ngesang Dorje
Ling contain some surprising information. This text was written by the Fifth Dalai
Lama for a monastery that had previously sided with those who opposed the

Mongolian troops that had helped the Dalai Lama gain temporal power. While the text does not call on the monastic authorities to undermine state law, it declares: "When there are 'criminals' who have broken other [people's] laws and ask for refuge, one should be of benefit."[208] The text, unfortunately, offers no context for this statement, making it difficult to explain. What can be noted from this remark, however, is that in the late seventeenth century even the highest political authority, the Dalai Lama himself, was aware that his government did not have the power to submit all wrongdoers to justice, thereby acknowledging the legal plurality that Tibetan areas had known for centuries.

While state interference in monastic affairs has clear historical precedent, current governmental regulations in Tibetan areas are perceived by monks as going against monastic rule,[209] in particular with regard to the expulsion of monks. The age limits set for monks entering the monastery and the appointment of those to high positions serve as further examples. With the exception of murder, treason, and forgery, on the whole, the historical monastic guidelines demonstrate that monasteries themselves had the authority to make these types of decisions.[210] This is exemplified by the fact that the individual monastic guidelines contain such a wide range of regulations regarding legal issues.

## MONASTIC BUDDHIST NOTIONS OF JUSTICE

The distinctions between monastic law and secular law, which need further scrutiny, are occasionally clearly demarcated in the text and at other instances left unclear. Both the Dharma and law are concerned with maintaining a balance of power, ultimately bringing about wide-reaching effects, the primary of which is the happiness and welfare of sentient beings. A Bhutanese law code lays bare the connections that are less visible in the monastic guidelines: "Well-being in all the lands depends on the state law being in accord with the Dharma. The prophecy of the Dharma-cakravartin on governing the state can be truly seen in the Teachings of the Buddha; other than that what else is there?"[211]

In many ways, law may be seen as promising justice and social order, but within Tibetan society there seems to have been awareness that secular law is not separable from cosmic effects and that social order thus is not dependent on this type of justice alone. The passage from monastic guidelines from 1918 cited earlier, connecting the purity of the Sangha, the happiness of the land, and the adherence to the sixteen pure "human rules" further illustrates this point.

Monks, we know from other sources, were part of the legal system in Tibet, but the influence of monastic ideology on legal structures has not yet been established, although there are indications suggesting that this influence was substantial.[212] The monastic guidelines that have stronger links to the state authorities tend to show more involvement in the execution of justice, but on the whole most monasteries, regardless of their affiliation, demonstrate an awareness of both their rights and responsibilities. Meting out punishments was one of those responsibilities, which clearly never had "a return to inner morality" as an objective.[213] Rather, according to the texts, penalties served "to make an example" of the perpetrator, preventing others from doing the same in the future. Failing to carry out that duty of punishing led to further punishment. This may have some correspondences to descriptions of the ideal behavior of Bodhisattvas that feature in some Indic Buddhist texts. In the *Bodhisattvabhūmi,* for example, the Bodhisattva is not simply required to correct the behavior of others by punishing: he commits a fault if he neglects to do so.[214] The emphasis in the monastic guidelines also lies on a fair but pragmatic application of the rules: justice is not done at all costs. It should be noted that karma, the *law* of cause and effect, is not engaged at any level in the monastic guidelines.

Notions of fairness and justice—if at all mentioned in Buddhist Studies literature—are often addressed in terms of the workings of karma. Tempting though it may be to then conclude that for Buddhists the natural law of karma can be equated with all types of justice, such as social, punitive, and conciliatory justice, it is clearly mistaken to conflate a doctrinal issue with actual practice. Collins argues this point in the following way:

> In the European-Christian case, everyone is intimately aware, as a matter of day-by-day experience, of the continuous and changing way ideals and the *Lebenswelt* coexist, of their sometimes stark, sometimes subtle and nuanced relations of contradiction, complementary opposition, or agreement; and so it is easy to see immediately that such an abstract and simplistic deduction from universal and ideal premises—God will punish, therefore there should be no need for law—is quite inappropriate for historical understanding, however admirable the ideals may (or may not) be. The Buddhist case is just the same.[215]

The way in which monastic law is understood by monastic authors themselves is rather similar, if not identical to law outside of the Tibetan monastery. Laws—and by extension justice—serve to secure social order, making it "particularly effective as an instrument of government."[216] In the Tibetan societies, where the government has traditionally been a symbolically prominent yet functionally absent factor, the distinctions between law and custom,[217] or law and morality, are less easily made.[218] Buddhist morality and secular law ultimately are both "normative social practices that set standards for desirable behavior and proclaim symbolic expressions of social values."[219]

Religion is often seen as providing a means of social control, which implies "a system of rewards and punishments, either internalized during socialization or externally supplied by institutions, or both."[220] The monastic guidelines emphasize externally supplied punishments, but not because karma is not part of the equation, or not believed in. In other words, the goal of promoting justice—by, for example, making a monk do prostrations—is not in order to allow him to accumulate merit, thereby cancelling out his misdeeds. Rather, it serves to keep the peace, to restore the reputation, to promote a sense of cohesion, and to strengthen the identity of the monastic community. While Buddhism is regularly both praised and vilified for its individualist tendencies, on a monastic level the execution of justice was a communal exercise and karma played only a minor part. This notion of justice as being communal and for the sake of social order is strongly connected to the perceived responsibility of the monastic community in society.

# 8

# Maintaining (the) Order

## Conclusions

### THE MONASTIC INSTITUTION AND TIBETAN
### SOCIETY IN AN AGE OF DECLINE

While this book focuses on Tibetan monasteries in pre-modern times, many issues or themes that are addressed here are widespread among Buddhist cultures. One of these is that—as we live in the *kaliyuga* (*snyigs dus*), the degenerate age—the Buddhist Teachings are seen to be in decline. In fact, over the course of history, Buddhists have always seen themselves as living in the degenerate age. Another important issue shared by many cultures that have monastic Buddhism is the notion that the Sangha—the community of monks and nuns—is the guardian and protector of the Buddhist Teachings. There are many Buddhist texts written in different times and places that contain a message similar to "as long as the Sangha remains, so will the Dharma." The Tibetan monastic guidelines also motivate their audience to behave well, employing similar rhetoric. It is even suggested, among others in the 1918 *chayik* for Tengpoche, that keeping to the rules of (monastic) discipline could extend the Buddhist Teachings' limited lifespan ever so slightly: "One should, solely motivated by the pure intention to be able to extend the precious Teachings of the Victor even a little bit in this time that is nearing the end of the five hundred [year period],[1] assume the responsibility to uphold one's own discipline."[2]

In the Mindröl Ling *chayik*, maintaining and protecting the Teachings of the Buddha and striving for the enlightenment of oneself and others were seen to depend upon whether individuals knew restraint based on pure moral discipline.[3] Clearly, the Dharma and the Sangha were perceived to have a strong symbiotic relationship. While the two concepts mentioned above—that of the decline of the Dharma and that of the Sangha's role as the custodian of the Teachings—no doubt greatly influenced Buddhist societies and their (notions of) social policy, the sources at hand only substantiate this for Tibetan societies.

Often, when speaking of one's social responsibilities in a Buddhist context, the finger is pointed to karma. It is seen as an explanatory model for the way a Buddhist society dealt, and still deals, with societal inequalities and injustices. Spiro sums up this view succinctly: "inequalities in power, wealth, and privilege are not inequities," as these inequalities are due to karma, and thus "represent the working of a moral law."[4] While karma indeed works as an explanatory model for how things became the way they are now, it does not explain why things *stay* the way they are. In the context of Tibet, the limited degree of societal change throughout history is remarkable[5] and the influence of monastic Buddhism on this phenomenon is great. Even today's monks are concerned with limiting change, as Gyatso remarks: "The principal task that monks set themselves is self-perpetuation of their traditions and the institutions that safeguard them."[6] It can thus be argued that the monasteries were "extremely conservative" and that, while there was a pressing need to "adapt to the rapid changes of the twentieth century, religion and the monasteries played a major role in thwarting progress."[7]

The dominance or, in other words, the religious monopoly of the monasteries meant that they had—theoretically—the potential to use their organizational power and skills toward the development of things like education and healthcare accessible to all, poverty relief, and legal aid. However, history teaches us that the institutions which political scientists and others generally see as promoting social welfare were never established in Tibet.[8] It is too simplistic to explain the urge for self-perpetuation and the lack of institutional social activism in terms of the greed and power that large corporations are often seen to display. Rather, I propose that the two very pervasive notions alluded to previously—that of the Dharma in decline and the Sangha as the protector of Buddhism—are much more nuanced explanations as to why certain things often stayed the way they were.

Connecting the decline of the Buddha's Teachings to a penchant toward conservatism is not new. Nattier suggests that the perspective that the Teachings will eventually and inevitably disappear from view "could lead to the viewpoint we actually find in much of South, Southeast, and Inner Asian Buddhism; namely, a fierce conservatism, devoted to the preservation for as long as possible of the Buddha's teachings in their original form."[9] East Asia is excluded from this list, because, as Nattier argues, there the age of decline meant that one had to just try harder. Tibetan understandings of this notion are varied and have not been sufficiently explored, but generally they seem to vacillate between the idea that the Teachings *will* disappear and the belief that being in an age of decline means that being good is more challenging.[10] Indeed, the two concepts are not mutually exclusive. Pointing to the notion that we live in the age of decline (*kaliyuga*), which makes life (and thus maintaining discipline) more difficult, or emphasizing the belief that the Dharma will one day not be accessible to us anymore, are pervasive tropes and even justifications in Tibetan culture, both in pre-modern texts and among contemporary Tibetan Buddhists, be they laypeople or monks.[11]

Further contributing to the conservatism provoked by living in an age of decline is the monopoly position of Tibetan Buddhism. Throughout the documented history of Tibet, monks and monasteries have played dominant roles. They hardly ever had to compete with other religions or obstinate rulers. Not having any competition means not having to adapt or change. In that sense, Tibetan Mahāyāna monasticism is more akin to the monasticism of Theravāda countries such as Thailand, Burma, and Sri Lanka and less like that of Mahāyāna countries like China, Korea, and Japan, making the categories of Mahāyāna and Theravāda less meaningful when looking at monastic Buddhism in a comparative way. While this book only examines the Tibetan situation in some detail, it is likely that this theory explaining why societal change was rare, slow, or difficult is also applicable to most Buddhist societies where monasticism was widespread and where Buddhism had a monopoly position. It is for scholars of other types of Buddhism to test this theory.

### MONASTIC GUIDELINES FOR AND AGAINST CHANGE

*If we want things to stay as they are, things will have to change.*
—TOMASI DI LAMPEDUSA [1958] 2007: 19

The monastic guidelines presented in this book show the internal organization of the monastery: where to sit, what rituals to perform, who to appoint as monk official, and how to punish bad behavior. More importantly, these monastic guidelines convey the position of the monastery in society and its perceived role. The texts display a strong need for the monasteries to maintain their traditions. The changes that the monk authors implement in these texts are mostly geared toward the monastic institution remaining the same.

The guidelines show that the monastic authorities were willing to take measures that, in the modern day and age, appear at times rather harsh, politically incorrect, or even unjust. Some examples of these measures are given in this study: people from the lowest classes were sometimes barred from becoming monks, thereby preventing those classes from employing the monastery as a vehicle for social mobility. At other times, boys were levied from families as a sort of "monk tax."[12] Often, monasteries gave out loans with rather high levels of interest (between ten and twenty percent), which in some cases caused families to be indebted for generations to come. Some monastic institutions permitted lay residents, who worked the monastic estates; in fact, the monasteries had the prerogative to make these people perform corvée labor on monastic grounds. In other instances, the institutions were able to penalize the laity for not adhering to the rules that were in place on monastic territory.

The reasons for proposing or implementing these policies were clearly not primarily motivated by greed but by the urge for self-perpetuation and by adherence to the Vinaya rules. Still, the existing levels of inequality were often maintained and reinforced in this way.[13] The close association of religion with the status quo is, of course, neither exclusively Tibetan nor Buddhist; it is a feature of organized religions all over the world. Martin Luther King, expressing his disappointment, famously remarked: "Is organized religion too inextricably bound to the status quo to save our nation and the world?"[14]

Throughout Tibet's recorded history, the dominant position of the monastery was rarely challenged openly by ordinary people. Is this because both monks and laypersons perceived the existing societal structures in place as just or justifiable? One can only hypothesize. In order to do that, we need to return to the two concepts mentioned earlier: the age of decline and the Sangha as the custodian of the Dharma. If the Dharma is in danger of decline and the members of the Sangha are the only ones who can safeguard it, is it not right that the monastery does everything in its power to continue itself, even if that means making sure that lower-class people do not become monks, because their presence in the community would deter potential upper-class benefactors and potentially upset local deities? Even if it means forcing boys to become monks when the monk population was seen to drop? Surely, desperate times call for desperate measures. And in the *kaliyuga*—the age of decline—times are almost always desperate. It appears that most, if not all, policy was ultimately focused on the preservation of the Sangha, which in actual practice translated to the maintenance of the monasteries that facilitated the monkhood.

Was this safeguarding of the Sangha seen as serving society as a whole? And if so, how? These are equally difficult questions to answer, because almost all Tibetan authors were products of Buddhist monasticism—alternative voices are hardly ever heard. We do know that—despite the fact that there was a degree of force and social pressure—the ordinary population has always willingly contributed to the continuation of the monkhood. Ultimately, even the simplest Tibetan farmer would be aware that Buddhism—in any form—contributed to his happiness and his prosperity. If the Sangha, then, was as pivotal in the upkeep of that vehicle of utility, ordinary people knew they could contribute by making sure that the Sangha survive the test of time. Thus, the monks were (and are) a field of merit (S. *puṇyakṣetra*), not just because they enabled others to give—on the basis of which people could accumulate merit—but also because the monks perpetuated this very opportunity of accumulating merit. And monks maintained their status as a field of merit by upholding the Vinaya rules, their vows. This highlights the fact that, while it is often thought not to have had a clear societal function, the Vinaya *did* impact Tibetan society, albeit implicitly. This makes the view that Tibetan monasticism existed solely to perpetuate itself one-sided, to say the least.[15]

Aside from being a field of merit, Tibetan monks were also involved in other ways to serve laypeople, namely by performing rituals to appease the many spirits that were seen to reside in Tibet and the Himalayas. These worldly deities wreaked havoc when angered and could cause untimely rains, hail, and earthquakes. Important here is that these spirits particularly disliked change. The author of the monastic guidelines for the whole of Sikkim, Sidkeong Tulku, who introduced many religious and economic reforms, met with an untimely death in 1914 at the age of thirty-four. A highly placed Sikkimese Buddhist related the account of his death to Charles Bell and explained this unfortunate event by saying that Sidkeong Tulku, at that time the Mahārāja of Sikkim, had angered the spirits by his new ideas, resulting in his passing.[16]

Spirits, often addressed as Dharma protectors but also occasionally as local protectors (*sa bdag, gzhi bdag*), feature prominently in the monastic guidelines. Often, in the closing lines of the monastic guidelines they are called upon to protect those who follow the rules set out in the work and to punish those who go against them, according to one work, "both financially and by miraculous means."[17] Some of the surviving scrolls containing the monastic guidelines depict the school's or lineage's most important protectors at the bottom.[18] In this study I have argued that the spirits warranted the maintenance of traditions and purity in the monasteries. This is probably one of the reasons why some monasteries did not admit aspiring monks from the lower classes. To please the protector deities was to keep things as they were.

Again, the monks' role in all of this was to preserve the balance, to maintain the status quo. And again, the preservation of the monastic vows was as important— if not more important—than performing the right kinds of rituals. A Bhutanese legal code, written in 1729, for example, presents a prophecy that says: "When the discipline of the Vinaya declines, vow-breakers fill the land / With that as its cause the happiness of beings will disappear."[19] Viewed in this light, lay Buddhists and monks both had a stake in the maintenance of the Vinaya and in the appeasement of the spirits.

Commenting on the situation in Ladakh in recent times, Mills remarks that "the tantric powers of a monastery which lacked firm discipline were occasionally questioned by laity."[20] While the laity is clearly underrepresented in Tibetan sources, a number of scholars and travelers report on the spirits' influence over the lives of ordinary Tibetans. Tucci notes: "The entire spiritual life of the Tibetan is defined by a permanent attitude of defence, by a constant effort to appease and propitiate the powers whom he fears."[21] Ekvall mentions the soil owners (*sa bdag*) as the spirits who exercised "the most tyrannical control over the activities of the average Tibetan."[22] This presented monks and laypeople with a common cause: to preserve Buddhism at any cost, thereby maintaining equilibrium. This contrasts with Mills's contention with regard to Geluk monasticism that the monastery's religious and ritual authority is conceived of primarily in terms of "subjugation" or disciplining the surroundings, which—according to him—includes the laypeople.[23] In the light of information presented here, it appears more fitting to think of the monasteries' religious authority as geared toward *negotiation* rather than subjugation. The monks' role was to negotiate the spirits, the laypeople, and change in general. Monasteries did not only hold power and authority; they were also burdened with the responsibility of taking care of their surroundings.

Perhaps the Tibetan monastic institutions were, just like the early Benedictine monasteries, perceived as "living symbols of immutability in the midst of flux."[24] However, the overall reluctance to change did not mean that there was no change. To present past Tibetan societies as static would be ahistorical. Throughout this study, I have pointed out when the monastic guidelines indicate organizational and societal changes. At the same time, change—the focus of most contemporary historical research—has not been the main concern of this book. In this, I am in agreement with Dumont, who states: "The modern mind believes in change and is quite ready to exaggerate its extent."[25]

The Tibetan situation echoes Welch's observations of the situation of Chinese Buddhist monasteries during the early twentieth century, noting that "the monastic system was always in the process of slight but steady change."[26] While slight change is more difficult to ascertain than widely reported historical events, no doubt detecting and understanding continuity has a greater effect on our understanding of any given society.

Miller has argued that many of the institutional roles commonly attributed to the monastic system in Tibet were not really inherent to it, but that it varied in accordance with the differing social, political, and economic contexts.[27] While these varying contexts have been remarked upon throughout this book, it needs to be noted that Miller's statement is not entirely correct. When looking at the monastic guidelines that are centuries and hundreds of miles apart, themes and roles that are shared in common can be distinguished. Possibly the most pervasive cause for this remarkable level of continuity and relative homogeneity throughout time and place highlighted here is the Vinaya that all monks in Tibetan societies share.

Summing up, I have argued that the perceived need to protect the Dharma in the age of decline has influenced Tibetan societies for centuries, resulting in a comparatively low level of social change. The general motivation to do so is, I believe, ultimately based on wanting the good for all members of society—all sentient beings. When trying to understand social phenomena in pre-modern Tibetan societies, one thus should never neglect the influence of religious practices and sentiments. It therefore does not make sense simply to reduce policy—be it governmental or monastic policy—to being solely politically or economically motivated.

For Tibetan Buddhists, and it appears that this is also the case for many Buddhists elsewhere in Asia, what is seen as morally just—or in other words simply the right thing to do—is ultimately connected to what is believed to maximize the highest level of well-being. A question political scientists and philosophers have attempted to answer is whether a just society promotes the virtue of its citizens. The current view—endorsed by, among others, Rawls—is that a society should stimulate freedom, not virtue.[28] Based on the monastic guidelines, the Tibetan monastic understanding regarding this issue is that a just society *requires* virtue: the two, virtue and justice, cannot exist without each other. These are then seen to bring about the well-being of sentient beings. Of course, ritual service was an important contribution of the Tibetan monkhood to society, but rituals are only truly effective when the performers were sufficiently virtuous: that is, upholding their vows and precepts. While this book has not directly addressed the political implications of Tibetan monasticism, particularly from the mid-seventeenth century onward, the ritual role of the (Geluk) monks made government and administration subordinate to the Geluk hierarchy. Incoming taxes were spent on funding these rituals. This is because, as Schwieger asserts, "the prayers and ritual services of the Gelukpa monks were regarded as essential to the welfare of Tibet."[29]

In other words, to maintain the Dharma is to stimulate virtue and justice and thereby general well-being. The Sangha is charged with the important task of keeping the Dharma intact. Accordingly, while there can be no doubt that karma is a factor *implicitly,* the monastic authors of the sources at hand *explicitly* stress preserving the Dharma against the test of time as absolutely vital to bringing about the welfare of all.

# APPENDIX

## I. POSTSCRIPT: MATTERS FOR FUTURE RESEARCH

This study has focused on pre-modern Tibetan monastic organization, policy, and ideology, for which the *chayik* are superb sources. However, there are many more facets of Tibetan society on which these works could shed light. As they contain numerous references to quantities of goods, measurements, weights, and money, they might be useful sources for an analysis of a more quantitative nature. The absence of a trustworthy resource that informs us about how much, for example, a *nyag* of butter cost in the market, or what one could buy with one *dngul srang,* however, has hindered my research somewhat. The texts will also be of use when employing methods of network analysis. The often ill-understood relations between "mother monasteries" and their branches may be clarified by looking at the respective monastic guidelines and their authors. Related to this is the political employment of the *chayik* that has been hinted at in this book, but which is in need of further research.

Moreover, there exist many more *chayik* than have been discussed here. Some of these are gradually being made available by the Buddhist Digital Resource Center (formerly, the Tibetan Buddhist Resource Centre, TBRC; www.tbrc.org), whereas others may remain in their original monasteries in various states of decay. Collecting and cataloguing these texts is an important task to be carried out sooner rather than later. Toward the end of the writing of this book, the online repository BDRC made the collection of mainly Geluk *chayik,* referred to in this work as *bCa' yig phyogs bsgrigs,* available in a searchable format. The further digitization of more sets of monastic guidelines of different schools will yield important information on, for example, monastic organizational positions and the citing of canonical texts, and so on.

During my fieldwork, I was able to collect a number of recently composed *chayik.* To study them was beyond the scope of this project, however. To examine contemporary *chayik,* on their own but also in light of older "versions," will help us better understand contemporary Tibetan monasticism, inside and outside Tibet. The way in which contemporary monasteries are now studied emphasizes change, not continuity, and tends not to engage with the often less easily perceivable or understandable Buddhist ideological frameworks. Reading both the old and new monastic guidelines may, to a certain extent, remedy these limitations.

For this study it was important to look at Vinaya works—preferably materials that Tibetans themselves read and wrote. While of course these texts are plentiful and available, they are not easily consulted as they are difficult to read. Unfortunately, very limited scholarly attention has been paid to native Tibetan Vinayic works and their usage. This study has demonstrated the lasting relevance of the Vinaya for monastic life. It is my hope that this will stimulate others to examine these Tibetan texts in more detail—possibly in conjunction with the monastic guidelines.

Another topic hardly touched upon is the position of women, nuns, and nunneries in pre-modern Tibetan monasticism. Admittedly, this study has no more than peripherally engaged the topic of gender. Even in instances when the "lay society" was discussed, the agents were in most cases just half of the population: men. This is mostly due to the nature of the sources I was able to consult. While these texts mention women fairly often, works written for or mentioning nunneries and nuns are comparatively few. Hopefully, more pre-modern *chayik* written for nunneries—for I am sure there are many more than the two or three that this book mentions—will come to light in the future.

Last of all, the influence of monastic rule-making on secular laws in Tibet has not yet been established. The scantily studied Tibetan legal texts need to be viewed with the understanding that monastic thinking greatly affected their authors and their work. Such a study would shed further light on the relationship between the monastics and the state and between the religious and the secular in Tibet.

## II. FIELDWORK: THE INFORMANTS AND THEIR BACKGROUNDS

The fieldwork referred to in this study was mainly conducted in July and August 2012 in North India and Ladakh, while a disastrous "pre-fieldwork" trip to Kham in March 2011, which included a not quite voluntary "free" trip back from Dergé to China proper provided by the Public Security Police, showed me what was and—more importantly—what was *not* possible with regard to doing research in Tibetan areas. All interviews were held in Tibetan without the use of interpreters or field assistants. Most, but not all, interviews were recorded: it was up to the informant to state their preference. In total, I conducted twenty interviews, although not all informants were equally informative; only those who have been referred to in this work are mentioned by name. All of the interviewed monks gave oral consent to being cited in this work. The names of the monks are given in alphabetical order and for some their titles are given, while the names of others who did not introduce themselves along with their titles, or were not introduced by others as having a certain title, are left as is.

### LOBZANG DÖNDRUP (BLO BZANG DON GRUB)

Lobzang Döndrup, around seventy-five, normally lives at Samkar monastery (Geluk), but at the time of the interview he had temporarily moved to Spituk for the rain retreat. When he was eight he was made a monk at Samkar, a branch monastery of Spituk. It was obligatory for young monks from Spituk and affiliated institutions in Ladakh to study in Drepung Loseling for at least three years. Between his fifteenth and twentieth year he lived in Drepung monastery in Lhasa, until he was forced to go back to Ladakh in 1959.

### THE DIRECTOR (DBU 'DZIN) OF DRIGUNG JANGCHUB LING MONASTERY

This monk, in his fifties, did not give me his name. He did disclose he was born in Kham Gawa and first became a monk in a branch monastery of Drigung called Kham Gyok gonpa (Khams mgyogs dgon pa). He had been a disciplinarian there before arriving from Tibet fourteen years previously.

### GEN RINCHEN (RGAN RIN CHEN)

Gen Rinchen was introduced as the director (dbu 'dzin) of Dolma Ling (sGrol ma gling) nunnery (Rimè) in Dharamsala. He was originally from Kandzé in Kham and his mother monastery was Sera Je. At the time of fieldwork, he was in his mid-fifties.

### KHENPO CHÖYING LHÜNDRUP (MKHAN PO CHOS DBYINGS LHUN GRUB)

Khenpo Chöying Lhundrup did not fulfill any identifiable official post at Khampa Gar (Khams pa sgar) in Bir (Drukpa Kagyü, official name: dPal phun tshogs chos 'khor gling), but was referred to by his peers as being the most knowledgeable on the topic of *chayik* and discipline. When I interviewed him, he was in his early thirties. He was born in Lhatho in Chamdo district (Kham), where he became a monk at the original Khampa Gar. He arrived in India in 2004.

### KHENPO KÖNCHOK CHÖKYAB (MKHAN PO DKON MCHOG CHOS SKYABS)

Khenpo Könchok Chökyab, in his mid-forties when interviewed, was at that time the abbot of the educational college (*bshad grwa*) of Drigung Kagyü monastery. He was born in Ladakh and was made a monk at Phiyang when he was eleven. To further his education he went to Drigung Kagyü in Rajpur.

### LAMA TSÜLTRIM (BLA MA TSHUL KHRIMS)

This senior monk, who explicitly requested anonymity, was working as, in his own (English) words, the "spare tire" of a Nyingma monastery in India, meaning that he was asked to do various (organizational) jobs when there was a need for them. He was in his fifties at the time of fieldwork. He was born in India and had traveled abroad a number of times. He interlaced his Tibetan with a fair amount of English.

### KÖNCHOK CHÖNYI (DKON MCHOG CHOS NYID)

Könchok Chönyi, around seventy-five, was a retired ritual specialist (*slob dpon zur pa*) at Phiyang. He was born in the area around this monastery. His father died when he was very young and his mother did not remarry and worked as a farmer. He was made a monk when he was eight. When he was fourteen he, along with a group of young monks, traveled to Central Tibet to study at Yangri Gar, a Drigung Kagyü monastery specializing in ritual practices. He was forced to leave in 1959, when he was twenty years old.

### NGAWANG PELJIN (NGAG DBANG DPAL SBYIN)

Ngawang Peljin was the disciplinarian at Nechung monastery (non-affiliated) at the time of fieldwork. He was in his mid-forties and originally from Central Tibet. He was a monk in Drepung in Tibet.

### NGAWANG SANGYÉ (NGAG DBANG SANGS RGYAS)

Ngawang Sangyé was the disciplinarian at Gyütö (Geluk) in Dharamsala, having just been appointed one month beforehand. He was in his early forties and originally from Arunachal Pradesh. Prior to his position as disciplinarian he was a monk official (*'gan 'dzin*) at a branch monastery of Gyütö in Arunachal Pradesh.

### GESHÉ NGAWANG ZÖPA (DGE BSHES NGAG DBANG BZOD PA)

Geshé Ngawang Zöpa was not an informant during my fieldwork, but is a teacher of Buddhism currently residing in the Netherlands. Now in his fifties, he was born in South India and was made a monk at Sera Je when he was twelve. I have been one of his regular interpreters since 2006 and we occasionally discuss my research and monastery life in general.

### GESHÉ PENDÉ GYENTSEN (GE BSHES PHAN BDE RGYAL MTSHAN)

Geshé Pendé Gyentsen was the abbot of the nunnery Genden Chöling (Geluk) at the time of fieldwork. He was in his late fifties and from Lithang in Kham. His home monastery is Sera Je in South India.

### RENDO SENGGÉ (RE MDO SENGGE)

Rendo Senggé was born in Rendo, Amdo. He became a monk in 1984 at Kirti monastery in Amdo Ngawa. He received his *dge bshes rab 'byams pa* degree in 1997. He was a teacher at the Kirti monastery in Dharamsala and one of the authors of the new *chayik* for both the Tibetan and exile Kirti monasteries. He is also the author of *Bod kyi shes yon lam lugs dang srid byus* [The Tibetan education system and its policies]. At the time of fieldwork he was in his late thirties.

### SHÉRAP GYATSO (SHES RAB RGYA MTSHO)

Shérap Gyatso was an elderly monk who lived in Sakya Chökhor Ling (Sa skya chos 'khor gling) in Rajpur. He was in his late seventies at the time of fieldwork. He was born near Sakya in Tibet and his parents had been farmers and were occupants (*mi ser*) of the Sakya estate. He became a monk at Sakya when he was around seventeen years old. When the Chinese took over power he was made to undergo reeducation for two years. He went into exile in 1962.

### SÖNAM CHÖGYEL (BSOD NAMS CHOS RGYAL)

Sönam Chögyel was a junior secretary at Sakya Chökhor ling in Rajpur. He was in his late twenties at the time of fieldwork and did not disclose any personal information.

### TENDZIN DRUKDRA (BSTAN 'DZIN 'BRUG SGRA)

Tendzin Drukdra was the serving disciplinarian at Tsechok Ling (Geluk) in Dharamsala at the time of fieldwork. When I interviewed him, he was in his early thirties. He was born in India.

### TUPTEN YARPEL (THUB BSTAN YAR 'PHEL)

Tupten Yarpel was the general secretary (*drung spyi*) at Namgyel Dratsang (Geluk) in Dharamsala at the time of fieldwork. He was in his forties and originally from Shigatse but had also lived in Lhasa for some years. Previously, he served the monastery as a secretary (*drung yig*) for many years and was a teacher of written Tibetan language at Sara College in Himachal Pradesh.

# NOTES

## INTRODUCTION

1. Silber 1985: 252.

2. Spiro 1971: 428. While Spiro's research generally focuses on Burmese Buddhism, some of his comments—like this one—he considered applicable to all Buddhist societies.

3. Spiro also makes this point; ibid.: 287.

4. Ibid.: 425.

5. Collins 1982: 6–7.

6. "Tibet" here refers to "ethnographic Tibet," an area encompassing much more space than the Tibet on any map, however contested its borders may be. For the current purpose, the unifying factor is the presence and dominance of monastic Buddhism. While this study mainly addresses Tibetan Buddhist societies, Bon monasticism is also occasionally referred to. Because Bon monastic organizational features are largely identical with Buddhist monasticism, the two Tibetan religions often will be consciously conflated. See also Kvaerne 1970: 188. While the phrase is used throughout this work, I am aware that a singular "Tibetan society" does not, and never did, exist. Furthermore, all concepts of society should be seen in the context of a specific time and space.

7. This is also argued by Gombrich [1988] 2006: 113.

8. It is most likely that by "priests" Kawaguchi means monks, but this is not entirely certain when one takes the notion of "priests" in Japan into account.

9. Kawaguchi 1909: 373.

10. This appears to be a view expressed by Parenti (2003: 590), who regards pre-modern Tibet as "little more than a despotic retrograde theocracy of serfdom and poverty, so damaging to the human spirit, where vast wealth was accumulated by a favored few who lived high and mighty off the blood, sweat, and tears of the many."

11. Chayet (2003: 86) notes ruefully that "it is true that the economic and social history of Tibet has still to be written."

12. Carrasco 1959: 218.

13. See, for example, Bataille 1988; Parenti 2003: 579–90.

14. *Bod kyi shes yon*: 67. Here political Tibet is taken to consist of the current-day Tibet Autonomous Region, Kham and Amdo.

15. A fair number of documents valuable to social historians that have escaped destruction have been catalogued and published at www.dtab.uni-bonn.de/tibdoc/index1.htm and in many collections edited by Schuh. Manuscripts found on the periphery of the Tibetan state also have been collected. See, for example, Ramble and Drandul 2008. Many valuable sources are not available to (most) academics and are kept in Beijing and in the Lhasa archives (*Lha sa yig tshags khang*). It is unrealistic to expect that access to them will be possible in the foreseeable future.

16. Ellingson 1990: 218.

17. For works that attempt to understand contemporary monastic Tibetan Buddhism in part through the lens of its history, see Caple 2011; Makley 2007; Mills 2003; Hillman 2005.

18. Gyatso 2003: 236.

19. For example, *gdan rabs* or *dkar chag*.

20. Monastic guidelines from outside the Tibetan polity can be equally informative on monastic policies. A collection of manuscripts that contains a small number of monastic guidelines for Sikkimese monasteries is found in Schuh and Dagyab 1978.

21. For example, through the Buddhist Digital Resource Center (BDRC) at www.tbrc.org.

22. Silk 2008: 65.

23. Clarke (2014: 164) simultaneously points out that by choosing the word "monk" as a translation of *bhikṣu*, the Buddhist renunciate is burdened with "unwanted cultural baggage." In many works, the term *bhikṣu* is translated as "fully ordained monk," probably referring to the fact that this person has taken the full gamut of vows (*bsnyen par rdzogs pa*, S: *upasaṃpadā*) (ibid.: 171n2).

24. Students and scholars of Buddhism are less likely to conflate the Buddhist monk with his younger Christian counterpart, the latter of whom has taken vows of poverty, obedience, stability, and so on. I ask other readers to keep an open mind every time the word "monk" is mentioned.

25. On the—equally problematic—term "monastery" see later in this chapter.

26. Various spellings of this loanword exist. According to Snellgrove ([1987] 2002: 419n17), it is derived from the Sanskrit *vandya*, from which the anglicized Japanese term "*bonze*" is also derived. However, there is now a consensus that the word *ban de* is more likely to represent the honorary Sanskrit appellation *bhadanta* (T. *btsun pa*). Davidson (2005: 11) mentions a group of historical agents called the Bendé (*ban de*) who were intimately associated with the ancient royal dynasty, describing them as "part clergy, part laity, and intermittently observing some monastic traditions." Later, it appears that the word became somewhat less ambiguous; a prominent example is the Fifth Dalai Lama's penname *Za hor gyi ban dhe*: "the monk from Za hor." The development and use of the term *ban de* is in need of further investigation.

27. The word *bla ma* (in this work mainly written as "lama" for ease of reading) is another very problematic term. The multifarious nature of this word has caused no end of serious

misunderstandings (see, for example, Hillman 2005: 34n16). While acknowledging that this term is in desperate need of a thorough examination on the basis of emic descriptions from both written and oral materials, here, when "lama" is used and the context is not immediately obvious, I mention whether the word refers to the category of "monks" or otherwise.

28.  While the translation often given for this term is "novice," the English term does not cover the ontological status of a *dge tshul*. The word "novice" suggests that one will, one day, become something more than that—that it is just the start of something. In most Tibetan traditions, however, many monastics never take *dge slong* ordination, nor do they intend to, for various reasons. One will thus find many elderly "novices" in Tibetan monasteries, who will have been in robes for almost their entire lives. For this reason—and for lack of a better translation—when the texts clearly differentiate *dge slong* from *dge tshul* I give the Tibetan or Sanskrit, instead of an ambiguous or misleading English translation.

29.  For this and other reasons it is problematic, even for scholars of Indian Buddhism, to translate *dge bsnyen* (S. *upāsaka*) as "householder" or "layman," as is oftentimes done. An *upāsaka* is someone who has taken certain vows, which sets him apart from other nonmonastics, who are usually referred to as *khyim pa* (S. *gṛhin*) or *khyim bdag* (S. *gṛhapati*) in the Indic traditions. See also Seyfort Ruegg 2004: 24–26.

30.  Ibid.: 24.

31.  In certain contexts, these people also lived in "*dgon pa*," a word most commonly translated as monastery. For more on these communities in Southwest Tibet, see Aziz 1978: 76–92. *Tshig mdzod chen mo* glosses the word *ser khyim pa* as laypeople who wear yellow, i.e., people who look like monks but have wives (p. 2948). It appears that these "yellow householders" were, in their earliest guise, a type of wayward or runaway monk. Chennga Drakpa Jungné (sPyan snga grags pa 'byung gnas, 1175–1255) instructs the monks in his thirteenth-century *chayik* for Drigung Til ('*Bri gung mthil*, also spelled *thil* or *thel*), to make the *ser khyim pa* in the area of the monastery retake their vows, and if they refuse, to expel them from the monastic estate. See '*Bri gung mthil bca' yig*: 250a.

32.  The "politically correct" term in use for these practitioners is "the white-clad, long-haired ones" (*gos dkar lcang lo can*), whereas colloquially they are often known as *sngags pa*.

33.  For the rules and regulations of a contemporary community of such practitioners in Amdo, see Dhondup 2013.

34.  See Cabezón 2004. He states that a monk is either "a renunciate" (*rab 'byung*), by which he means someone who has taken the *dge bsnyen/ upāsaka* vows), a novice (*dge tshul*), or someone with full ordination (*dge slong*).

35.  There the word *ban de* is commonly used to indicate monks.

36.  Personal communication with Rendo Senggé, Dharamsala, July 2012.

37.  Collins 1988: 106.

38.  Spiro 1971: 294.

39.  In this study, I use "Vinayic" to refer to anything derived from either the canonical Vinaya ('*dul ba/ 'dul ba'i lung*) or commentaries and subcommentaries on monastic discipline.

40.  Gombrich [1988] 2006: 150.

41.  Dreyfus 2003: 45.

42.  Personal communication with Tupten Yarpel, Dharamsala, July 2012.

43.  Schopen 1996a: 123.

44. According to one of my informants, however, a *dgon pa* becomes a *dgon pa chen mo* if it carries out the three rituals (*gzhi gsum cho ga*), mentioned previously.

45. *Bod kyi shes yon*: 53–54.

46. According to a Tibetan dictionary, a *grwa tshang* is a rather big division among a community of monks; see *Tshig mdzod chen mo*: 417. A *dgon pa* is either a secluded place at least one *krośa* (about two miles) removed from the village (as a translation of *araṇya*) or the residency of the Sangha; see ibid.: 461.

47. *gdan sa gsum*. The Three Great Seats refer to the three large Geluk monasteries in Central Tibet: Drepung, Ganden, and Sera.

48. Examples of this are the *chayik* for the "forest hermitage" (*nags khrod*) of Pabongka (*Pha bong kha bca' yig*) and the "temple" of Ramoche (*Ra mo che bca' yig*). The latter's title actually calls this institution a *grwa tshang*.

49. Gyatso 2003: 219.

50. Dreyfus 2003: 52.

51. For a critique of this notion, see Samuel 1993: 142–46.

52. Samuel (1993: 578–82) provides an overview of the number of monks in different areas based on secondary sources and thereby concludes that overall the monk population consisted of perhaps ten to twelve percent in the agricultural areas and a considerably lower number in other areas.

53. I also make this argument in Jansen 2013a: 121–22.

54. Ellingson 1990: 206.

55. Childs 2005: 5.

56. Sewell 1993: 25.

## 1.   DOCUMENTS THAT ESTABLISH THE RULES

1. Aside from the mentioned Indic predecessor of the *chayik*, the *kriyākāraṃ*, similar works also exist in the Theravāda as well as in East Asian Buddhist traditions; see Jansen 2015.

2. Articles that expand this chapter have been published in Jansen 2015, 2016a.

3. An example of this is the *bCa' yig chen mo*, a work seen as the earliest Bhutanese constitution written by the founder of Bhutan, Zhabs drung Ngag dbang rnam rgyal (1594–1651). It is claimed that this work itself was based on monastic *chayik* that the author had written previously. However, the later text was intended for the Bhutanese population as a whole (Aris 1979: 215). The date of this law code is uncertain.

4. It is tempting to translate *khrims* as "law." However, it is important to note that this word has both secular and religious connotations.

5. The earliest *kriyākāraṃ* is the "*bhichu samgasa kriyakara*," the largest part of which has been lost (Schopen 1996b: 589n45).

6. For example, monks who did not attend ceremonies, who wore householder's clothes, or who hit other monks had to pay fines amounting to a certain number of rolls of silk (Burrow 1940: 95n489).

7. Schopen 2002: 360–62.

8. Tatz 1986: 66–67.

9. *bKa' gdams rin po che'i chos 'byung rnam thar nyin mor byed pa'i 'od stong*, written by Lo dgon pa bsod nams lha'i dbang po (1423–1496).

10. Vetturini [2007] 2013: 165–66, 375.

11. Ellingson 1990: 208.

12. This text can be found in *dPal ldan tshal pa bka' brgyud kyi bstan pa'i mnga' bdag zhang g.yu brag pa brtson 'grus grags pa'i gsung 'bum rin po che*: bKa' thor bu: shog dril chen mo (Kathmandu: Shree Gautam Buddha Vihar, 2004): 176–81.

13. I am grateful to Erden Chuluu at Kyoto University for drawing my attention to this. He has kindly shared an example of one such text with me, regarding a monastery in Inner Mongolia from the nineteenth century, which is in a book containing old Mongolian legal texts (Čige, *Erten-ü mongyol-un qauli čayajă-yin teüke* [Ancient Mongolian legal history], 330–47, Shenyang: Liyouning-un ündüsüten-ü keblel-ün qoriya, 2004). A recent Mongolian language article focuses on these texts. Unfortunately, I did not have access to it (see Gombodorž 2016). The development and implementation of such rules in a Mongolian monastery in the eighteenth century are alluded to by Humphrey and Ujeed 2013: 144.

14. Chandra 1980: 3617–30; 3473–75; 3469–73.

15. Ellingson 1990: 205.

16. Ibid.: 210.

17. Examples of this are: *dBen gnas 'khyung rdzong ri khrod pa rnams kyi khrims su bca' ba'i yi ge thar pa'i them skas*, in bCa' yig sde brgyad la springs yig lam yig sko 'ja' sogs kyi rim pa phyogs gcig tu bsgrigs (bsKal bzang rgya mtsho [the Seventh Dalai Lama] *gSung 'bum*, vol. 3): 434–45, and *De mo srid skyong dang pos dar nor ri khrod la bstsal ba'i bca' yig* (1757), in *bCa' yig phyogs bsgrigs*: 151–55.

18. For example, *Rong zom bca' yig*. For a treatment of this *chayik*, see Sur 2017.

19. See Whitecross 2017.

20. Personal communication with Ciulan Liu, Taipei, June 2011.

21. Grothmann 2012: 137–39.

22. Kun mkhyen rig pa 'dzin pa chos kyi grags pa (1595–1659) wrote the *bKa' 'gyur bzhengs dus dpon yig rnams kyi bca' yig*, in *gSung 'bum*, vol. 2: 175–80. This text is briefly discussed in Schaeffer 2009: 31–33. He translates the title as "Guidelines for Chief scribes [*sic*] During the Production of a Kangyur."

23. Cüppers, 2011; see also Whitecross 2014: 352 for the use of this term in Bhutan.

24. For example, the facsimiles of two *chayik* found in Schuh and Dagyab 1978: 250–67, 272, 278.

25. *Chos sde chos dbyings 'od gsal gling bca' yig*: 434.

26. See Schneider 2002: 416 and French 1995a: 125, plate 23.

27. *dge 'dun gyi khrims*.

28. Personal communication with Tendzin Drukdra, Dharamsala, July 2012.

29. Personal communication with Rendo Senggé, editor in chief of the latest *chayik* for Kirti byes pa monastery (in Tibet), Dharamsala, July 2012. He mentioned that in the old Tibet, abiding by the country's rule was never a problem for the monks, but that this has now become difficult because of the current Chinese government's policies, which effectively prevent monks from following the traditional monastic education. For many monks, upholding the traditional education system is paramount to abiding by Chinese law.

30. Tshe ring dpal 'byor et al, eds., *Bod kyi snga rabs khrims srol yig cha bdams bsgrigs* (Lhasa: Bod ljongs mi dmangs dpe skrun khang, 1989).

31. For example, Seneviratna 2000: 187.

32. Ellingson 1990: 209.

33. Blackburn 1999: 286.

34. Ibid.

35. Cabezón 2004: 6. This rule was not a Tibetan invention: study by non-*bhikṣu*s was prohibited in the Vinaya texts themselves.

36. Dreyfus 2003: 114.

37. D4117 (P5619). For an English summary and the Sanskrit of the first chapter of this text, see Bapat 1982. A commentary to that text *'Dul ṭīk nyi ma'i 'od zer legs bshad lung rigs kyi rgya mtsho* by the thirteenth-century Kadam master Kun mkhyen mtsho sna ba shes rab bzang po is used in all Tibetan Buddhist traditions. See also Nietupski 2017.

38. Dreyfus 2003: 117.

39. Ibid.: 40.

40. *dPal yul gdan rabs*: 360–61.

41. Huber 2004: 135.

42. Cabezón 1997: 337.

43. *dGa' ldan thub bstan rab rgyas gling bca' yig*: 159.

44. Bechert 1970: 772.

45. Personal communication, July 2012. However, the *Mūlasarvāstivāda vinaya* clearly states that *individual* monks could not alter the *kriyākāraṃ*: communal rules could only be changed by communal effort (see Schopen 2007: 112). The early Sri Lankan Sangha *sāsana,* which Seneviratna (2000: 199) describes as liberal, and whose rules were rather flexible, appears similar, however: "It allowed the monks to get together and decide for themselves what rules and regulations should be adopted."

46. Smith 2001: 156.

47. *Pha bong kha bca' yig*: 248.

48. Personal communication with Ngawang Peljin, Dharamsala, July 2012.

49. Bechert 1970: 765.

50. Schopen 1994b: 147.

51. *bKra shis dga' ldan chos 'phel gling bca' yig*: 498.

52. Blackburn 1999: 281–309.

53. For a treatment and complete translation of this *chayik* see Jansen 2014.

54. *dPal 'khor chos sde bca' yig*: 413. This monastery is likely to be located in Gyantse (rGyal rtse).

55. *bKra shis chos rdzong bca' yig*: 412.

56. Interview with Ngawang Choseng (no. 91), Tibetan Oral History Project, 2007: 38. This source unfortunately only provides the English translation, while the interview was conducted in Tibetan.

57. Personal communication with Rendo Senggé, Dharamsala, July 2012.

58. *Bod kyi dgon sde*: 92.

59. This finding accords with that of Sullivan, who researches the history of Geluk monasteries in Amdo. He told me it was often difficult, if not impossible, to gain access to the *chayik*. Personal communication, Taipei, June 2011.

60. Personal communication with Rendo Senggé, Dharamsala, July 2012. The idiom "*rtsa chen po*" does not merely refer to something rare or expensive, but has an added connotation of sacrality.

61. The entire city of Lhasa would be under the rule of Drepung monastery during that festival. The overarching disciplinarian would have final authority over the population of monks and laypeople at that time. For an eyewitness account see Bell [1948] 1998: 58.

62. Personal communication with Ngawang Peljin, Dharamsala, August 2012.

63. Schopen 2010a: 108.

64. Wickremasinghe 1928: 281.

65. This is the *bCa' yig mi chog brgyad cu*. Personal communication with monks at Pelyul, Kandzé prefecture, March 2011.

66. Personal communication with Tupten Yarpel, Dharamsala, July 2012.

67. Personal communication with Lobzang Döndrup, Spituk, August 2012. For a recent anthropological study of the monastic organization of Spituk, see Bridges 2017.

68. Personal communication with Tendzin Drukdra, Dharamsala, July 2012.

69. See Schuh 1984: 291–311.

70. Pirie 2010: 214.

71. Gutschow 2004: 63. The *chayik* in question was reportedly written by the fifteenth-century Geluk master Shes rab bzang po and his disciple Slob dpon mdo sde rin chen.

72. Nietupski 2011: 64.

73. Silk 2003: 177.

74. See chapter 6 for more on the relationship between laypeople and monks.

75. For example, *Se ra theg chen gling rtsa tshig*: 182.

76. *dPal yul dar thang bca' yig*: 199.

77. Examples of these orally transmitted histories can be found in Jackson 1984; see also Jansen 2010: 59–62.

78. Cabezón 1997: 337–38. The book, actually called *Byang chub lam rim che mo dang 'brel ba'i ser byas mkhan snyan grwa tshang gi bca' khrims che mo* (Bylakuppe: Ser jhe Printing Press, 1991), contains *The Great Exhortation* (5–108), as well as the ritual calendar for the debate ground (*grwa tshang gi chos ra'i mdzad rim*) (109–18).

79. For example, ibid.: 108.

80. Cabezón 1997: 339.

81. Reportedly, a thousand copies of this text were printed, compared to a population in excess of 3,500 monks.

82. Personal communication with Geshé Ngawang Zöpa, Amersfoort, February 2012.

83. Cech 1988: 71.

84. Personal communication with Rendo Senggé, Dharamsala, July 2012.

85. Personal communication with Ngawang Sangyé, Dharamsala, August 2012.

86. In Gyütö monastery, this position of an older monk responsible for a new monk is called *khrid mkhan dge rgan* (the accompanying teacher). In other monasteries the person in charge of teaching the new monk how to behave could be the *shag dge rgan* (the living-quarter's teacher) or the *kham tshan dge rgan* (the regional house's teacher).

87. In fact, Das ([1893] 1965: 7) reports that in Tashi Lhunpo in the late nineteenth century, if a new novice monk misbehaved and was turned out, his "tutor" received "ten stripes of the cane" and needed to pay "a fine of 40 lbs of butter within three days."

88. Ellingson 1990: 210. This is reiterated by Tupten Yarpel, who said that the rules are mainly communicated orally (*ngag rgyun*). Personal communication, Dharamsala, July 2012. See also *'Bras spungs bca' yig*: 316.

89. *Pha bong kha bca' yig*: 237.
90. *Bod kyi dgon sde*: 108.
91. *Chos sde chos dbyings 'od gsal gling bca' yig*. This text was written by Blo bzang rta mgrin (1867–1937). The location of this monastery is unknown to me.
92. *dPal yul gdan rabs*: 402.
93. Ibid.: 405.
94. Silk 2007: 277.
95. Schopen 1994a: 60.
96. Ortner 1989: 171.
97. *'Bras ljongs bca' yig*: 269.
98. Ratnapala 1971: 164.
99. Minogue [1998] 2005: 262–63.

## 2. HISTORICAL AND DOCTRINAL FRAMEWORKS OF MONASTIC ORGANIZATION IN TIBET

1. Snellgrove [1987] 2002: 240.
2. Kapstein 2000: 60.
3. Kern 1896: 72.
4. Davidson 2005: 64.
5. This is not to say that there were no disagreements on how to interpret the *pratimokṣa* vows, in particular in combination with the other two sets of vows. On the interpretation of the *trisaṃvara*, see Sobisch 2002.
6. Kapstein 2000: 25.
7. Wangdu and Diemberger (2000: 2, 11) furthermore remark that the style of the text appears to be in transition: from archaic Dunhuang-style Tibetan to early "classical" Tibetan.
8. Ibid.: 64–69. *sBa bzhed*: 17b.
9. For an overview of state involvement in the patronage of the Sangha, see Dargyay 1991: 111–28.
10. *sBa bzhed*: 63.
11. *Bod kyi dgon sde*: 169. The primary source the authors used is probably the *dBa' bzhed*; see Wangdu and Diemberger 2000: 73. It is difficult to tell how much these allowances amounted to, as the measurements of the unit *khal* fluctuated over the centuries and could differ from region to region.
12. Aris's foreword to Martin and Bentor 1997: 9.
13. See chapter 6 for a more elaborate treatment of this topic.
14. The discussion of the recent developments of the monastic economy among Tibetans in the PRC is based on Caple 2011. Caple views the drive toward self-sufficiency as coming from Tibetans themselves and argues that it is not necessarily part of the dynamics between the state and the monasteries. This view is perhaps not entirely warranted: one of my informants was told by the Chinese during Communist reeducation in the early 1960s that the monks in the old Tibet had been eating other people's food, and that they should actually be self-sufficient (*rang kha gso dgos*) (personal communication with Shérap Gyatso, Rajpur, August 2012). This is why the monks who were allowed to remain at the monasteries (up until the Cultural Revolution) were made to do farmwork. Initially, at least, self-sufficiency was forced upon the Tibetan monks by the PRC government.

15. The wording is *dam pa'i chos kyi me ro* or *bstan pa'i me ro*. One of the earlier works in which this story features is the text by lDe'u jo sras written in the thirteenth century; see *lDe'u chos 'byung*: 390–92.

16. Davidson 2005: 65–72.

17. Ibid.: 71, translating *Chos 'byung me tog snying po sbrang rtsi'i bcud*: 446.

18. Halbwachs [1941] 1992.

19. *btsun pa*, S. *bhadanta*.

20. *dGa' ldan thub bstan rab rgyas gling bca' yig*: 160. Quoted from the *Vinayottara-grantha* (D7): 234b.

21. Ibid.: 161.

22. *Rin chen sgang bca' yig*: 210. A similar point is made in Snellgrove [1987] 2002: 306.

23. *dPal yul dar thang bca' yig*: 187.

24. Gombrich [1988] 2006: 19.

25. This same notion was also widespread in Chinese Buddhism; see Walsh 2010: 7.

26. For more on the widespread Buddhist narrative of decline, see Nattier 1991.

27. Personal communication with Tendzin Drukdra, Dharamsala, July 2012.

28. Personal communication with Geshé Pendé Gyentsen, Dharamsala, July 2012. One of these relaxations is that one needs a smaller group of *bhikṣu*s present at an ordination. In central lands one needs ten, whereas in outer regions one needs just five "*vinayadharas*." See *Vinayavastu* (D1): 52a. However, the perception that Tibet was counted among those foreign regions was one not readily entertained by Tibetan authors.

29. Personal communication with Lama Tsültrim, Dehradun, August 2012. He reported that the monks even have a brief phrase to brush off any such criticisms: "*dus dpags*" (considering the times . . .). On the age of decline this monk says that "it is not the Dharma that is changing, or that the Dharma is not as good as it used to be. The Dharma remains the same—it is the individual who changes and worsens. These days, there are just more delusions (*nyon mongs*) around."

30. Again, this is not just a Tibetan custom, nor was it only prevalent in more recent times. In ninth-century Japan the author of the *Mappō-tōmyōki* (末法燈明記) argued that the government should not punish those monks with poor discipline, because one could not be expected to adhere fully to the rules in such a decadent age. See Nattier 1991: 138.

31. Davidson 2005: 102.

32. Shakya 1999: 419.

33. Kapstein 2000: 9.

34. See for example van der Kuijp 1987: 69n13.

35. For an exploration of the ways in which Tibetans adapted Buddhism, see Kapstein 2000.

36. Gombrich [1988] 2006: 12.

37. These factors are further discussed in chapter 6.

38. Anderson and Tollison 1992: 374.

39. Ibid.: 390.

40. Ibid.: 374. In *The Wealth of Nations*, Adam Smith ([1776] 1976: 311, 377) argued that state-supported, monopoly religions produced inferior services for their followers, but he did not look at the overall societal benefits of such religions.

41. Goldstein 2009: 10.

42. See Viehbeck 2016.

43. *vaiyāpṛtyakara bhikṣu.*

44. Silk 2008: 27.

45. The important post is discussed in detail in Chapter 3.

46. I assume that this refers to the ordination lineage.

47. *bKra shis lhun po bca' yig*: 86.

48. *dbu mdzad chen mo.* This was the same rank as disciplinarian.

49. *dPal yul gdan rabs*: 358–59. Apparently, other positions that had a more prosaic character, such as treasurer (*phyag mdzod*) or "manager"/steward (*gnyer pa*), do not seem to have required a particular level of religious education or practice. The technical terms are further discussed in Chapter 4.

50. Dagyab 2009: 55.

51. This is likely a translation of *geshé*, which was the highest scholastic degree in the Sakya tradition.

52. Cassinelli and Ekvall 1969: 206.

53. Personal communication with Shérap Gyatso, Rajpur, August 2012.

54. Wangchuk 2005: 227.

55. Silk 2008: 10.

56. This text, which has been translated into English as *Words of My Perfect Teacher,* explains how during the harvesting of tea leaves many insects are killed, and that the tea is transported by people on foot until Dar rtse mdo (a Tibeto-Chinese border town in modern Sichuan also known as Kangding). These people carry the loads strapped to their heads, which causes the skin to peel, so that their white skulls become visible. This tea is then loaded onto pack animals, who also suffer under the weight. The readers are not implored to do something about these exploitative practices, but rather to think of the dissatisfactory nature of *saṃsāra. Kun bzang bla ma'i zhal lung*: 74.

57. In the section that discusses compassion, the author of the *Kun bzang bla ma'i zhal lung* criticizes the mistreatment of animals, especially by so-called lamas and monks, each of whom is meant to be the refuge, savior, and defender of all living beings, but instead all of whom are only involved in protecting their patrons who give them food and gifts by bestowing initiations and blessings onto them. Ibid.: 198.

58. Ibid.: 233.

59. Heubner and Garrod 1993: 179.

60. Spiro 1971: 429.

61. See Walsh 2010: 10–11.

62. Cf. McCleary and van der Kuijp 2010: 149–80.

63. Walsh 2007: 373.

64. R. Miller 1961: 436.

65. For example, Cassinelli and Ekvall 1969: 74.

66. *Homo Hierarchicus*: 277, as quoted in Collins 1988: 116.

67. Goldstein 1998: 22.

68. Cf. Gombrich [1988] 2006: 113.

69. This expression is alluded to in *Gong ra nges gsang rdo rje gling bca' yig*: 227, *Kong stod dung dkar dgon bca' yig*: 594, and *sKu 'bum rgyud pa grwa tshang bca' yig*: 275. The complete saying is: *sbal pa rma can gcig gis sbal tshang phung*; see Cüppers 1998: 178.

70. Collins 1988: 115.

71. *kham tshan.* This word is spelled in various ways (e.g., *khang tshan / khams tshan / kham tshan*).

72. In the larger monasteries intercollegiate feuding was a regular occurrence. For more on this "'communal violence," see chapter 7 and Jansen 2013a: 122 et seq.

73. This dual model is further elaborated upon in chapter 5.

74. Silk 2008: 31.

75. Schopen 2001: 111.

76. Ashman and Winstanley 2007: 86.

77. Ishii 1986: 6.

78. Ashman and Winstanley 2007: 83.

79. Velasquez 2003: 531–62.

80. Ashman and Winstanley 2007: 92.

81. Sayer 2008: 148.

82. Maher 2012: 271.


## 3.   ENTRANCE TO THE MONASTERY

1. This chapter is an adaptation of Jansen 2013b: 137–64.

2. Bell 1931: 169.

3. Gyatso 2003: 222.

4. Goldstein's coining of the phrase "the ideology of mass monasticism" has contributed to the notion that the monkhood in Tibet was open to all; see Goldstein 1998, 2009. For a critique of this position see Jansen 2013a: 111–39.

5. Ratnapala 1971: 259.

6. Ibid.: 141.

7. Das [1893] 1965: 4.

8. Ibid.: 7.

9. According to various Vinaya commentaries, the five sexual "disabilities" that preclude ordination are: (1) male and female hermaphrodites (S. *paṇḍaka, pho mo ma ning*); (2) people with diseased genitals (*mtshan dug*); (3) people without genitals; (4) people who have changed sexes three or more times; (5) eunuchs or impotent men (S. *saṇḍha, za ma*) (Cabezón 2017: 381–84).

10. That is, killing a human being, having sexual intercourse, lying (usually the false claim of spiritual accomplishments), and stealing (something of value).

11. Bapat and Gokhale 1982: 20, S.116–48. Gernet notes that in China slaves were not to be ordained and that this seems to be supported by the Vinaya (referring to Rhys Davids and Oldenberg 1881–85, Mahavagga vol. I: 47, 199), not because of their lowly state but because they were owned by someone else; see Gernet [1956] 1995: 129, 351n171.

12. *Vinayasūtra ('Dul ba'i mdo* D4117): 4b. The relevant section in the Sanskrit text can be found in Bapat and Gokhale 1982: S.149–64.

13. Guṇaprabha's auto-commentary, the *Vinayasūtravṛtti*, does contain this group of excluded people. *Vinayasūtravṛttyabhidhānasvavyākhyāna ('Dul ba'i mdo'i 'grel pa mngon par brjod pa rang gi rnam par bshad pa* D4119): zhu 24b.

14. *'Dul ba'i mdo'i rgya cher 'grel pa (*Vinayasūtraṭīka) (D4120): 'u 36b. To my knowledge, a Sanskrit version of this text is not extant.

15. Iwao 2012: 66.

16. Richardson 1983: 137.

17. This appears to be a misreading for *pukkasa,* which is understandable because graphically *bu/pu* may appear very similar.

18. *Tshig mdzod chen mo*: 2624.

19. Ibid.: 1354.

20. *bKra shis lhun po bca' yig*: 35–158.

21. It should be noted here that people requesting admission to the monastery could be either laymen in search of ordination or monks from other monasteries.

22. The named villages are Zhol, rNams sras, and bDe legs. *bKra shis lhun po bca' yig*: 68.

23. Sandberg 1906: 122.

24. Cech 1988: 70.

25. Restricting people from entering the monastery on the basis of regional origin did not occur only in Tibetan Buddhist areas; in Korea, during the Koryŏ dynasty (918–1392), not just slaves but the inhabitants of entire regions were prevented from ordination. See Vermeersch 2008: 155.

26. *'Bras spungs bca' yig*: 302.

27. Ibid. See also Jansen 2013a: 109–39.

28. This is the *chayik* written for Namgyel Dratsang by the Seventh Dalai Lama, bsKal bzang rgya mtsho, in 1727.

29. *hi ma la ya'i rigs brgyud.*

30. Personal communication, Dharamsala, July 2012. One notable exception to this rule is of course Georges Dreyfus, who was admitted to this monastery at the behest of the Dalai Lama himself, but whose admittance met with some resentment from the other monks. See Dreyfus 2003: 32.

31. Carrasco 1959: 188.

32. Risley 1894: 292.

33. Carrasco 1959: 188.

34. For a description of a monk's admission into the monastery see Dreyfus 2003: 59. It should be noted here that actually entering and living at a monastery and gaining official admission to the monastery are separate occasions, and it is likely that certain monks living at a monastery at particular times were never officially enrolled at the institution. On semi-monks and unofficial monks in Drepung see Jansen 2013a: 109–39.

35. In some cases, a chronic lack of new monks at a powerful monastery resulted in the levying of the "monk tax" (*grwa khral*). On the topic of monk tax, see Jansen (forthcoming) 2018.

36. *rdzong dpon.*

37. *'khrol tham.* Surkhang 1986: 22.

38. Dargyay 1982: 21.

39. *nyag lcags khal.*

40. *sgrig ja.*

41. *mTshur phu dgon gyi dkar chag*: 257–58. The guidelines for *dGa' ldan mdo sngags chos 'phel 'chi med grub pa'i byang chub gling* from 1949 also enumerate the gifts a new monk was supposed to offer. See *'Chi med grub pa'i byang chub gling bca' yig*: 649.

42. *ṭam ka.*

43. Nornang 1990: 267n16.

44. Personal communication with Könchok Chönyi, Phiyang, August 2012.

45. Cabezón 1997: 350.

46. *kham tshan.*

47. Snellgrove and Richardson [1968] 1986: 238.

48. *grwa zhing.*

49. Carrasco 1959: 32–33. A comparable system appears to have been in place at Dunhuang in the ninth and tenth centuries. Monks and nuns possessed fields and they hired laborers to farm their land; see Gernet [1956] 1995: 132.

50. To this day, Sri Lankan monasteries also only allow new recruits from the landholding caste; see Gombrich [1988] 2006: 166. Kemper (1984: 408) makes a similar point, saying that except for a brief period of time only members of the Goyigama caste could become monks. It is not clear, however, whether in contemporary Sinhalese society the decisive factor is one's birth in such a caste or the actual ownership of fields.

51. Personal communication, Phiyang, August 2012. An interesting parallel to this is a Chinese decree issued in 955, which states those who cannot be supported by their parents may not enter the order; see Gernet [1956] 1995: 45.

52. *'Bri gung mthil bca' yig*: 248a.

53. Goldstein 1986: 96.

54. Spencer Chapman ([1938] 1984: 179) further notes that a high physical standard was also required of monks-to-be.

55. *'Bri gung mthil bca' yig*: 248a.

56. Ibid.: 248a, b.

57. Kawaguchi 1909: 435–36.

58. The concept of class as developed and defined by socialist thinkers did not exist in Tibet until modern times. In modern Tibetan *gral rim* is a neologism that denotes "class." See Kolås 2003: 181–200, for an examination of notions of class in Tibetan society.

59. Personal communication with Lama Tsültrim, Dehradun, August 2012.

60. Cassinelli and Ekvall 1969: 269.

61. Kolås 2003: 188.

62. Spencer Chapman [1938] 1984: 179.

63. *bKra shis lhun po bca' yig*: 68.

64. This phrase (*mi nag*) commonly refers to people who commit nonvirtuous actions.

65. *Se ra byes bca' yig*: 579.

66. Ibid.: 571.

67. Fjeld 2008: 113.

68. Rauber-Schweizer 1976: 80–81.

69. *me lam chu lam.*

70. The same practice occurs in Te, Mustang, where it is called *me bcad chu gcad* (to cut off the fire, to cut off the water). In addition to not being allowed access to water and fire, villagers may not share any food and drink with those who are being boycotted; see Ramble 2008: 178–79.

71. Tsering and Ishimura 2012: 5–9.

72. Thargyal and Huber 2007: 67.

73. Gombo 1983: 50.

74. Schopen 2010b: 231.

75. While I previously used the word "outcaste" as a translation of *pukkasa / g.yung po,* here the word "outcast" is more apt, for in the Tibetan context the people who were turned away from the monastery were often those who had been banned or cast out of their village or tribe as a punishment for certain misdeeds.

76. This is not to say that the model of karma is never used to justify the manner in which lower classes of people are treated in the Tibetan Buddhist world. An example of such reasoning, passed on orally and after 1959, can be found in Mumford 1989: 47–49.

77. *chos skyong, chos srung, srung ma, bstan srung.*

78. *Rong zom bca' yig.*

79. *sMin grol gling bca' yig*: 313. For a more extensive treatment of this text see Townsend 2017.

80. *sku rten.*

81. This must have been the Eighth Dalai Lama Jampel Gyatso ('Jam dpal rgya mtsho, 1758–1804)·

82. *bSam yas lcog grwa bca' yig.*

83. Schopen (1995a: 478) makes a similar argument in the context of the Vinaya literature: "The Vinayas are actually preoccupied, if not obsessed, with avoiding any hint of social criticism and with maintaining the status quo at almost any cost."

84. The question as to whether these deities were merely "invented" to justify certain political or economic policies is irrelevant here. Hubert and Mauss noted the existence of a *sphère imaginaire de la religion,* arguing that because religious ideas are believed, they exist and thereby become social facts (cited in Collins 1998: 73).

85. One may argue that these people usually also had political power and that it was thus not necessarily their religious position that made change possible. I suspect, however, that particularly in the larger monasteries, the politically and economically significant posts were usually not given to the religiously influential monks, because holding such an office was seen as a potential threat to their religious standing.

86. There appears to be a parallel between marriage and entering the monkhood. Even though people from various classes intermarried, the lowest strata were endogamous, and thus were excluded from marrying up, which presented yet another limitation to social mobility for them.

87. A similar point is made in the context of contemporary Spiti by Tsering and Ishimura 2012: 6.

88. Access to education is further discussed in chapter 6.

89. Thargyal and Huber 2007: 205.

90. Cassinelli and Ekvall 1969: 83.

## 4.   MONASTIC ORGANIZATION

1. Ferguson and Shalardchai 1976: 104–5. In the context of monastic Buddhism "seniority" always refers to the time since ordination, not to age.

2. Nietupski 2009: 11.

3. For example, Rawls [1971] 1999: 264: "The principle of fair equality of opportunity goes against the ideas of a hierarchical social structure with a governing class."

4. See for example Dumont 1980: 231–38.

5. Thailand is another example where the concept of hierarchy is associated with order and harmony. See Ferguson and Shalardchai 1976: 140.

6. In the *Mūlasarvāstivāda vinaya* seniority was the most decisive factor. Schopen (2004c: 177) describes this as follows: "This rule of seniority in its broadest form dictated that a monk's access to places, goods, and services be determined by his monastic age or the length of time he has spent as an ordained monk."

7. This text, *Tshogs kyi bzhugs gral bca' yig chen mo* [The great monastic guidelines on the seating arrangements at the assembly], is mentioned in *bKra shis lhun po bca' yig*: 87.

8. *'Bri gung byang chub gling bca' yig*: 402.

9. This concept is further elaborated in chapter 5.

10. *'Bras spungs bca' yig*: 301.

11. *'Bras ljongs bca' yig*: 270.

12. The *sKu mchod 'phrul thos grol chen mo* ritual, about which not much is known. Judging from the name, it may have involved the recitation of the *Bar do thos grol* [The Tibetan book of the dead].

13. *Thos grol chen mo sgrig yig*: 385. The word here translated as "training" (*bslab*) is ambiguous, for in monastic contexts it often also refers to vows (S. *śikṣā*).

14. Penjore 2011: 17.

15. *'Bras spungs bca' yig*: 300–301.

16. *dPal yul dar thang bca' yig*: 194. The word *zur tshogs* could have multiple meanings. It may refer to a less prominent spot (possibly on the "side rows") when assemblies are held, but it might also indicate a less important assembly, i.e., a different occasion altogether. The latter interpretation is more likely, because in the monastic guidelines for Pabongka hermitage the context clearly indicates that *zur tshogs* is a minor assembly that does not require the entire monk community, *Pha bong kha bca' yig*: 246.

17. There is a parallel here with the narrative found among others in the *Cullavagga* IX, in which the Buddha perceives the presence of someone in the assembly who was not pure. This impure person is explained as someone without vows and without precepts. This man was not allowed to partake in the recitation of the *prātimokṣa* and was removed from the assembly; see Rhys Davids and Oldenberg, vol. IX, 1881–1885: 299–319.

18. This is also apparent in Tibetan wedding ceremonies; see Jansen 2010.

19. In the Tibetan context, the advantage of sitting in front is obvious: the butter in the tea that is served during the assembly usually collects on top (partially due to the cold climate), and thus those who are first in line get the portion high in caloric value, whereas the tea of those at the back contains hardly any butter.

20. Gombo 1983: 52.

21. For the terms *karmadāna* and *vihārapāla* see Silk 2008: 127–35, 136–46. The Indic use of these terms seems to diverge significantly from the twelfth-century Chinese use.

22. Yifa 2002: 151–53.

23. Pachow [1955] 2000: 230.

24. This information is largely based on my fieldwork and pertains to the contemporary situation in Namgyel Dratsang, Nechung, and Gyütö. The *chayik* barely report on this voting process. That voting is a continuation of older practices and not influenced by modern (or Western) processes is speculative, but in my opinion likely nonetheless.

25. *bKra shis lhun po bca' yig*: 85.

26. *Bod kyi dgon sde*: 86.

27. Goldstein 1968: 220.

28. Michael (1982: 119) naively states that "for the monk or nun social origin was, of course, no longer relevant."

29. Stein [1962] 1972: 140; see also Carrasco 1959: 216.

30. Dreyfus 2003: 51.

31. Cabezón 1997: 348. Rendo Senggé, Könchok Chönyi, and Lobzang Döndrup all claim that the robes worn by the *chos mdzad* were the same as those of ordinary monks.

32. *gzhon khral* (literally: youth tax) or *gsar khral* (new tax). This is also noted in Dagyab 2009: 111. In Tsurpu this tax was also called *grwa khral* (monk tax); see *mTshur phu dgon gyi dkar chag*: 259. See also Jansen (forthcoming) 2018.

33. *mTshur phu dgon gyi dkar chag*: 258.

34. Personal communication with Rendo Senggé, Dharamsala, July 2012.

35. *kham tshan*.

36. *mang ja*.

37. Personal communication with Blo bzang don sgrub, Spituk, August 2012.

38. Cech 1988: 77.

39. Das's gloss of *sger rigs* is correct here; it must refer to *sger pa*—private landowners and the lower aristocracy. In other cases, *sger pa* indicated all (lay) nobility. Travers 2011: 155–74.

40. This may refer to a type of hereditary chief or to military officials.

41. Das [1893] 1965: 8.

42. *bKra shis lhun po bca' yig*: 73–74.

43. This is not dissimilar to what was common practice during the Koryŏ dynasty (918–1392) in Korea. The sons of the concubines of the king would often become monks. When they were ordained they automatically obtained a high administrative rank (i.e., *samjung* 三重) (Vermeersch 2008: 171).

44. *sku drag gi gtong sgo. bKra shis lhun po bca' yig*: 74.

45. Ibid.

46. Goldstein 1968: 156–57.

47. Ibid.: 155.

48. Gombo 1983: 65n10.

49. Bunnag 1973: 43.

50. Mills 2000: 17–34; McCleary and van der Kuijp 2010: 164.

51. Cassinelli and Ekvall 1969: 74; Goldstein and Tsarong 1985: 21.

52. Welch 1967: 116 et seq.

53. Dagpa (2003: 177), for example, notes that "'[d]iscipline, hierarchy and studies characterized the large Tibetan monasteries."

54. Bell [1946] 1998: 199.

55. Miller 1958: 250.

56. Goldstein 2009: 12.

57. Personal communication with Gen Rinchen, Dharamsala, August 2012. Presumably, a smaller institution could also rely more on information being passed orally; see Chapter 3.

58. *mi tshan*.

59. Jansen 2013a: 118–23.

60. *bKra shis lhun po bca' yig*: 82–83.

61. This is also noted by Gyatso (2003: 228) in the context of contemporary Geluk monasteries.

62. This relationship is examined in more detail in chapter 6.

63. This term is not just a modern one: it is mentioned in the *chayik* written in the late sixteenth century; *dPal ri chos sde bca' yig*: 457.

64. For example, *bKra shis lhun po bca' yig*.

65. For example, *'Bri gung byang chub gling bca' yig. las sne pa* also occurs. This is short for *las kyi sne mo (pa)*. In other instances, this term may refer to monks who are involved in monastic service as opposed to education. In the *sMin grol gling bca' yig*, for example, the monk who repeatedly fails his exams is threatened to be made into a *las sne*, in all likelihood someone tasked to do menial labor. *sMin grol gling bca' yig*: 288.

66. For example, *gDan sa chen po'i bya ba las kyi sne mor mngags rnams kyi bca' yig*.

67. For example, *sMin grol gling bca' yig*.

68. For example, *'Bri gung mthil bca' yig*. The term *mkhan slob* is of course a contraction of *mkhan po* and *slob dpon*. However, it is clear from the context that it is used to denote all those in official positions.

69. Jagou 2004: 327nn81, 82.

70. An example of this is the *'Bri gung mthil bca' yig*, written between 1235 and 1255, which displays at least two unusual terms denoting certain official posts, namely *sgom pa ba* and *dpon las*. I take the former term as equivalent to *sgom pa*. This was a high civil and military function within the Drigung Kagyü school, the so-called "seat of civil power"; see Sperling 1987: 39. This official generally was a layperson and had considerable power, but this *chayik* clearly shows that he ultimately answered to the abbot (here: the author of the text).

71. Nowadays, in the larger Tibetan monasteries in India, only the more senior and high-level *geshés* are considered for the posts of abbot and disciplinarian; see Gyatso 2003: 230.

72. *Dung dkar gsung rtsom*: 69.

73. Dagyab 2009: 55.

74. Cassinelli and Ekvall 1969: 206.

75. Khenpo Könchok Chökyab mentions that, currently, repeat-offending monks, who have stained their record by having been caught multiple times with alcohol and cigarettes, are not eligible to become monastic functionaries in the future. Personal communication, Rajpur, August 2012.

76. For example, *bKra shis lhun po bca' yig*: 85–86.

77. *'Bri gung byang chub gling bca' yig*: 403.

78. This illustrates the potential influence of monastic administrators. In some areas these monks also chose the headmen of the villages. Goldstein 1968: 133.

79. *'Bri gung byang chub gling bca' yig*: 404–5.

80. *sMin grol gling bca' yig*: 312.

81. *gDan sa chen po'i bya ba las kyi sne mor mngags rnams kyi bca' yig*: 319.

82. *Pace* Cassinelli and Ekvall 1969: 143–44.

83. In Dakpo Shedrup Ling this team consisted of the chant master (*dbu mdzad*) and eight monks. This council selected the abbot. See Nornang 1990: 253. The term *lhan rgyas*

is also regularly used to refer to a committee consisting of laypeople, e.g., *gzhis rgan lhan rgyas* (*mTshur phu dgon gyi dkar chag*: 583). In exile, contemporary guidelines are compiled jointly by the members of the *lhan rgyas*. Personal communication with Ngawang Peljin, Dharamsala, July 2012.

84. Nornang 1990: 263–69. In 1920 Sera monastery (full name: Se ra theg chen gling) had two offices, the *spyi so* and the *gnyer tshang*; see *Se ra theg chen gling rtsa tshig*: 186. Sera's individual colleges naturally had their own organizational committees.

85. Ibid.: 253. This term *zhal ta pa* also features "an administrative monk," as the translation of *vaiyāpṛtyakara*, although in some contexts this office was not filled by a monk. See Silk 2008: 39–73, and 44 in particular. According to *brDa dkrol gser gyi me long*, it can be equated with *do dam pa*, which can be roughly translated as "manager." See *brDa dkrol gser gyi me long*: 765.

86. *Se ra byes bca' yig*: 569.

87. For example, Dagyab 2009: 56–57; *Bod kyi dgon sde*: 86.

88. *bla spyi* is likely to be an abbreviation of *bla brang spyi sa*, as evidenced in *dGon khag gi dge 'dun pa rtsa tshig*: 303.

89. R. Miller 1961: 427–28. This "jisa mechanism" or "model" is explained to underlie all Tibetan Buddhist monastic economies. Chapter 5 deals further with this topic.

90. For example, *Rong po rab brtan dgon bca' yig*: 538. Here the word is used in a way similar to *spyi pa*, on which more later on in this chapter.

91. For example, *Ra mo che bca' yig*: 139.

92. For example, Dagyab 2009: 57.

93. In smaller monasteries, the monastic authorities may be referred to simply as *bla brang*. Here this word does not refer to the estates held by wealthier incarnations. See for example *Pha bong kha bca' yig*: 241.

94. Dakpa 2003: 171–72.

95. For example, *gDan sa chen po'i bya ba las kyi sne mor mngags rnams kyi bca' yig*.

96. Silk 2008: 211.

97. Michael 1982: 44.

98. *dge skos/ bskos; chos khrims pa; zhal ngo.*

99. *dbu mdzad.*

100. *gnyer pa; spyi ba; spyi gnyer.*

101. *phyag mdzod, mdzod pa.*

102. For example, *dkon gnyer, nor gnyer pa, mchod dpon*, etc.

103. While these terms are derived from non-Bon sources, the hierarchical system and its terms appear remarkably similar in (current) Bon monasteries; see Karmay and Nagano 2003. While the latter two types of monks, the treasurer and maintenance personnel, feature frequently in the *chayik*, they will not be dealt with here. This is partly due to the limited role they played in the actual organization of the monastery and partly due to constraints of space.

104. *mkhan po.*

105. Gyatso 2003: 230.

106. On the role of the abbot, see later in this chapter.

107. Bunnag 1973: 129.

108. Pardue notes it was common to have lay supervisors at the monastery who had to report back to the state on the quality of conduct; see Pardue 1971: 121. The Christian monasteries employed laypeople as managers and otherwise, in very similar ways; see for example Smyrlis 2002: 245–61.

109. Welch 1967: 374. This does not necessarily reflect a historical reality.

110. Thargyal and Huber (2007: 49) speculate that the administration of the Dergé kingdom was modeled on that of the monasteries.

111. The spelling *dge bskos* also occurs regularly. For the sole reason of consistency, I refer to *dge skos*. For a more elaborate treatment of the role of the disciplinarian in the Tibetan monastery, see Jansen 2016b.

112. Silk 2008: 103–4; Schopen 1996a: 117; and Schopen 2004b: 68–69, 103–4.

113. The role of the *upadhivārika* varied in the different narratives in the *Mūlasarvāstivāda vinaya* from having a rather elevated status to being little more than a janitor. See Schopen 1996a: 97n35.

114. Takeuchi 1993: 56–57. The source used is Pt 1119. In Pt 1297, the disciplinarian (*dge skos*) of Weng shi'u temple (*weng shi'u si'i* (si = 寺) also loans out grains (*gro nas*).

115. Gyatso 2003: 230.

116. The *dge skos* should therefore not be confused or equated with the term *vinayadhara*, which refers to someone who has memorized and has extensive knowledge of the Vinaya.

117. *Bod kyi dgon sde*: 86.

118. *'Bri gung mthil bca' yig*: 248b.

119. The so-called *sgrogs med* monks; see Nornang 1990: 251.

120. By this I assume the author means the nonscholar monks, without *dge slong* ordination.

121. Snellgrove and Richardson [1968] 1986: 241.

122. This six-month term is also in place in Gyütö monastery in India, while I was informed that in Tibet the disciplinarian's position used to change four times a year. Personal communication with Ngawang Sangyé, Dharamsala, August 2012. The maximum term appears to be three years, which is in place in Drigung Jangchub Ling ('Bri gung byang chub gling) in India. Personal communication with the director of Drigung Jangchub Ling, Rajpur, August 2012.

123. *sMin grol gling bca' yig*: 309.

124. *mTshur phu dgon gyi dkar chag*: 280.

125. *sMin grol gling bca' yig*: 238. What the disciplinarian is meant to do with the forbidden objects is not specified.

126. *Bod kyi dgon sde*: 87.

127. This is one of the lower-level *geshé* degrees at Drepung; see Tulku 2000: 17, 19.

128. *'Bras spungs bca' yig*: 308.

129. *rgyun drang*. I take this to refer to his ordination lineage. No mention is made, however, if having *dge slong* ordination was a prerequisite. The elderly monk Shérap Gyatso of Sakya noted that one did not have be a *dge slong* to be a disciplinarian there. Personal communication, Rajpur, August 2012.

130. This physical quality is also mentioned by an anonymous monk officer in Drukpa Kargyü ('Brug pa dkar [sic] rgyud) monastery in Clement Town, Dehradun. He said that while the chant master needs to be well educated, the disciplinarian has to be strong and imposing.

131. *tham ga.*

132. *bKra shis lhun po bca' yig:* 86. In contemporary Namgyel Dratsang, the new disciplinarian, during his appointment ceremony, recites a prayer (*smon lam*), the wording of which is not set. In this prayer he promises to follow the Vinaya and to serve the monastery. Personal communication with Ngawang Peljin, Dharamsala, July 2012.

133. *bKra shis lhun po bca' yig:* 86.

134. *dge skos chen mo.*

135. *do dam pa. brDa dkrol gser gyi me long:* 765.

136. Aris 1976: 690.

137. *bKra shis lhun po bca' yig:* 71.

138. Travers 2008: 14. This is further specified as a military commander in charge of a group of twenty-five people. *Tshig mdzod chen mo:* 2379.

139. *bKra shis lhun po bca' yig:* 84.

140. They were called *dge skos* or *chos khrims pa.* The usage of the two terms cannot be understood as being based on school or regional preference. It appears, however, that monasteries in Ladakh prefer *chos khrims pa.*

141. *dGa' ldan khri pa.*

142. I was told that in Gyütö monastery the great chant master (*bla ma dbu mdzad*) could become the abbot and only retired abbots could become Ganden Tripa. Personal communication with Ngawang Sangyé, Dharamsala, August 2012.

143. Karmay and Nagano 2003: 508.

144. *'Bras spungs bca' yig:* 305. In other words, they would receive respectively five or six times the amount of donations than would an ordinary monk.

145. *gdangs dbyangs.*

146. This is a paraphrase of *bKra shis lhun po bca' yig:* 84.

147. *tshogs chen dbu mdzad.*

148. *bKra shis lhun po bca' yig:* 87.

149. *dPal yul gdan rabs:* 359.

150. *bla sgam.*

151. *lha rams dge bshes.* Possibly contradictory information is given here: www.berzinar chives.com/web/en/archives/study/history_buddhism/buddhism_tibet/gelug/brief_histo ry_gyumay_gyuto_tantric_college.html (accessed February 2, 2014), where it is mentioned that the *bla ma dbu mdzad* are chosen from among the former disciplinarians.

152. Personal communication with Ngawang Sangyé, Dharamsala, August 2012. The great chant master of Gyütö monastery in India was abroad during the time of my field-work. The monks at the monastery recommended him as the most knowledgeable on the topic of *chayik.* Their set of monastic guidelines, the *rGyud stod bca' yig chen mo,* is said to be the original scroll from the fifteenth or sixteenth century that had been taken from Tibet to India. It is only taken out of its box when the *bla ma dbu mdzad* decides to read it aloud in the presence of the assembly. This is not for a special occasion, but only when it seems appropriate, at least once every three years. My informant, the disciplinarian at the time, believes that over time new rules have been added to the original manuscript.

153. Powers 1995: 481, 530. The author further explains the hierarchy at the Gyütö monastery.

154. *'Bras spungs bca' yig*: 305. I have not come across this title elsewhere. It is likely that it refers to the foreman of the kitchen staff (*lag bde*). Alternatively, it could mean the "graceful" *dbu mdzad*. In any case, this post is clearly distinct from that of chant master, who is paid much higher wages, namely five shares.

155. *Rin chen sgang bca' yig*: 214.

156. For example, in the colophon of Kunga Lodrö's (1729–1783) *dPal rdo rje gzhon nu'i byin 'bebs kyi rol yig mthon ba rang grol gsal byed mdzes rgyan*. In *gSung 'bum, vol. 3, 926* (Kathmandu: Sa skya rgyal yongs gsung rab slob gnyer khang, 2008). This text, a so-called *dbyangs yig*, was written at the behest of the chant master (*dbu byed*). Although little is known about the organization of nunneries, contemporary cases suggest that titles of officials and the like are the same as in the monasteries; e.g., Schneider 2009: 285.

157. *mchod gral pa*. *dPal yul gdan rabs*: 359.

158. Ibid.

159. Nornang 1990: 253.

160. For an extensive treatment of this role in Indic textual material, see Silk 2008: 38–73.

161. *do dam pa*.

162. The variants *zhal ta ba* and *zhal ta* also occur.

163. Alternatively, one finds *zhal ba byed pa*; e.g., in *dPal yul dar thang bca' yig*: 193, where this type of service clearly refers to physical labor such as fixing roofs and painting the buildings.

164. *bar shar*.

165. *sMin grol gling bca' yig*: 310.

166. *gdan gnyer*.

167. Ibid.: 311.

168. Elsewhere in the same text, the monks are warned that the kitchen (*rung khang*) is the domain of its staff (*zhal ta'i las byed*) and that they cannot simply enter it and stay near the stove. See *sMin grol gling bca' yig*: 286.

169. *Se ra byes bca' yig*: 586; *Se ra byes bca' yig 2*: 83.

170. *dung mkhan*.

171. *zhal ta ba lag gtsang ba*. This term *lag gtsang ba* could refer to the literal sense of maintaining a certain level of hygiene, which may well be important when the *zhal ta ba* are to handle food and drink. However, more figuratively it could have the sense of being honest and incorruptible, which may be equally, if not more, important here.

172. *dkon gnyer*.

173. *chab ril ba*.

174. *Gangs dkar gling bca' yig*: 147. Interestingly, in this work (p. 149) the steward (*gnyer pa*), the disciplinarian, the chant master, the *zhal ta ba*, the two hornblowers, and the shrine-keeper are all allotted equal shares. This may be a typical feature of a smaller monastery.

175. *phyag bde ba*.

176. *sTeng po che bca' yig*: 462/5b.

177. For example, *Byams pa gling bca' yig*: 251a.

178. *dge 'dun gyi zhal ta pa*.

179. *mTshur phu bca' yig*: 706/4a.

180. *'Bras spungs bca' yig*: 302. The post of *zhal ta dpon* does not seem to be in use in other texts.

181. *dge slong zhal ta byed pa.*

182. *Vinayavastu ('Dul ba'i gzhi*, D1): 97b; Silk 2008: 55–56.

183. In contrast, in a work on the history of Labrang monastery in Amdo the *tshogs chen spyi ba* is translated as "the general accounting office," which collected taxes on every load-bearing animal; see Nietupski 2011: 91.

184. *chos khrims.*

185. *Rin chen sgang bca' yig*: 214.

186. Ibid.

187. *dPal ri chos sde bca' yig*: 458.

188. *spyi khrims.*

189. *sMin grol gling bca' yig*: 307. The word *gzhis,* here translated as "base," may refer to either the place where the monks have set up camp or the home monastery.

190. *sMin grol gling bca' yig*: 282.

191. Bunnag 1973: 33.

192. Ekvall 1964: 195.

193. Ibid.: 195–96. For a more detailed examination of the role of the individual monk within the larger context of the monastic economy, see chapter 5.

194. *bla brang.* On this phenomenon see chapter 5.

195. *rDo phud chos 'khor gling bca' yig*: 568.

196. *Se ra byes bca' yig*: 578. This is in accord with the Vinaya regulations on the acceptance of gifts that are either unsuitable or useless to the Sangha. Items that are not of any use to monks, such as perfume, still need to be used in some way. See Schopen 1995b: 107.

197. *Ra mo che bca' yig*: 131.

198. Ibid. The issue of monks dealing with (lay) sponsors is further discussed in chapter 6.

199. The term *spyi so,* when referring to an individual, is not used as such in the *Tshig mdzod chen mo,* where it is described as the office of those who manage the general income of each of the monasteries in the olden days. *Tshig mdzod chen mo*: 1680. While both spellings appear with equal regularity in the *chayik, spyi bso,* in which the second syllable *bso* might be the future tense of the verb *gso ba*—i.e., to make grow, to restore, to nourish—appears to make more etymological sense. Literally then, *spyi bso* stands for either an office or someone in charge of caring for the general welfare of the Sangha. Elsewhere, the spelling *spyi gso* also occurs; e.g., Karmay and Nagano 2003: 756. Here it is rendered as "accountant."

200. This is also confirmed in Dagyab 2009: 56, 58.

201. Dakpa 2003: 171.

202. *Kong stod dung dkar dgon bca' yig*: 597.

203. *mchod gnyer.*

204. *Rong po rab brtan dgon bca' yig*: 538.

205. Ibid.: 537.

206. For more on these types of "offerings" see chapter 6.

207. *phogs deb.*

208. See Jansen 2013a: 131–32; *'Bras spungs bca' yig*: 306–7. For more on these ledgers, see chapter 6.

209. *Se ra byes bca' yig*: 581.
210. Here: *chos khrims pa*; the two then get abbreviated to *spyi chos*.
211. *'Bri gung byang chub gling bca' yig*: 404.
212. Personal communication with Khenpo Chöying Lhundrup, Bir, August 2012.
213. Personal communication with Sönam Chögyel, Rajpur, August 2012.
214. The full name of this monastery is 'Bri gung yang ri sgar thub bstan sde bzhi rab rgyas gling.
215. Personal communication with Könchok Chönyi, Phiyang, August 2012.
216. Dagyab 2009: 60.
217. The Mongolian term that is closely related to *gnyer pa* is *hetsuu hun,* meaning "clever one"; see Purevjav 2012: 262.
218. von Hinüber 1995: 11.
219. The greater implications for the monastic economy and the Tibetan society as a whole of this "rule" are explored in chapter 6.
220. *chos gzhis/ mchod gzhis.*
221. *Bod kyi dgon sde*: 172. Similar to the Tibetan *gnyer pa,* in Korea, during the Koryŏ period the steward (直 歲 *chikse*) was in charge of collecting rents from the temple's estates, while the treasurer (典 座 *chŏnjwa*) had the function of providing for the material needs of the monastery; see Vermeersch 2008: 217.
222. *dngul gnyer.* Perhaps the difference between the *gnyer pa* and the *dngul gnyer* is simply that the latter only dealt with monetary issues, whereas the former apparently also dealt with farmlands.
223. *'ded pa.*
224. Dagyab 2009: 61. While it does not say whether these people were lay or ordained, there are accounts of monks collecting debts for their monastery. For an account of a monk collecting debts, see Gyatso 1998.
225. *'Bras spungs bca' yig*: 314. As mentioned earlier, ordinary monks were not allowed to keep animals.
226. *sMin grol gling bca' yig*: 309–10.
227. According to Cassinelli and Ekvall (1969: 275), all the monasteries in the Sakya polity made loans to the laity on a regular basis. They were handled by the monastery's "business manager."
228. Interestingly, the role of *gnyer pa* in Mindröl Ling monastery was more like that of a janitor. "The jobs concerning the general monastic compound (*gling*), such as the willow fence, [are taken care of] in consultation with the *gnyer pa*. According to older custom restoration and masonry work was done in the spring." *sMin grol gling bca' yig*: 311.
229. This may be akin to the post of *phan tshun che mo*: the supervisor of political and economic matters in Bon monasteries; see Karmay and Nagano 2003: 756.
230. *rgyun ja.*
231. Kvaerne 1970: 189.
232. Or simply *'go ba.* Caple 2010: 201. This has been translated as "manager."
233. Nietupski 2011: 63.
234. Personal communication with Könchok Chönyi, Phiyang, August 2012.
235. Personal communication with Lobzang Döndrup, Spituk, August 2012.

236. For example, in Mustang; see Ramble 2008: 286. Sherring ([1916] 1974: 170 et seq.) gives a description of his dealing with what he calls "Nirba," who are unmistakably lay administrators. In Dergé, the cabinet ministers, usually belonging to the class of aristocrats, were also called *gnyer pa* (or *gnyer chen*); see Thargyal and Huber 2007: 49.

237. Joldan 2006: 73.

238. *ban log;* elsewhere: *grwa log.*

239. Ekvall 1959/60: 217.

240. Dargyay 1982: 74.

241. French 1995a: 241.

242. Michael 1982: 158.

243. As found in *Bod kyi dgon sde*: 172, previously cited above.

244. *gnyer tshang.*

245. *spyi bso.*

246. Nornang 1990: 250–51, 256. Separate economies based on the source of the income are not unusual and—as shall be further explored in chapter 5—resonate in Vinayic materials.

247. Another common term is *grwa log.*

248. Ekvall 1959/60: 210.

249. Ibid.: 219.

250. Ibid.: 217.

251. Cassinelli and Ekvall 1969: 144.

252. Ibid.: 69.

253. Gunawardana 1979: 99. An interesting parallel is found in Cistercian monasteries in thirteenth-century England. The Cistercian monks had a group of middlemen, who were laymen, to conduct the business they were not allowed to conduct. See Madden 1963: 344.

254. On the extent of monks handling money in the *Mūlasarvāstivāda vinaya,* see for example Schopen 2006: 225–45.

255. For the case of the Fifth Dalai Lama dealing with these "vowless" monks, see Jansen 2013a: 115–21.

256. On the expulsion of monks and their reentry, see chapter 7.

257. *dPal yul dar thang bca' yig*: 193–94.

258. Gyatso 2003: 233.

259. In other Buddhist cultures disrobing is (and was) a very common feature of the monkhood. Bunnag (1973: 157) describes how in Thailand when a monk disrobed, his personal sponsor, who had given him a monthly allowance when he was a monk, would equip him for life outside the monastery by giving him money and clothes.

260. Dargyay 1982: 21.

261. Personal communication with Shérap Gyatso, Rajpur, July 2012.

262. Cech (1988: 85) also notes that the Bon *chayik* she examined does not often mention the abbot. However, she extrapolates from this that he did not have much to do with the enforcement of rules.

263. *khri pa* or *khri chen.*

264. *bstan pa'i bdag po* or *bstan bdag.*

265. In fact, the Sakya author Kunga Lodrö refers to the Dalai Lama (*Gong sa mchog,* here in all likelihood the Eighth Dalai Lama) as "the owner of the complete Teachings"

(*yongs rdzogs bstan pa'i bdag po*), the ultimate authority. See *bSam yas lcog grwa bca' yig*: 408.

266. Mills 2003.

267. Nietupski 2011: 140.

268. *'Bri gung mthil bca' yig* a: 249a.

269. Cassinelli and Ekvall 1969: 318.

270. Bunnag 1973: 94–95.

271. Notable exceptions here are the Fifth, Thirteenth, and Fourteenth Dalai Lama.

272. Cassinelli and Ekvall 1969: 318.

273. *mtshan nyid grwa tshang*.

274. *Thor rgod rgyal po bca' yig*: 368.

275. Schram [1954] 2006: 373–74.

276. *dPal yul dar thang bca' yig*: 199.

277. Ibid.

278. Bell [1946] 1998: 200.

279. *dPal yul gdan rabs*: 357.

280. *gdan rabs*. The owner of the Teachings (*bstan pa'i gdag po*) was then also called the *gdan rabs 'dzin pa'i khri rin po che*. Ibid.: 358.

281. Reynolds 1979: 225; Foulk 2004: 291.

282. Personal communication with Lama Tsültrim, Dehradun, August 2012.

283. Mills 2003: 315.

284. Cf. Mills 2003.

285. Kurzman 1998: 43.

286. Southern 1970: 29.

287. We can see a parallel in the corporate world, as the question of who can ultimately be held accountable or responsible (with all its legal implications) is one that is still very much a matter of debate. For an interesting discussion of this issue, see Ashman and Winstanley 2007: 83–95.

## 5.  MONASTIC ECONOMY AND POLICY

1. B. Miller 1961: 438.

2. Dreyfus 2003: 348n54.

3. In that sense, one could argue that to do this is to return to the roots of economics, as this field was originally a subset of moral philosophy. This is convincingly argued in Sedlacek 2011.

4. Hann and Hart 2011: 94.

5. Sayer 2004: 2.

6. Shakya 1999: 252.

7. Hillman 2005: 33–34.

8. Goldstein (1989b: 34) remarks on the Tibetan situation that monks had to provide their own food and that there were no monastery- or college-run communal kitchens.

9. Dreyfus 2003: 65.

10. *Pha bong kha bca' yig*: 239.

11. Dreyfus 2003: 47.

12. "The monasteries chose to hoard the resources and not distribute them. In local monasteries the circumstances were better" (ibid.: 351n28). Cassinelli and Ekvall (1969: 330) note: "Hoarding was a marked feature of Tibetan economic behavior."

13. Stein [1962] 1972: 148.

14. Here one might expect a discussion of feudalism and serfdom. Because these are such contentious issues, in which semantics appear to play a big role, I do not expect to be able to settle them, nor are they particularly relevant to the picture I try to paint here. I merely intend to describe and analyze the way the monastery dealt, and thought it dealt, with its surroundings. I leave it to the reader to judge whether these circumstances should be considered feudal. For more on this discussion, see Goldstein 1971b, 1986, 1987, 1989a; Miller 1987, 1988; Mills 2003: 331–47.

15. That is, the physical representations of enlightened beings.

16. *Dung dkar gsung rtsom*: 68.

17. Schopen 2001: 131.

18. For more on these distinctions in an Indian Buddhist context see Silk 2002: 175–77.

19. *sMin grol gling bca' yig*: 286–87.

20. *spyi 'bul. Gong ra nges gsang rdo rje gling bca' yig*: 228–29.

21. *sMin grol gling bca' yig*: 284.

22. *Byams pa gling bca' yig*: 251b.

23. This is in contrast with the observation that in Buddhist India property rights were not affected by becoming a monk; see Wayman 1984: 49.

24. *rNam rgyal grwa tshang bca' yig*: 67.

25. The topic of the judicial position of the monastery among the lay population is discussed in chapter 7.

26. There is plenty of narrative evidence from the *Mūlasarvāstivāda vinaya* that property held by individual members of the Sangha was common; e.g., Schopen 2000a: 7.

27. *'Bras spungs bca' yig*: 314. This two-month period seems relatively lenient compared to the rules given in the fourteenth-century guidelines for Jampa Ling, which state that animals may not be kept in the compound beyond three days. *Byams pa gling bca' yig*: 251b.

28. "[T]he monks' obligation to use what is 'given' to them is, in fact, their obligation to make merit for their donors—they are one and the same" (Schopen 1996a: 112).

29. This is also mentioned in Goldstein 2009: 11.

30. This is the allowance provided to the monasteries by the government of Sikkim.

31. *'Bras ljongs bca' yig*: 271.

32. Kvaerne 1970: 190.

33. This was arguably the largest expense; see Goldstein 2009: 11.

34. Ekvall 1964: 195.

35. Hovden 2013: 223–24.

36. This was equally the case in Bon monasteries; see Kvaerne 1970: 189.

37. Similarly, in contemporary Theravāda law the difference between property owned by the Sangha on an institutional level and that held by monks individually is recognized. Generally speaking, people regard an offering to the Sangha to be more meritorious than when the same is given to an individual monk. Nonetheless, both parties receive donations on a regular basis. Gombrich [1988] 2006: 161.

38. I have learned from personal experience that this is still the case in Tibetan monasteries, both in Tibet and in exile: a donation can never be simply given. The monk officials receiving the gifts always ask the benefactor what their gift is for. Individuals may have specific ideas as to where they wish their money to be spent, but often people ask the monks what the monastery is in need of the most. Separate funds thus are kept, ranging from providing food for the monks, to medical care, to the restoration of halls or the construction of a new stūpa.

39. *mTshur phu bca' yig*: 708/5a.

40. This phenomenon was called *thebs rtsa*; see Dagyab 2009: 108. The author translates this word as "Zinsverwendungsspende."

41. Tambiah 1970: 68.

42. Stein [1962] 1972: 140 (emphasis added).

43. *Dung dkar gsung rtsom*: 74. While it informs on the normative notions regarding the early funding of monks, the historicity of this claim is of course in doubt. That the monks were in fact subsidized is likely, but that they possessed no fields or cattle is not in line with historical trends among other contemporary Buddhist communities in China and India.

44. Dung dkar, among others, argues that Tibet was not well suited for alms begging, as the population was too sparse and villages were too spread out; see *Dung dkar gsung rtsom*: 75. The issue of begging for alms is discussed in chapter 6.

45. For example, Caple 2011.

46. *chos phogs*.

47. *Bod kyi dgon sde*: 178.

48. Most guidelines, however, contain information on the pro rata distribution of donations, e.g., how much an ordinary monk would receive in relation to, for example, the abbot. As briefly mentioned in the previous chapter this was expressed in shares (*skal*). This "income disparity" is also noted by Ekvall (1964: 197), who comments that "the lama [here meaning *sprul sku*] may receive a share, which, in recognition of his special status, is five, nine, or even more times the share of the individual monk." In Thekchen Damchö Gatsel Ling monastery in 1898 a lama received ten shares of donations (*'gyed*), a disciplinarian or a chant master five, whereas the water-dispensers and tea-makers were given one share. *Theg chen dam chos dga' tshal gling bca' yig*: 401.

49. Here I understand *zhing* to mean *bsod nams kyi zhing* (S. *puṇyakṣetra*).

50. *bSam gtan chos mchog gling gi bca' yig*: 671.

51. *Theg chen dam chos dga' tshal gling bca' yig*: 401.

52. *bKra shis chos rdzong bca' yig*: 410. With this rule the author probably intended to prevent monks from sharing their allocation of offerings with those who did not deserve them.

53. *dngul srang*.

54. *'Chi med grub pa'i byang chub gling bca' yig*: 648.

55. While this may have been the ideal in medieval Benedictine monasteries, the relative self-sufficiency and focus on monastic labor of these institutions seems to have been exaggerated. Raftis (1961: 457) notes: "It has been a romantic notion only with difficulty dispelled by historical research, that the typical (or perhaps ideal) monk labored in the fields so as to be almost self-supporting. The truth of the matter was far different. Even in

the general recommendations of the rule of St Benedict manual labor was only part, and not a necessary part, of a programme of moral culture." Similarly, the self-sufficiency of the Chan monasteries is equally questionable, for as early as the tenth century the "Pure Rules" written by Xuefeng Yicun convey that most of the monastic income came from donations and the monastic estates on which lay people worked; see Poceski 2003: 45–46.

56. For example, *bKra shis chos rdzong bca' yig*: 408.

57. *'bru phogs.*

58. *mTshur phu dgon gyi dkar chag*: 258.

59. Kvaerne 1970: 191.

60. Schuh and Dagyab 1978: 270.

61. Ibid.

62. Goldstein 2009: 13.

63. *ldab ldob.*

64. Khedrup, Richardson, and Skorupski 1986: 79. In fact, the *chayik* for Tashi Lhunpo from 1876 also notes these intruders. While it is not explicitly mentioned that these imposter-debaters were after financial gain, it is a likely scenario: "When the great disciplinarian and the disciplinarian of the debate ground make their rounds at the debate ground, aside from the few genuinely studious ones, most of them are only those who merely clap their hands, and who discuss goats and sheep (i.e., irrelevant subjects)." *bKra shis lhun po bca' yig*: 70.

65. Goldstein 2009: 10.

66. Personal communication with Shérap Gyatso, Rajpur, August 2012.

67. *spag.*

68. These were performed at the houses of sponsors.

69. Personal communication with Könchok Chönyi, Phiyang, August 2012.

70. It is significant that the informant never used the verb *tshong rgyag pa* (to do business) but instead calls what the monks did *'tsho stangs skyel ba*: to make a living.

71. Personal communication with Khenpo Chöying Lhundrup, Bir, July 2012.

72. Personal communication with Sönam Chögyel, Rajpur, July 2012.

73. *Kun 'phel gling bca' yig*: 558.

74. *grwa zhing.* Also called "lama's field"; e.g., Diack [1897] 1994 III: 88.

75. Jahoda 2007: 229n26.

76. A parallel can be found in Sri Lanka: according to the *katikāvata*s there seems to have been a custom of laypeople granting land to a *vihara* and then using the surplus for themselves. This type of "tax avoidance" was possible because people made sure that the monk population consisted of relatives; see Ratnapala 1971: 227.

77. Carrasco 1959: 33.

78. Personal communication with Lobzang Döndrup, Spituk, August 2012.

79. See Mills 2000: 27.

80. Personal communication with Könchok Chönyi, Phiyang, August 2012. This system is very similar to that described as salary fields (*phogs zhing*) in Tsarong 1987: 59.

81. There is, however, an interesting parallel with the Dunhuang of the ninth and tenth centuries, where monks and nuns possessed land that was farmed by hired laypeople. This effectively provided the monastic owner with his livelihood. Gernet [1956] 1995: 132–33.

82. Goldstein 1964: 137–38. Dagyab (2009: 22) similarly maintains that the Central Tibetan monasteries before 1959 were obliged to supply each monk with his livelihood,

regardless of whether one was involved in studying or not. Textual evidence suggests, however, that this cannot have been universally true. It is more likely that such an obligation was the exception rather than the rule.

83. Michael (1982: 111) suggests, however, that his informants maintained that "Lhasa financially supported all monasteries of all sects and backed their disciplinary authority." This assertion seems highly unlikely.

84. Carrasco 1959: 178.

85. *phogs yig* or *phogs deb*.

86. See Sullivan 2013: 195.

87. This is likely to be dGe 'phel hermitage (*ri khrod*), which is situated in the mountains above Drepung monastery.

88. This originally was an early Kadam monastery in Tsang.

89. *'Bras spungs bca' yig*: 306–7. See also Jansen 2013a: 131–32.

90. *Tshogs chen phogs yig*.

91. *bKra shis lhun po bca' yig*: 83.

92. *Thob rgyal rab rgyas gling dgon bca' yig*: 454.

93. There is a document called *phogs yig lag 'dzin* (Document no. 1709) that is accessible at www.dtab.uni-bonn.de. This text, however, appears to contain the allowances allotted to the master and servant (*ngo g.yog*) of the bKras ljongs (*bKra shis ljong) incarnation in 1817. This document merits further research.

94. With the possible exception of Tashi Lhunpo, which functioned in many ways mostly independent from the Ganden Phodrang government.

95. *Se ra byes bca' yig*: 569.

96. Generally speaking, not much is known about this nunnery, which in 1947 housed 110 nuns. Even then they received "special distributions." This number may have simply been an ideal one, for elsewhere in the same source it is reported that there were only 50 nuns living there. Cassinelli and Ekvall 1969: 397, 404.

97. *rje btsun sgrol ma'i dgongs rdzogs*.

98. *snyung gnas*.

99. *Rin chen sgang bca' yig*: 213.

100. *sbyor 'jags*.

101. See *mNga' ris khyung rdzong dkar po'i nye 'dabs kyi nam gling dgon sde'i dkar chag*. In *Rig 'dzin tshe dbang nor bu'i gsung 'bum*, vol. 5 (Dalhousie 1976–77): 653–59. This text is partially translated in Michael 1982: 181–82.

102. *mchod gzhis*. Surkhang 1986: 23.

103. Goldstein 1973: 448.

104. Walsh 2010: 185n2.

105. For an account of how a lama meticulously recorded and spent his wealth, see Wood 2013.

106. Stein [1962] 1972: 148.

107. *lcags po 'brug lo*. In the *bCa' yig phyogs bsgrigs* this is erroneously dated as 1920. The author was the regent of Tibet between 1819 and 1844. See Zhabs-dkar 1994: 676.

108. *Se ra theg chen gling rtsa tshig*: 182.

109. *gzhis gnyer*.

110. *lugs gnyis*: the secular (*srid*) and religious (*chos*) systems.

111. *Se ra theg chen gling rtsa tshig*: 186–87.

112. Ibid.: 187.

113. Ibid.

114. Naturally, here the issue is the inheritance of individual "simple" monks. With regard to the inheritance of whole monasteries during the twelfth century for example, the legality of the ownership was often challenged, as witnessed by the instances of a number of early Kadam monasteries. The solution was sought in securing the inheritance of religious property from father to son and in the case of celibate masters, uncle to nephew. See Davidson 2005: 290.

115. Schopen 2008: 640. The basic ruling found here is that the attendant of the dying monk received his six standard belongings, and in case of there being more than one attendant, all were to receive equal shares. The rest was to be divided and shared with the other monks; see ibid.: 635. For more on Indian Buddhist "property and inheritance laws," see Schopen 1995a, 2000a: 11–12, 2001.

116. Ratnapala 1971: 170. For more on Sinhalese inheritance and property rights in later times see Evers 1967.

117. Bunnag 1973: 120.

118. *prativastu*. Schopen 2008: 640n45.

119. Yifa 2002: 207–8.

120. This is also noted by Cassinelli and Ekvall (1969: 234), who comment that "each monastery had different regulations regarding possessions of deceased monks. In most monasteries the things went on to the monastery."

121. Ibid.: 307.

122. Personal communication with Shérap Gyatso, Rajpur, August 2012. In contrast, Khedrup et al. note that "quite a lot of monks" owned land and other property such as livestock. They could become quite rich, in part because they "did not have to pay much by way of taxation." However, when these rich monks died, most of their property would go to their college and not to their family. Khedrup, Richardson, and Skorupski 1986: 66.

123. Diack [1897] 1994 III: 88.

124. In contrast, in contemporary Ladakh these living quarters are owned and maintained by the "natal household estates" of the monks. These households are able to sell them on to other estates, if deemed appropriate (Mills 2000: 27). Nonetheless, the process of "inheriting" the living quarters was no doubt similar. To complicate matters further, Könchok Chönyi reports that the Ladakh branches (*yan lag gi dgon*) of Yangri Gar in Central Tibet used to own a hundred living quarters in this monastery, so that the monks sent out to study there would have a place to live. Personal communication, Phiyang, August 2012.

125. Goldstein 2009: 6.

126. Ekvall 1959/60: 209, 1964: 195.

127. *ldab ldob skyid sdug*.

128. Khedrup, Richardson, and Skorupski 1986: 51.

129. For research on monks inheriting in the *Mūlasarvāstivāda vinaya* see Schopen 1995b, 2001. According to the latter work (2001: 112) "vinayadharas did not want to give up their right to inheritance."

130. For example, Cassinelli and Ekvall 1969: 239. Speaking of Ladakh, Mills (2003: 313) notes that "when monks enter the monastery they lose the right to inherit."

131. French 1995a: 174. Interestingly, on page 173 the author details the account of a person "who did not inherit because he had taken religious vows," i.e., had become a monk. On page 333, she gives the life story of the monk Thubten Sangye, who states that "monks cannot inherit."

132. Cassinelli and Ekvall 1969: 234. Conversely, in Sri Lanka a monk could inherit family land, which would then become monastic property after his death; see Kemper 1984: 408.

133. Here the most obvious parallel is the way merchants and monks traveled on the Silk Route.

134. Chen 1949: 100. In contrast, Slobodnik (2004: 8), writing about Amdo, remarks that according to a Chinese (propagandist) source, the main income for the monastery was the taxes paid to them by the people, demonstrating the people's subordination to the monastery.

135. Michael 1982: 49–50. In contrast, a source of income for Chinese monasteries during the Song dynasty was the organizing of religious festivals, which were accompanied by market fairs; see Walsh 2010: 59. This (conscious) attempt to accrue wealth appears not to have been common practice in Tibetan monasteries. Similarly, there are indications that Chinese monasteries occasionally owned shops at the market. In the ninth century the monastery of Da Xiang Si (大像寺) in western Shanxi had such a shop, either as a branch of the monastic treasury or as an outlet to sell the monastery estate's produce; see Twitchett 1957: 539–40. Tibetan monasteries' ownership of shops appears to be a more recent phenomenon, however. See Caple 2011 and Dagyab 2009: 127–29.

136. Schopen 2001: 120.

137. Desideri [1937] 2011: 333.

138. Schopen 2004: 32.

139. Schopen 2000a: 14.

140. *Vinayavibhaṅga* (D3 Cha): 156b.

141. *'Bri gung mthil bca' yig*: 249b.

142. This issue is further discussed in chapter 6.

143. It is sometimes argued that, while other schools were lax in this regard, one of the major accomplishments of Tsongkhapa is that the movement he spearheaded was the only one without a laissez-faire attitude toward alcohol consumption by monks. See for example Norman 2009: 156. The above passage (*'Bri gung mthil bca' yig*: 249b), however, clearly shows that strict regulations toward monastic alcohol consumption were in place some two hundred years before Tsongkhapa's time.

144. *Se ra byes bca' yig*: 550.

145. Cassinelli and Ekvall 1969: 401.

146. Patrul Rinpoche 1998: 105.

147. *bKra shis lhun po bca' yig*: 116.

148. Makley 2007: 191.

149. *'Bras spungs bca' yig*: 307.

150. *bKra shis chos rdzong bca' yig*: 410.

151. On various occasions, the *Mūlasarvāstivāda vinaya* paints a picture of "a Buddhist monk who accepts, handles, and disperses what must have been considerable, or even very large sums of money" (Schopen 2006: 236). However, the money is always handled for the benefit of the larger community.

152. Gernet [1956] 1995: 163.

153. *Ra mo che bca' yig*: 137. A similar sentiment is expressed in a *chayik* from 1930 written by the Thirteenth Dalai Lama; see *Rong po rab brtan dgon bca' yig*: 538.

154. *Pha bong kha bca' yig*: 243.

155. *'O chu dgon bca' yig*: 177. In the *bCa' yig phyogs bsgrigs* this text is wrongly dated 1798; in the *bCa' yig phyogs bsgrigs* 2 this error has been corrected.

156. *grwa pa sgrig gis 'tsho*. Phuntsho 2004: 572.

157. *mTshur phu bca' yig*: 708/5a.

158. *'Bras spungs bca' yig*: 313–34.

159. *bKra shis lhun po bca' yig*: 117.

160. Ibid.: 118.

161. Ibid.: 83.

162. Cech 1988: 77.

163. *chos khrims khang*.

164. *bKra shis lhun po bca' yig*: 118.

165. *rgyal khrims* or *srid khrims*.

166. That is, do not pursue people.

167. *sMin grol gling bca' yig*: 282.

168. Schram [1954] 2006: 374.

169. Dōgen 1996: 110.

170. Here we see that the problem was the mixing of the sacred and the profane, not the business itself. Similarly, Jesus once chased men buying and selling and exchanging money out of the temple (John 2:14), but he did not pursue them once they were outside of the temple. Sedlacek 2011: 139.

171. Miller 1958: 187–88.

172. In the previous chapter the need for the financial managers to possess capital of their own is mentioned. In a similar way it seems that business monks most likely came from the wealthier strata of society.

173. Personal communication with Shérap Gyatso, Rajpur, August 2012.

174. For example, a modern work on the history of Tsurpu claims that at the time of the Thirteenth Dalai Lama each monk received about four hundred silver coins from him. See *mTshur phu dgon gyi dkar chag*: 269. It is likely that this was a yearly amount. While it is difficult to calculate the value of money, as the value of silver fluctuated greatly, this still appears to have been a substantial amount.

175. Spencer Chapman ([1938] 1984: 178), traveling through Central Tibet in the 1920s, claims: "Practically half the revenue of the State is devoted to the upkeep of the monasteries, either in the form of grants of land or in gifts of barley, butter and tea."

176. *Bod kyi dgon sde*: 174. Naturally, in the context of Tibet, for most transactions actual currency was hardly ever used—to facilitate the discussion the word "money" is therefore used in a rather broad way.

177. Chen (1949: 138) also notes this logic: the "lamaseries" in Kham loaned out more cash than the wealthy families, "due to their involvement in trade."

178. Monks clearly did not only loan goods and money out to laypeople; they also gave credit to their fellow monks. A number of loan contracts between mostly higher-placed monks can be found at www.dtab.uni-bonn.de.

179. The text itself states that both the previous year and the year before that, famines had taken place. *gDan sa bca' yig*: 127. For some of the historical context, see Martin 2010.

180. *gDan sa bca' yig*: 127–28.

181. *mTshur phu bca' yig*: 708/5a.

182. Cassinelli and Ekvall 1969: 235. For more on cases in which monks were punished under secular law see chapter 7.

183. *sMin grol gling bca' yig*: 281–82.

184. *mi zad pa*, S. *\*akṣaya*.

185. *rab tu sbyor ba*, S. *pra√yuj/ \*prayojayati*. For a discussion of this term see Schopen 2004b: 56–57.

186. *Vinayavibhaṅga* (D3 Cha): 155a. The narrative reasoning given for this ruling by the redactors of the *Mūlasarvāstivāda vinaya* can be found in Schopen 2004a: 29–30, 2004b: 48–50.

187. Schopen 2000a: 7.

188. As in the example of Rinchen Gang nunnery given earlier.

189. Whether these managers were monks is not confirmed, although it is likely that they were. In the *Mūlasarvāstivāda vinaya* conflicting narratives exist. In the *Uttaragrantha* the *ārāmika* (often a layperson) provided the loans, whereas in the *Vinayavibhaṅga* monks themselves are depicted as handing them out. See Schopen 2001: 102.

190. *Chab mdo dga' ldan theg chen byams pa gling bca' yig*: 549.

191. Dagyab 2009: 108.

192. Ibid.: 179.

193. Chen 1949: 139.

194. *Bod kyi dgon sde*: 174.

195. Probably written in either 1899 or 1959.

196. *dngul ṭam rdo*.

197. Manuscript 110: 0614_AA_1_1_66_9 at www.dtab.uni-bonn.de/tibdoc/termdoc/term2.htm.

198. Chen 1949: 138.

199. Dagyab 2009: 61.

200. Welch 1967: 27.

201. Exercising (any type of) force was not always an option for monasteries that were less powerful. Bunnag (1973: 124), for example, reports several cases in which tenants refused to pay rent, because they knew the monastery was unlikely to pursue the matter.

202. Bell [1946] 1998: 200.

203. This (purposely anonymized) account is based on what I have heard during my stay in India between 2000 and 2005 and from later conversations with monks. This incident most definitely merits further research, for it may prove to be very informative on the contemporary nature of monk–lay relations in exile.

204. Dagyab 2009: 183.

205. Nowadays, this term is used to denote interest rates that are exorbitant. This—much more recent—gloss of the word "usury" has no place in this discussion.

206. See Kaye 2000: 86–87.

207. Aristotle, *Politics*, 1258a39–1258b7, as cited in Sedlacek 2011: 85.

208. Walsh 2010: 14 (emphasis added).

209. Graeber 2011: 496. Similar attitudes to usury can be found in non-Buddhist Indian texts such as the *Manusmṛti*. It is said there that to lend out goods so business can be conducted is not permitted unless it is for a "religious purpose" (S. *dharmārtha*). See Schopen 2004b: 57–58. In this article it is suggested that Vinaya and Dharmaśāstra materials contain significant parallels in this regard.

210. Caple 2010: 210.

211. Dagyab 2009: 118.

212. Ibid.: 174.

213. Gernet [1956] 1995: 359n73. This remark pertains not just to China but also to India.

214. Ekvall 1964: 198.

215. As some of the examples I have given throughout this study suggest, the aristocracy and the monastic institutions cannot comfortably be seen as separate agents, although the exact nature of this relationship remains opaque. This lacuna in scholarship is in need of further research.

216. For example, Parenti 2003. For an overview of these types of sources see Powers 2004.

217. Ekelund et al. 1996: 116.

218. Le Goff 1988: 69.

219. This is of course not dissimilar to the role of the Christian Church and its monasteries in medieval Europe. See Ekelund et al. 1996: 175.

220. Wiley 1986: 9.

221. Weber [1922] 1978: 586.

222. Caple 2011: 261.

223. Dreyfus 2003: 74.

224. *Dung dkar gsung rtsom*: 78.

225. On this issue, see Ornatowski 1996.

226. This is what Tambiah (1970: 213) called the double negation of reciprocity. For its occurrence in the Vinaya see Schopen 1995b: 107. According to the Vinaya, monks are not only to accept whatever they are given, they are also to *use* what they are given (meaning that they cannot trade or sell it). This latter stipulation is apparently disregarded by the authors of certain *chayik*. According to the earlier-cited instance from the monastic guidelines for Drepung monastery, for example, monks were required to sell on the horses they were given but not allowed to keep; see *'Bras spungs bca' yig*: 314.

227. Walsh 2010: 14.

228. This argument is compellingly made in Graeber 2011: 56 et seq.

229. Gernet [1956] 1995: 247.

## 6.  RELATIONS WITH THE LAITY

1. Goldstein 2009: 3.

2. Ekvall 1959/60: 217.

3. Gyatso 2003: 239–40.

4. Kapstein 2004: 233–34.

5. This is in parallel with "the preoccupation of the compilers of the Buddhist *Vinaya*s with their public image" (Schopen 2006: 243). Put another way, "Sensitivity about

lay-monk relations is one of the fundamental parameters of the Vinaya" (Bailey and Mab-bett 2006: 181).

6. Miller 1961: 199.

7. For example, Hovden 2013; Ramble 2008; Ortner 1989.

8. Bechert 1984: 274.

9. Goldstein and Tsarong 1985: 17.

10. For rules on eating see for example Pachow [1955] 2000: 59.

11. Accordingly, in an ideal Buddhist world, "there are two 'occupations' for a monk: meditation and recitation" (Schopen 2006: 241).

12. This is a feature found throughout the monastic Buddhist world. For example, whereas some of the rules in the seventeenth-century Qing Code (*Da Qing lü* 大 清 律) enforced the specific religious rules, "others were intended to distance the sangha from ordinary people" (Dicks 2014: 237).

13. For the importance of these boundaries in Pāli Buddhism see Kieffer-Pülz 2011.

14. This term, in Tibetan *khrims grogs*, is frequently mentioned in similar discussions. The thirteenth-century Vinaya commentator mTsho sna ba shes rab bzang po explains that this is a friend who prevents one from committing a *pārājika*, who is not nonhuman, mute, stupid, insane, a hermaphrodite, or blind. See Jam mgon kong sprul and International Translation Committee 2003: 378n133. In practice, however, a monk companion was invariably simply a monk of reasonably good standing.

15. *nyag*—the exact weight or measure is not known.

16. *sMin grol gling bca' yig*: 279.

17. Wickremasinghe 1928: 278.

18. A lengthy discussion on behavior and movement during the summer and winter retreats is found in Tsongkhapa's *Byams pa gling bca' yig*: 250b-1a.

19. Cech 1988: 75.

20. While the topic of gender is beyond the scope of this study, the *chayik* are informative regarding monastic contact with women.

21. *dPal yul dar thang bca' yig*: 194.

22. Wessels 1924: 74.

23. While limiting movements in monastic compounds in more densely populated areas was of course not always feasible or even desired, we can see the often unrestricted access that Tibetan laity are allowed to most monasteries today in both the PRC and exile communities as a significant development.

24. Strenski 1983: 470. Sihlé (2015: 369–73) questions the universal centrality of gift-giving in Buddhist cultures posited by Strenski, using as an example a contemporary Tibetan Buddhist community, in which the transactions to do with ritual service take prominence over straightforward donations. I think this is likely to be a historical continuity and the *chayik* material also points in that direction. From the emic point of view, however, such *quid pro quo* transactions are still viewed as offerings.

25. Tambiah 1970: 68.

26. Spiro 1971: 465.

27. As will be indicated later in this chapter, there are many exceptions to this generalization.

28. Schopen 1996a: 115 (emphasis added). For more on how to handle donations in the Indian commentarial traditions, see Silk 2002: 129–83.

29. Schopen 1996a: 112.

30. Schopen 1995b: 108n20.

31. Nietupski 2011: 20.

32. By contrast, Khedrup et al. (1986: 241) describes the Tibetan "fighting" monks (*ldab ldob) and their proclivity for giving: "they were characterized not only by generosity in their own group, but often by light-hearted, almost reckless charity to those in great material need, the beggars and the poor."

33. Welch 1967: 16.

34. *Se ra theg chen gling rtsa tshig*: 185.

35. This quotation is given by the Fifth Dalai Lama in his *chayik* for Drepung. *'Bras spungs bca' yig*: 299. See also Jansen 2013a: 116. This same quotation is also found in guide-lines for Namgyel Dratsang written by the same author; see *rNam rgyal grwa tshang bca' yig*: 66–67.

36. *sTag brag dgon pa bca' yig*: 631.

37. The exemption of this latter category is found in *bKra shis chos rdzong bca' yig*: 409.

38. *'Bras spungs bca' yig*: 304.

39. *spyi'i dge 'dun gyi 'du sgo 'phrogs pa*.

40. *nye ba'i mtshams med lnga. Tshig mdzod chen mo*: 961; see also Silk 2007: 265.

41. *'Bras spungs bca' yig*: 310.

42. Ibid.: 319–20.

43. *Byams pa gling bca' yig*: 251a.

44. *Kong stod dung dkar dgon bca' yig*: 588.

45. *sMin grol gling bca' yig*: 286.

46. Ibid.: 283–84.

47. *dkyil 'khor*, S. maṇḍala.

48. *Rong zom bca' yig*: 400.

49. *sbyin pa*, S. dāna.

50. In recent times in Thailand, the more prominent monks also occasionally help out their poorer relations by giving them money; see Bunnag 1973: 120. Gernet ([1956] 1995: 218–19), in considering earlier Chinese Buddhist communities, detects a devel-opment, with monks first being the recipient and then becoming the donors, as there were a number of documents recording the monastics' generosity to the sick and the poor. One wonders, however, whether there was ever truly a "development" as such or whether this dual role of recipient and donor always existed synchronously, considering that monks and nuns as the donors of religious items are well attested in early material culture in India.

51. Schopen 1994b: 158.

52. Silk 1999: 368.

53. *'u lag*.

54. This is witnessed by Khedrup et al. (1986: 79), who note that in Sera monastery "the tea was made in kitchens where the lay servants worked. They were a wild and often dishon-est lot and stole as much of the supplies as they could."

55. The corvée-worker explains the origins for this status: "Tradition said that we were descendants from former monks who had married and had been made to render *'u lag* service for the maintenance of the monastery"; see Dhondub and the Information Office of H.H. the Dalai Lama 1978: ii.

56. This duty is explained as "a *khral* or tax in the form of compulsory labor" and as something "not paid for, as it was seen as a sort of payment for the personally owned land that had been given to them by the monastery"; see ibid.: i–ii.

57. Ibid.: ii–iii.

58. Personal communication with Lobzang Döndrup, Spituk, August 2012.

59. Nornang 1990: 257.

60. *Gong ra nges gsang rdo rje gling bca' yig*: 226.

61. Cassinelli and Ekvall 1969: 200.

62. *Byams pa gling bca' yig*: 251b–52a.

63. *dPal yul dar thang bca' yig*: 193.

64. For an interesting account of the division of labor between monks and laypeople in Limi, Nepal, in the last hundred or so years, see Hovden 2013: 216–18, 224–27.

65. Nietupski 2011: 89.

66. *qiu fu* 求福. Welch 1967: 33–35.

67. Dargyay 1982: 79.

68. Personal communication with Lobzang Döndrup, Spituk, August 2012.

69. Dhondub and the Information Office of H.H. the Dalai Lama 1978: ii.

70. I have no doubt that the author Terdak Lingpa, who was close to the Fifth Dalai Lama, modeled this section on the *chayik* the latter wrote for traveling government representatives; see Cüppers 2007.

71. *'gro mgon.*

72. *sMin grol gling bca' yig*: 308.

73. The unusual phrase *bla ma la dmigs pa'i sdig kham po che* in all likelihood refers to a deed so negative that it would disappoint one's teacher.

74. *Byams pa gling bca' yig*: 252a.

75. *'Bras spungs bca' yig*: 310. See also Jansen 2013a: 130.

76. *ja nyag.*

77. *Se ra byes bca' yig*: 566–67; *Se ra byes bca' yig* 2: 83.

78. *Ra mo che bca' yig*: 131.

79. *grong chog.*

80. *Pha bong kha bca' yig*: 245.

81. *Theg chen dam chos dga' tshal gling bca' yig*: 401.

82. *dPal yul dar thang bca' yig*: 194.

83. Ibid.: 196–97.

84. Here it needs to be noted that the verb invariably used when referring to buying Buddhist paraphernalia is *blu ba*—a verb signifying respect toward the object being purchased. Its more archaic meaning is "to ransom," which is also used in rituals. This verb usage indicates that the transaction is not a clear-cut business deal.

85. Cassinelli and Ekvall 1969: 401.

86. Presumably the printer's own wishes.

87. Here this indicates not the butter for the lamps but the actual receptacles.

88. *sMin grol gling bca' yig*: 312.

89. Ekelund et al. 1996: 85.

90. By contrast, in China, according to the *Gazetteer of Qixia Monastery* from 1704, begging for alms was still held as the ideal, while owning property was seen as necessary only if there were too many monks to be fed on alms; see Brook 2014: 217.

91. Cassinelli and Ekvall 1969: 302.

92. *bka' khrims.*

93. Here the word *rdzong* (fort) refers to the local secular authorities.

94. Aris 1986: 150–52 (110b). The translation of the same passage in a colonial work on Bhutan reads: "All Jongpens [\**rdzong dpon*] and Head Lamas of monasteries shall not try to realise any gifts by going round visiting raiyats [land-holding farmers]" (White [1909] 1971: 305). My translation here differs slightly from that of Aris's.

95. Diack [1897] 1994 III: 88.

96. French 1995a: 320.

97. Bell [1946] 1998: 58.

98. Pardue 1971: 21–22.

99. *bsod snyoms pa chen po.* Heimbel 2013: 224.

100. *'Bri gung mthil bca' yig*: 249b. For the translation of this passage, see chapter 5.

101. Wood 2013: 43.

102. *spyi don.*

103. *'Bras spungs bca' yig*: 313.

104. *slong mo byed pa.*

105. *Se ra byes bca' yig* 2: 111.

106. Jansen 2013a: 130–31.

107. *sgrig rim.*

108. *Rin chen sgang bca' yig*: 214.

109. Caple 2011: 121.

110. Ibid.: 125. See also Caple 2010: 178–219.

111. *mTshur phu bca' yig*: 707/4b.

112. The sources that refer to these rounds are numerous; e.g., *bKra shis lhun po bca' yig*: 90 and Zongtse 1995: 578.

113. *khyim (pa) sun 'byin pa*, P. *kuladūsaka*, C. *wu jia* 污家. This term is not unproblematic. See Oldenberg [1879] 1964, vol. 1: xvii; Frauwallner 1956: 140–41; Horner 1949, vol. 1: 326; Yamagiwa 2001: 58–59.

114. *dge 'dun gyi lhag ma'i chos bcu gsum.* Literally, "remnants of the Sangha." Being guilty of breaking these rules would mean a temporary removal from the monastic community for six days and nights. For more on the technicalities of the *Saṅghāvaśeṣa* in mainly the Pali Vinaya, see Kieffer-Pülz 2014: 49.

115. Horner 1949, vol. 1: 314–29.

116. *Vinayottarāgamaviśeṣāgamapraśnavṛtti* ('*Dul ba lung bla ma'i bye brag lung zhu ba'i 'grel pa*) (D4116): 278b.

117. In more recent times in Thailand there have been one or two cases in which a monastic community lost its day-to-day support of the laypeople in the vicinity due to "the real or alleged misdemeanours of one or more of its members" (Bunnag 1973: 112).

118. In the context of the *chayik*, the phrase is invariably *khyim (pa) sun 'byin pa* (and alternatives to this spelling).

119. *rNam rgyal grwa tshang bca' yig*: 72.

120. For an interesting account of one master's attempt to deal with offerings ethically, see Wood 2013.

121. *bKra shis chos 'phel gling bca' yig*: 358.

122. *chos spyod*. For example, in *Kaṃ tshang chos spyod sogs kha ton gces btus*, 2001, compiled by Shes rab rgyal mtshan, Delhi: 653–66.

123. The author repeats this almost verbatim in another *chayik* for the same monastery: *Se ra theg chen gling bca' yig*: 104–5.

124. *Se ra byes bca' yig*: 566.

125. The text simply gives the word *bu lon* (loan/debt) without clarifying whose debt—the layperson's or the monk's—is being referred to.

126. *sMin grol gling bca' yig*: 281.

127. Ibid.: 306.

128. *paṇ zhwa*.

129. *sTag lung brang mang thos bsam bstan gling bca' yig*: 196.

130. *Ra mo che bca' yig*: 130.

131. *Gong ra nges gsang rdo rje gling bca' yig*: 227.

132. *bKra shis lhun po bca' yig*: 81.

133. sKyid na was a special school at Tashi Lhunpo that trained civil servants in the Panchen Lama's administration.

134. *dGu rtsegs ma'i char 'bebs*. This is in all likelihood a type of festival during which prayers were held, which were sponsored by the local population. *Char 'bebs* is likely an abbreviation for a cycle of prayers or a specific prayer. It may refer to the prayers recited during the festival called *bKra shis dgu rtsegs* held at the end of the year. See Tucci [1970] 1988: 150.

135. *than*.

136. *bKra shis lhun po bca' yig*: 89.

137. Ibid.: 100–101.

138. To play in the water is the 64th *prāyaścitta* (*sor gshags*), an offense requiring confession.

139. This version is a copy (*ngo bshus*) along with corrections (*zhu dag*) of the *chayik* written by the Thirteenth Dalai Lama in 1926; see *Byams gling grwa tshang bca' yig*: 484.

140. Ibid.: 482.

141. In the brief explanation of the 253 "vows" by the Fifth Dalai Lama, this is number 163: "to skip while going [somewhere]"; *So thar gyi tshul khrims rnam gsal sgron me*: 25.

142. *bKra shis dga' ldan chos 'phel gling bca' yig*: 498, 9.

143. The monastery in question is called Hor yul dur bde [*sic*: bed] wang gi bkra shis rdzogs ldan dge rgyas gling. I have not been able to locate this monastery. *Dur bed* probably refers to Dörbet, a tribe found predominantly in Mongolia, but also in Kalmykia and parts of China. The memoirs of Dorjiev suggest that this Dörbet or Dorbed, as a place, was situated in current-day Kalmykia; see Norbu and Martin 1991.

144. *gos sbubs can*, literally cylindrical clothes.

145. *sgom thag*. These were ropes that were meant to tie one's leg in the correct position for meditation.

146. *Rong po rab brtan dgon bca' yig*: 538.

147. *bKra shis bsam gtan gling bca' khrims*: 531.

148. *dge 'dun gyi nang khrims*: this phrase must here refer to the Vinaya rules.

149. *Kun 'phel gling bca' yig*: 557–58.

150. In fact, the smoking of tobacco by monks and laypeople alike had been forbidden throughout Tibet by the Thirteenth Dalai Lama in 1918. For more on this prohibition and further attitudes toward smoking in Tibet, see Berounsky 2013.

151. *rgyang grags. rDo phud chos 'khor gling bca' yig*: 566.

152. *gcus zhwa.*

153. Ibid.: 569.

154. *Thob rgyal rab rgyas gling dgon bca' yig*: 454.

155. *Pha bong kha bca' yig*: 243.

156. *skrod pa*, S. *pravāsana*. The commentaries on the *Mūlasarvāstivāda vinaya* do not agree on how to interpret when and how the actual act of *kuladūṣaka* is actually committed, however.

157. This is not to say that the Tibetan tradition had forgotten what this phrase was meant to signify. The Fifth Dalai Lama states, in his explanation of the *Prātimokṣa* rules: "*kuladūṣaka* occurs when someone has, due to bad behavior, caused a householder to turn back on his faith in the Sangha, and when he, due to that fault, has been banished, disputes the Sangha who has banished him and does not pay heed, despite others' having refuted him"; *So thar gyi tshul khrims rnam gsal sgron me*: 10. This corresponds largely to the contents of the *Sarvāstivāda prātimokṣa*. See Pachow [1955] 2000: 85–86.

158. Schopen 2001: 137.

159. Silk 2008: 10.

160. Goldstein and Tsarong 1985: 25.

161. B. Miller 1961: 409.

162. For example, Tambiah 1970; Spiro 1971; Bunnag 1973; Gombrich [1988] 2006.

163. *Se ra byes bca' yig*: 582.

164. The text reads *skor sbyong*, which I emend to *dkor sbyong*. As mentioned in an earlier chapter, *dkor* refers to monastic wealth, but often has a negative connotation. For example, someone who "eats *dkor*" (*dkor bza' mkhan*) in colloquial (and written) Tibetan is someone who sponges off the monastic amenities without doing anything in return. Furthermore, the Thirteenth Dalai Lama describes the materials given by the sponsors out of faith as a kind of debt that is to be repaid by being a good monk. See *bKra shis dga' ldan chos 'phel gling bca' yig*: 498.

165. *bKra shis chos rdzong bca' yig*: 408. This is also a word used to refer to arhats.

166. On this motivation for building Buddhist temples, see for example Gyatso 1989.

167. The early *chayik* for a tantric community by Rongzom Chözang does connect upsetting the protectors with obstacles and unfavorable circumstances; see *Rong zom bca' yig*: 399.

168. *chos khrims.*

169. *mi yi chos.*

170. Aris 1986: 140. The translation is an adaptation from that of Aris's.

171. *dPal ri chos sde bca' yig*: 458.

172. One of the most comprehensive discussions of this concept is by Seyfort Ruegg 1991.

173. Kvaerne 1970: 190.

174. *sbyin 'dzin pa.*

175. Nietupski 2011: 90.

176. Clarke 2014: 24. While Clarke also looks at the monks' relationship with their re-productive family (i.e., wife, husband, children), I here mainly treat the family unit in the sense of the monk's parental home. I have dealt with the former type of family in some detail in Jansen 2014.

177. Clarke 2014: 26.

178. Schopen 2001: 117.

179. 'das pa, S. atyaya. Schopen 2007: 123–24. The translated passage found in 'Dul ba (Pa): 112b.

180. Silk 2008: 58.

181. Goldstein 2009: 6.

182. The comparison between a monastery and a boarding school is also made in Das [1893] 1965: 6.

183. Nietupski 2011: 23.

184. Ibid.: 24.

185. The impact that these monastic networks had on politics, trade, and social relations has been little researched to date.

186. Personal communication with anonymous monks in Pelyul, March 2011.

187. For the international status of Drepung monastery in the late seventeenth century see Jansen 2013a: 120–25.

188. khyim nas khyim med par rab tu byung ba; this sūtric phrase is common to describe the process of becoming ordained.

189. The latter point is made by Cassinelli and Ekvall 1969: 235.

190. sMin grol gling bca' yig: 287. The text goes on to state the punishments one would incur by arriving back at the monastery later than the agreed-upon date.

191. While we tend to assume that this regulation served to maintain monastic identity, Ramble's (2008: 67) research in Te, Mustang, suggests that while monks and nuns were, generally speaking, exempt from communal duties, they were also not to stay at home overnight, so that they could not benefit their families economically and thereby put other households at a disadvantage.

192. sMin grol gling bca' yig: 279.

193. Ibid.: 286.

194. Miller 1958: 145. This point is also made in Carrasco 1959: 104. However, here it is pointed out that they could never work the monastery's land. This is contradicted by infor-mation provided by Cassinelli and Ekvall 1969: 402. They note that monks who were not good at their studies became menial workers within their monasteries and, similarly, could not plow but they could reap and sow.

195. sKu 'bum byams pa gling bca' yig: 10.

196. 'Bras spungs bca' yig: 319. See also Jansen 2013a: 116–17.

197. Aris 1986: 158–59.

198. Kawaguchi (1909: 434), traveling in Tibet in the early 1900s, also notes this reality: "The Tibetan monks do farming and the 'young rowdies' do the work of ordinary soldiers."

199. Schopen 2008: 637.

200. Dreyfus 2003: 36. The Bhutan law code qualifies this restriction and states that monks who have no knowledge should not be doctors, nor do divinations (mo). See Aris 1986: 160.

201. That is, *pañca sahā dhārmika: bhikṣu, bhikṣunī, śīksamāna, śrāmaṇera, śrāmāṇerī.*

202. Ratnapala 1971: 181. See also Seneviratna 2000: 201: "Bhikkus are furthermore prohibited to attend sick people and from practicing medicine."

203. Gombrich [1988] 2006: 156.

204. Schopen 1995a: 495.

205. Schopen 1994b: 158.

206. There is, however, mention of the existence of "hospices" (*'gron khang*) from around the twelfth century onward, where the sick were cared for. They were often set up by lamas (Stein [1962] 1972: 147).

207. Arya 2009: 3. This was not the case for all medical colleges, as the *chayik* written by the Fifth Dalai Lama for Drang srong 'dus pa'i gling (in Shigatse) clearly indicates; see *bCa' yig phyogs bsgrigs* 2: 79. Nonetheless, part of the title of this place was "Medical Monastic College" (gSo ba rig pa'i grwa tshang), and the rules this text contains are very similar to monastic *chayik,* although it stipulates different regulations for the lay and monastic members, an example of which is their respective dress codes.

208. Meyer 2003: 11. A later *chayik* for the same college from 1740 written by Pho lha ba bsod nams stobs rgyal can be found in *bCa' yig phyogs bsgrigs* 2: 162–65. Van Vleet (2016) discusses what may be the first *chayik* written for a medical institution, authored by the Fifth Dalai Lama.

209. The *sman pa grwa tshang* called *gSo rig gzhan phan gling.*

210. Anonymous, *Labulengsi Monastery,* 1989: 34.

211. This was also the case for monasteries in Song-era China, which often produced medicines, with an intention both to help and to make a profit. See Walsh 2010: 60, 157n31.

212. See Gyatso 2015.

213. *rgyun ja. sTag lung brang mang thos bsam bstan gling bca' yig*: 200.

214. *sTag brag dgon pa bca' yig*: 639–40.

215. *nad g.yog.*

216. *rim gro. sMin grol gling bca' yig*: 284.

217. *dPal ri chos sde bca' yig*: 457.

218. *rim gro byed*; this phrase is ambiguous as it could merely refer to any type of help or more specifically to "healing rituals."

219. *Gong ra nges gsang rdo rje gling bca' yig*: 228.

220. *Kong stod dung dkar dgon bca' yig*: 589.

221. *Ra mo che bca' yig*: 130–31.

222. The *chayik* for Drepung, however, does mention the post of *sman sbyin pa,* the giver of medicines. This person may have been a chemist of some sort, but unfortunately no information is given. See *'Bras spungs bca' yig*: 304.

223. Khedrup et al. (1986: 78) notes that in Sera it was usually the "rogue" monks who would take care of the aging. He recounts that they had come across an elderly monk who had been dead in his room for a long time without anyone noticing.

224. For the interaction between Buddhism and medicine in Tibet see Garrett 2008: 37–56.

225. Ratnapala 1971: 156–57.

226. Gombrich [1988] 2006: 147.

227. Spiro 1971: 307.

228. Dicks 2014: 242.

229. See Travers 2016 on the Tibetan pre-modern education system(s).

230. Kawaguchi 1909: 435.

231. Spencer Chapman [1938] 1984: 95.

232. Cassinelli and Ekvall 1969: 271; French 1995a: 329.

233. Diack [1897] 1994 III: 91.

234. Cassinelli and Ekvall 1969: 323.

235. Miller 1958: 141. In particular among Tibetan Buddhist families in Nepal, the practice of sending young boys to the monastery only to call them back when they reach adulthood or are needed to help the family is widespread.

236. *bla brang slob grwa*.

237. Presumably, those of the "Tashi Lhunpo government," not the Ganden Phodrang.

238. Das [1893] 1965: 9–10. The Ganden Phodrang also set up similar schools: the rTse slob grwa for aspiring monk officials and the rTsis slob grwa for aspiring lay officials. See Travers 2011: 167. These schools were generally accessible only to the elite.

239. *Bod kyi shes yon*: 67.

240. Again, the education of laypeople in historical Tibet is very much understudied, which, in part, may have to do with the lack of sources, but see Travers 2016.

This citation is found in a *chayik* by the Fifth Dalai Lama, *Gong ra nges gsang rdo rje gling bca' yig*: 222: *dge slong mchog yin dge tshul 'bring / khyim na gnas pa tha ma yin/*. This is cited from an unnamed text. The quote is generally attributed to the *Śrīkālacakragarbhanāmatantra*. It can be located in *bsDus pa'i rgyud kyi rgyal po dus kyi 'khor lo'i 'grel bshad / rtsa ba'i rgyud kyi rjes su 'jug pa stong phrag bcu gnyis pa dri ma med pa'i 'od ces bya ba* (D845): 262a: *gsum las dge slong mchog yin zhing / 'bring ni dge tshul zhes bya ste / khyim gnas de las tha ma'o /*; and alternatively in *Trisaṃvaraprabhāmālā (sDom gsum 'od kyi phreng ba)* (D3727): 55a: *rten ni gsum las dge slong mchog / 'bring ni dge tshul yin par 'dod / khyim na gnas pa tha ma'o /*. It is usually cited in the context of the quality of vows, but here it is more like an encouragement for monks to hold to their vows.

241. For Christian monasticism in a comparative perspective, see for example Silber 1985: 264. From a diachronic perspective, perhaps the social (and legal) position of Chinese Buddhist monks was most subject to change. See for example Barrett 2014.

242. Miller 1958: 138.

243. Horner 1949, vol. 1: xxix.

244. This point is also made by Miller 1958: 149.

245. Bailey and Mabbett 2006: 181.

246. Gyatso 2003: 243.

247. Sedlacek 2011: 78.

248. Wangchuk 2005: 228.

249. Schwartz 1994: 733.

250. Ibid.: 731.

251. Ibid.: 730.


7.  JUSTICE AND THE JUDICIAL ROLE OF THE MONASTERY

1. French 1995a: 169.

2. Carrasco 1959: 121.

3. Vermeersch 2008: 151.

4. French 1995a: 47.

5. Personal communication with Rendo Senggé, Dharamsala, July 2012.

6. Ellingson 1990: 205.

7. *sGrig lam rnam gzhag*. Penjore 2011: 23.

8. In terms of chronology, naturally "Tibetan secular law preceded ecclesiastic law," which only began with the first ordinations at Samyé in the middle of the second half of the eighth century; see van der Kuijp 1999: 289.

9. French 1998: 519n40.

10. French 1995a: 345.

11. Ibid.: 344.

12. Schopen 1995b: 117.

13. *mKhas pa'i dga' ston*.

14. As found in Tucci 1950: 53, 102.

15. Richardson 1985: 94–99.

16. Stein [1962] 1972: 143–44. The text used by Stein is recorded as *Bod kyi rgyal po khri srong lde'u bstan gyis chos khrims bsdams pa'i le'u* and is found in the *Padma bka' thang*: 397–402.

17. Uebach 1992: 829.

18. *mNga' ris rgyal rabs*.

19. *chos rtsigs*.

20. Vitali 2003: 57.

21. Similarly, in Sri Lanka, the monasteries were at first under direct jurisdiction of the king, while from the tenth century onward monasteries were allowed or perhaps even required to manage their own property (Gunawardana 1979: 4).

22. Dargyay 1982: 74.

23. *Zhal lce bcu drug*.

24. *Zhal lce bcu gsum*.

25. *Me long gdong*.

26. Schuh 1984: 298.

27. Variations of this text were reproduced and circulated widely throughout Tibet, well into the twentieth century; see Pirie 2013: 239–41.

28. *mi chos gtsang ma bcu drug*. See Roesler 2015.

29. *'O chu dgon bca' yig*: 178.

30. *sMin grol gling bca' yig*: 312. Here the term "human rules" (*mi chos*) is more likely to refer to local lay sensibilities, customs, or rules.

31. According to Goldstein (1998: 19), this was also the case for Drepung.

32. Bell [1946] 1998: 201. This is reiterated by French 1995b: 103. This issue is discussed in further detail later.

33. Heirman and De Rauw 2006: 73.

34. *chos srid zung 'brel*.

35. Bell [1946] 1998: 157.

36. Arguments found in various canonical sources are given in Zimmerman 2006.

37. *Se ra theg chen gling rtsa tshig*: 183.

38. *sil bu'i dus*.

39. *Chos 'byung me tog snying po sbrang rtsi'i bcud*: 446. See also Davidson 2005: 71; Wangdu and Diemberger 2000: 91n349.

40. This imagery is also found in Aris 1976: 623. In the Bhutanese governmental decree that Aris discusses, the two—secular law and religious law—are said to make up "the good legal system" of the country, which is presented as a prerequisite for happiness in the land.

41. *gser gyi gnya' shing.*

42. *rNam rgyal grwa tshang bca' yig*: 64.

43. That is, religious (*chos lugs*) and worldly traditions (*rjig rten gyi lugs*).

44. *bKra shis lhun po bca' yig*: 38. The title can be translated as "The magnificent golden vajra-yoke that adds and makes up for deficiencies of the life force of the two orders: a work definitely necessary for the whole central population of the Sangha and the subsidiaries, such as the internal estates of Tashi Lhunpo."

45. Elsewhere in the same text, however, the imagery of the golden yoke is used, quoting the *Bodhicaryāvatāra,* in the analogy of the blind turtle, to describe the rarity of attaining a precious human life. See *bKra shis lhun po bca' yig*: 60.

46. This is a play on words: *bkur ba* means both "to carry" and "to respect."

47. *bKra shis dga' ldan chos 'phel gling bca' yig*: 498–99.

48. *'Bras spungs bca' yig*: 321.

49. Aris 1986: 126, 102b.

50. By contrast, in Sri Lanka in the 1970s, a high-ranking monk is quoted as saying that monastic law, "unlike secular law, is not strictly enforced if it is not suitable for the specific occasion" (Ferguson and Shalardchai 1976: 126). Equally, Tibetans monks in exile are said to have a "remarkably pragmatic approach, such that whenever a clash between (at least minor) religious observations and some practical imperative occurs, the latter prevails" (Gyatso 2003: 237). To the extent that contemporary monastic tradition is a continuity of previous practices, this may indicate a divergence between theory and practice.

51. Incidentally, John Locke ([1690] 1980: 38) conveys a similar notion, namely that there is tacit consent to the laws of the country, which is to say that anyone who travels on a highway implicitly consents to and is bound by the local laws.

52. French 1995a: 101.

53. *rgya sdom pa.*

54. Huber 2004: 133.

55. The meaning of *nag bcangs* is not clear. It may refer to cremating the bodies of lay-people.

56. *Se ra byes bca' yig*: 581.

57. *Pha bong kha bca' yig*: 244.

58. *rgyang grags*; this is about two miles.

59. *Kong stod dung dkar dgon bca' yig*: 589.

60. Huber 2004: 133.

61. *dPal 'khor chos sde bca' yig*: 433: Interestingly, the wording describing the territory of the monastery and the rules concerning killing is identical to that found in the fifteenth-century *chayik* for the same monastery (here named rGyal rtse chos sde), as cited in Huber 2004: 134. This suggests that not only the anonymous authors of this twentieth-century text used older *chayik*, but also that, presumably, the territory described in so much detail had remained the same for almost five hundred years.

62. *Rong po rab brtan dgon bca' yig*: 538. The translation is from Huber 2004: 135.

63. *mgon khang.* Ibid.: 136.

64. The full name of this monastery is sPo stod phu dgon chos lding rin chen spungs. Interestingly, the monastery is affiliated with the Karma Kagyü school and is a branch of Tsurpu, while the *chayik* was presumably written by someone at the central government.

65. *Phu lung dgon bca' yig*: 610.

66. *bKra shis lhun po bca' yig*: 124.

67. *Rwa sgreng bca' yig*: 498.

68. *dPal yul dar thang bca' yig*: 188.

69. Ibid.

70. *sMin grol gling bca' yig*: 283.

71. *mTshur phu dgon gyi dkar chag*: 281.

72. *nag chang.*

73. That is, Sera, Drepung, Ganden, Gyütö, and Gyümè.

74. Note that the verb *sbyin pa* here denotes religious giving.

75. *dGon khag gi dge 'dun pa rtsa tshig*: 345.

76. *Pha bong kha bca' yig*: 435.

77. *mTshur phu dgon gyi dkar chag*: 280.

78. *'Bras spungs bca' yig*: 312. Again, the *chayik* for Sera Je by the Seventh Dalai Lama uses nearly identical wording, except that in this version only laypeople are addressed; see *Se ra byes bca' yig*: 578.

79. *Byams gling grwa tshang bca' yig*: 482.

80. *sTeng po che bca' yig*: 463/6a.

81. *Thob rgyal rab rgyas gling dgon bca' yig*: 454.

82. There is a possible parallel with the regulations in place in the 840s in China. The *Tiwei boli jing* 提 謂 波 利 經 was one of the main texts written to provide rules for laypeople who were under the authority of monks. See Barrett 2014: 209.

83. *mTshur phu dgon gyi dkar chag*: 291.

84. *gzu ba.*

85. Stein [1962] 1972: 146–48.

86. For information about monastic mediation and reconciliation in "early Buddhism," see Bailey and Mabbett 2006: 219–31.

87. Nietupski 2011: 81. More generally, monks appear to have been seen as more trustworthy. Bell ([1946] 1998: 199) reports that when there was a legal dispute between a layman and a monk, justice was usually in favor of the monk.

88. Goldstein 1971: 175. Goldstein also notes on p. 177 that the term for "mediation" is *bar zhugs* and for adjudication *bka' bcad gnang.* A similar process is described in *mTshur phu dgon gyi dkar chag.* This modern-era work notes that going to the *phyag khang* (presumably the monastery's treasurer's office) was a step taken only when all else had failed. See *mTshur phu dgon gyi dkar chag*: 583.

89. Diack [1897] 1994 III: 92.

90. French 1995a: 324.

91. *sMin grol gling bca' yig*: 312.

92. *dPal yul dar thang bca' yig*: 198–99.

93. Ibid.: 189. The text goes on to mention that the more important incarnations and "owners of the Teachings" (*bstan bdag*) are exempted from the rule on horse-riding.

94. *gso sbyong.*

95. *dbyar gnas. dPal yul dar thang bca' yig*: 190.

96. Personal communication with Könchok Chönyi, Phiyang, August 2012.

97. *'Bras spungs bca' yig*: 311.

98. Ibid. See also Jansen 2013a: 122.

99. *Gong ra nges gsang rdo rje gling bca' yig*: 226.

100. Gyatso 2003: 231.

101. *dPal yul dar thang bca' yig*: 194.

102. *sMin grol gling bca' yig*: 281.

103. *dge 'dun gyi dbyen.*

104. *bstan bshig.*

105. *rNam rgyal grwa tshang bca' yig*: 71.

106. The last three ways of punishing monks are similar to the three possible penalties for monks described by the *Daoseng ge*. Offending monks are (1) made to do odd jobs inside the monastic community, (2) forced to return to lay life, (3) referred to the civil authorities for trial; see Heirman and De Rauw 2006: 77n83.

107. For more on corporal punishment in Tibet, see Schwieger 2015a.

108. *gsum tshan.* It is not clear what needs to be paid here.

109. *sder mo.* This word usually refers to animal claws, but here it might indicate a specific type of weapon.

110. *'Bri gung byang chub gling bca' yig*: 403.

111. *nag mtho.* This must refer to a specific boundary marker.

112. Ibid.

113. This is to indicate that he acknowledges he is no longer a monk at that point.

114. Ibid.: 404.

115. For another interesting instance of readmittance after sexual conduct see Wood 2016.

116. Ibid.

117. *sMin grol gling bca' yig*: 281.

118. *Phu lung dgon bca' yig*: 612.

119. *Pha bong kha bca' yig*: 242.

120. Bunnag 1973: 95.

121. Welch 1967: 119–20.

122. Lempert 2006: 23.

123. Personal communication with Khenpo Könchok Chökyab, Rajpur, August 2012.

124. Yifa 2002: 19.

125. In Sri Lanka, a similar type of "public humiliation" as punishment for an injunction was carrying a hundred boxes of sand to the assembly; see Ratnapala 1971: 177.

126. Huber 2004: 135. This is complicated by the fact that, although the verb that is most often used when fines of any sort are suggested is "*bul ba*," its most basic meaning is a self-deprecating honorific verb denoting "to give." In the case of ordinary, misbehaving monks being made to do prostrations in front of the assembly, it would be the *only* correct verb to use.

127. Personal communication with Ngawang Peljin, Dharamsala, July 2012.

128. Wijayaratna 1990: 143.

129. Pachow [1955] 2000: 62.

130. Gethin 2007: 64.

131. Presumably *spyi ba.*

132. Pereira 1912: 417.

133. Schram [1954] 2006: 374.

134. Goldstein 1964: 137.

135. Personal communication with Shérap Gyatso, Rajpur, August 2012.

136. The same informant also told me that it was this houseteacher who initially told the new monks all of the "local" regulations to which they must adhere.

137. Personal communication, Lobzang Döndrup, Spituk, August 2012.

138. *sTeng po che bca' yig:* 464/6b.

139. *bKra shis chos rdzong bca' yig:* 496.

140. Personal communication with the director of Drigung Jangchub Ling, Rajpur, August 2012.

141. Also see Dreyfus 2003: 58.

142. Personal communication with Lama Tsültrim, Dehradun, August 2012.

143. *bKra shis lhun po bca' yig:* 99.

144. mDo khams sho mdo dgon dga' ldan bshad sgrub gling. This monastery is in Sho mdo, Lhorong country, in Chamdo prefecture. While it is currently included within the Tibet Autonomous Region, the Thirteenth Dalai Lama considered it to be in mDo smad (commonly understood to refer to Eastern Tibet).

145. *Sho mdo dga' ldan bshad sgrub gling bca' yig:* 527.

146. *grwa shag la / sgo the* [sic: *them*] *sbyar ba.* Literally, to attach a threshold to the monks' quarters. It means that he is locked either in his room or out of his room.

147. A *gaṇḍi* is a piece of wood used in the monastery to signal both daily activities and exceptional circumstances; see Helffer 1983: 114.

148. *Mang spro dgon bca' yig:* 63–64.

149. French 1995a: 324.

150. *gnas dbyung.*

151. White clothes are emblematic of householders. They thus signify that the person is no longer a monk.

152. *Phu lung dgon bca' yig:* 609.

153. *srang,* a type of currency.

154. *Chab mdo dga' ldan theg chen byams pa gling bca' yig:* 548.

155. Cech 1988: 73.

156. *rta thab.* This is an abbreviation of *rta thab g.yog,* servants who take care of the horses and the fire.

157. *khral bzo.* The exact meaning of this word is not clear; it may also denote "tax collector."

158. *mTshur phu dgon gyi dkar chag:* 285.

159. Presumably, this is the name of the text that is deemed lost.

160. *skyid sdug 'then pa.*

161. *rgya ma.*

162. Ibid.

163. *smar zho.* Schuh and Dagyab 1978: 246.

164. *gnang chen.*

165. *Se ra theg chen gling rtsa tshig*: 187.

166. It can be no coincidence that this is also the case in the Vinayas; see Clarke 2009b: 116.

167. For an example of such a *chayik,* see Jansen 2014.

168. *sMin grol gling bca' yig*: 279.

169. For example, Willis 1989: 101: "Of the four schools, only the dGe-lugs-pa enjoins strict celibacy." In other instances, a similar sentiment is couched in more innocuous terms, such as that the Geluk monasteries "emphasize celibacy and purity"; see Samuel 2013: 11. Another recent reiteration of this myth can be found in Clarke 2014: 116.

170. *zom nyer bzhag.* This exact phrase does not occur in the dictionaries, but *zom lus* (leaving one's boot, i.e., leaving something behind unintentionally) does; see Goldstein, *The New Tibetan–English Dictionary of Modern Tibetan*: 963. Here it must refer to any business the ex-monk may have in the monastery. The phrase may have some parallels in the well-known narrative of Hwa shang Mahāyāna leaving one of his shoes behind at Samyé, i.e., some of his views remained current in Tibet.

171. *sTeng po che bca' yig*: 464/6b.

172. *rDo phud chos 'khor gling bca' yig*: 565.

173. Cassinelli and Ekvall 1969: 234.

174. *zhu ngo mgron brgyud med pa.* This is a "government" term for reporting to a higher official through an aid. See Goldstein, *The New Tibetan–English Dictionary of Modern Tibetan*: 933.

175. *Byams gling grwa tshang bca' yig*: 482–83.

176. Personal communication with Khenpo Könchok Chökyab, Rajpur, August 2012.

177. *Gong ra nges gsang rdo rje gling bca' yig*: 225.

178. *rDo phud chos 'khor gling bca' yig*: 565.

179. Clarke 2009b: 116–19.

180. According to the *Mahāvyutpatti, gnas nas dbyung* is a translation of *utkṣepanīya*: to get thrown out. See Lokesh Chandra, *Tibetan–Sanskrit Dictionary*: 1369.

181. Clarke 2014: 162.

182. Clarke 2009a: 30.

183. See, for example, *rDo phud chos 'khor gling bca' yig*: 564. This is also stated in the guidelines for Kumbum's Tantric college; see *sKu 'bum rgyud pa grwa tshang bca' yig*: 276.

184. Clarke 2014: 103.

185. This means that the person in question loses seniority.

186. Schuh and Dagyab 1978: 246.

187. This rendering of the spelling Risley explains as the "the iron letter," in the sense of the "inflexible rule." This may have been a local etymology or merely Risley's flight of imagination; see Risley 1894: 300.

188. Ibid.: 302.

189. *dPal yul dar thang bca' yig*: 193.

190. Ibid.

191. *'cham dpon.*

192. The terms used are *rgyal khrims, srid khrims, spyi khrims,* and *nag khrims.*

193. Goldstein 1968: 234–35. In Thailand too, homicide was the concern of state authorities. Unlike in Tibet, however, also all "criminal" cases that involved laypeople were to be reported to the state as well; see Bunnag 1973: 53.

194. Goldstein 1964: 133.

195. *sMin grol gling bca' yig*: 307.

196. Bell [1946] 1998: 332.

197. See http://tibet.prm.ox.ac.uk/photo_1998.286.53.2.html.

198. *Se ra theg chen gling rtsa tshig*: 184.

199. Ibid.: 186.

200. Ibid.

201. The relationship between the Sangha and the state in Mongolia is a complex one, and seems to have fluctuated greatly over time. Wallace's article on law and the monkhood in Mongolia is very informative on this matter, but a further investigation, particularly with a comparison to Tibetan practices, is a desideratum. See Wallace 2014.

202. Here I am in agreement with Samuel 1993: 33.

203. As translated by Cabezón 2017: 192.

204. Ibid.: 188.

205. Travers 2009: 372–73.

206. Gunawardana 1979: 4.

207. Gernet [1956] 1995: 223–24: "officials denounced the remote Buddhist establishments as hideouts for convicts and draft-evaders."

208. *Gong ra nges gsang rdo rje gling bca' yig*: 228.

209. Schwartz 1994: 730. This is further confirmed by Rendo Sengge's remarks noted earlier.

210. In fact, in Amdo in the nineteenth century, Tibetan monastics frequently interfered with laws and legal practices of the (Qing) state; see Oidtmann 2016.

211. The translation is after Aris 1986: 124, 101b.

212. Further research might, for example, shed light on whether the situation was comparable to the Western European one, where ecclesiastical courts were the first modern legal system. See North and Gwin 2010: 136.

213. French 1995a: 344.

214. Naturally, the text, along with its commentary by Tsongkhapa, states the usual caveats; see Tatz 1986: 82, 238.

215. Collins 1998: 435.

216. Pirie 2010: 228.

217. Ramble 2008: 41.

218. A similar remark can be made with regard to Burma; see Huxley 1995: 81.

219. Wallace 2014: 332.

220. Gombrich 1975: 218.


## 8.    MAINTAINING (THE) ORDER

1. Nattier notes the various mentions of this five-hundred-year period in different sūtras. She questions the translation "the last five hundred years" given by Conze for

*paścimāyāṃ pañcaśatyāṃ,* which appears in the *Vajracchedikā-sūtra,* arguing that *paścima* can also mean "that which follows." See Nattier 1991: 33–37. In Tibetan this word, usually rendered *tha ma* (or alternatively *mtha' ma*), definitely means "last" or "the end." When the whole phrase *(dus) lnga brgya mtha' ma,* which features widely in the Kanjur, is mentioned in later Tibetan texts, it most definitely points to the last five-hundred-year period or to the end of a five-hundred-year period.

   2. *sTeng po che bca' yig:* 464/6b.

   3. *sMin grol gling bca' yig:* 274–75.

   4. Spiro 1971: 439.

   5. Only aristocrats are known to have tried to implement major societal changes. The sole attempt at a revolution—i.e., changing the system and not the people in charge—was masterminded by an aristocrat in 1933. See Goldstein 1973: 455.

   6. Gyatso 2003: 237.

   7. Goldstein 1989b: 37.

   8. This is not the same as saying that there was no social welfare in pre-modern Tibet. My research has shown that on an institutional level there were no policies promoting these issues in place, but that on an individual level people generally took good care of each other.

   9. Nattier 1991: 136–37.

   10. Gyatso (2003: 235–36) also points out this notion regarding contemporary Tibetan monasticism in exile: "Standards in discipline are perceived to have slipped. But this is perceived to be indicative of a more general 'natural' process of corruption."

   11. There is no consensus in Buddhist canonical texts on the finality of this decline; see Nattier 1991: 223. On the whole, however, in the Tibetan Buddhist tradition there is the understanding that the Teachings will merely *appear* to disappear.

   12. For more on this topic, see Jansen (forthcoming) 2018.

   13. According to Goldstein (1968: 254), "almost all the elements in the ruling elite had crucial vested interests in maintaining the basic status quo." Naturally, this ruling elite also included the aristocracy. The relationships and networks between the two types of "elite" are in need of further research.

   14. King 1964: 96.

   15. Goldstein (1989b: 37) views the reasons for the monasteries' opposition to change in ideologies of a more materialist kind: "Furthermore, the mass monk ideology and the annual cycle of prayer festivals led the monasteries continually to seek more land and endowments and vigorously to oppose any attempt on the part of the government to decrease their revenues. It also made them advocates of the serf-estate economic system and, thus, extremely conservative." I have called the ideology of mass monasticism into question elsewhere; see Jansen 2013a.

   16. Bell 1931: 20.

   17. For example, *'Chi med grub pa'i byang chub gling bca' yig:* 655. Also see *Pha bong kha bca' yig:* 244; *'O chu dgon bca' yig:* 178; *Sho mdo dga' ldan bshad sgrub gling bca' yig:* 528; and *dPal yul dar thang bca' yig:* 201. Another example of this can be found in the guidelines for Eren monastery; see Sullivan 2015: 96.

   18. For a picture of such a *chayik,* see www.aaoarts.com/asie/VDL/.

   19. Translation is after Aris 1986: 138(107a).

   20. Mills 2003: 317.

21. Tucci [1970] 1988: 187.
22. Ekvall 1964: 79.
23. Mills 2003: 330.
24. Southern 1970: 29.
25. Dumont 1980: 218.
26. Welch 1967: 107.
27. Miller 1958: viii.
28. See for example Sandel 2009: 9.
29. Schwieger 2015b: 220.

# SOURCES

## WORKS IN TIBETAN

*sBa' bzhed*

sBa gsal snang (9th century). N.d. *sBa bzhed ces bya ba las sba gsal snang gi bzhed pa bzhugs*. Edited by mGon po rgyal mtshan. Beijing: Mi rigs dpe skrun khang, 1982.

*Bla brang bkra shis 'khyil gyi 'grig yig*

'Jigs med dam chos (18th century) and dKon mchog rGyal mtshan (1764–1853). N.d. N.p.

*Bod kyi dgon sde*

Tshe rgyal, Tshe ring 'bum, and dBang drag rdo rje. 2005. *Bod kyi dgon sde'i rig gnas spyi bshad me tog phreng ba*. Xining: mTsho sngon mi rigs dpe skrun khang.

*Bod kyi shes yon*

Re mdo sengge. 2011. *Bod kyi shes yon lam lugs dang srid byus*. Dharamsala: Bod kyi shes rig las khung.

*Bod kyi snga rabs khrims srol yig cha bdams bsgrigs*

Tshe ring dpal 'byor, ed. 1989. Lhasa: Bod ljongs mi dmangs dpe skrun khang.

*'Bras ljongs bca' yig*

Srid skyong rnam rgyal sprul sku. 1909. In *Urkunden, Erlasse und Sendschreiben aus dem Besitz Sikkimesischer Adelshäuser und des Klosters Phodang*, edited by Dieter Schuh and L.S. Dagyab, 267–71. St Augustin: VGH Wissenschaftsverlag, 1978.

*'Bras spungs bca' yig*

Ngag dbang blo bzang rgya mtsho. 1682. "Chos sde chen po dpal ldan 'bras dkar spungs pa'i dgon gyi bca' yig tshul 'chal sa srung 'dul ba'i lcags kyo kun gsal me long." In *Bod kyi snga rabs khrims srol yig cha bdams bsgrigs*, edited by Tshe ring dpal 'byor, 275–323. Lhasa: Bod yig dpe rnying dpe skrun khang, 1989.

### *'Bri gung byang chub gling bca' yig*
'Bri gung bstan 'dzin padma'i rgyal mtshan. 1802. "'Bri gung byang chub gling gi bca' yig thar pa'i gru rdzings." In *Bod kyi snga rabs khrims srol yig cha bdams bsgrigs*, 398–406. Lhasa: Bod ljongs mi dmangs dpe skrun khang, 1989.

### *'Bri gung mthil bca' yig a*
sPyan snga grags pa 'byung gnas (1175–1255). N.d. "Magha dha rdo rje gdan 'bri gung byang chub gling gi bca' khrims." In *gSung 'bum, vol. 1*, 247–50. Delhi: Drikung Kagyu, 2002.

### *'Bri gung mthil bca' yig b*
sPyan snga grags pa 'byung gnas (1175–1255). N.d. "rDo rje gdan 'bri gung byang chub gling gi rtsa khrims." In *'Bri gung bka' brgyud chos mdzod chen mo, vol. 34*, edited by A mgon rin po che, 390–94. Lhasa, 2004.

### *Byams gling grwa tshang bca' yig*
Thub bstan rgya mtsho. 1927. "Byams gling grwa tshang gi bca' yig ngo ma byams blar song ba'i ngo bshus zhus dag song." In *Bod sa gnas kyi lo rgyus dpe tshogs bca' yig phyogs sgrigs*, edited by Bod rang skyong yig tshags khang, 478–84. Lhasa: Bod ljongs mi dmangs dpe skrun khang, 2001.

### *Byams pa gling bca' yig*
Blo bzang grags pa'i dpal (Tsongkhapa). 1417. "Byams pa gling na bzhugs pa'i spyi'i dge 'dun la khrims su bca' ba'i yi ge." In *gSung 'bum, vol. 2 (Zhol)*, 250b–58a. New Delhi: Mongolian lama Gurudeva, 1978–79.

*Byang chub lam rim che mo dang 'brel ba'i ser byas mkhan snyan grwa tshang gi bca' khrims che mo.* Anonymous. 1991. Bylakuppe: Ser jhe Printing Press.

### *dByar gnas nang khrims*
Tshul khrims bzang po (1884–c.1957). N.d. "dByar gnas dge 'dun nang khrims." In *gSung 'bum, vol. 8*, 655–66. N.p.

### *bCa' yig mi chog brgyad chu*
dPal chen 'dus pa rtsal (1887–1932). N.d. "bCa' yig mi chog brgyad chu." In *dPal yul rnam rgyal chos gling gi gdan rabs*, edited by Mu po, 401–3. Taipei: Corporate Body of the Buddha Educational Foundation, 2007.

### *bCa' yig phyogs bsgrigs*
Bod rang skyong yig tshags khang, ed. 2001. *Bod sa gnas kyi lo rgyus dpe tshogs bca' yig phyogs sgrigs*. Lhasa: Bod ljongs mi dmangs dpe skrun khang.

### *bCa' yig phyogs bsgrigs 2*
Bod rang skong ljongs yig tshags khang, ed. 2013. *bCa' yig phyogs bsgrigs: Bod kyi lo rgyus yig tshags dpe tshogs, vol. 27*. Lhasa: Bod ljongs mi dmangs dpe skrun khang.

### Chab mdo dga' ldan theg chen byams pa gling bca' yig
Thub bstan rgya mtsho. 1932. "Tā la'i bla ma sku phreng bcu gsum pas chab mdo dga' ldan theg chen byams pa gling du bstsal ba'i bca' yig." In *Bod sa gnas kyi lo rgyus dpe tshogs bca' yig phyogs bsgrigs*, edited by Bod rang skyong ljongs yig tshags khang, 540–50. Lhasa: Bod ljongs mi dmangs dpe skrun khang, 2001.

### 'Chi med grub pa'i byang chub gling bca' yig
Srid skyong stag brag. 1949. "dGa' ldan mdo sngags chos 'phel 'chi med grub pa'i byang chub gling bca' yig." In *Bod sa gnas kyi lo rgyus dpe tshogs bca' yig phyogs bsgrigs*, edited by Bod rang skyong ljongs yig tshags khang, 647–56. Lhasa: Bod ljongs mi dmangs dpe skrun khang, 2001.

### Chos 'byung me tog snying po sbrang rtsi'i bcud
Nyang ral nyi ma 'od zer (1124–1192). N.d. Lhasa: Bod ljongs mi dbang dpe bskrun khang, 1988.

### Chos sde chos dbyings 'od gsal gling bca' yig
Blo bzang rta mgrin (1867–1937). N.d. "Chos sde chos dbyings 'od gsal gling gi 'dzin grwa gtugs tshul gyi bca' yig." In *gSung 'bum, vol. 3*, 433–39. New Delhi: Mongolian lama Gurudeva, 1975–76.

### gDan sa bca' yig
Zhang brtson 'grus grags pa (1123–1193). N.d. "gDan sa nyams dmas su gyur ba'i skabs mdzad pa'i bca' yig." In *dPal ldan tshal pa bka' brgyud kyi bstan pa'i mnga' bdag zhang g.yu brag pa brtson 'grus grags pa'i gsung 'bum rin po che: bka' thor bu, shog dril chen mo*, 176–81. Kathmandu: Shree Gautam Buddha Vihar, 2004.

### gDan sa chen po'i bya ba las kyi sne mor mngags rnams kyi bca' yig
Kun dga' blo gros (1729–1783). N.d. Kathmandu: Sa skya rgyal yongs gsung rab slob gnyer khang (2008): 333–60.

### lDe'u chos 'byung
lDe'u jo sras (13th century). N.d. "mKhas pa lde'us mdzad pa'i rgya bod kyi chos 'byung rgyas pa." In *rGya bod kyi chos 'byung rgyas pa*, 31–442. Lhasa: Bod ljongs mi dmangs dpe skrun khang, 1987.

### rDo phud chos 'khor gling bca' yig
Srid skyong rwa sgreng. 1938. "rDo phud chos 'khor gling dgon bstsal ba'i bca' yig." In *Bod sa gnas kyi lo rgyus dpe tshogs bca' yig phyogs bsgrigs*, edited by Bod rang skyong ljongs yig tshags khang, 563–71. Lhasa: Bod ljongs mi dmangs dpe skrun khang, 2001.

### 'Dul ṭīk nyi ma'i 'od zer legs bshad lung rigs kyi rgya mtsho
Kun mkhyen mtsho sna ba shes rab bzang po (13th century). N.d. Cazadero: Ye shes sde'i chos 'khor 'phrul par khang, 2003.

### Dung dkar gsung rtsom
Dung dkar blo bzang phrin las. 1997. *Dung dkar blo bzang phrin las kyi gsung rtsom phyogs bsgrigs*. Beijing: Krung go'i bod kyi shes rig dpe skrun khang.

*dGa' ldan thub bstan rab rgyas gling bca' yig*

Ngag dbang blo bzang rgya mtsho. 1664. "dGa' ldan thub bstan rab rgyas gling gi bca' yig." In *Gangs can rig brgya'i sgo 'byed lde mig ces bya ba bzhugs so: bca' yig phyogs sgrig*, edited by mGon po dar rgyas, 159–68. Beijing: Mi rigs dpe skrun khang, 1989.

*Gangs dkar gling bca' yig*

De mo srid skyong dang po (Ngag dbang 'jam dpal bde legs rgya mtsho). 1757. "Gangs dkar gling gi bca' yig sa bon de mo srid skyong dang po'i dam phab kyis me glang lor bstal ba." In *Bod sa gnas kyi lo rgyus dpe tshogs bca' yig phyogs bsgrigs*, edited by Bod rang skyong ljongs yig tshags khang, 143–49. Lhasa: Bod ljongs mi dmangs dpe skrun khang, 2001.

*dGon khag gi dge 'dun pa rtsa tshig*

Kun gling rgyal thog gnyis pa. 1882. "Kun gling rgyal thog gnyis pas se 'bras dga' dang rgyud grwa stod smad sogs dgon khag gi dge 'dun pas nag chang sogs mi dge ba'i spyod tshul dang chas gos khyim pa spyi mtshungs byed mkhan la lta rtog 'jug gnon dgos pa'i rtsa tshig." In *Bod sa gnas kyi lo rgyus dpe tshogs bca' yig phyogs bsgrigs*, edited by Bod rang skyong ljongs yig tshags khang, 343–47. Lhasa: Bod ljongs mi dmangs dpe skrun khang, 2001.

*Gong ra nges gsang rdo rje gling bca' yig*

Ngag dbang blo bzang rgya mtsho. 1664. "Gong ra nges gsang rdo rje gling gi bca' yig." In *Gangs can rig brgya'i sgo 'byed lde mig ces bya ba bzhugs so: bca' yig phyogs sgrig*, edited by mGon po dar rgyas, 220–33. Beijing: Mi rigs dpe skrun khang, 1989.

*bKa' 'gyur bzhengs dus dpon yig rnams kyi bca' yig*

Kun mkhyen rig pa 'dzin pa chos kyi grags pa (1595–1659). N.d. In *gSung 'bum*, vol. 2, 175–80. Kulhan: Drikung Kagyu Institute, 1999.

*Kaṃ tshang chos spyod sogs kha ton gces btus*

Shes rab rgyal mtshan, ed. 2001. Delhi: N.p.

*Kong stod dung dkar dgon bca' yig*

Srid skyong stag brag. 1943. "Kong stod dung dkar dgon la bstsal ba'i khrims su bca' ba'i yi ge." In *Bod sa gnas kyi lo rgyus dpe tshogs bca' yig phyogs bsgrigs*, edited by Bod rang skyong ljongs yig tshags khang, 583–601. Lhasa: Bod ljongs mi dmangs dpe skrun khang, 2001.

*bKra shis chos rdzong bca' yig*

Anonymous ("the community of lamas and monks," *bla ma grwa tshogs spyi thog*). 1900. "Dung dkar bkra shis chos rdzong dgon gyi bca' yig." In *Bod sa gnas kyi lo rgyus dpe tshogs bca' yig phyogs bsgrigs*, edited by Bod rang skyong ljongs yig tshags khang, 404–12. Lhasa: Bod ljongs mi dmangs dpe skrun khang, 2001.

*bKra shis chos 'phel gling bca' yig*

Thub bstan rgya mtsho. 1888. "Tā la'i bla ma'i bcu gsum pas bkra shis chos 'phel gling dgon la bstsal ba'i bca' yig." In *Bod sa gnas kyi lo rgyus dpe tshogs bca' yig phyogs bsgrigs*, edited by Bod rang skyong ljongs yig tshags khang, 348–64. Lhasa: Bod ljongs mi dmangs dpe skrun khang, 2001.

*bKra shis dga' ldan chos 'phel gling bca' yig*
Thub bstan rgya mtsho. 1927. "*mDo smad dgon gsar bkra shis dga' ldan chos 'phel gling.*" In *Bod sa gnas kyi lo rgyus dpe tshogs bca' yig phyogs bsgrigs*, edited by Bod rang skyong ljongs yig tshags khang, 498–500. Lhasa: Bod ljongs mi dmangs dpe skrun khang, 2001.

*bKra shis lhun po bca' yig*
bsTan pa'i dbang phyug. 1876. "bKra shis lhun po dpal gyi bde chen phyogs thams cad las rnam par rgyal ba'i gling gi dge 'dun dbu dmangs dang / bla brang nang ma sogs lto zan khongs gtogs dang bcas pa spyi khyab tu nges dgos pa'i yi ge khrims gnyis srog gi chad mthud rab brjid gser gyi rdo rje'i gnya' shing dge." In *Gangs can rig brgya'i sgo 'byed lde mig ces bya ba bzhugs so: bca' yig phyogs sgrig*, edited by mGon po dar rgyas, 35–158. Beijing: Mi rigs dpe skrun khang, 1989.

*bKra shis lhun po bca' yig 2*
bsTan pa'i dbang phyug. 1876. "Paṇ chen sku phreng brgyad pas bkra shis lhun po dgon la bstsal ba'i bca' yig." In *Bod sa gnas kyi lo rgyus dpe tshogs bca' yig phyogs bsgrigs*, edited by Bod rang skyong ljongs yig tshags khang, 216–342. Lhasa: Bod ljongs mi dmangs dpe skrun khang, 2001.

*bKra shis bsam gtan gling bca' khrims*
Thub bstan rgya mtsho. 1930. "Byang bya do bkra shis bsam gtan gling dgon la btsal ba'i bca' khrims." In *Bod sa gnas kyi lo rgyus dpe tshogs bca' yig phyogs bsgrigs*, edited by Bod rang skyong ljongs yig tshags khang, 529–33. Lhasa: Bod ljongs mi dmangs dpe skrun khang, 2001.

*Kun 'phel gling bca' yig*
Srid skyong rwa sgreng. 1934. "dGe dgon kun 'phel gling la bstsal ba'i bca' yig." In *Bod sa gnas kyi lo rgyus dpe tshogs bca' yig phyogs bsgrigs*, edited by Bod rang skyong ljongs yig tshags khang, 555–63. Lhasa: Bod ljongs mi dmangs dpe skrun khang, 2001.

*Kun bzang bla ma'i zhal lung*
rDza dpal sprul rin po che (O rgyan 'jigs med chos kyi dbang po, 1808–1887). N.d. *rDzogs pa chen po klong chen snying tig gi sngon 'gro'i khrid yig kun bzang bla ma'i zhal lung dang / rdzogs pa chen po sems nyid ngal gso bcas bzhugs so* (with Kun mkhyen klong chen rab 'byams). Edited by Sogen Rinpoche, 2–355. New Delhi, 2003.

*sKu 'bum byams pa gling bca' yig*
Ngag dbang blo bzang rgya mtsho. 1653. "rGyal dbang lnga bas sku 'bum byams pa gling la bstal ba'i bca' yig." In *Bod sa gnas kyi lo rgyus dpe tshogs bca' yig phyogs bsgrigs*, edited by Bod rang skyong ljongs yig tshags khang, 8–11. Lhasa: Bod ljongs mi dmangs dpe skrun khang, 2001.

*sKu 'bum rgyud pa grwa tshang bca' yig*
bsKal bzang rgya mtsho. 1726. "Yid kyis srung 'dul ba'i bca' yig dran pa'i lcags kyo rnam par bkod pa." In *bCa' yig sde brgyad la springs yig lam yig sko 'ja' sogs kyi rim pa phyogs gcig tu bsgrigs, gSung 'bum, vol. 3*, 270–87. Gangtok: Dodrup Sangye, 1975–83.

*Mang spro dgon bca' yig*
Nyi ma rnam rgyal. 1711. "Urkunden des Klostes Mado (Maṅ-spro): Dokument XLVII." In *Urkunden und Sendschreiben aus Zentraltibet, Ladakh und Zanskar: Edition der Texte, vol. 2,* edited by Dieter Schuh, 61–64. St Augustin: VGH-Wissenschaftsverlag, 1979.

*sMin grol gling bca' yig*
gTer bdag gling pa. 1698. "O rgyan smin grol gling gi 'dus sde'i bca' khrims kyi yi ge blang dor gsal bar byed pa'i nyi ma." In *O rgyan smin grol gling gi dkar chag,* edited by bsTan pa'i sgron me, 272–316. Xining: Krung go'i bod kyi shes rig dpe skrun khang, 1992.

*rNam rgyal grwa tshang bca' yig*
bsKal bzang rgya mtsho. 1727. "rNam rgyal grwa tshang la bstsal ba'i bca' yig gser gyi gnya' shing." In *Bod sa gnas kyi lo rgyus dpe tshogs bca' yig phyogs sgrigs,* edited by Bod rang skyong yig tshags khang, 64–73. Lhasa: Bod ljongs mi dmangs dpe skrun khang, 2001.

*rNam rab mthong smon dwags po grwa tshang bca' yig*
Thub bstan rgya mtsho. 1928. "rNam rab mthong smon dwags po grwa tshang gi dge 'dun rnams la bstsal ba'i bca' yig." In *Bod sa gnas kyi lo rgyus dpe tshogs bca' yig phyogs bsgrigs,* edited by Bod rang skyong ljongs yig tshags khang, 513–17. Lhasa: Bod ljongs mi dmangs dpe skrun khang, 2001.

*mNga' ris khyung rdzong dkar po'i nye 'dabs kyi nam gling dgon sde'i dkar chag*
Rig 'dzin tshe dbang nor bu (1698–1755). N.d. *gSung 'bum, vol. 5,* 653–59. Dalhousie, 1976–77.

*'O chu dgon bca' yig*
rTa tshag rje drung ho thog thu ngag dbang thub bstan skal bzang bstan pa'i sgron me. 1798. "'O chu dgon gyi 'dul khrims bca' yig bstal zin." In *Bod sa gnas kyi lo rgyus dpe tshogs bca' yig phyogs bsgrigs,* edited by Bod rang skyong ljongs yig tshags khang, 174–79. Lhasa: Bod ljongs mi dmangs dpe skrun khang, 2001.

*O rgyan smin sgrol gling gi dkar chag*
bsTan pa'i sgron me. 1992. Xining: Krung go'i bod kyi shes rig dpe skrun khang.

*Padma bka' thang*
Anonymous. N.d. Chengdu: Si khron mi rigs dpe skrun khang, 1996.

*dPal rdo rje gzhon nu'i byin 'bebs kyi rol yig mthon ba rang grol gsal byed mdzes rgyan*
Kun dga' blo gros (1729–1783). N.d. In *gSung 'bum, vol. 3,* 903–8. Kathmandu: Sa skya rgyal yongs gsung rab slob gnyer khang, 2008.

*dPal 'khor chos sde bca' yig*
Anonymous (the "office," *yig tshang*). 1903. "Yig tshang gis dpal 'khor chos sde'i bca' yig thub bstan gsal ba'i sgron me." In *Bod sa gnas kyi lo rgyus dpe tshogs bca' yig phyogs bsgrigs,* edited by Bod rang skyong ljongs yig tshags khang, 413–38. Lhasa: Bod ljongs mi dmangs dpe skrun khang, 2001.

*dPal ri chos sde bca' yig*
Shes rab 'od zer (1518–1584 or –1572). N.d. "Grwa tshang gi bca' yig bstan pa'i nyi 'od." In *gSung 'bum,* edited by Gonpo Tseten, 455–60. Gangtok: n.p., 1977.

### dPal yul dar thang bca' yig

dPal yul dar thang mchog sprul rin po che 'jam dpal dgyes pa'i rdo rje (20th century). N.d. "Phan bde'i rtsa ba bca' yig gi skor." In *dPal yul dar thang mchog sprul rin po che 'jam dpal dgyes pa'i rdo rje'i gsung 'bum legs bshad nor bu'i bum bzang*, 186–225. Chengdu: Si khron dpe skrun khang, 2008.

### dPal yul gdan rabs

Mu po, ed. 2007. *dPal yul rnam rgyal chos gling gi gdan rabs*. Taipei: Corporate Body of the Buddha Educational Foundation.

### Pha bong kha bca' yig

Ye shes blo bzang bstan pa'i mgon po (1760–1810). N.d. "Kun gling rgyal thog dang po rta tshag rje drung ho thog thu ye she's blo bzang bstan pa'i mgon pos pha bong kha byang chub shing gi nags khrod la bstsal ba'i bca' yig nyes brgya'i klung rgyan 'gog pa'i chu lon." In *bCa' yig phyogs bsgrigs: Bod kyi lo rgyus yig tshags dpe tshogs, vol. 27*, edited by Bod rang skong ljongs yig tshags khang, 232–50. Lhasa: Bod ljongs mi dmangs dpe skrun khang, 2013.

### 'Phags yul 'bri gung bka' brgyud gtsug lag slob gnyer khang gi khungs gtogs slob phrug rnams kyi blang dor sgrig gzhi

Anonymous. N.d. (201?). Dehradun: Drikung Kagyu Institute.

### Phu lung dgon bca' yig

Anonymous (government issued). 1947. "sPo stod phu dgon chos lding rin chen spungs bca' yig." In *Bod sa gnas kyi lo rgyus dpe tshogs bca' yig phyogs bsgrigs*, edited by Bod rang skyong ljongs yig tshags khang, 602–13. Lhasa: Bod ljongs mi dmangs dpe skrun khang, 2001.

### Ra mo che bca' yig

bsKal bzang rgya mtsho. 1740s. "Ra mo che bzhi sde grwa tshang dga' ldan bsam gtan gling gi bca' yig." In *Bod sa gnas kyi lo rgyus dpe tshogs bca' yig phyogs bsgrigs*, edited by Bod rang skyong ljongs yig tshags khang, 117–42. Lhasa: Bod ljongs mi dmangs dpe skrun khang, 2001.

### Ri khrod bca' yig

De mo srid skyong dang po (Ngag dbang 'jam dpal bde legs rgya mtsho). 1757. "De mo srid skyong dang pos dar nor ri khrod la bstsal ba'i bca' yig." In *Bod sa gnas kyi lo rgyus dpe tshogs bca' yig phyogs bsgrigs*, edited by Bod rang skyong ljongs yig tshags khang, 151–55. Lhasa: Bod ljongs mi dmangs dpe skrun khang, 2001.

### Rin chen sgang bca' yig

Anonymous. 1845. "Rin chen sgang btsun ma grwa tshang gis bca' sgrig lag tu len dgos kyi tho yig blang dor gsal ba'i sgron me." In *Bod sa gnas kyi lo rgyus dpe tshogs bca' yig phyogs bsgrigs*, edited by Bod rang skyong ljongs yig tshags khang, 209–15. Lhasa: Bod ljongs mi dmangs dpe skrun khang, 2001.

*Rong po rab brtan dgon bca' yig*

Thub bstan rgya mtsho. 1930. "Tā la'i bla ma sku phreng bcu gsum pas rong po rab brtan dgon la btsal ba'i bca' yig gsal byed nor bu'i 'od snang." In *Bod sa gnas kyi lo rgyus dpe tshogs bca' yig phyogs bsgrigs*, edited by Bod rang skyong ljongs yig tshags khang, 538–40. Lhasa: Bod ljongs mi dmangs dpe skrun khang, 2001.

*Rong zom bca' yig*

Rong zom chos bzang (1012–1088). N.d. "Rong zom chos bzang gis rang slob dam tshig pa rnams la gsungs pa'i rwa ba brgyad pa'i bca' yig." In *gSung 'bum, vol. 2*, 399–414. Chengdu: Si khron mi rigs dpe skrun khang, 1999.

*Rwa sgreng bca' yig*

Ngag dbang blo bzang rgya mtsho (1617–1682). Written or reworked in the wood monkey year (*shing sprel lo*). "gDan sa chen po rwa sgreng rgyal ba'i dben gnas kyi bca' yig gong sa mchog nas bstsal ba'i zhal bshus 'khrul med." In *bCa' yig phyogs bsgrigs: Bod kyi lo rgyus yig tshags dpe tshogs, vol. 27*, edited by Bod rang skong ljongs yig tshags khang, 486–500. Lhasa: Bod ljongs mi dmangs dpe skrun khang, 2013.

*bSam gtan chos mchog gling gi bca' yig*

Si tu padma nyin byed dbang po. 1825. "sGrub sde bsam gtan chos mchog gling gi bca' yig." In *gSung 'bum, vol. 3*, 643–72. Upper Bhattu: dPal spungs gsung rab nyams gso khang, 2006.

*bSam yas lcog grwa bca' yig*

Kun dga' blo gros (1729–1783). N.d. "bSam yas lcog grwa'i bca' yig." In *gSung 'bum, vol. 3*, 419–28. Kathmandu: Sa skya rgyal yongs gsung rab slob gnyer khang, 2008.

*Se ra byes bca' yig*

bsKal bzang rgya mtsho. 1737. "Se ra theg chen gling gi sgrig khrims gnon sdems skor rgyal mchog bdun pa chen pos me sbrul lor btsal ba'i bca' yig gser tham chen mo 'byar ma'i ngo bshus." In *History of the Sera Monastery of Tibet, 1418–1959*, edited by Champa Thupten Zongtse, 561–82. New Delhi: International Academy of Indian Culture and Aditya Prakashan, 1995.

*Se ra byes bca' yig 2*

bsKal bzang rgya mtsho. 1737. "rGyal mchog bdun pa chen pos se ra theg chen gling la stsal ba'i khrims su bca' ba'i yi ge rab gsal nor bu'i me long zhes bya ba bzhugs so." In *Bod sa gnas kyi lo rgyus dpe tshogs bca' yig phyogs bsgrigs*, edited by Bod rang skyong ljongs yig tshags khang, 96–117. Lhasa: Bod ljongs mi dmangs dpe skrun khang, 2001.

*Se ra theg chen gling rtsa tshig*

Tshe smon gling rgyal thog gnyis pa (Ngag dbang 'jam dpal tshul khrims). 1820. "Tshe smon gling rgyal thog gnyis pas se ra theg chen gling gi chos khrims sogs byed sgo'i skor btsal ba'i rtsa tshig." In *Bod sa gnas kyi lo rgyus dpe tshogs bca' yig phyogs bsgrigs*, edited by Bod rang skyong ljongs yig tshags khang, 180–90. Lhasa: Bod ljongs mi dmangs dpe skrun khang, 2001.

*Sho mdo dga' ldan bshad sgrub gling bca' yig*

Thub bstan rgya mtsho. 1920s. "Tā la'i bla ma sku phreng bcu gsum pas mdo khams sho mdo dgon dga' ldan bshad sgrub gling la bstsal ba'i bca' yig 'dul ba 'bum sde'i dgongs don rnam par bkra ba." In *Bod sa gnas kyi lo rgyus dpe tshogs bca' yig phyogs bsgrigs*, edited by Bod rang skyong ljongs yig tshags khang, 524–28. Lhasa: Bod ljongs mi dmangs dpe skrun khang, 2001.

### *So thar gyi tshul khrims rnam gsal sgron me*

Ngag dbang blo bzang rgya mtsho (1617–1682). N.d. "So thar gyi tshul khrims la dga' ba'i dpyod ldan tshogs la phan byed nyung ngu rnam gsal sgron ma." In *Gangs can rig brgya'i sgo 'byed lde mig ces bya ba bzhugs so: bca' yig phyogs sgrig*, edited by mGon po dar rgyas, 8–34. Beijing: Mi rigs dpe skrun khang, 1989.

### *sTag brag dgon pa bca' yig*

Srid skyong stag brag. 1947. "Srid skyong stag brag gis stag brag dgon par bstsal ba'i bca' yig." In *Bod sa gnas kyi lo rgyus dpe tshogs bca' yig phyogs bsgrigs*, edited by Bod rang skyong ljongs yig tshags khang, 620–56. Lhasa: Bod ljongs mi dmangs dpe skrun khang, 2001.

### *sTag lung brang mang thos bsam bstan gling bca' yig*

rTa tshag ngag dbang blo bzang bstan pa'i rgyal mtshan. 1899. "rTa tshag ngag dbang blo bzang bstan pa'i rgyal mtshan nas stag lung brag mang thos bsam bstan gling la bstsal ba'i bca' yig." In *Bod sa gnas kyi lo rgyus dpe tshogs bca' yig phyogs bsgrigs*, edited by Bod rang skyong ljongs yig tshags khang, 191–208. Lhasa: Bod ljongs mi dmangs dpe skrun khang, 2001.

### *Theg chen dam chos dga' tshal gling bca' yig*

Thub bstan rgya mtsho(?). 1898. "Chos sde chen po theg chen dam chos dga' tshal gling gi khrims su bca' ba'i yi ge phyag na padmo'i zhal lung blang dor rab gsal me long." In *Bod sa gnas kyi lo rgyus dpe tshogs bca' yig phyogs bsgrigs*, edited by Bod rang skyong ljongs yig tshags khang, 387–403. Lhasa: Bod ljongs mi dmangs dpe skrun khang, 2001.

### *Thob rgyal rab rgyas gling dgon bca' yig*

Thub bstan rgya mtsho. 1913. "Thob rgyal rab rgyas gling dgon gyi bca' khrims bstsal brgyu'i snyan zhur tā la'i bcu gsum pa'i chog mchan 'khod pa." In *Bod sa gnas kyi lo rgyus dpe tshogs bca' yig phyogs bsgrigs*, edited by Bod rang skyong ljongs yig tshags khang, 449–55. Lhasa: Bod ljongs mi dmangs dpe skrun khang, 2001.

### *Thor rgod rgyal po bca' yig*

Thub bstan rgya mtsho. 1889. "Thor rgod rgyal pos zhu ltar mtshan nyid grwa tshang gi dgon sde gsar btab zhu rgyu'i skyabs mgon rtse nas gser tham chen mo phab pa'i bca' yig." In *Bod sa gnas kyi lo rgyus dpe tshogs bca' yig phyogs bsgrigs*, edited by Bod rang skyong ljongs yig tshags khang, 365–79. Lhasa: Bod ljongs mi dmangs dpe skrun khang, 2001.

### *Thos grol chen mo sgrig yig*

dPal chen 'dus pa rtsal (1887–1932). N.d. "sKu mchod 'phrul thos grol chen mo gtong skabs kyi sgrig yig." In *dPal yul rnam rgyal chos gling gi gdan rabs*, edited by Mu po, 381–400. Taipei: Corporate Body of the Buddha Educational Foundation, 2007.

*sTeng po che bca' yig*

Ngag dbang bstan 'dzin nor bu. 1918. "Shar khum bu steng po che gsang sngags theg mchog chos gling gi bca' yig kun gsal me long." In *gSung 'bum, vol. 4,* 497–510. Kathmandu: Ngagyur dongak choling monastery, 2004.

*Tshig mdzod chen mo*

Yisun Zhang, ed. 1993. *Bod rgya tshig mdzod chen mo.* Beijing: Mi rigs dpe skrun khang.

*mTshur phu bca' yig*

Mi bskyod rdo rje (1507–1554). N.d. *dGa' tshal karma gzhung lugs gling dang por sgar chen 'dzam gling rgyan du bzhugs dus kyi 'phral gyi bca' yig. gSung 'bum, vol. 3,* 700–15. Lhasa: n.p., 2004.

*mTshur phu dgon gyi dkar chag*

Rin chen dpal bzang. 1995. *mTshur phu dgon gyi dkar chag kun gsal me long.* Beijing: Mi rigs dpe skrun khang.

## WORKS IN OTHER LANGUAGES

Anderson, Gary M., and Robert D. Tollison. 1992. "Morality and Monopoly: The Constitutional Political Economy of Religious Rules." *Cato Journal* 12: 373–92.

Anonymous. 1989. *Labulengsi Monastery (bla brang dgon pa).* Edited by Cultural Relics and Archaeology Research Institute of Gansu Province and Cultural Relics Preserving Committee of Labulengsi Monastery. Beijing: Cultural Relics.

Aris, Michael. 1976. "The Admonition of the Thunderbolt Cannon-ball and Its Place in the Bhutanese New Year Festival." *Bulletin of the School of Oriental and African Studies* 39(3): 601–35.

———. 1979. *Bhutan.* Warminster: Aris & Philips.

———. 1986. *Sources for the History of Bhutan.* Vienna: Arbeitskreis für tibetische und buddhistische Studien.

Arya, Pasang Y. 2009. "Schools and Medical Training of Physicians and Medical Ethics in Tibetan Medicine." www.tibetanmedicine-edu.org/images/stories/pdf/medicine_schools.pdf

Ashman, Ian, and Diana Winstanley. 2007. "For or Against Corporate Identity? Personification and the Problem of Moral Agency." *Journal of Business Ethics* 76(1): 83–95.

Aziz, Barbara Nimri. 1978. *Tibetan Frontier Families: Reflections of Three Generations from D'ing-ri.* Durham, NC: Carolina Academic Press.

Bailey, Greg, and Ian Mabbett. 2006. *The Sociology of Early Buddhism.* Cambridge: Cambridge University Press.

Bapat, P.V., and V.V. Gokhale. 1982. *Vinaya-sūtra and Auto-commentary on the Same by Guṇaprabha: Chapter 1: Pravrajyā-vastu.* Patna: Kashi Prasad Jayaswal Research Institute.

Barrett, T.H. 2014. "Buddhism and Law in China: The Emergence of Distinctive Patterns in Chinese History." In *Buddhism and Law: An Introduction,* edited by Rebecca Redwood French and Mark A. Nathan, 201–16. New York: Cambridge University Press.

Bataille, Georges. 1988. "The Unarmed Society: Lamaism." In *The Accursed Share: An Essay on General Economy,* 93–110. New York: Zone Books.

Bechert, Heinz. 1970. "Theravāda Buddhist Sangha: Some General Observations on Historical and Political Factors in Its Development." *Journal of Asian Studies* 29(4): 761–78.

———. 1984. "Buddhist Revival in East and West." In *The World of Buddhism: Buddhist Monks and Nuns in Society and Culture*, edited by Heinz Bechert and Richard F. Gombrich, 273–85. New York: Facts on File.

Bell, Charles Alfred. 1931. *The Religion of Tibet*. Oxford: Clarendon Press.

———. [1946] 1998. *Portrait of a Dalai Lama: The Life and Times of the Great Thirteenth*. Delhi: Book Faith India.

Berounsky, Daniel. 2013. "Demonic Tobacco in Tibet." *Mongolo-Tibetica Pragensia* 6(2): 7–34.

Blackburn, Anne M. 1999. "Looking for the Vinaya: Monastic Discipline in the Practical Canons of the Theravāda." *Journal of the International Association of Buddhist Studies* 22(2): 281–309.

Bourdieu, Pierre. 1984. *Distinction: A Social Critique of the Judgement of Taste*. Cambridge, MA: Harvard University Press.

Bridges, Alex W. 2017. "Two Monasteries in Ladakh: Religiosity and the Social Environment in Tibetan Buddhism." PhD dissertation, Case Western Reserve University.

Brook, Timothy. 2014. "The Ownership and Theft of Monastic Land in Ming China." In *Buddhism and Law: An Introduction*, edited by Rebecca Redwood French and Mark A. Nathan, 217–33. New York: Cambridge University Press.

Bunnag, Jane. 1973. *Buddhist Monk, Buddhist Layman: A Study of Urban Monastic Organization in Central Thailand*. Cambridge: Cambridge University Press.

Burrow, T. 1940. *A Translation of the Kharoṣṭhī Documents from Chinese Turkestan*. London: Royal Asiatic Society.

Cabezón, José Ignacio. 1997. "The Regulations of a Monastery." In *Religions of Tibet in Practice*, edited by Donald S. Lopez, 335–51. Princeton, NJ: Princeton University Press.

———. 2004. "Monks." www.thlib.org/#!essay = /cabezon/sera/people/monks/s/b1

———. 2017a. *The Just King: The Tibetan Buddhist Classic on Leading an Ethical Life*. Boulder, CO: Snow Lion.

———. 2017b. *Sexuality in Classical South Asian Buddhism*. Somerville: Wisdom.

Caple, Jane. 2010. "Monastic Economic Reform at Rong-bo Monastery: Towards an Understanding of Contemporary Tibetan Monastic Revival and Development in A-mdo." *Buddhist Studies Review* 27(2): 179–219.

———. 2011. "Seeing beyond the State? The Negotiation of Moral Boundaries in the Revival and Development of Tibetan Buddhist Monasticism in Contemporary China." PhD dissertation, University of Leeds.

Carrasco, Pedro. 1959. *Land and Polity in Tibet*. Seattle: University of Washington Press.

Cassinelli, C.W., and Robert B. Ekvall. 1969. *A Tibetan Principality: The Political System of Sakya*. Ithaca, NY: Cornell University Press.

Cech, Krystyna. 1988. "A Bonpo *bča'-yig*: The Rules of sMan-ri Monastery." In *Tibetan Studies: Proceedings of the 4th Seminar of the International Association for Tibetan Studies, Schloss Hohenkammer–Munich 1985*, edited by Helga Uebach and Panglung Jampa Losung, 69–85. Munich: Kommission für Zentralasiatische Studien, Bayerische Akademie der Wissenschaften.

Chandra, Lokesh. 1980. *Multi-lingual Buddhist Texts in Sanskrit, Chinese, Tibetan, Mongolian and Manchu, vol. 8*. New Delhi: Sharada Rani.

Chayet, Anne. 2003. "17th and 18th Century Tibet: A General Survey." In *Tibet and Her Neighbours: A History*, edited by Alex McKay, 83–89. London: Hansjörg Mayer.

Chen, Han-Seng. 1949. *Frontier Land Systems in Southernmost China: A Comparative Study of Agrarian Problems and Social Organization among the Pai Yi People of Yunnan and the Kamba People of Sikang*. New York: Institute of Pacific Relations.

Childs, Geoff. 2005. "Methods, Meanings, and Representations in the Study of Past Tibetan Societies." *Journal of the International Association of Tibetan Studies* 1(1): 1–13.

Čige. 2004. *Erten-ü mongyol-un qauli čayajā-yin teüke* [Ancient Mongolian legal history]. Shenyang: Liyouning-un ündüsüten-ü keblel-ün qoriya.

Clarke, Shayne. 2009a. "Monks Who Have Sex: *Pārājika* Penance in Indian Buddhist Monasticisms." *Journal of Indian Philosophy* 37(1): 1–43.

———. 2009b. "When and Where Is a Monk No Longer a Monk? On Communion and Communities in Indian Buddhist Monastic Law Codes." *Indo-Iranian Journal* 52(2/3): 115–41.

———. 2014. *Family Matters in Indian Buddhist Monasticisms*. Honolulu: University of Hawai'i Press.

Collins, Steven. 1982. *Selfless Persons: Imagery and Thought in Theravāda Buddhism*. Cambridge: Cambridge University Press.

———. 1988. "Monasticism, Utopias and Comparative Social Theory." *Religion* 18(2): 101–35.

———. 1998. *Nirvana and Other Buddhist Felicities: Utopias of the Pali Imaginaire*. Cambridge: Cambridge University Press.

Cüppers, Christoph. 2007. "Die Reise- und Zeltlagerordnung des Fünften Dalai Lama." In *Pramāṇakīrtiḥ: Papers Dedicated to Ernst Steinkellner on the Occasion of His 70th Birthday*, edited by Birgit Kellner, Helmut Krasser, Horst Lasic, Michael Torsten Much, and Helmut Tauscher, 37–51. Vienna: Arbeitskreis für tibetische und buddhistische Studien.

———. 2011. "Tibetische Regierungsverordnungen." www.tibet-encyclopaedia.de/regierung sverordnung.html

——— and Per K. Sørensen. 1998. *A Collection of Tibetan Proverbs and Sayings: Gems of Tibetan Wisdom and Wit*. Stuttgart: Steiner.

Dagyab, Namri. 2009. "Vergleich von Verwaltungsstrukturen und wirtschaftlichen Entscheidungsprozessen tibetisch-buddhistischer Klöster in der Autonomen Region Tibet, China und Indien." PhD dissertation, Rheinischen Friedrich-Wilhelms-Universität.

Dakpa, Ngawang. 2003. "The Hours and Days of a Great Monastery: Drepung." In *Lhasa in the Seventeenth Century: The Capital of the Dalai Lamas*, edited by Françoise Pommaret, 167–78. Leiden: Brill.

Dargyay, Eva K. 1982. *Tibetan Village Communities: Structure and Change*. Warminster: Aris & Philips.

———. 1991. "Sangha and State in Imperial Tibet." In *Tibetan History and Language, Studies Dedicated to Uray Geza on His Seventieth Birthday*, edited by Ernst Steinkellner, 111–28. Vienna: Arbeitskreis für tibetische und buddhistische Studien.

Das, Sarat Chandra. [1893] 1965. *Indian Pandits in the Land of Snow*. Calcutta: Firma K.L. Mukhopadhyay.

Davidson, Ronald M. 2005. *Tibetan Renaissance: Tantric Buddhism in the Rebirth of Tibetan Culture*. New York: Columbia University Press.

Desideri, Ippolito. [1937] 2011. *An Account of Tibet: The Travels of Ippolito Desideri of Pistoia, S.J., 1712–1727*. Translated by Filippo de Filippi. London: Routledge.

Dhondub, Choedon, and Information Office of H.H. the Dalai Lama [translation]. 1978. *Life in the Red Flag People's Commune*. Dharamsala: Information Office of H.H. the Dalai Lama.

Dhondup, Yangdon. 2013. "Rules and Regulations of the Reb kong Tantric Community." In *Monastic and Lay Traditions in North-Eastern Tibet*, edited by Yangdon Dhondup, Ulrich Pagel, and Geoffrey Samuel, 117–40. Leiden: Brill.

Diack, Alexander Henderson. [1897] 1994. *Gazetteer of the Kangra District, Parts II to IV: Kulu, Lahul and Spiti, 1897.* Delhi: Indus.

Dicks, Anthony. 2014. "Buddhism and Law in China: Qing Dynasty to the Present." In *Buddhism and Law: An Introduction*, edited by Rebecca Redwood French and Mark A. Nathan, 234–53. New York: Cambridge University Press.

Dōgen, Taigen. 1996. *Dōgen's Pure Standards for the Zen Community: A Translation of the Eihei Shingi.* Translated by Daniel Leighton and Shohaku Okumura. Albany: State University of New York Press.

Dreyfus, Georges. 2003. *The Sound of Two Hands Clapping: The Education of a Tibetan Buddhist Monk.* Berkeley: University of California Press.

Dumont, Louis. 1980. *Homo Hierarchicus: The Caste System and Its Implications.* Chicago: University of Chicago Press.

Ekelund, Robert B., et al. 1996. *Sacred Trust: The Medieval Church as an Economic Firm.* New York: Oxford University Press.

Ekvall, Robert B. 1959/60. "Three Categories of Inmates within Tibetan Monasteries: Status and Function." *Central Asiatic Journal* 5: 206–20.

———. 1964. *Religious Observances in Tibet: Patterns and Function.* Chicago: University of Chicago Press.

Ellingson, Ter. 1990. "Tibetan Monastic Constitutions: The bCa' yig." In *Reflections on Tibetan Culture: Essays in Memory of Turrell V. Wylie*, edited by Lawrence Epstein and Richard F. Sherburne, 205–29. Lewiston, NY: Edward Mellen Press.

Evers, Hans-Dieter. 1967. "Kinship and Property Rights in a Buddhist Monastery in Central Ceylon." *American Anthropologist* 69(6): 703–10.

Ferguson, John P., and Ramitanondh Shalardchai. 1976. "Monks and Hierarchy in Northern Thailand." *Journal of the Siam Society* 64(1): 104–49.

Fjeld, Heidi. 2008. "Pollution and Social Networks in Contemporary Rural Tibet." In *Tibetan Modernities: Proceedings of the Tenth Seminar of the IATS, 2003*, edited by Robert Barnett and Ronald Schwarz, 113–37. Leiden: Brill.

Foulk, T. Griffith. 2004. "*Chanyuan qinggui* and Other 'Rules of Purity' in Chinese Buddhism." In *The Zen Canon: Understanding the Classic Texts*, edited by Steven Heine and Dale S. Wright, 275–312. Oxford: Oxford University Press.

Frauwallner, Erich. 1956. *The Earliest Vinaya and the Beginnings of Buddhist Literature.* Rome: Istituto italiano per il Medio ed Estremo Oriente: Serie orientale Roma (vol. 8).

French, Rebecca Redwood. 1995a. *The Golden Yoke: The Legal Cosmology of Buddhist Tibet.* Ithaca, NY: Cornell University Press.

———. 1995b. "The Cosmology of Law in Buddhist Tibet." *Journal of the International Association of Buddhist Studies* 16(1): 97–116.

———. 1998. "Lamas, Oracles, Channels, and the Law: Reconsidering Religion and Social Theory." *Yale Journal of Law & the Humanities* 10: 505–35.

Garrett, Frances. 2008. *Religion, Medicine and the Human Embryo in Tibet.* London: Routledge.

Gernet, Jacques. [1956] 1995. *Buddhism in Chinese Society: An Economic History from the Fifth to the Tenth Centuries.* Translated by Franciscus Verellen. New York: Columbia University Press.

Gethin, Rupert. 2007. "Buddhist Monks, Buddhist Kings, Buddhist Violence: On the Early Buddhist Attitudes to Violence." In *Religion and Violence in South Asia: Theory and Practice,* edited by John Hinnells and Richard King, 62–82. London: Routledge.

Goldstein, Melvyn C. 1964. "A Study of the Ldab Ldob." *Central Asiatic Journal* 9(2): 123–41.

———. 1968. "An Anthropological Study of the Tibetan Political System." PhD dissertation, University of Washington.

———. 1971a. "The Balance between Centralization and Decentralization in the Traditional Tibetan Political System." *Central Asiatic Journal* 15(3): 170–82.

———. 1971b. "Serfdom and Mobility: An Examination of the Institution of Human Lease in Traditional Tibetan Society." *Journal of Asian Studies* 30(3): 521–34.

———.1973. "The Circulation of Estates in Tibet: Reincarnation, Land and Politics." *Journal of Asian Studies* 32(3): 445–55.

———. 1986. "Reexamining Choice, Dependency and Command in the Tibetan Social System: 'Tax Appendages' and Other Landless Serfs." *Tibet Journal* 11(4): 79–112.

———. 1987. "On the Nature of the Tibetan Peasantry: A Rejoinder." *Tibet Journal* 13(1): 61–65.

———. 1989a. "Freedom, Servitude and the 'Servant-serf' Nyima: A Re-rejoinder to Miller." *Tibet Journal* 14(2): 56–60.

———. 1989b. *A History of Modern Tibet, 1913–1951: The Demise of the Lamaist State.* Berkeley: University of California Press.

———. 1998. "The Revival of Monastic Life in Drepung Monastery." In *Buddhism in Contemporary Tibet: Religious Revival and Cultural Identity,* edited by Melvyn C. Goldstein, 15–52. Berkeley: University of California Press.

———. 2009. "Tibetan Buddhism and Mass Monasticism." In *Moines et moniales de par le monde: La vie monastique au miroir de la parenté,* edited by A. Herrou and G. Krauskopff. Paris: L'Harmattan.

——— and Paljor Tsarong. 1985. "Tibetan Buddhist Monasticism: Social, Psychological and Cultural Implications." *Tibet Journal* 10(1): 14–31.

Gombo, Ugen. 1983. "Cultural Expressions of Social Stratification in Traditional Tibet: 'Caste' and Casteism in a Non-Hindu Context." *Anthropology* 7: 43–77.

Gombodorž, M. 2016. "Comparative Study of Several Monastic Codes of Rules by Mongolian Lamas." *Kul'tura Central'noj Azii: pis'mennye istočniki* 9: 35–50.

Gombrich, Richard F. 1975. "Buddhist Karma and Social Control." *Comparative Studies in Society and History* 17(2): 212–20.

———. [1988] 2006. *Theravāda Buddhism: A Social History from Ancient Benares to Modern Colombo.* London: Routledge.

Graeber, David. 2011. *Debt: The First 5,000 Years.* New York: Melville House.

Grothmann, Kerstin. 2012. "Migration Narratives, Official Classifications, and Local Identities: The Memba of the Hidden Land of Pachakshiri." In *Origins and Migrations in the Extended Eastern Himalayas,* edited by Toni Huber and Stuart H. Blackburn, 125–51. Leiden: Brill.

Gunawardana, R.A.L.H. 1979. *Robe and Plough: Monastic and Economic Interest in Early Medieval Sri Lanka*. Tuscon: University of Arizona Press.

Gutschow, Kim. 2004. *Being a Buddhist Nun: The Struggle for Enlightenment in the Himalayas*. Cambridge, MA: Harvard University Press.

Gyatso, Janet. 1989. "Down with the Demoness: Reflections on a Feminine Ground in Tibet." In *Feminine Ground: Essays on Women and Tibet*, edited by Janice Dean Willis, 38–53. Ithaca, NY: Snow Lion.

———. 2015. *Being Human in a Buddhist World: An Intellectual History of Medicine in Early Modern Tibet*. New York: Columbia University Press.

Gyatso, Lobsang, and Gareth Sparham. 1998. *Memoirs of a Tibetan Lama*. Ithaca, NY: Snow Lion.

Gyatso, Sherab. 2003. "Of Monks and Monasteries." In *Exile as Challenge: The Tibetan Diaspora*, edited by Dagmar Bernstorff and Hubertus von Welck, 213–43. Hyderabad: Orient Longman.

Halbwachs, Maurice. [1941] 1992. *On Collective Memory*. Translated by Lewis A. Coser. Chicago: University of Chicago Press.

Hann, Chris, and Keith Hart. 2011. *Economic Anthropology: History, Ethnography, Critique*. Cambridge: Polity Press.

Heimbel, Jörg. 2013. "The Jo gdan tshogs sde bzhi: An Investigation into the History of the Four Monastic Communities in Śākyaśrībhadra's Vinaya Tradition." In *Nepalica-Tibetica: Festgabe für Christoph Cüppers*, edited by Franz-Karl Ehrhard and Petra Maurer, 187–234. Andiast: International Institute for Tibetan and Buddhist Studies.

Heirman, Ann, and Tom De Rauw. 2006. "Offenders, Sinners and Criminals: The Consumption of Forbidden Food." *Acta Orientalia* 59(1): 57–83.

Helffer, Mireille. 1983. "Le gaṇḍi: Un simandre Tibétain d'origine Indienne." *Yearbook for Traditional Music* 15: 112–25.

Heubner, Ann M., and Andrew C. Garrod. 1993. "Moral Reasoning among Tibetan Monks: A Study of Buddhist Adolescents and Young Adults in Nepal." *Journal of Cross-Cultural Psychology* 24(June): 167–85.

Hillman, Ben. 2005. "Monastic Politics and the Local State in China: Authority and Autonomy in an Ethnically Tibetan Prefecture." *China Journal* 54: 29–51.

Horner, Isaline B. 1949. *The Book of the Discipline, vol. 1: Suttavibhaṅga*. London: Pāli Text Society: Luzac.

Hovden, Astrid. 2013. "Who Were the Sponsors? Reflections on Recruitment and Ritual Economy in Three Himalyan Village Monasteries." In *The Tibetans Who Escaped the Historian's Net: Studies in the Social Hisory of Tibetan Societies*, edited by Charles Ramble, Peter Schwieger, and Alice Travers, 209–30. Kathmandu: Vajra Books.

Huber, Toni. 2004. "Territorial Control by 'Sealing': A Religio-Political Practice in Tibet." *Zentralasiatischen Studien* 33: 127–52.

Humphrey, Caroline, and Hürelbaatar Ujeed. 2013. *A Monastery in Time: The Making of Mongolian Buddhism*. Chicago: University of Chicago Press.

Huxley, Andrew. 1995. "Studying Theravāda Legal Literature." *Journal of the International Association of Buddhist Studies* 20(1): 63–91.

Ishii, Yoneo. 1986. *Sangha, State, and Society: Thai Buddhism in History*. Translated by Peter Hawkes. Honolulu: University of Hawai'i Press. Monographs of the Center for Southeast Asian Studies, Kyoto University.

Iwao, Kazushi. 2012. "Organisation of the Chinese Inhabitants in Tibetan-ruled Dun-huang." In *Old Tibetan Studies: Dedicated to the Memory of RE Emmerick, Proceedings of the Tenth Seminar of the IATS, 2003, vol. 14*, edited by Cristina Scherrer-Schaub, 65–75. Leiden: Brill.

Jackson, David. 1984. *The Mollas of Mustang: Historical, Religious, and Oratorical Traditions of the Nepalese-Tibetan Borderland*. Dharamsala: Library of Tibetan Works & Archives.

Jagou, Fabienne. 2004. *Le 9e Panchen Lama (1883–1937): Enjeu des relations sino-tibétaines*. Paris: École française d'Extrême-Orient.

Jahoda, Christian. 2007. "Socio-Economic Organisation of Village Communities and Mon-asteries in Spiti, H.P., India: The Case of a Religious Administrative Unit (*chos gzhis*)." In *Discoveries in Western Tibet and the Western Himalayas: Essays on History, Literature, Archaeology and Art, Proceedings of the Tenth Seminar of the IATS, 2003, vol. 8*, edited by Amy Heller and Giacomella Orofino, 215–40. Leiden: Brill.

'Jam mgon Kong-sprul Blo-gros-mtha'-yas and International Translation Committee founded by Kalu Rinpoche. 2003. *Buddhist Ethics*. Ithaca, NY: Snow Lion.

Jansen, Berthe. 2010. "A Tibetan Nuptial Oratorical Tradition: The Molla from Dingri." MPhil thesis, Oxford University, 2010.

———. 2013a. "How to Tame a Wild Monastic Elephant: Drepung Monastery According to the Great Fifth." In *The Tibetans Who Escaped the Historian's Net*, edited by Charles Ramble, Peter Schwieger, and Alice Travers, 109–39. Kathmandu: Vajra Books.

———. 2013b. "Selection at the Gate: Access to the Monkhood and Social Mobility in Tradi-tional Tibet." In *Current Issues and Progress in Tibetan Studies: Proceedings of the Third International Seminar of Young Tibetologists, Kobe 2012* (Journal of Research Institute, vol. 51), edited by Tsuguhito Takeuchi, Kazushi Iwao, Ai Nishida, Seiji Kumagai, and Meishi Yamamoto, 137–64. Kobe: Kobe City University of Foreign Studies.

———. 2014. "The Monastic Guidelines (bCa' yig) by Sidkeong Tulku: Monasteries, Sex and Reform in Sikkim." *Journal of the Royal Asiatic Society* 24(4): 597–622.

———. 2015. "Monastic Organizational Guidelines." In *Brill's Encyclopedia of Buddhism, vol. 1*, edited by Jonathan Silk et al., 442–49. Leiden: Brill.

———. 2016a. "Monastic Guidelines (*bCa' yig*): Tibetan Social History from a Buddhist Studies Perspective." In *Social Regulation: Case Studies from Tibetan History* (Proceed-ings of the International Association of Tibetan Studies Conference, Ulan Baatar, 2013), edited by Jeannine Bischoff and Saul Mullard, 64–98. Leiden: Brill.

———. 2016b. "The Disciplinarian (*dge skos / dge bskos / chos khrims pa / zhal ngo*) in Tibetan Monasteries: His Role and His Rules." *Revue d'Etudes Tibétaines* 37: 145–61.

———. (forthcoming) 2018. "A Preliminary Investigation into Monk-tax: *grwa khral / btsun khral / ban khral* and Its Meanings." In *Tax, Corvée and Community Obligations in Tibetan Societies*, edited by Alice Travers, Peter Schwieger, and Charles Ramble. Leiden: Brill.

Joldan, Sonam. 2006. "Traditional Ties between Ladakh and Buddhist Tibet: Monastic Or-ganization and Monastic Education as a Sustaining Factor." *Tibet Journal* 31(2): 69–88.

Kapstein, Matthew. 2000. *The Tibetan Assimilation of Buddhism: Conversion, Contestation, and Memory*. New York: Oxford University Press.

———. 2004. "A Thorn in the Dragon's Side: Tibetan Buddhist Culture in China." In *Govern-ing China's Multiethnic Frontiers*, edited by Morris Rossabi, 230–84. Seattle: University of Washington Press.

Karmay, Samten Gyaltsen, and Yasuhiko Nagano, eds. 2003. *A Survey of Bonpo Monasteries and Temples in Tibet and the Himalaya: Bon Studies, vol. 7.* Osaka: National Museum of Ethnology.

Kawaguchi, Ekai. 1909. *Three Years in Tibet: with the Original Japanese Illustrations.* Madras: Theosophist Publishing Society, Benares and London.

Kaye, Joël. 2000. *Economy and Nature in the Fourteenth Century: Money, Market Exchange and the Emergence of Scientific Thought.* Cambridge: Cambridge University Press.

Kemper, Steven. 1984. "The Buddhist Monkhood, the Law, and the State in Colonial Sri Lanka." *Comparative Studies in Society and History* 26(3): 401–27.

Kern, Hendrik. 1896. *Manual of Indian Buddhism.* Strassburg: K.J. Trübner.

Khedrup, Tashi, Hugh Richardson, and Tadeusz Skorupski. 1986. *Adventures of a Tibetan Fighting Monk.* Bangkok: Tamarind Press.

Kieffer-Pülz, Petra. 2011. *Sīmāvicāraṇa: A Pali Letter on Monastic Boundaries by King Rāma IV of Siam.* Bangkok: Fragile Palm Leaves Foundation, Lumbini International Research Institute.

———. 2014. "What the Vinayas Can Tell Us about Law." In *Buddhism and Law: An Introduction*, edited by Rebecca Redwood French and Mark A. Nathan, 46–62. New York: Cambridge University Press.

King, Martin Luther. 1964. "Letter from Birmingham Jail." In *Why We Can't Wait.* New York: Harper and Row.

Kolås, Åshild. 2003. "'Class' in Tibet: Creating Social Order before and during the Mao Era." *Identities: Global Studies In Culture and Power* 10(2): 181–200.

Kurzman, Charles. 1998. "Organizational Opportunity and Social Movement Mobilization: A Comparative Analysis of Four Religious Movements." *Mobilization: An International Quarterly* 3(1): 23–49.

Kvaerne, Per. 1970. "Remarques sur l'administration d'un monastère Bon-po." *Journal asiatique* 258: 187–92.

Le Goff, Jacques. 1988. *Your Money or Your Life: Economy and Religion in the Middle Ages.* New York: Zone Books.

Lempert, Michael P. 2006. "Disciplinary Theatrics: Public Reprimand and the Textual Performance of Affect at Sera Monastery, India." *Language & Communication* 26(1): 15–33.

Locke, John. [1690] 1980. *Second Treatise of Government.* Edited by Crawford Brough Macpherson. Indianapolis: Hackett.

Madden, Sister James Eugene. 1963. "Business Monks, Banker Monks, Bankrupt Monks: The English Cistercians in the Thirteenth Century." *Catholic Historical Review* 49(3): 341–64.

Maher, Derek F. 2012. "Tibetan Monastics and Social Justice." In *The Wiley-Blackwell Companion to Religion and Social Justice*, edited by Michael D. Palmer and Stanley M. Burgess, 268–79. Chicester: Wiley-Blackwell.

Makley, Charlene E. 2007. *The Violence of Liberation: Gender and Tibetan Buddhist Revival in Post-Mao China.* Berkeley: University of California Press.

Martin, Dan. 2010. "The Book-moving Incident of 1209." In *Edition, éditions: L'écrit au Tibet, évolution et devenir—Collectanea Himalayica 3*, edited by Anne Chayet, Cristina Scherrer-Schaub, Françoise Robin, and Jean-Luc Achard, 197–217. Munich: Indus Verlag.

——— and Yael Bentor. 1997. *Tibetan Histories: A Bibliography of Tibetan-Language Historical Works*. London: Serindia.

McCleary, Rachel M., and Leonard W.J. van der Kuijp. 2010. "The Market Approach to the Rise of the Geluk School, 1419–1642." *Journal of Asian Studies* 69(1): 149–80.

Meyer, Fernand. 2003. "The Golden Century of Tibetan Medicine." In *Lhasa in the Seventeenth Century: The Capital of the Dalai Lamas*, edited by Françoise Pommaret, 99–117. Leiden: Brill.

Michael, Franz H. 1982. *Rule by Incarnation: Tibetan Buddhism and Its Role in Society and State*. Boulder, CO: Westview Press.

Miller, Beatrice D. 1958. "Lamas and Laymen: A Historico-functional Study of the Secular Integration of Monastery and Community." PhD dissertation, University of Washington.

———. 1961. "The Web of Tibetan Monasticism." *Journal of Asian Studies* 20(2): 197–203.

———. 1988. "Last Rejoinder to Goldstein on Tibetan Social System." *Tibet Journal* 13(3): 64–67.

Miller, Robert James. 1961. "Buddhist Monastic Economy: The Jisa Mechanism." *Comparative Studies in Society and History* 3(4): 427–38.

Mills, Martin A. 2000. "Vajra Brother, Vajra Sister: Renunciation, Individualism and the Household in Tibetan Buddhist Monasticism." *Journal of the Royal Anthropological Institute* 6(1): 17–34.

———. 2003. *Identity, Ritual and State in Tibetan Buddhism: The Foundations of Authority in Gelukpa Monasticism*. London: Routledge Curzon.

Minogue, Kenneth. [1998] 2005. "Social Justice in Theory and Practice." In *Social Justice: From Hume to Walzer*, edited by David Boucher and Paul Kelly, 255–67. London: Routledge.

Mumford, Stan. 1989. *Himalayan Dialogue: Tibetan Lamas and Gurung Shamans in Nepal*. Madison: University of Wisconsin Press.

Nattier, Jan. 1991. *Once Upon a Future Time: Studies in a Buddhist Prophecy of Decline*. Berkeley: Asian Humanities Press.

Nietupski, Paul K. 2009. "Guṇaprabha's Vinayasūtra Corpus: Texts and Contexts." *Journal of the International Association of Tibetan Studies* 5: 1–19.

———. 2011. *Labrang Monastery: A Tibetan Buddhist Community on the Inner Asian Borderlands, 1709–1958*. Lanham, MD: Lexington Books.

———. 2017. "Guṇaprabha on Monastic Authority and Authoritative Doctrine." *Journal of Buddhist Ethics* 24: 169–224.

Norbu, Thubten Jigme, and Dan Martin. 1991. "Dorjiev: Memoirs of a Tibetan Diplomat." *Hokke-Bunka Kenkyū* 17: 1–105. Accessed via https://sites.google.com/site/tibetological/dorjiev

Norman, Alexander. 2009. *Secret Lives of the Dalai Lama: Holder of the White Lotus*. London: Abacus.

Nornang, Ngawang L. 1990. "Monastic Organization and Economy at Dwags-po bShad-grub-gling." In *Reflections on Tibetan Culture: Essays in Memory of Turrell V. Wylie*, edited by Lawrence Epstein and Richard F. Sherburne, 249–68. Lewiston, NY: Edward Mellen Press.

North, Charles M., and Carl R. Gwin. 2010. "Religion and the Emergence of the Rule of Law." In *Religion, Economy, and Cooperation*, edited by Ilkka Pyysiainen, 127–58. Berlin: De Gruyter.

Oidtmann, Max. 2016. "A 'Dog-eat-dog' World: Qing Jurispractices and the Legal Inscription of Piety in Amdo *Extrême-Orient Extrême-Occident* 1: 151–82.

Oldenberg, Hermann. [1879] 1964. *The Vinaya Piṭakam: One of the Principal Buddhist Holy Scriptures in the Pāli Language: The Mahāvagga, vol. 1*. London: Pāli Text Society, Luzac.

Ornatowski, Gregory K. 1996. "Continuity and Change in the Economic Ethics of Buddhism: Evidence from the History of Buddhism in India, China and Japan." *Journal of Buddhist Ethics* 3: 198–240.

Ortner, Sherry B. 1989. *High Religion: A Cultural and Political History of Sherpa Buddhism*. Princeton, NJ: Princeton University Press.

Pachow, W. [1955] 2000. *A Comparative Study of the Pratimoksa: On the Basis of Its Chinese, Tibetan, Sanskrit, and Pali Versions*. Delhi: Motilal Banarsidass.

Pardue, Peter A. 1971. *Buddhism: A Historical Introduction to Buddhist Values and the Social and Political Forms They Have Assumed in Asia*. New York: Macmillan Press.

Parenti, Michael. 2003. "Friendly Feudalism: The Tibet Myth." *New Political Science* 25(4): 579–90.

Patrul, Rinpoche. 1998. *The Words of My Perfect Teacher*. Translated by Padmakara Translation Group. Walnut Creek, CA: AltaMira Press.

Penjore, Dorji. 2011. "Rows of Auspicious Seats: The Role of *bzhugs gral phun sum tshogs pa'i rten 'brel* Ritual in the Founding of the First Bhutanese State in the 17th Century." *Journal of Bhutan Studies* 24: 1–42.

Pereira, George. 1912. "A Visit to Labrang Monastery, South-West Kan-su, North-West China." *Geographical Journal* 40(4): 415–20.

Phuntsho, Karma. 2004. "Echoes of Ancient Ethos: Reflections on Some Popular Bhutanese Social Themes." In *The Spider and the Piglet*, edited by K. Ura and S. Kinga, 564–79. Thimphu: Centre of Bhutan Studies.

Pirie, Fernanda. 2010. "Law before Government: Ideology and Aspiration." *Oxford Journal of Legal Studies* 30(2): 207–28.

———. 2013. "Law and Religion in Historic Tibet." In *Religion in Disputes: Pervasiveness of Religious Normativity in Disputing Processes*, edited by Franz von Benda-Beckmann, Keebet von Benda-Beckmann, Martin Ramstedt, and Bertram Turner, 231–47. New York: Palgrave Macmillan.

Poceski, Mario. 2003. "Xuefeng's Code and the Chan School's Participation in the Development of Monastic Regulations." *Asia Major, Third Series* 16(2): 33–56.

Powers, John. 1995. *Introduction to Tibetan Buddhism*. Ithaca, NY: Snow Lion.

———. 2004. *History as Propaganda: Tibetan Exiles Versus the People's Republic of China*. Oxford: Oxford University Press.

Purevjav, Lkham. 2012. "Patterns of Monastic and Sangha Development in Khalkha Mongolia." In *Mongolians after Socialism: Politics, Economy, Religion*, edited by Bruce M. Knauft and Richard Taupier, 249–68. Ulaanbaatar: Admon Press.

Raftis, J.A. 1961. "Western Monasticism and Economic Organization." *Comparative Studies in Society and History* 3(4): 452–69.

Ramble, Charles. 2008. *The Navel of the Demoness: Tibetan Buddhism and Civil Religion in Highland Nepal*. New York: Oxford University Press.

——— and Nyima Drandul. 2008. *Tibetan Sources for a Social History of Mustang, Nepal, vol. 1: The Archive of Te; Part 1*. Halle (Saale): IITBS.

Ratnapala, Nandasena. 1971. *The Katikavatas: Laws of the Buddhist Order of Ceylon from the 12th Century to the 18th Century*, critically edited, translated, and annotated. Munich: Kitzinger.

Rauber-Schweizer, Hanna. 1976. *Der Schmied und sein Handwerk im traditionellen Tibet*. Rikon: Tibet-Institut.

Rawls, John. [1971] 1999. *A Theory of Justice*. Revised edition. Cambridge, MA: Belknap Press of Harvard University Press.

Reynolds, Craig J. 1979. "Monastery Lands and Labour Endowments in Thailand: Some Effects of Social and Economic Change, 1868–1910." *Journal of the Economic and Social History of the Orient* 22(2): 190–227.

Rhys Davids, T.W., and Hermann Oldenberg. 1881–1885. *Vinaya Texts*. Edited by Max Müller. Oxford: Clarendon Press.

Richardson, Hugh. 1983. "Notes and Communications." *Bulletin of the School of Oriental and African Studies* 46(1): 136–38.

———. 1985. *A Corpus of Early Tibetan Inscriptions*. London: Royal Asiatic Society.

Risley, Herbert Hope. 1894. *The Gazetteer of Sikhim*. Calcutta: Bengal Secretariat Press.

Roesler, Ulrike. 2015. "16 Human Norms (*mi chos bcu drug*)—Indian, Chinese, and Tibetan." In *The Illuminating Mirror: Tibetan Studies in Honour of Per K. Sørensen on the Occasion of His 65th Birthday*, edited by Olaf Czaja and Guntram Hazod, 389–409. Wiesbaden: Dr. Ludwig Reichert Verlag.

Samuel, Geoffrey. 1993. *Civilized Shamans: Buddhism in Tibetan Societies*. Washington, DC: Smithsonian Institution Press.

———. 2013. "Reb kong in the Multiethnic Context of A mdo: Religion, Language, Religion, and Identity." In *Monastic and Lay Traditions in North-Eastern Tibet*, edited by Yangdon Dhondup, Ulrich Pagel, and Geoffrey Samuel, 5–22. Leiden: Brill.

Sandberg, Graham. 1906. *Tibet and the Tibetans*. London: Society for Promoting Christian Knowledge.

Sandel, Michael J. 2009. *Justice: What's the Right Thing to Do?* London: Penguin Books.

Sayer, Andrew. 2004. "Moral Economy," 1–15. www.comp.lancs.ac.uk/sociology/papers/sayer-moral-economy.pdf

———. 2008. "Moral Economic Regulation in Organizations: A University Example." *Organization* 15(2): 147–64.

Schaeffer, Kurtis R. 2009. *The Culture of the Book in Tibet*. New York: Columbia University Press.

Schneider, Hanna. 2002. "Tibetan Legal Documents of South-Western Tibet: Structure and Style." In *Tibet, Past and Present: Tibetan Studies: Proceedings of the Ninth Seminar of the International Association for Tibetan Studies, Leiden 2000, vol. 1*, edited by Henk Blezer, 415–29. Leiden: Brill.

Schneider, Nicola. 2009. "Le monachisme comme alternative au mariage: Le cas des nonnes tibétaines d'une région nomade du Kham." In *Moines et moniales de par le monde: La vie monastique au miroir de la parenté*, edited by A. Herrou and G. Krauskopff, 279–91. Paris: L'Harmattan.

Schopen, Gregory. 1994a. "Ritual Rights and Bones of Contention: More on Monastic Funerals and Relics in the Mūlasarvāstivāda-vinaya." *Journal of Indian Philosophy* 22(1): 31–80.

———. 1994b. "The Monastic Ownership of Servants or Slaves: Local and Legal Factors in the Redactional History of Two Vinayas." *Journal of the International Association of Buddhist Studies* 17(2): 145–73.

———. 1995a. "Death, Funerals, and the Division of Property in a Monastic Code." In *Buddhism in Practice*, edited by Donald S. Lopez, 473–502. Princeton, NJ: Princeton University Press.

———. 1995b. "Monastic Law Meets the Real World: A Monk's Continuing Right to Inherit Family Property in Classical India." *History of Religions* 35(2): 101–23.

———. 1996a. "The Lay Ownership of Monasteries and the Role of the Monk in Mūlasarvāstivādin Monasticism." *Journal of the International Association of Buddhist Studies* 19(1): 81–126.

———. 1996b. "The Suppression of Nuns and the Ritual Murder of Their Special Dead in Two Buddhist Monastic Texts." *Journal of Indian Philosophy* 24(6): 563–92.

———. 2000a. "The Good Monk and His Money in a Buddhist Monasticism of 'the Mahāyāna Period.'" *Eastern Buddhist Society* 32(1): 85–105.

———. 2001. "Dead Monks and Bad Debts: Some Provisions of a Buddhist Monastic Inheritance Law." *Indo-Iranian Journal* 44(2): 99–148.

———. 2002. "Counting the Buddha and the Local Spirits In: A Monastic Ritual of Inclusion for the Rain Retreat." *Journal of Indian Philosophy* 30(4): 359–88.

———. 2004a. "Art, Beauty, and the Business of Running a Buddhist Monastery." In *Buddhist Monks and Business Matters: Still More Papers on Monastic Buddhism in India*, 19–44. Honolulu: University of Hawai'i Press.

———. 2004b. "Doing Business for the Lord: Lending on Interest and Written Loan Contracts in the Mūlasarvāstivāda-vinaya." In *Buddhist Monks and Business Matters: Still More Papers on Monastic Buddhism in India*, 45–90. Honolulu: University of Hawai'i Press.

———. 2004c. "On Buddhist Monks and Dreadful Deities: Some Monastic Devices for Updating the Dharma." In *Gedenkschrift J.W. de Jong: Studia Philologica Buddhica Monograph Series 17*, edited by H.W. Bodewitz and Minoru Hara, 161–84. Tokyo: International Institute for Buddhist Studies.

———. 2006. "On Monks and Menial Laborers: Some Monastic Accounts of Building Buddhist Monasteries." In *Architetti, Capomastri, Artigiani: L'Organizzazione dei Cantieri e Della Produzione Artistice nell' Asia Ellenistica*, edited by Gherardo Gnoli, 225–45. Rome: Istituto Italiano per l'Africa e l'Oriente.

———. 2007. "The Buddhist Bhikṣu's Obligation to Support His Parents in Two Vinaya Traditions." *Journal of the Pali Text Society* 29: 107–36.

———. 2008. "Separate but Equal: Property Rights and the Legal Independence of Buddhist Nuns and Monks in Early North India." *Journal of the American Oriental Society* 128(4): 625–40.

———. 2010a. "On Incompetent Monks and Able Urbane Nuns in a Buddhist Monastic Code." *Journal of Indian Philosophy* 38(2): 107–31.

———. 2010b. "On Some Who Are Not Allowed to Become Buddhist Monks or Nuns: An Old List of Types of Slaves or Unfree Laborers." *Journal of the American Oriental Society* 130(2): 225–34.

Schram, Louis M.J. [1954] 2006. *The Monguors of the Kansu-Tibetan Frontier.* Edited by Kevin Stuart. Xining: Plateau.

Schuh, Dieter. 1984. "Recht und Gesetz in Tibet." In *Tibetan and Buddhist Studies: Commemorating the 200th Anniversary of Alexander Csoma de Kőrös,* edited by Louis Ligeti, 291–311. Budapest: Akadémiai kiadó.

—— and L.S. Dagyab. 1978. *Urkunden, Erlasse und Sendschreiben aus dem Besitz Sikkimesischer Adelshäuser und des Klosters Phodang.* St Augustin: VGH Wissenschaftsverlag.

Schwartz, Ronald David. 1994. "Buddhism, Nationalist Protest, and the State in Tibet." In *Tibetan Studies: Proceedings of the Sixth Seminar of the International Association for Tibetan Studies,* edited by Per Kvaerne, 728–38. Oslo: Institute for Comparative Research in Human Culture.

Schwieger, Peter. 2015a. "Criminal Law and Corporal Punishment in Tibet." In *Secular Law and Order in the Tibetan Highland,* edited by Dieter Schuh, 145–58. Andiast: International Institute for Tibetan and Buddhist Studies.

——. 2015b. *Dalai Lama and the Emperor of China.* New York: Columbia University Press.

Sedlacek, Tomas. 2011. *Economics of Good and Evil: The Quest for Economic Meaning from Gilgamesh to Wall Street.* Oxford: Oxford University Press.

Seneviratna, Anuradha. 2000. "The Buddhist Monastic Law in Ancient Sri Lanka." *The Jurist* 60(1): 162–203.

Sewell, William H. 1993. "Toward a Post-materialist Rhetoric for Labor History." In *Rethinking Labor History: Essays on Discourse and Class Analysis,* edited by L.R. Berlanstein, 15–37. Urbana: University of Illinois Press.

Seyfort Ruegg, D. 1991. "*Mchod yon / yon mchod* and *mchod gnas / yon gnas*: On the Historiography and Semantics of a Tibetan Religio-Social and Religio-Political Concept." In *Tibetan History and Language: Studies Dedicated to Uray Geza on His Seventieth Birthday,* edited by Ernst Steinkellner, 441–53. Vienna: Arbeitskreis für tibetische und buddhistische Studien.

——. 2004. "Aspects of the Study of the (Earlier) Indian Mahāyāna." *Journal of the International Association of Buddhist Studies* 27(1): 3–62

Shakya, Tsering. 1999. *The Dragon in the Land of Snows: A History of Modern Tibet since 1947.* New York: Columbia University Press.

Sherring, Charles A. [1916] 1974. *Western Tibet and the Indian Borderland: The Sacred Country of Hindus and Buddhists; with an Account of the Government, Religion and Customs of Its Peoples.* Delhi: Cosmo.

Sihlé, Nicolas. 2015. "Towards a Comparative Anthropology of the Buddhist Gift (and Other Transfers)." *Religion Compass* 9 (11): 352–85.

Silber, Ilana Friedrich. 1985. "'Opting Out' in Theravāda Buddhism and Medieval Christianity: A Comparative Study of Monasticism as Alternative Structure." *Religion* 15(3): 251–77.

Silk, Jonathan. 1999. "Marginal Notes on a Study of Buddhism, Economy and Society in China." *Journal of the International Association of Buddhist Studies* 22(2): 361–96.

——. 2002. "Cui bono? or Follow the Money: Identifying the Sophist in a Pāli Commentary." In *Buddhist and Indian Studies: In Honour of Professor Sodo Mori,* 129–83. Hamamatsu: Kokusai Bukkyoto Kyokai.

———. 2003. "Dressed for Success: The Monk Kasyapa and Strategies of Legitimation in Earlier Mahayana Buddhist Scriptures." *Journal Asiatique* 291(1): 173–219.

———. 2007. "Good and Evil in Indian Buddhism: The Five Sins of Immediate Retribution." *Journal of Indian Philosophy* 35(3): 253–86.

———. 2008. *Managing Monks: Administrators and Administrative Roles in Indian Buddhist Monasticism*. New York: Oxford University Press.

Slobodnik, Martin. 2004. "Destruction and Revival: The Fate of the Tibetan Buddhist Monastery Labrang in the People's Republic of China." *Religion, State & Society* 32(1): 7–19.

Smith, Adam. [1776] 1976. *The Wealth of Nations*. Chicago: University of Chicago Press.

Smith, Adam, and Knud Haakonssen, eds. [1759] 2002. *The Theory of Moral Sentiments*. Cambridge: Cambridge University Press.

Smith, E. Gene. 2001. *Among Tibetan Texts: History and Literature of the Himalayan Plateau*. Boston: Wisdom.

Smyrlis, Konstantinos. 2002. "The Management of Monastic Estates: The Evidence of the Typika." *Dumbarton Oaks Papers* 56: 245–61.

Snellgrove, David L. [1987] 2002. *Indo-Tibetan Buddhism: Indian Buddhists and Their Tibetan Successors*. Boston: Shambhala.

——— and Hugh Richardson. [1968] 1986. *A Cultural History of Tibet*. Boston: Shambhala.

Sobisch, Jan-Ulrich. 2002. *Three-vow Theories in Tibetan Buddhism: A Comparative Study of Major Traditions from the Twelfth through Nineteenth Centuries*. Wiesbaden: Ludwig Reichert Verlag.

Southern, R.W. 1970. *Western Society and the Church in the Middle Ages*. Harmondsworth, UK: Penguin Book.

Spencer Chapman, Frank. [1938] 1984. *Memoirs of a Mountaineer: Lhasa the Holy City*. Gloucester: Alan Sutton.

Sperling, Elliot. 1987. "Some Notes on the Early 'Bri-gung-pa Sgom-pa." In *Silver on Lapis: Tibetan Literary Culture and History*, edited by Christopher Beckwith, 33–53. Bloomington, IN: Tibet Society.

Spiro, Melford E. 1971. *Buddhism and Society: A Great Tradition and Its Burmese Vicissitudes*. London: George Allen & Unwin.

Stein, Rolf A. [1962] 1972. *Tibetan Civilization*. Stanford, CA: Stanford University Press.

Strenski, Ivan. 1983. "On Generalized Exchange and the Domestication of the Sangha." *Man* 18(3): 463–77.

Sullivan, Brenton. 2013. "The Mother of All Monasteries: Gönlung Jampa Ling and the Rise of Mega Monasteries in Northeastern Tibet." PhD dissertation, University of Virginia.

———. 2015. "Monastic Customaries and the Promotion of Dge Lugs Scholasticism in Amdo and Beyond." *Asian Highlands Perspectives* 36: 82–105.

Sur, Dominic. 2017. "Constituting Canon and Community in Eleventh Century Tibet: The Extant Writings of Rongzom and His Charter of Mantrins (sngags pa'i bca' yig)." *Religions* 8(3): 1–29.

Surkhang, Wangchen Gelek. 1986. "Government, Monastic and Private Taxation in Tibet." *Tibet Journal* 11(1): 21–40.

Takeuchi, Tsuguhito. 1993. "Old Tibetan Loan Contracts." *Memoirs of the Research Department of the Toyo Bunko (the Oriental Library)* 51: 25–83.

Tambiah, Stanley Jeyaraja. 1970. *Buddhism and the Spirit Cults in North-East Thailand.* Cambridge: Cambridge University Press.

Tatz, Mark, Asanga, and Tsong-kha-pa (Blo-bzang-grags-pa). 1986. *Asanga's Chapter on Ethics with the Commentary of Tsong-Kha-Pa: The Basic Path to Awakening, the Complete Bodhisattva.* Lewiston, NY: Edwin Mellen Press.

Thargyal, Rinzin, and Toni Huber. 2007. *Nomads of Eastern Tibet: Social Organization and Economy of a Pastoral Estate in the Kingdom of Dege.* Leiden: Brill.

Tibet Oral History Project. 2007. "Interview # 91—Ngawang Choseng: July 7." www.tibet-oralhistory.org

Tomasi di Lampedusa, Guiseppe. [1958] 2007. *The Leopard.* London: Vintage Books.

Townsend, Dominique. 2017. "How to Constitute a Field of Merit: Structure and Flexibility in a Tibetan Buddhist Monastery's Curriculum." *Religions* 8(9): 1–20.

Travers, Alice. 2008. "Exclusiveness and Openness: A Study of Matrimonial Strategies in the Ganden Phodrang Aristocracy (1880–1959)." *Journal of the International Association of Tibetan Studies* 4: 1–27.

———. 2009. "Risk and Social Mobility among the Aristocracy: A Study of the Demotion and Dismissal Cases in the Careers of the Dga' ldan Pho brang Officials at the Beginning of the 20th Century (1885–1952)." In *Contemporary Visions in Tibetan Studies: Proceedings of the First International Seminar of Young Tibetologists, London, 9–13 August 2007,* edited by Brandon Dotson, Kalsang Norbu Gurung, Georgios Halkias, and Tim Myatt, 363–81. Chicago: Serindia.

———. 2011. "The Careers of the Noble Officials of the Ganden Phodrang (1895–1959): Organisation and Hereditary Divisions within the Service of State." *Revue d'Etudes Tibétaines* 21: 155–74.

———. 2016. "Between Private and Public Initiatives? Private Schools in Pre-1951 Tibet." *HIMALAYA, the Journal of the Association for Nepal and Himalayan Studies* 35(2): 118–35.

Tsarong, Paljor. 1987. "Economy and Ideology on a Tibetan Monastic Estate in Ladakh: Processes of Production and Reproduction and Transformation." PhD dissertation, University of Wisconsin–Madison.

Tsering, Tashi, and Gaku Ishimura. 2012. "A Historical Overview of Education and Social Change in Spiti Valley, India." *International Association for Ladakh Studies* 28(June): 4–16.

Tucci, Giuseppe. 1950. *The Tombs of the Tibetan Kings.* Rome: Istituto Italiano per il Medio ed Estremo Oriente.

———. [1970] 1988. *The Religions of Tibet.* Berkeley: University of California Press.

Tulku, Tarab. 2000. *A Brief History of Tibetan Academic Degrees in Buddhist Philosophy.* Copenhagen: NIAS.

Twitchett, D.C. 1957. "The Monasteries and China's Economy in Medieval Times." *Bulletin of the School of Oriental and African Studies* 19(3): 526–49.

Uebach, Helga. 1992. "Notes on the Section of Law and State in the *Chos-'byung* of lDe'u." In *Tibetan Studies Proceedings of the 5th Seminar of the International Association for Tibetan Studies, Narita 1989,* edited by S. Ihara and Z. Yamaguchi, 823–31. Narita: Naritasan Shinshoji.

van der Kuijp, Leonard W.J. 1987. "An Early Tibetan View of the Soteriology of Buddhist Epistemology: The Case of 'Bri-gung 'jig-rten mgon-po." *Journal of Indian Philosophy* 15(1): 57–70.

———. 1999. "The Yoke Is on the Reader: A Recent Study of Tibetan Jurisprudence." *Central Asiatic Journal* 43(2): 266–92.

Velasquez, Manuel. 2003. "Debunking Corporate Moral Responsibility." *Business Ethics Quarterly* 13(4): 531–62.

Vermeersch, Sem. 2008. *The Power of the Buddhas: The Politics of Buddhism during the Koryŏ Dynasty (918–1392)*. Cambridge, MA: Harvard University Press.

Vetturini, Gianpaolo. [2007] 2013. "The bKa' gdams pa School of Tibetan Buddhism: Historical Legacy of the bKa' gdams pas according to the bKa' gdams rin po che'i chos 'byung rnam thar nyin mor byed pa'i 'od stong (vols. 1 & 2)." PhD dissertation. London: SOAS.

Viehbeck, Markus. 2016. "An Indian Classic in 19th-Century Tibet and Beyond: Rdza Dpal sprul and the Dissemination of the *Bodhi (sattva) caryāvatāra*." *Revue d'Etudes Tibétaines* 36: 5–44.

Vitali, Roberto. 2003. "Events in the History of Mnga' ris skor gsum (Tenth–Fifteenth Centuries)." In *The History of Tibet, vol. II: The Medieval Period: c. 850–1895: The Development of Buddhist Paramountcy*, edited by Alex McKay, 53–89. London: Routledge.

Van Vleet, Stacey. 2016. "Medicine as Impartial Knowledge: The Fifth Dalai Lama, the Tsarong School, and Debates of Tibetan Medical Orthodoxy." In *The Tenth Karmapa & Tibet's Turbulent Seventeenth Century*, edited by Karl Debreczeny and Gray Tuttle, 263–91. Chicago: Serindia.

von Hinüber, Oskar. 1995. "Buddhist Law According to the Theravāda-Vinaya: A Survey of Theory and Practice." *Journal of the International Association of Buddhist Studies* 18(1): 7–45.

Wallace, Vesna. 2014. "Buddhist Laws in Mongolia." In *Buddhism and Law: An Introduction*, edited by Rebecca Redwood French and Mark A. Nathan, 319–33. New York: Cambridge University Press.

Walsh, Michael J. 2007. "The Economics of Salvation: Toward a Theory of Exchange in Chinese Buddhism." *Journal of the American Academy of Religion* 75(2): 353–82.

———. 2010. *Sacred Economies: Buddhist Monasticism and Territoriality in Medieval China*. New York: Columbia University Press.

Wangchuk, Dorji. 2005. "Das dPal-yul-Kloster in Geschichte und Gegenwart: Die Wiederbelebung der klösterlichen Tradition der rNying-ma-Schule." *Buddhismus in Geschichte und Gegenwart* 11: 213–34.

Wangdu, Pasang, and Hildegard Diemberger. 2000. *dBa' bzhed: The Royal Narrative Concerning the Bringing of the Buddha's Doctrine to Tibet*. Vienna: Verlag der Österreichischen Akademie der Wissenschaften.

Wayman, Alex. 1984. *Buddhist Insight: Essays by Alex Wayman*. Delhi: Motilal Banarsidass.

Weber, Max. [1922] 1978. "Religious Rejections of the World and Their Directions." In *Economy and Society: An Outline of Interpretive Sociology*, translated by Ephraim Fischoff et al. Berkeley: University of California Press.

Welch, Holmes. 1967. *The Practice of Chinese Buddhism: 1900–1950*. Cambridge, MA: Harvard University Press.

Wessels, C. 1924. *Early Jesuit Travellers in Central Asia, 1603–1721*. The Hague: Nijhoff.

White, J. Claude. [1909] 1971. *Sikhim and Bhutan: Twenty-one Years on the North-East Frontier, 1887–1908*. Delhi: Vivek.

Whitecross, Richard W. 2014. "Buddhism and Constitutions in Bhutan." In *Buddhism and Law: An Introduction*, edited by Rebecca Redwood French and Mark A. Nathan, 350–67. New York: Cambridge University Press.

———. 2017. "Law, 'Tradition' and Legitimacy: Contesting Driglam Namzha." In *Development Challenges in Bhutan Perspectives on Inequality and Gross National Happiness*, edited by Johannes Schmidt, 115–34. Cham: Springer International.

Wickremasinghe, Don M. de Zilva, ed. 1928. *Epigraphia Zeylanica: Being Lithic and Other Inscriptions of Ceylon 1912–1927, vol. 2*. London: Oxford University Press.

Wijayaratna, Môhan. 1990. *Buddhist Monastic Life: According to the Texts of the Theravāda Tradition*. Cambridge: Cambridge University Press.

Wiley, Thomas W. 1986. "Macro Exchanges: Tibetan Economics and the Roles of Politics and Religion." *Tibet Journal* 11(1): 3–20.

Willis, Janice Dean. 1989. "Tibetan Ani-s: The Nun's Life in Tibet." In *Feminine Ground: Essays on Women and Tibet*, edited by Janice Dean Willis, 96–117. Ithaca, NY: Snow Lion.

Wood, Benjamin. 2013. "The Scrupulous Use of Gifts for the Saṅgha: Self-Ennoblement through the Ledger in Tibetan Autobiography." *Revue d'Etudes Tibétaines* 26: 35–55.

———. 2016. "Coming to Terms with a Monk's Seduction: Speculations on the Conduct of Sgra tshad pa Rin chen rnam rgyal (1318–1388)." *Journal of Indian Philosophy* 45(2): 207–34.

Wylie, Turrell. 1959. "A Standard System of Tibetan Transcription." *Harvard Journal of Asiatic Studies* 22: 261–67.

Yamagiwa, Nobuyuki. 2001. *Das Pāṇḍulohitakavastu: Über die verschiedenen Verfahrensweisen der Bestrafung in der buddhistischen Gemeinde*. Marburg: Indica et Tibetica Verlag.

Yifa. 2002. *The Origins of Buddhist Monastic Codes in China: An Annotated Translation and Study of the Chanyuan Qinggui*. Honolulu: University of Hawai'i Press.

———. 2005. "From the Chinese Vinaya to Chan Regulations: Continuity and Adaptation." In *Going Forth: Visions of Buddhist Vinaya: Essays Presented in Honor of Professor Stanley Weinstein*, edited by William M. Bodiford, 124–35. Honolulu: University of Hawai'i Press.

Zhabs-dkar (Tshogs-drug-rang-grol). 1994. *The Life of Shabkar: The Autobiography of a Tibetan Yogin*. Edited by Constance Wilkinson et al. Translated by Matthieu Ricard et al. Albany: State University of New York Press.

Zimmerman, Michael. 2006. "Only a Fool Becomes a King: Buddhist Stances on Punishment." In *Buddhism and Violence*, edited by Michael Zimmerman, 213–42. Lumbini: Lumbini International Research Institute.

Zongtse, Champa Thupten. 1995. *History of the Sera Monastery of Tibet (1418–1959)*. New Delhi: International Academy of Indian Culture and Aditya Prakashan.

## CONSULTED DICTIONARIES

*Bod rgya tshig mdzod chen mo*. Zhang Yisun, ed. 1993. Beijing: Mi rigs dpe skrun khang.

*Buddhist Hybrid Sanskrit Grammar and Dictionary*. Franklin Edgerton. [1953] 2004. Delhi: Motilal Banarsidass.

*brDa dkrol gser gyi me long*. bTsan lha ngag dbang tshul khrims. 1997. Beijing: Mi rigs dpe skrun khang.

*The New Tibetan-English Dictionary of Modern Tibet.* Melvyn Goldstein, ed. 2001. Berkeley: University of California Press.

*A Sanskrit-English Dictionary.* Monier Monier-Williams. [1872] 1999. Delhi: Motilal Banarsidass.

*Tibetan-Sanskrit Dictionary.* Lokesh Chandra. [1958–60] 1971. Kyoto: Rinsen Book.

## CITED WEBSITES

www.aaoarts.com/asie/VDL/
www.berzinarchives.com
www.dtab.uni-bonn.de
https://sites.google.com/site/tibetological/dorjiev
http://himalaya.socanth.cam.ac.uk
http://tbrc.org/
www.thlib.org
www.tibetoralhistory.org
http://tibet.prm.ox.ac.uk/photo_1998.286.53.2.html

# INDEX

*Abbatial History of Pelyul* (dPal yul gdan rabs): on the authority of the abbot, 82–83; on the comprehensive nature of *chayik* rules, 19; on the great chant master position, 38, 71, 72; on *The Eighty Prohibitions* (bCa' yig mi chog brgyad cu), 28

agriculture and farming: forced on monks by the PRC government, 194n14; by hired laypeople on land owned by monks and nuns in Dunhuang, 199n49, 214; inheritance of agricultural lands, 140; by the lay community for monasteries, 124; monk fields, 49, 94; by monks to support themselves, 64, 93; by nuns at Rinchen Gang, 97; and the post of *spyi pa*, 75–76; restrictions on, 141; scarcity of agricultural laborers in Central Tibet, 99

alcohol: government decree on alcohol and women written for Geluk monasteries in the Lhasa area, 155–156, 232n73; and *kuladūṣaka* (behaving badly in full view of the laity), 133; as payment for construction work, 123; punishment of monks caught multiple times with, 164, 203n75

allowances: and contemporary Tibetan monasteries, 91; distribution of, 91–93, 96; during the time of Songtsen Gampo, 91; during the time of Trisong Detsen, 32; ledgers of, 76, 89, 95–96; in Sikkimese monasteries, 58, 212n30; and the steward's office, 79, 96; supplied to monks by sponsors in Thailand, 210n259; at the Three Great Seats, 86, 95

Ashman, Ian, and Diana Winstanley, 42

behaving badly in full view of the laity. *See kuladūṣaka* (T. *khyim (pa) sun 'byin pa*)

Bell, Charles Alfred, 151–152; on the correlation between a monastery's size and the level of monastic discipline, 64; on the death of Sidkeong Tulku, 180; on legal disputes between a layman and a monk, 232n87; on looting by Drepung monks, 128; on the punishment of monks by secular powers, 171; on social mobility in Tibet, 44

Bhutan: *chayik* used for legal codes in, 16; ideal rule viewed as a combination of secular and religious traditions, 149, 153, 173; law code of 1729 of, 127, 141, 180; restrictions on monks who have no knowledge, 227n200; restrictions on soliciting alms, 127, 224n94; seating-arrangement ritual in, 59; *zhal ngo* (hereditary chiefs), 70

Bhutanese *chayik* (bKra shis chos rdzong bca' yig), 192n55, 214n56, 217n150, 225n142, 234n139; on arhats, 226n165; authorship attributed to monastic officials and the community of monks, 21; exemption, 222n37; on monks sharing their allocation of offering, 213n52

monks leaving the monastery's premises, 74, 117; on monks visiting relatives, 140; prerequisites for *zhal ta pa*, 72–73; on punishment of those carrying alcohol to the monastery, 155; on the role of *spyi pa/ba* in confiscating "unsuitable" items of clothing of travelling monks, 74; *rtsis 'dzin pa* of the treasury at, 78; on women entering monastic residencies, 141. *See also* Terdak Lingpa
*mkhan po* (abbots): authority of, 42–43, 81–83; on donations attracted by, 98; lack of mention of the abbot in the *chayik* Bon monastery of Menri, 210n262; selection of abbots of the Three Great Seats, 60; supervisory function of, 82
monastic boundaries: and the connection between territorial control and monastic guidelines, 153–154; putting down a *sīmā* (monastic "border"), 8–9; and the redistribution of goods beyond the monastic community, 121; restrictions on the laity's killing animals within the vicinity of the monastic territory, 154–155; restrictions on the laity's movement across the monasteries' boundary markers, 118; and restrictions on the physical movement of monks, 74, 117–118; unrestricted access of Tibetan laity in the PRC and exile communities, 221n23. *See also* Sangha
monastic economics in Song-era China: merit as a material religio-economic commodity, 114; and the participation of monks and nuns, 110–111; and the production of medicines, 228n211
monastic fighting: addressed in the *chayik* of Gongra Ngesang Dorje Ling, 158–159; and Drepung monastic guidelines, 158; and Mindröl Ling monastic guidelines, 159; and secular law, 159
monastic guidelines. *See chayik*
monastic institutions: as a crucial agent in Tibetan society, 10–11, 39–40; and the aristocracy, 91, 111, 220n215, 237n13; celibacy at its center, 8, 235n169; terms for, 8–10
monastic organization: establishment of a Sangha by putting down a *sīmā* (monastic "border"), 8–9; and the Ganden Phodrang government, 6; hierarchy reflected in rituals at monasteries, 59; *lhan rgyas* (committee consisting of laypeople), 203–204n83; and the maintenance of the status quo, 5, 54–55, 84, 145, 177, 179; the medieval

Catholic Church as corporation compared with Buddhist institutions, 40, 41; and the performance of three monastic rituals (*gzhi gsum cho ga*), 8; and religious figures of authority, 42–43, 81–83; and the term *dgon pa*, 9; and the term *vihāra*, 9; titles and officials at nunneries, 207n156; and voting to select the disciplinarian, 60, 201n24. *See also* chant masters (*dbu mdzad*); discipline at monasteries; individuality; monks; Sangha; *spyi pa/ba*; *spyi so*; *zhal ta pa* (*vaiyāpṛtyakara*)
monastic purity: benevolence of the protectors related to, 54, 56, 180; and celibacy, 8, 167, 235n169; and sitting in the assembly hall, 59, 201n17; and "The Sixteen Pronouncements," 151, 173; and Vinaya rules, 117. *See also* celibacy
Mongolia: debating sessions discussed in *Chos sde chos dbyings 'od gsal gling bca' yig*, 28, 194n91; Dörbet (Dur bed) tribe in, 225n143; gift to Labrang by prince Erdeni Jinong, 119; guidelines for monks' attire for a monastery in, 134; old Mongolian legal texts, 101n13; prince Erdeni Jinong, 119; the process of creating guidelines for a monastery in, 16–17; relation between the Sangha and the state in, 236n201; term *hetsuu hun* ("clever one") compared with *gnyer pa*, 209n217
monks: as a pacifying force, 138; as a field of merit (S. *puṇyakṣetra*), 137–138, 179; *dge slong* (*śrāmaṇera*) and *dge tshul* (*bhikṣu*) used for, 7, 66, 78, 189n28, 189n28, 189n34; an alternative etymological explanation of *grwa pa* (Central Tibetan word for "monk"), 8; high number in Tibet of, 10–11; Joden Dézhi (Jo gdan sde bzhi) members, 128; and local lay populations, 65, 86–87, 91, 95, 101, 111–113, 123–124, 134; and seniority, 200n1, 201n6; Tibetan terms referring to (male) inhabitants of a monastery, 7. *See also* education of monks; ex-monks; families and family ties; *kuladūṣaka*; *prātimokṣa* (monks' vows); Sangha
*Mūlasarvāstivāda vinaya*, 80; activities that annoy laypeople mentioned in the *Prātimokṣa* of, 134; on buying and selling without seeking gain, 101; on collecting interest on loans, 219n186, 219n189; on healthcare for ill monks, 141; and the homogenous monastic identity among Tibetan Buddhists, 32; *kriyākāraṃ* in,

the entrance to the assembly hall, 23. *See also Abbatial History of Pelyul* (dPal yul gdan rabs)

Pelyul Darthang *chayik,* 223n63, 223n82; monastic disruptions due to regional differences addressed in, 158, 159; on punishment for selling of alcohol on monastic grounds, 155; on the readmission of ex-monks, 170; recitation of, 25; restrictions on ex-monks who retook their vows, 80; restrictions on killing animals within the vicinity of the monastic territory, 155; restrictions on laypeople entering the grounds, 118; restrictions on monks carrying arms, 170; on the role of the disciplinarian, 157–158; on the supervisory function of the abbot, 82; word *zur tshogs* in, 59, 201n16

Pelyul Namgyel Chöling (dPal yul rnam rgyal chos gling) Nyingma monastery. *See Abbatial History of Pelyul*

Pereira, George, 163

period of fragmentation (*sil bu'i dus*), 33–34, 34, 152

Phiyang monastery (Phyi dbang bkra shis rdzong): sliding entry fee at, 49. *See also* Könchok Chönyi

Phodang *chayik (Pho ldang bca' yig)* by the Fourteenth Karmapa (1846), 167; on reentering the monastery, 169

Phulung *chayik (Phu lung dgon bca' yig)* (1947), 154, 161

Pirie, Fernanda, 24

pollution: and the appeasement of protectors, 54, 56. *See also* monastic purity; outcasts and caste

*prātimokṣa* vows, 17; activities that annoy laypeople mentioned in, 134; and the creation of a uniform set of morals, 2–3; and the function of *chayik* in the upholding of, 19–20; impure persons barred from the recitation of, 201n17; keeping of vows as a matter of life and death, 138; rulings against buying and selling, 101

property and inheritance: and contemporary Theravāda law, 212n37; *dkor* (monastic wealth), 58, 138, 164n164; land and property owned by rich monks, 100, 216n122; by monks in Sri Lanka, 217n132; natal household estates of monks, 216n124; of ordinary monks, 89, 100, 212n26; and religious property, 88–90, 99–100, 216n114; rights to inheritance lost by monks entering a monastery, 140, 216n130

protectors: calling on Pehar as a witness, 150; fear of offending local protector deities, 53–54. *See also* local protectors

punishment: and the absolving of the Sangha as a whole from wrongdoing, 98; banning access to water and fire, 52, 199n70; breaking of the thirteen *Saṅghāvaśeṣa dharma*s (*dge 'dun gyi lhag ma'i chos bcu gsum*), 130, 224n114; corporal punishment, 161–165; expulsion of vow breakers, 168; keeping the peace as the ultimate goal of, 174–175; of laypeople for killing animals in the vicinity of the monastic territory, 154–155; for leaving a monastery without permission, 164; limited role in purifying negative karma of, 149–150; of managers for failure to punish *pārājika* offenses, 66; of monks caught multiple times with alcohol and cigarettes, 160, 164, 203n75; offering of a communal tea-round as punishment for killing animals, 154; practices in Tibetan secular courts, 164; and the privileged legal status of Tibetan monks, 150–151; range of types of, 163–164; related to interactions with women, 166–167; of women for interacting with monks, 166–167

Raftis, J.A., 213–214n55

Ramble, Charles: on monks and nuns in Te, Mustang, 227n191; on "Nirba" (lay administrators), 210n236

Ramoché *chayik (Ra mo che bca' yig),* 190n48, 208n197, 218n153, 223n78; guidelines on begging for alms, 132; guidelines on offerings, 126; on repaying medical debts, 143

Rawls, John, 200n3

religious law, silken knot imagery of, 152

Rendo Senggé (Re mdo Sengge): about, 186; on access to the *chayik* at Kirti, 22, 197n60; an alternative etymology of the word *grwa pa* by, 9; on the *chos mdzad,* 61, 202n31; on the recitation of the Kirti monastery *chayik,* 26; on the relationship of *chayik* to the secular law, 17, 148, 191n29; on the the Tibetan system of monastic learning, 145; on the word *dgon pa,* 9

Reting *chayik,* on protecting monastic grounds and surrounding wild life, 155

Rinchen Gang *chayik (Rin chen sgang bca' yig;* Sakya nunnery, 1845): *dbu byed* as the title of the nun in charge of leading the assembly, 72; and the nunnery's financial instability, 97,

South Asia Across the Disciplines is a series devoted to publishing first books across a wide range of South Asian studies, including art, history, philology or textual studies, philosophy, religion, and the interpretive social sciences. Series authors all share the goal of opening up new archives and suggesting new methods and approaches, while demonstrating that South Asian scholarship can be at once deep in expertise and broad in appeal.

*Extreme Poetry: The South Asian Movement of Simultaneous Narration*, by Yigal Bronner (Columbia)

*The Social Space of Language: Vernacular Culture in British Colonial Punjab*, by Farina Mir (UC Press)

*Unifying Hinduism: Philosophy and Identity in Indian Intellectual History*, by Andrew J. Nicholson (Columbia)

*The Powerful Ephemeral: Everyday Healing in an Ambiguously Islamic Place*, by Carla Bellamy (UC Press)

*Secularizing Islamists? Jama'at-e-Islami and Jama'at-ud-Da'wa in Urban Pakistan*, by Humeira Iqtidar (Chicago)

*Islam Translated: Literature, Conversion, and the Arabic Cosmopolis of South and Southeast Asia*, by Ronit Ricci (Chicago)

*Conjugations: Marriage and Form in New Bollywood Cinema*, by Sangita Gopal (Chicago)

*Unfinished Gestures: Devadāsīs, Memory, and Modernity in South India*, by Davesh Soneji (Chicago)

*Document Raj: Writing and Scribes in Early Colonial South India*, by Bhavani Raman (Chicago)

*The Millennial Sovereign: Sacred Kingship and Sainthood in Islam*, by A. Azfar Moin (Columbia)

*Making Sense of Tantric Buddhism: History, Semiology, and Transgression in the Indian Traditions*, by Christian K. Wedemeyer (Columbia)

*The Yogin and the Madman: Reading the Biographical Corpus of Tibet's Great Saint Milarepa*, by Andrew Quintman (Columbia)

*Body of Victim, Body of Warrior: Refugee Families and the Making of Kashmiri Jihadists*, by Cabeiri deBergh Robinson (UC Press)

*Receptacle of the Sacred: Illustrated Manuscripts and the Buddhist Book Cult in South Asia*, by Jinah Kim (UC Press)

*Cut-Pieces: Celluloid Obscenity and Popular Cinema in Bangladesh*, by Lotte Hoek (Columbia)

*From Text to Tradition: The Naisadhīyacarita and Literary Community in South Asia*, by Deven M. Patel (Columbia)

*Democracy against Development: Lower Caste Politics and Political Modernity in Postcolonial India*, by Jeffrey Witsoe (Chicago)

*Into the Twilight of Sanskrit Poetry: The Sena Salon of Bengal and Beyond*, by Jesse Ross Knutson (UC Press)

*Voicing Subjects: Public Intimacy and Mediation in Kathmandu*, by Laura Kunreuther (UC Press)

*Writing Resistance: The Rhetorical Imagination of Hindi Dalit Literature*, by Laura R. Brueck (Columbia)

*Wombs in Labor: Transnational Commercial Surrogacy in India* by Amrita Pande (Columbia)

*I Too Have Some Dreams: N.M. Rashed and Modernism in Urdu Poetry* by A. Sean Pue (UC Press)

*The Place of Devotion: Siting and Experiencing Divinity in Bengal-Vaishnavism* by Sukanya Sarbadhikary (UC Press)

*We Were Adivasis: Aspiration in an Indian Scheduled Tribe by Megan Moodie* (Chicago)

*Writing Self, Writing Empire: Chandar Bhan Brahman and the Cultural World of the Indo-Persian State Secretary* by Rajeev Kinra (UC Press)

*Landscapes of Accumulation: Real Estate and the Neoliberal Imagination in Contemporary India* by Llerena Searle (Chicago)

*Polemics and Patronage in the City of Victory: Vyasatirtha, Hindu Sectarianism, and the Sixteenth-Century Vijayanagara Court,* by Valerie Stoker (UC Press)

*Hindu Pluralism: Religion and the Public Sphere in Early Modern South India* by Elaine M. Fisher (UC Press)

*Negotiating Languages: Urdu, Hindi, and the Definition of Modern South Asia* by Walter N. Hakala (Columbia)

*Building Histories: The Archival and Affective Lives of Five Monuments in Modern Delhi* by Mrinalini Rajagopalan (Chicago)

*Reading the Mahavamsa: The Literary Aims of a Theravada Buddhist History* by Kristin Scheible (Columbia)

*Modernizing Composition: Sinhala Song, Poetry, and Politics in Twentieth-Century Sri Lanka* by Garrett Field (UC Press)

*Language of the Snakes: Prakrit, Sanskrit, and the Language Order of Pre-modern India* by Andrew Ollett (UC Press)

*The Hegemony of Heritage: Ritual and the Record in Stone* by Deborah L. Stein (UC Press)

*The Monastery Rules: Buddhist Monastic Organization in Pre-Modern Tibet,* by Berthe Jansen (UC Press)

.

CPSIA information can be obtained
at www.ICGtesting.com
Printed in the USA
LVHW11s0730230918
591080LV00001B/1/P